Southern Biography Series

Bertram Wyatt-Brown, Editor

Gerald W. Johnson

From Southern Liberal to National Conscience

Vincent Fitzpatrick

Louisiana State University Press
Baton Rouge

Copyright © 2002 by Louisiana State University Press
All rights reserved
Manufactured in the United States of America
First printing
11   10   09   08   07   06   05   04   03   02
5   4   3   2   1

Designer: Amy Holcomb
Typeface: Bembo
Typesetter: Coghill Composition Co. Inc.
Printer and binder: Thomson-Shore, Inc.

ISBN 0-8071-2750-7

Frontispiece: Gerald W. Johnson at age sixty. Photograph by A. Aubrey Bodine.
Copyright © Jennifer B. Bodine, Denton, Md.

The published and unpublished works of Gerald W. Johnson are quoted by
permission of Kathryn Johnson Sliger, Executrix of the Gerald Johnson Estate.
Excerpts from published and unpublished works and letters of H. L. Mencken
are used by permission of the Enoch Pratt Free Library in accordance with the
terms of the will of Henry Louis Mencken.

The paper in this book meets the guidelines for permanence and durability of
the Committee on Production Guidelines for Book Longevity of the Council
on Library Resources. ∞

Contents

Photographs

Preface

Eleanor Roosevelt was unable to attend but sent a telegram of congratulations. Gilbert Harrison of the *New Republic* and Irita Van Doren of the *New York Herald Tribune Books,* forums graced for decades by Gerald White Johnson's prose, traveled to Baltimore's Enoch Pratt Free Library for the ceremony. A former governor of Maryland spoke, as did a number of other dignitaries. The recipient of all this attention was an author for whom silence was unthinkable. He had already published over ten million words, and his career would stretch nearly two more decades. His prose had helped to distinguish Mencken's *American Mercury* during its heyday, and he had cavorted with the iconoclastic Baltimorean on the *Evening Sun.* His ideas had influenced W. J. Cash's monumental *Mind of the South.* His writing had pleased Presidents Franklin Roosevelt and Harry S. Truman. It had also, not surprisingly, outraged thousands of others. He extolled the reflective life and scorned those philistine, materialistic Americans who knew little of plain living and high thinking. About suffering he was never indifferent, and he believed that a writer must speak for those incapable of speaking for themselves. He was a remarkable man, and it was an impressive group who gathered in 1960 to celebrate Johnson's seventieth birthday.[1]

James H. Bready of the *Baltimore Sun,* who perceptively discussed Johnson's writing for decades and helped Kate Coplan of the library staff to plan this gathering, had arranged for a surprise guest who had been out on the presidential campaign trail stumping for John F. Kennedy. Johnson's face took on a look of "utter joy" when Adlai Stevenson entered the room. An "unreconstructed Stevensonian," Johnson had assisted in a variety of ways during the presidential campaigns of 1952 and 1956. Johnson, Stevenson remarked

1. Dorothy Johnson van den Honert to author, June 8, 1995; "Gerald W. Johnson Lauded by Stevenson and Others," *BS,* October 25, 1960; Donald Kirkley, "Man of 10 Million Words," *BS,* April 11, 1954. Johnson's birthday was on August 6, but the party was held on October 24 to accommodate those who had been on vacation during the summer.

warmly, was "loved by all enemies of cant, hypocrisy and boredom." He thanked his friend for "a thousand rescues in an age where humor is suspect and conformity a virtue" and celebrated Johnson as "the critic and conscience of our time."[2]

Stevenson was not swelling a scene, for the 1950s had been an especially contentious, highly public time for Johnson. Bemoaning what he saw as a brave country's descent into an age of anxiety, he served as one of the most eloquent spokespersons for America's adversary culture. He attacked Senator Joseph McCarthy long before it became safe to do so and used a variety of forums to lambaste the Republicans in general and President Eisenhower in particular. Johnson had never concerned himself with drubbing lightweights and had always shown a healthy indifference to public approval. These same features of courage and humanitarianism that marked the prose of the fifties also distinguished the writing of the other decades of Johnson's lengthy and controversial career.

He was born in Riverton, North Carolina, twenty-five years after Appomattox in a South still experiencing the effects of Reconstruction. One of his cousins had ridden with Confederate general Joseph Wheeler's cavalry. Johnson lived to see a man walk on the moon. He voted for Woodrow Wilson and Jimmy Carter. He elegized William Jennings Bryan in 1925 and vilified James Jones in 1978. He was six years old when the Supreme Court made legal the doctrine of "separate but equal" in *Plessy v. Ferguson,* lived twenty-six years beyond *Brown v. Board of Education,* and witnessed Baltimore burning after the assassination of Dr. Martin Luther King in 1968. All three events proved highly significant for him. Both Icarus and Nestor, he published over a span of seventy-five years, and to our present age of literary specialization, the number and diversity of Johnson's roles seem staggering.

He served as a televison commentator and professor of journalism and lectured all over North America. He wrote forty-four books—the output of several lifetimes for ordinary writers—among them histories and biographies, novels and series for children. He always thought of himself as primarily a journalist and wrote for newspapers in North Carolina, Baltimore, and New York City. He believed, correctly, that the essay was his forte and contributed

2. James H. Bready, interview by author, tape recording, Baltimore, August 6, 1990; Bready, "Gerald W. Johnson: Looking Back over Thirty Years," *BS,* March 30, 1980; GWJ to Adlai Stevenson, October 31, 1960, AES Papers. The typescripts of Stevenson's speech and those given by other dignitaries are housed with the GWJ Papers at Wake Forest.

to magazines as diverse as *Look* and the *American Scholar*. Fred Hobson has called Johnson "one of the outstanding essayists of any age."[3]

His vision could hardly have ranged more widely. As a regional writer, he watched the South. While he was never obsessed with his native land, he loved to dissect it for his fellow Southerners and explain it to the Yankees. He played a considerable part in the Southern literary renaissance during the 1920s, decried the senseless violence in Southern mill towns, and caused considerable controversy in attacking the Agrarian manifesto *I'll Take My Stand* (1930). He flayed those Southerners who attacked the New Deal, scoffed at the Dixiecrats as unenlightened reactionaries, and excoriated the murderers of civil rights activists. He colorfully likened the practice of liberalism in the South to "manning the rapids." As a national writer, he watched America; as an internationalist, he looked upon the world. These roles were frequently intertwined, and Johnson's skill as a comparative historian—he ranged across continents and through the centuries—proved one of his greatest strengths.[4]

Johnson saw himself as a generalist, a popularizer, and he felt most comfortable with the common reader. He scoffed at intellectuals whose prose proved unintelligible to the plain people. The "keenest wit," he explained, "the subtlest ironist, the cleverest juggler of paradox are futile and impotent as against the writer who puts in plain language what the reader has been thinking all along, but lacks the words to express." Once Johnson found his authentic voice—there was a youthful infatuation with Mencken's rollicking hyperbole and seductive cadences—his prose was luminous. Johnson remarked sagely that "the culminating point of great art is the concealment of artifice so completely that the finished work appears to be no art at all, but a simple statement of a simple truth." Discussing a concert or a political campaign, a murder or a novel, the tragic drowning of two youngsters or Chamberlain's act of betrayal at Munich, Johnson could make his readers rage and reflect, laugh and cry.[5]

No matter what the forum, the style, or the decade, Johnson remained

---

3. GWJ, Address to the National Press Club, April 22, 1953, GWJ Papers; James Walt, "Tale of Another Liberal's Progress," *Maryland English Journal* 4 (fall 1965): 60; Fred Hobson, introduction to *South-Watching: Selected Essays by Gerald W. Johnson* (Chapel Hill and London: University of North Carolina Press, 1983), vii.

4. Sam Ragan, interview by author, tape recording, Southern Pines, N.C., June 18, 1991.

5. GWJ, *Incredible Tale: The Odyssey of the Average American in the Last Half Century* (New York: Harper and Brothers, 1950), 201; GWJ, "Mencken and the Art of Boob Bumping," *NR* 168 (May 19, 1973): 8.

above all else a civil libertarian. He hated Big Brother—the totalitarianism of the political right was as repugnant as that of the political left—and he insisted upon the right of all Americans to speak freely. Believing that "we cannot guarantee the freedom of Alfred M. Landon without guaranteeing that of Earl Browder, too," Johnson argued that "as long as we defend resolutely the right of every silly ass to spread nonsense, we make doubly secure our right to speak words of wisdom, beauty, and truth." To try to eradicate communism by denying free speech was, in Johnson's lively trope, "to roast the pig by burning the house." Throughout his canon, he celebrated John Milton, John Stuart Mill, Thomas Jefferson, and Justice Oliver Wendell Holmes.[6]

Johnson believed that democracy, for all its flaws, was the most humane form of government, and that the common people, if kept properly informed, could choose intelligently. He believed that humankind, if not capable of perfection, was at least capable of improvement. No Pollyanna, he recognized the horrors of his age; he called the twentieth century "the most terrible since the Hundred Years' War." However, he labored, usually with success, to show an affirming flame.[7]

He saw the American experience as a morality play and believed unashamedly in heroes— Robert E. Lee, for example, Woodrow Wilson and Franklin Delano Roosevelt—bold individuals who did not fear taking that proverbial next step. Like Thomas Carlyle, whose writing he knew well, Johnson was a yea-sayer who urged Americans to think the best of themselves and their noble political experiment. Know right from wrong, he challenged his readers, and don't hesitate to label them such. Tell the truth plainly. Take responsibility for your life; beware of false gods who would have you follow them and tell you what to do. Never forget the bravery of the founding fathers, but understand that the American dream of freedom has been corrupted by greed and fear. For all of his moralism, however, Johnson was never conventionally religious. In the end, his religion was his art, and his devotion his utter dedication to this craft.

Such dedication led to the crafting of nine biographies that appeared between 1927 and 1967. The first, *Andrew Jackson: An Epic in Homespun,* proves

6. GWJ, "When to Build a Barricade," in GWJ, *America-Watching: Perspectives on the Course of an Incredible Half-Century* (Owings Mills, Md.: Stemmer House, 1983), 119; GWJ, "This Terrifying Freedom," in *America-Watching: Perspectives in the Course of an Incredible Century* (Owings Mills, Md.: Stemmer House, 1976), 106.

7. GWJ, "On Voting Democratic: Confession of a Party-Liner," *NR* 170 (June 22, 1974): 16–18.

the most engaging, and it was also the first book to bring Johnson national attention. He also reviewed biographies for decades and had very definite ideas on the biographer's art, ideas that bear noting here. Reviewing a life of Woodrow Wilson, Johnson dismissed both hagiography and debunking: "Liars have lied in the highest, widest, and most handsome fashion, both those who would embalm [Wilson] in goose grease and those who would corrode him with vitriol." Johnson believed that the competent biographer is "content to advance for his subject only such claims as can be substantiated and is not unwilling to submit his subject's failings"; he argued that such a biographer depicts his subject "warts and all."[8]

This is what I have tried to accomplish here. He proved a writer with clear strengths and weaknesses; the paradoxes he was so enamored of as a stylist are obvious in his career. He proved, for example, both prescient and myopic, both catholic and parochial in his opinions. He could sacrifice content for style; the canon is uneven in quality, and his moralism could prove bothersome to his readers. This man who believed that nothing is so constant as change refused, as the twentieth century progressed, to change his views on racial segregation. In brief, he was imperfect like the rest of us. I have tried here to depict Johnson as he was, not Johnson laundered. To his credit, he would have wanted it no other way.

He generalized that "writers don't have interesting lives" and that "it is far more difficult to write an interesting biography of a man of ideas rather than a man of action." For the most part, Johnson was such a man of ideas. Responding to a request for biographical information, he remarked colloquially, "Outside the list of books there is flatly nothing to report. Adventurous, amorous, or in arms, just ain't. I live the dullest life on the dullest street in the dullest city in America; and it suits me just fine." In saying so, he exaggerated a bit, but when he chose to dissent, it was from ideas rather than from decorum. There were no embarrassing public spectacles, no breakdowns, no problems with drugs or alcohol; he was happily married for nearly fifty-eighty years and left behind no skeletons to be rattled by posterity. In the end, his writing shaped his life. He once praised Eleanor Roosevelt for "her ability to live serenely in the eye of a hurricane."[9] The same trope can be applied to

---

8. GWJ, "Portrait of a Man Whose Life Was Grandly Tragic," *NYHTB,* February 23, 1958, p. 1; GWJ, "Once the World's Wonder," *NYHTB,* October 31, 1943, p. 20; GWJ, "Clean Harry: He Left Office a Poorer but Better Man," *BS,* January 27, 1974.

9. James H. Bready, "Books and Authors," *BS,* April 1, 1965; GWJ, "Selected New Books in Review," *BES,* April 21, 1955; GWJ to Richard Walser, March 3, 1952, Richard Gaither Walser Papers, Southern Historical Collection, Wilson Library, University of North

Johnson's career, with the hurricane being the tumult of the twentieth century and the eye being the equanimity of his study, where he wrote with astonishing productivity about everything that interested him. Johnson's life here is more interesting than he would have us believe.

His sense of decorum and modesty have made this first biography about him more difficult. A publisher proposed an autobiography, but Johnson refused: "Writing my memoirs would be indecent exposure." A librarian offered to compile a Johnson bibliography, but he refused again: "A few personal friends may exhume some of my work and write a monograph for the Modern Library Association. But an enduring reputation that would justify your labor? Not a chance." With the exception of a period in France right after his service in World War I had ended, he never kept a diary. And unlike his colleague Mencken, Johnson consigned no material to time lock; there was no attempt to manage his reputation from the grave. This book consequently entailed considerable archival work, precisely the sort of archaeological dig that Johnson the biographer chose not to undertake. His interests lay elsewhere.[10]

Johnson's career proves especially interesting in light of several large social and artistic issues. Who, for example, tells most convincingly about the South, and what is the best vantage point for telling the story? Johnson fell between the polarities of the doomsayer and the apologist and thought that he could see the South most clearly and whole from a distance.[11] Second, his career emphasizes the ephemerality of so much of the writing that is done for newspapers and magazines. Today's copy—goes an old newspaper joke—wraps tomorrow's fish. This month's magazine article is finally consigned to a dusty volume filling a shelf in a long line of library stacks. Finally, Johnson's career forces us to confront once again an old, sad story: the plight of many American authors who have struggled to make a living. Faulkner took a job

---

Carolina at Chapel Hill; GWJ, "A Summing Up by Mrs. F.D.R.," *NYHTB,* September 8, 1963, p. 6.

10. GWJ to Wingate Johnson, May 23, 1963, GWJ Papers; John Adam Moreau, "Gerald W. Johnson to Forego Memoirs as 'Indecent Exposure,' " *BS,* April 15, 1973; GWJ to Adler, September 26, 1962, BA Papers. It was the Atheneum Press that wanted Johnson to write an autobiography, and it was Betty Adler, curator of the H. L. Mencken Collection at Baltimore's Enoch Pratt Free Library, who wanted to compile a Johnson bibliography.

11. For a thorough and valuable discussion of "the radical need of the Southerner to explain and interpret the South," see Fred Hobson, *Tell About the South: The Southern Rage to Explain* (Baton Rouge and London: Louisiana State University Press, 1983).

in the post office in Mississippi and wrote screenplays in Hollywood; Melville worked in the Custom House; the poet John Berryman taught in a prep school where he was assigned an office in the men's room—such a list stretches a long way. To help pay the bills, Johnson churned out hack work that consumed time and energy which could have been spent more profitably elsewhere. Moreover, financial problems worsened his already difficult final decade.

Johnson seems in some ways very much one of us. In other ways he seems the product of another time and milieu. "Presentism" and "generational chauvinism" had not been coined while Johnson was writing, but he clearly grasped the concepts and understood the pitfalls. "My grandfather," he wrote with uncharacteristically bludgeoning irony, "was a fiend in human form, and how it would have startled the old gentleman to know it! . . . He was a ruling elder in the Presbyterian church. . . . But he also owned Negroes, so we know that he was a fiend in human form. Which just goes to show you how much a man's character can be changed after he's dead." Elsewhere, Johnson explained more temperately that "every man is to some extent the creation of his own time, affected by the temper of his time, destined to bear, in the eyes of posterity, the stamp of his time."[12] I have tried here to avoid viewing the past through the lens of the present. He generated much controversy during his career, and portions of his story will most probably prove controversial to posterity. We live in a fiercely egalitarian, highly sensitive age. Johnson would have applauded the former and guffawed at the latter.

12. GWJ, "All Government Investigations Should Be Rigorously Controlled," *GDN* January 6, 1952; GWJ, "Schooling for Ancestors: 2051 A.D.," *Vogue* 117 (February 1, 1951): 188.

Acknowledgments

I am grateful for the assistance offered by a number of generous and highly capable people. First, I would like to thank Gerald Johnson's family, who were most helpful and cooperative. Kathryn Hayward Johnson graciously met with me for an extended interview conducted over the course of three days. I am grateful for the hospitality extended to my wife and me in Valparaiso, Indiana, by Mrs. Johnson, Johnson's son-in-law and daughter Kathryn (Mr. and Mrs. Frederick Allen Sliger), and by his granddaughter Susan Sliger. I am grateful to Mrs. Sliger, the executrix of her father's estate, for giving me permission to quote from his writing; I also appreciate her kindness in answering my many questions. Johnson's daughter Dorothy (Mrs. Leonard van den Honert of Pittsfield, Massachusetts) has generously taken the time to respond to numerous queries, and I appreciate her kind permission to quote from her letters as well as from the remarks that she made about her father on several public occasions. Gerald van den Honert, Johnson's grandson, generously shared with me his research on the family genealogy. Lois Johnson, Gerald's sister, granted me a lengthy and very helpful interview in Southern Pines, North Carolina, a session also attended by Charles Lambeth, Esq. (Johnson's nephew), and by Catharine Lambeth Carlton (his niece). I appreciate Mr. Lambeth's kindness in sharing with me his extensive correspondence with Johnson. I am also grateful for his courtesy in allowing me to quote from his mother's memoir, "Sketch of the Life of Gerald Johnson by His Sister, Mamie, Mrs. Charles Lambeth of Thomasville, N.C., 1939." Mrs. Carlton took considerable trouble in conducting a tour of Riverton and explaining the history of the community. Another of Johnson's nephews, the Honorable John Webb of Wilson, North Carolina, kindly took the time to speak with me about his uncle's career. This is a remarkable family, and it has been my good fortune to make their acquaintance.

I would like to thank the highly skilled and very helpful people at the Louisiana State University Press. I am grateful to Bertram Wyatt-Brown, Sylvia Frank Rodrigue, and John Easterly, all of whom offered invaluable suggestions. I also wish to thank Eivind Boe, whose diligence and skill in copyediting the manuscript are much appreciated.

I wish to thank Robert Stump, Coordinator of Social Work for the Baptist Children's Homes of North Carolina, for the courtesies extended when I visited this very important Johnson site in Thomasville. I am grateful for the assistance of Edith L. Whitt, Registrar of Mars Hill College in Mars Hill, North Carolina; Hallie Arrington, Associate Registrar of Wake Forest University; Sharon Lambeth, Director of Personnel for the Thomasville Public Schools; Jonathan Harding, Archivist of the Century Club in New York City; Eleanor Carlucci, Archivist at Random House; and Jennifer Powell, the Director of Human Resources at WJZ television in Baltimore.

Portions of this book have appeared in different form in the *Baltimore Sun,* in two essays in the *Virginia Quarterly Review,* and in my introduction to Johnson's *By Reason of Strength* (Laurinburg, N.C.: St. Andrews Press, 1994). I am grateful for permission to make use of this material.

I would like to thank Jennifer B. Bodine, the daughter of A. Aubrey Bodine, for her kind permission to use Mr. Bodine's photograph of Gerald W. Johnson.

During the course of my research, I have examined manuscripts, microfilm, and microfiche in a variety of collections. The Franklin D. Roosevelt Library in Hyde Park, New York, was most helpful regarding the correspondence generated by Johnson's *Roosevelt: Dictator of Democrat?* I appreciate the expert assistance provided at the Seeley G. Mudd Manuscript Library and the Firestone Library at Princeton University and the Special Collections Department of the Alderman Library at the University of Virginia. The Johnson papers in the Z. Smith Reynolds Library at Wake Forest University are quite extensive, and I spent many pleasant and productive days there. I wish to thank John R. Woodard and his very able assistants Julia Bradford, Myrtle Lytle, and Francisc Haber. I also had a pleasant and productive time working with the manuscripts in the Southern Historical Collection in the Wilson Library at the University of North Carolina at Chapel Hill, and I wish to thank especially John E. White. I am grateful to Gaylor Callahan, Kelly Swindell, and Laura Hayworth at the Jackson Library at the University of North Carolina at Greensboro. Robert Beall, the librarian at the *Greensboro (N.C.) News and Record,* generously provided material concerning the newspaper's history. Larry Lyon, editor of the *Lexington (N.C.) Dispatch,* kindly facilitated my access to the newspaper's archives.

The kind people at the *Baltimore Sun* were helpful in the greatest degree. I am grateful to the librarians—especially Carolyn Hardnett, Mary A. Schultz, and Dee Lyon—who assisted me during the many days when I researched Johnson's columns. I am also grateful to John S. Carroll, the former editor, and to Patricia T. McLellan, Harold Piper, Frederick N. Rasmussen, Edward Hewitt, and Vivian Kramer.

Johnson had a long and friendly relationship with the Enoch Pratt Free Library and was grateful for the expertise of its staff. I am similarly grateful for the skill and generosity of the many people who helped me in various ways. I wish to thank the Pratt Library, especially the gracious Averil J. Kadis, for permission to quote from the writing of H. L. Mencken. With this book, as with others, Kenneth White was most patient and helpful in finding material for me through interlibrary loan. I also wish to thank John Sondheim, Marcia Dysart, Ralph Clayton, Faye Houston, Shirley Viviano, Harriet Jenkins, Robert Burke, Wesley Wilson, Jeff Korman, Ed Mantler, Judy Cooper, Ofelia Racelis, Michael Donnelly, Thomas Himmel, Johnnie Fields, Carolyn Lee, David Levy, Margaret Gers, Bruce Edelman, Chris Graybill, Rachel Kubie, Tonia Curry, Neil Jordahl, and Wilbur McGill.

Numerous Baltimoreans kindly took the time to discuss different aspects of Johnson's career. James H. Bready knew Johnson well and wrote about him for decades. I am grateful for Mr. Bready's support for this book, the conversations that have proven so fruitful, and his kind permission to quote from his remarks at Johnson's memorial service. Harold A. Williams, historian of the *Baltimore Sun,* sat for an extremely valuable interview, kindly shared material with me, and suggested an avenue of research—one that I would not have thought of myself—that proved very rewarding. Mr. and Mrs. R. P. Harriss knew Johnson well for decades; I am grateful to Mrs. Harriss for allowing me to read and quote from her husband's diary and for giving me permission to quote from his remarks during Johnson's memorial service. Philip Wagner, Johnson's editor on the *Baltimore Evening Sun* during part of 1938, kindly took the time to share his recollections of this very important period. Barbara Holdridge, publisher of Johnson's *America-Watching,* kindly discussed the book's genesis and editorial process. Frank Shivers, the historian of Bolton Hill, graciously made the contacts that allowed me to tour the houses where Johnson lived. Walter Sondheim, prominent civic leader and Johnson's close friend, kindly made time in his very busy schedule to sit for an interview. Jesse Glasgow, journalist and Wake Forest alumnus, generously shared material with me and patiently answered my questions about the university. Dr. Thomas B. Turner graciously sat for a very helpful interview and shared his writing with me. I also wish to thank C. Hammond Brown, Charles A. Fecher, Lee Gordon, Arthur J. Gutman, Madeline Hebbel, Reuben Kramer, Terry Levering, Frank Mason, Stanislav Rembski, Laurence Roberts, Marion E. Rodgers, Gilbert Sandler, Philip Sherman, Mrs. Gervais Stoors, Virginia Tracey, and James Weitzel.

I am grateful to John Thompson of New York City; Bruce Clayton, the biographer of W. J. Cash; and Lisa Bell of the *London (England) Express,* who went to considerable trouble to research a query. A variety of people in Johnson's native North Carolina have proven most generous with their time and assistance. I would like to thank Wint Capel of the *Thomasville Times,* Roy Parker of the *Fayetteville Observer-Times,* and Sam Ragan of the *Southern Pines Pilot.* I also wish to thank Walter Beeker, Cathy Blomstrom, Joyce Gibson, Mrs. Catherine Huffman, Jay Jenkins, Hassie Jones, Shelby Stephenson, William C. Vincent, and Millie Yongue. I am grateful to Bynum Shaw for giving me a very helpful interview and for sharing with me the remarks that he made during Johnson's introduction into the North Carolina Literary Hall of Fame.

I am very grateful for the editorial advice and support offered during various stages of this project by three highly skilled and generous individuals. I wish to thank John Herbert Roper for his many kindnesses during the early stages of this book; he was most helpful. Fred Hobson first suggested that I consider writing a life of Johnson. He supported this book from its inception, graciously shared his correspondence with Johnson, and took the time, in the midst of many other duties, to read my manuscript in its entirety. He suggested judgments and interpretations that led me to rethink a number of my own. I admire Fred Hobson's writing and value his friendship. Robert J. Brugger, a gentleman and a scholar, edits as skillfully as he writes, and I have had the good fortune to have him as my editor on another book. He generously took the time to read this manuscript and offered invaluable editorial advice. This book has benefited greatly from the assistance of these men. Its faults are, of course, entirely my own.

Finally, I would like to thank my wife, Carol. Since 1985, we have written, co-authored, or co-edited ten books, several of which have run to multiple editions, and there have been frequent contributions to newspapers and magazines. Not surprisingly, we have found ourselves on numerous occasions laboring to meet multiple deadlines. For some people, such close collaboration and such a hectic writing schedule might lead to contention, perhaps even to lunacy, but thanks to her impeccable North Carolina manners, calm demeanor, and sense of humor, there has rarely even been a cross word. Far more important, in the midst of all this, she has given birth to a son who is as bright and kind and attractive as she is. Carol's editorial skills far surpass my own, and, more than once, she has led me out of mazes of my own creation. She knows very well the difference between good prose and bad and, bless her, always tells me the truth. I have had the good fortune to marry, to borrow Gerald Johnson's phrase, "a lady of quality."

Abbreviations

AM	*American Mercury*
AES Papers	Adlai E. Stevenson Papers, Seeley G. Mudd Manuscript Library, Princeton University, Princeton, N.J.
BA Papers	Betty Adler Papers, H. L. Mencken Collection, Enoch Pratt Free Library, Baltimore
BES	*Baltimore Evening Sun*
BS	*Baltimore Sun*
GDN	*Greensboro (N.C.) Daily News*
GWJ	Gerald W. Johnson
GWJ Papers	Gerald White Johnson Papers, North Carolina Baptist Historical Collection, University Archives, Personal Collection, Z. Smith Reynolds Library, Wake Forest University, Winston-Salem, N.C.
HLM Papers	H. L. Mencken Papers, H. L. Mencken Collection, Enoch Pratt Free Library, Baltimore
HTLFBS	*How Things Look from Bolton Street*
HTLFBS Papers	*How Things Look from Bolton Street* Papers, Maryland Department, Enoch Pratt Free Library, Baltimore
HWO Papers	Howard W. Odum Papers, Southern Historical Collection, Wilson Library, University of North Carolina at Chapel Hill
JSF	*Journal of Social Forces*

LD	*Lexington (N.C.) Dispatch*
NR	*New Republic*
NYHT	*New York Herald Tribune*
NYHTB	*New York Herald Tribune Books*
NYS	*New York Star*
SS	*Smart Set*
VQR	*Virginia Quarterly Review*

Gerald W. Johnson

I Home
1807–1896

Our sympathies are rooted somewhere in some particular locality, although we may spend our lives in a distant part of the world. As a rule the spot where we first become aware of things outside ourselves is the place where our roots are fixed; and as long as they are firmly in the earth our sympathies will not wither, however far distant may be the place where they blossom.

—*Gerald Johnson, ''The Provincial Scholar,'' delivered to the Phi Beta Kappa Society of Davidson College, April 26, 1955*

''Nothing is ever forgotten,'' the wise grandfather, a secular saint redolent of whiskey and tobacco, explains to Lucius Quintus Cincinnatus Priest near the end of William Faulkner's *The Reivers*. ''Nothing is ever lost. It's too valuable.'' Gerald Johnson concurred. A good Southerner, he always understood that where he was going was influenced by where he had been. With his strong sense of the past, he was intrigued by his ancestry and discussed it in newspapers, magazines, lectures, and books. In his eulogy for Dr. William Louis Poteat, a professor of biology and president of Wake Forest College, Johnson explained that his mentor viewed the past ''not with wistful longing for the irrevocable, but speculatively, seeking conspicuous landmarks to align with the present in order to make a reasonable guess at the future.''[1] Describing Dr. Poteat's position, Johnson was actually setting forth his own. In the end, the past for this fourth-generation American was neither an albatross nor a shrine.

Johnson was pure Scot and proud of it. (His surname was initially ''MacIan'' before it became anglicized, and he chose to publish his first magazine article, at age fifteen, under the pseudonym Ian M'Ian.) The ancestral heritage had been passed down, in written form and through the stories spun out

1. William Faulkner, *The Reivers* (New York: New American Library, 1962), 220; GWJ, ''The Future and Dr. Poteat,'' *Biblical Recorder*, June 29, 1938, pp. 4–5.

during meals and before the hearth, and Johnson knew it thoroughly. After the British victory at Culloden in 1746, many of the supporters of Charles Edward Stuart ("Bonnie Prince Charlie") made their way to the Cape Fear Valley in southeastern North Carolina. These immigrants, Johnson explained, "were Highlanders for the most part, political refugees driven out of their country by the troubles." They encountered more trouble in the New World, for these refugees, before being allowed to emigrate, had sworn to support the British crown. These Scots raised the largest Tory force in the colonies and fought for the British during the American Revolutionary War.[2] Clearly, these forebears knew all too well about unpopular positions and defeat and resiliency. So would Johnson.

A sizable number of these immigrants were Presbyterians, and it was a religious calling, not self-interest, that drove Johnson's paternal great-great-grandparents to America at the beginning of the nineteenth century. They proved a memorable couple. Daniel Whyte was born in Scotland sometime between 1776 and 1784. (His surname, anglicized to "White," would become Johnson's middle name.) He converted to the Baptist religion in 1800, married Catharine Campbell in 1806, and emigrated the following year. They reached Charleston, South Carolina, in early October, traveled north to Wilmington, North Carolina, and proceeded to Lumber Ridge in Robeson County, where Whyte preached his first Sunday sermon in America in early November.[3]

On May 23, 1813, he established the Old Spring Hill Baptist Church in

2. Lois Johnson, interview by author, tape recording, Southern Pines, N.C., August 15, 1989; GWJ, "Flora McDonald of the Lost Causes," *BES,* May 28, 1925; R. P. Harriss's speech at Johnson's seventieth birthday party at Baltimore's Enoch Pratt Free Library, GWJ Papers. For further discussion of the Scottish immigrants, see GWJ, "Centennial of the Founding of the Spring Hill Baptist Church," in Mary Rebecca Watson Powers et al., *Our Clan of Johnsons* (Kinston, N.C.: 1940), 104–13; GWJ, "Flora McDonald College Is Pride of Scots of North Carolina," *Edinburgh (Scotland) Weekly Scotsman,* reprinted in *GDN,* January 1, 1922; R. P. Harriss, "Gerald W. Johnson: Journalist and Author," *Gardens, Houses, and People* 22 (September 1947): 12; and Harriss, "The Sage of Bolton Hill," *BS* February 28, 1988.

3. GWJ, "Take Heart," *NR* 146 (February 19, 1962): 9–10. A number of sources, some of them contradictory, discuss the early life, marriage, and emigration of Daniel Whyte (sometimes referred to as "Donald") and Catharine Campbell; see Duncan McNeill, *Life of Reverend Daniel Whyte: With Incidents in Scotland and America* (Raleigh, N.C.: Broughton, 1879), 3–4; GWJ, "Centennial of the Founding of the Spring Hill Baptist Church," 104–13; and Catherine Jackson, "The Road to Riverton: From Persecution in Old Scotland to a Storied Little Community on the Lumbee River," *The State,* April 1982, pp. 12–15.

what is now Scotland County. Fusing the Old World and the New, sermons were preached in English during the morning and in Gaelic during the afternoon. Shortly after Whyte and Catharine settled in Spring Hill, he was called to the Welch Neck Church in South Carolina, where the family stayed for several years. Thereafter, he and his family returned to Spring Hill and settled permanently. He died in 1824 while on a missionary trip to New Hanover County. He was "a flaming evangel," Johnson explained, "a missionary who burnt himself out in a desperate endeavor to make good the words of his Master." Catharine continued his work, but with a considerable difference, for more than four decades prior to her death in 1867. She "gave ease to suffering bodies," Johnson remarked, "and balm to broken hearts." She was physician and nurse and counselor; fighting the plague, salving the wounds of a slave, she walked boldly where many feared to tread. "While her husband strove against sin," Johnson explained, "she strove against suffering."[4] Johnson's priorities are clear in this beautifully balanced sentence; he could well have chosen the second clause as his own epitaph. This world would always mean more to him than the next; he would respond to human anguish before raising his eyes heavenward. He meant no blasphemy here but rather a focus upon more pressing concerns. Like Catharine, Johnson would try his utmost to be a healer.

Daniel and Catharine's sense of duty and their belief in causes greater than themselves were passed on to their progeny. Their oldest daughter, Mary, married Charles Livingston. Catharine Whyte Livingston, the daughter of Mary and Charles, was born in 1826 and married Duncan Johnson. These were Johnson's paternal grandparents. Like their ancestors, they faced considerable hardship, not from the wilderness of the New World but rather from the cauldron of the Civil War. In late September 1862—after the Peninsula Campaign and Second Manassas and General Lee's first Maryland Campaign resulting in the bloody draw at Sharpsburg—Catharine Johnson told a correspondent: "We have beautiful weather these days, but I expect it is cold where all our boys are in Virginia. But why do I say all our boys? Nearly all

4. Joyce M. Gibson, *Scotland County Emerging, 1750–1900: The History of a Small Section of North Carolina* (Marceline, Mo.: Walsworth, 1995), 48; GWJ, "The Lumbee River," 3, GWJ Papers; GWJ, "Centennial of the Founding of the Spring Hill Baptist Church," 105. "The Lumbee River" was read by Johnson to the Gerald Johnson Book Club in Red Springs, N.C., on May 15, 1947, and is reprinted in part under the same title in *Pembroke Magazine* 15 (1983): 94–97. Spring Hill in 1813 was in Richmond County; Scotland County was created in February 1899 (Gibson, *Scotland County Emerging,* 223).

of them are now buried in Virginia's soil." Johnson was not the only member of this clan to understand the merits of the plain style.[5]

"My own people were . . . all wearers of the gray," Johnson wrote proudly more than a half century later, and at least one of his ancestors died for the Confederacy. The homes of both sets of Johnson's grandparents lay in the path of General William T. Sherman, whose men did considerable damage in Scotland County, including defiling a church. "In childhood," Johnson said, "I was an avid listener to tales that convinced me that he was a fiend in human form." As an adult, Johnson would conclude that the South faced far more dangerous enemies than this Yankee general.[6]

Given this ancestry, his own strong sense of the past, and his writer's need to commit his thoughts to paper, it is hardly surprising that he would analyze the war throughout his canon. He would lay blame where deserved and give praise where merited. On the one hand, he would harbor no romantic notions about the Lost Cause. He would conclude that the war was an avoidable tragedy, and that Yankee Abolitionists and Southern Fire-Eaters were equally responsible for the carnage. On the other hand, he would take great pride in the service record of North Carolina; the state provided one-fifth of the Confederacy's soldiers and sustained one-third of the casualties. These soldiers, he would publicize the state's boast, were "first at Bethel, farthest at Gettysburg, and last at Appomattox." People would interest him more than abstractions did, and his elegiac writing about the war would prove more winning than his polemics. He would celebrate the bravery of those cadets of the Virginia Military Institute who fell during the Battle of New Market, and he would capture the grandeur of General Lee: "He was great in war, greater in peace, greatest in defeat. He was brave and gentle; he was honorable and tolerant; he was manful and stainless. He won without gloating and lost without complaining. He maintained discipline and yet made allowance for

5. Catharine Whyte Livingston Johnson to Emeline Phillips, September 27, 1862, photocopy in the possession of Mrs. Frederick Allen Sliger, Valparaiso, Ind.

6. GWJ, "On Recognizing a Stain," *BES,* November 23, 1939; Gibson, *Scotland County Emerging,* 134–37. Various sources offer different figures for the ancestry killed in the war. According to the family tree, two of Johnson's great-uncles were killed (photocopy in the possession of Mrs. Frederick Allen Sliger, Valparaiso, Ind.); see also Fred Hobson, introduction to *South-Watching: Selected Essays by Gerald W. Johnson,* ed. Fred Hobson (Chapel Hill: University of North Carolina Press, 1983), ix; GWJ, *By Reason of Strength* (New York: Minton, Balch, 1930), 162–72; and GWJ, *American Heroes and Hero-Worship* (New York: Harper and Brothers, 1943), 12.

human error."[7] Johnson would grasp the enormity of the achievements of the Army of Northern Virginia, those brave men who did so much with so little for four long years, laid down their arms, and then manfully faced Reconstruction. In the end, this tragedy for the South would provide the occasion for some of Johnson's more compelling prose.

Johnson's father, Archibald, was born on August 9, 1859, in Riverton. He was thus a boy of five during that epic meeting at Appomattox. As a child, adolescent, and young adult, he endured the peace that, as his son would remark decades later, proved "more disastrous to the South than the peace of 1918 [was] to Germany. Not until about 1880 were the last looters sent packing and the South given the chance to start reconstruction . . . instead of destruction." Riverton lay a short distance from Spring Hill, and the traditional values of Daniel Whyte and Catharine Campbell were passed down among the closely knit Scottish community. The church offered spiritual guidance: Archibald "learned of the goodness of God—also his wrath. He chose early his path, the straight and narrow one, and he never deviated one iota." The Richmond Temperance and Literary Society taught him to be abstemious and articulate. And at the Spring Hill Academy, a private school on the church grounds "reputed to be one of the finest in that section of the state," he received the equivalent (in years, at least) of our modern high school education. However, Archibald's education "continued throughout his life" and taught his son that "the measure of a man is in his character, not in his diplomas." The recipient of numerous honorary doctoral degrees, Johnson would never slight an autodidact.[8]

Early in his career, Archibald taught school. Working at his half-brother's institution in Whiteville, North Carolina, he met Flora Caroline McNeill. Two years Archibald's senior, this fellow teacher was the daughter of Sheriff Hector McNeill of Cumberland County and had been educated at Floral College in Robeson County. This institution was, as Joyce M. Gibson has explained, "one of the first four-year colleges for women chartered by the

7. GWJ, "This Is the Way It Was," *NYHTB,* January 13, 1946; GWJ, "Retirement of a Press Agent," *BES,* June 25, 1931; GWJ, "Lost Leader," *BES,* June 1, 1933.

8. GWJ, "Mill Men Who Were Statesmen," *Cotton and Its Products* 3 (July 1925): 72–73; "Archibald Johnson," *Charity and Children* 45 (January 10, 1935): 2; Robert Melvin, "Livingston Johnson: A Study of a Baptist Editor's Role in Controversial Issues" (master's thesis, Southeast Baptist Theological Seminary, 1952), chapter 2, p. 16; GWJ to John Webb, July 23, 1975, photocopy in the possession of Mr. Charles Lambeth, Thomasville, N.C. See Gibson, *Scotland County Emerging,* 95, 121–23.

North Carolina legislature." Flora and Archibald married in 1885, and this union was "nearly as ideal as human alliances ever become. . . . They never attained wealth and ease, but they did win happiness.[9] This marriage would endure for forty-nine years until Archibald's death.

In 1882, he and a partner opened a hardware store in nearly Laurinburg. It failed, and the creditors agreed to accept partial payment. "Thank you," Archibald said, "but a just debt with me has not been settled until it has been paid one hundred cents to the dollar." He paid in full and passed on such probity to his son. About seven years later, Archibald turned to farming and "hated it." His son would never have any romantic vision of life on the land, and this attitude would prove very significant in later literary combat. Prior to the time of Gerald's birth, then, Archibald's career was marked by false starts. He had not yet discovered the calling that would make him famous: editing *Charity and Children,* the newspaper that would allow him to exert considerable influence throughout the state and lead him to be extolled as the "friend of the fatherless."[10]

It would be difficult to exaggerate Archibald's influence upon his son. There were differences, of course. Gerald would scoff at the Temperance movement and, unlike his father, would question the virtues of laissez-faire capitalism. Moreover, the son would never prove formally religious as the father was. In far more important ways, however, Gerald would unquestionably prove his father's son. Both showed contempt for worldly things, wrote prolifically, and never hesitated to say what they thought. "I would rather be wrong than nothing," Archibald liked to remark, and Gerald would concur. Archibald's concern for the orphans would manifest itself in Gerald's compassion for life's unfortunates. "I like a good man and loathe a holy one," Gerald would remark. Archibald was the former.[11]

What's bred in the bone, goes an old adage, is born in the flesh. Johnson's ancestry clearly helped to shape him. From Daniel Whyte and Catharine Campbell, he learned that America is no country for the timid, and that freedom, while costly and dangerous, is superior to safety. The response of his region and his family during the Civil War taught him that the good citizen defends his country, and he would enlist in the army immediately after

9. Mary Rebecca Watson Powers et al., "Archibald Johnson," in *Our Clan of Johnsons* (Kinston, N.C.: 1940), 71; Gibson, *Scotland County Emerging,* 99, 161, 165.

10. W. R. Cullom, "Archibald Johnson, 1859–1934," pamphlet, GWJ Papers; GWJ, "A Letter from Gerald Johnson," *LD,* March 15, 1978.

11. Lois Johnson, interview; GWJ to Wingate Johnson, April 4, 1957, GWJ Papers.

America entered World War I. Those values of "love and honor and pride and pity and compassion and sacrifice" that Faulkner later celebrated so famously in his Nobel Prize address were no glib abstractions for the Johnson clan; these values actually governed their lives.[12] Given his heritage, it would have been astonishing if Johnson had proven mercenary or dishonest, selfish or timid. With Archibald as well as with Livingston Johnson, the uncle who edited the *Biblical Recorder,* and with cousin John Charles McNeill, who became the poet laureate of North Carolina, the family gave Johnson a literary tradition to continue. Johnson's ancestry, in the end, helped to make him the type of writer that he was, helped to shape a career where love and need met serendipitously. He was suitably grateful, for when he looked back upon what had made him, he found it good and wrote it well.

He proved equally grateful to Riverton, the tiny community where he was begotten, born, and shaped. It was here that Johnson "looked on life and found it golden," and the place colored his ideas for the rest of his life. Johnson spent his first six years here in the Upper Cape Fear Valley. This would prove his land of lost content, and its resonances would tug at him in the same way that Fern Hill entranced Dylan Thomas.[13]

On August 6, 1890, Johnson was born, as he remarked later, "of white parents in a county in the Black Belt of North Carolina." He was the second of five children, and the only boy. An older brother had been stillborn. Mary Johnson, the oldest child of Flora and Archibald, had been born on December 30, 1885. Katherine, Lois, and Ella, Johnson's younger sisters, were born in 1892, 1894, and 1897. According to Mary, it was a "hot August morning" when Johnson was delivered at home: "We were all proud that he was a boy, especially my father. Of course his name should have been Duncan or Hector, but Mother didn't care for Duncan, nor Father for Hector, so the latter was allowed to exercise his romantic inclination for Gerald, to the scandal of the family in the eyes of our Scotch relatives." Certainly a more memorable name than "Gerald," "Hector" would have proven especially apt for this writer whose career would prove bellicose indeed. As a child, Johnson was called "Chunny," but the nickname did not stick.[14]

12. Joseph Blotner, *Faulkner: A Biography* (New York: Random House, 2:1974), 1357.

13. GWJ, "The Lumbee River," 7, GWJ Papers.

14. GWJ, "A Tilt with Southern Windmills," *VQR* 1 (July 1925): 184–92; Mary Johnson Lambeth, "Sketch of the Life of Gerald Johnson by His Sister, Mamie, Mrs. Charles Lambeth of Thomasville, N.C., 1939," 1, GWJ Papers; Charles Lambeth to author, August 17, 1989.

The country into which Johnson was born was very much in a state of transition. The gap between wealth and poverty had increased to the point where laissez-faire capitalism, previously considered sacrosanct, was being challenged, and the year of Johnson's birth saw the passage of the Sherman Anti-Trust Act. The American frontier, so portentous for the national myth of freedom, was closed later that decade. Only a little more than a century after the ratification of the Constitution, an older America was dying, and a new one struggling to be born.

The South into which Johnson was born was struggling as well. Its traditional agricultural economy was becoming increasingly industrialized. Between 1890 and 1900, the number of factories in North Carolina increased more than sevenfold. By the later date, the state had about one-third of the region's approximately 100,000 textile workers. Six years prior to Johnson's birth, there were six cotton mills in Scotland County alone. The region, like the country, experienced a significant demographic shift. In seven of the eleven former Confederate states, the urban population more than doubled between 1880 and 1890. Violence plagued the region; the South during this time, as C. Vann Woodward has remarked, "seems to have been one of the most violent communities of comparable size in all Christendom." Finally, the South struggled under the pall of the depression that plagued America in 1893 and 1894. In the South, its effects were felt as early as 1890 and 1891.[15]

North Carolina was experiencing significant political change and considerable racial tensions. In 1876, Democrats won control of the state government, but the Republicans retained control of Scotland County until 1884. In 1894, the Democrats lost control of both houses of the state legislature to the Fusionists, a coalition of Republicans and Populists. The following year, as William Alexander Mabry has pointed out, "race relations in the 'Black Belt' became strained almost to the breaking point." In 1896, the Republican candidate, Daniel E. Russell, was elected governor. White supremacists maintained a highly visible and violent presence during the political campaign and election of 1898. On November 10 of that year, racial violence in

15. Gaines M. Foster, *Ghosts of the Confederacy: Defeat, the Lost Cause, and the Emergence of the New South, 1865–1913* (New York: Oxford University Press, 1987), 79; Edward L. Ayers, *The Promise of the New South: Life after Reconstruction* (New York: Oxford University Press, 1992), 107, 111; Gibson, *Scotland County Emerging*, 153; C. Vann Woodward, *Origins of the New South, 1877–1913*, vol. 9, *A History of the South* (Baton Rouge: Louisiana State University Press, 1951), 159; Ayers, *The Promise of the New South*, 252–53, 283; see Woodward, *Origins of the New South*, 264.

Wilmington resulted in the death of approximately 100 African Americans. Two years later, North Carolina passed the Suffrage Amendment (also referred to as the "Disenfranchising Amendment"), which established a literacy requirement for voting in a state where more than 47 percent of the blacks were illiterate.[16]

When he looked back upon this tumultuous period of transition, Johnson would write forcefully. "Even in 1891," he remarked, "the scars of the great war that had ruined the South were still red and raw." Federal troops had been withdrawn in 1877, but as a boy Johnson still smelled, to use his strong olfactory image, "the cesspool of Reconstruction." The South of the 1890s, he recalled, was "mangy, flea-bitten, hungry, and . . . lynching became its favorite sport." Celebrating Archibald's bravery, Johnson said that "civilized white southerners, such as my father, took real and serious risks in denouncing the practice." The South of the 1890s also witnessed a portentous legal case begun in Louisiana. On June 7, 1892, Homer Adolph Plessy, reportedly seven-eighths white, bought a first-class railroad ticket but was later told by a conductor that he could not sit in the coach for white passengers. Plessy sued, and the case was ruled upon by the Supreme Court four years later. By a vote of seven to one, the court ruled against Plessy and said that the doctrine of "separate but equal" facilities for blacks and whites was indeed constitutional. To Johnson the child, this naturally meant nothing, but the decision would have huge implications for him later.[17]

For Johnson the child, Riverton proved a safe haven, a place of grace. Outwardly, this small farming community, on the outskirts of what would later be incorporated as the town of Wagram, about thirty-five miles southwest of Fayetteville, seemed inconsequential. The nearest railroad, a narrow-

16. William Alexander Mabry, *The Negro in North Carolina Politics since Reconstruction* (1940; reprint, New York: AMS Press, 1970), 23; Gibson, *Scotland County Emerging*, 145; Mabry, *The Negro in North Carolina Politics since Reconstruction*, 34–35, 40, 42, 47, 53–54, 70–71. See also Ayers, *The Promise of the New South*, 300–302; Woodward, *Origins of the New South*, 350; and Gibson, *Scotland County Emerging*, 206, 212–18.

17. GWJ, "A Commission from Raleigh," *Meredith College Quarterly Bulletin* 34 (March 1941): 4; GWJ, "War and Worse," *BES,* January 23, 1941; GWJ, "Note on Race Prejudice," *North American Review* 233 (March 1932): 226–33; GWJ, *Hod-Carrier: Notes of a Laborer on an Unfinished Cathedral* (New York: William Morrow, 1964), 209; "The Case of Homer Adolph Plessy," in *Race and Education: Integration and Community Control* (Middleton, Conn.: American Education Publications, 1969), 10–11; William B. Lockhart, Yale Kamisar, and Jesse H. Choper, *Constitutional Law: Cases—Comments—Questions* 3rd ed. (St. Paul: West, 1970), 1194–98.

gauge line for hauling lumber, lay nearly two miles away. Riverton was unincorporated and remained unmarked on many maps. (It remains so undesignated today.) The place was so small, Johnson joked, that its population was "six kin."[18]

But the joke, as Johnson well knew, told only part of the story. He celebrated Riverton as "more a state of mind" than an actual place and found the community remarkable for both its intellectual rigor and its quality of life. Riverton was marked by personal kindness and an absolute lack of pretense. The carpenter Jack McGirt built for Archibald a two-room cabin that became known prosaically as "The House That Jack Built." This proved the community center, and over the years Johnson came to think of it in much the same way that E. M. Forster thought of Howards End: a place of continuity, fellowship, and understanding. Producing doctors and lawyers, clergymen and teachers, editors and authors, Riverton took the life of the mind very seriously, and Johnson took considerable pride in the fact that "the community produced more books than there are houses."[19]

He read early and showed the vivid imagination that proved so useful later. He created an imaginary playmate named Jesse, who, as Mary Johnson Lambeth has recalled, "was almost a real person to the rest of the family." Gerald "talked to him, walked with him, and played with him for a long time. Then one day Jesse ceased to be. 'Jesse got lost in the swamp and an alligator ate him up,' Gerald said." He proved remarkably articulate as a child; when he was five or six, men gave him coins to make impromptu speeches on the street, and he used the money to buy books. He learned to laugh as well; he told his grandfather, a bald man with a long beard, that it would be better "if your beard grew on the top of your head."[20] Later, such drollery would enliven Johnson's prose.

Riverton balanced mind and body. It was a place of safety in a violent land for children to spend their lamb-white days. Tramping through the woods, picnicking, skinny-dipping in the Lumber River (everyone pronounced it "Lumbee"), these "sunburnt boys" were described for posterity by John

18. Ian M'Ian [GWJ], "Newport," *Biblical Recorder* 1 (November 1905); Lloyd Dennis, "Gerald Johnson: Man of Many Parts," *GDN,* March 22, 1964.

19. GWJ, "The Lumbee River," 2, 6, GWJ Papers; GWJ, "Letter to the Editor," *Laurinburg Exchange,* September 2, 1949.

20. Lambeth, "Sketch," 1–2; G.B., "Brilliant Baltimore Writer Never Forgets He's a Tar Heel," *GDN,* September 1, 1940.

Charles McNeill.[21] They were idyllic, these days of innocence for a young boy tucked away in a small and friendly corner of rural North Carolina.

But nothing so good could last. Johnson would later call Riverton "holy ground" and draw upon the Garden of Eden myth to speak of childhood. However, it was not puberty that drove him out of the garden. He left earlier, when Archibald's work took him elsewhere, and the family had to move. After he stopped farming in 1892, Archibald became editor of the nearby *Laurinburg Exchange.* Early in 1895, he founded the *Red Springs Citizen.* That summer, he agreed to edit *Charity and Children,* the house paper of the Thomasville Baptist Orphanage, and he moved to Thomasville in September 1895.[22]

The family joined him the following year. Much later, Johnson would explain that the "change in the environment and style of living was greater than would now be involved in a move from Thomasville to Seattle." He journeyed from the Coastal Plain to the Piedmont, from the land of cotton to the land of wheat, "from a predominately Highland Scotch community to one predominately Pennsylvania Dutch."[23] He saw no need to explain to his readers that, psychologically, this journey from one stage of life to another proved far more profound.

Unlike Thomas Wolfe, Johnson would conclude that he could indeed go home again. He would visit Riverton many times—as a boy and adolescent and college student during summer vacations, as a young journalist traveling down from Lexington and Thomasville, and as a middle-aged and elderly man making the trip down from Baltimore. He would never cease to revel in the annual summer reunions held in The House That Jack Built.

Far more important for his readers, he would return figuratively through the power of the imagination. And it is here especially that one wishes for that autobiography which Johnson chose not to write. He had a wonderful story to tell. He could have done with the Cape Fear Valley what Mencken does, in *Happy Days,* with Baltimore during the1880s and 1890s; what William Alexander Percy does, in *Lanterns on the Levee,* with Greenville, Missis-

21. McNeill's poem of this title is included in Powers, *Our Clan of Johnsons,* 87. For further discussion of the ambiance of Riverton, see GWJ to Louis Futtrell, August 22, 1914, GWJ Papers; and Margaret McMahan, "Lumbee—It Begins in Moore and Takes a Poetic Journey," *Southern Pines (N.C.) Pilot,* June 17, 1991, p. 11-B.

22. GWJ, "The Lumbee River," 2, GWJ Papers; GWJ, *Number Thirty-Six: A Novel* (New York: Minton, Balch, 1933), 266.

23. GWJ, "19th Century Thomasville Recalled," *LD,* [1946].

sippi; and what Willie Morris does with Yazoo City in both *North toward Home* and *My Dog Skip*. As Annie Dillard does with Pittsburgh, Johnson could have chronicled his own particular American childhood. While he chose to remain silent as an autobiographer, he would speak in other forums. Quite significantly, he would use his first publication to hymn the glories of Riverton—thus making the first payment on a debt that could never be repaid in full. And as an eighty-six-year-old journalist, he would fondly recall the yuletide of 1894 and give thanks for a child's Christmas in Riverton.[24]

Johnson's personal visits and professional career would merge most happily in 1947 when, long an author of national renown, he would return to address the Gerald Johnson Book Club in Red Springs. He would celebrate Riverton as a "fairy-haunted wood" and pause to ponder what was past and passing: "I am a little sorry for the children running through [The House That Jack Built] these days, because I cannot believe that their lot was ever as happy as mine was." With the land of his youth now "a land of memory," he would offer no lecture here but rather a prayer of thanksgiving.[25]

Johnson's end lay in his beginning. Both his life and work were marked by the best qualities of youth: optimism and curiosity, wonder and delight. As an elderly author, Johnson would conclude that there was no more important task than writing for children, and at seventy-eight he would join Eugene McCarthy's children's crusade. Youth is short, Johnson well knew, but art is long, and the canon of this native son grown famous testifies to the magnitude of a tiny place called Riverton—a place that, no matter where else Johnson happened to reside, he never ceased to think of as home.

24. M'Ian, "Newport"; GWJ, "The Indomitable Christmas Spirit," *Long Island (N.Y.) Newsday,* December 19, 1976.

25. GWJ, "The Lumbee River," 7, GWJ Papers.

2 The Education of Gerald Johnson
1896–1911

> When my father built this house in Thomasville, North Carolina, there was
> before it a sapling no taller than a schoolboy. Sixty years later the spot is occu-
> pied by a large hickory tree . . . emphatically not a sapling. The sapling is
> not there, although it never died; no more is the republic that existed when
> Washington was president existent now; and it is a reasonable assumption that
> the republic I know will not be existent when my youngest grandson is as old
> as I am now.
>
> —*Gerald Johnson,* Hod-Carrier

The Johnsons valued education highly. All five children were college graduates, Gerald from Wake Forest and his four sisters from Mere- dith College in Raleigh. The family took considerable pride in this accom- plishment, all the more remarkable because limited funds made tuition payments a struggle. In time, all five children would spend at least part of their careers as educators, and Lois Johnson would become the first dean of women at Wake Forest.[1]

Johnson proved grateful for the educational opportunities offered him in Thomasville, Mars Hill, and Wake Forest. He proved a successful student, but he never allowed schooling to get in the way of his education. One of those on whom nothing was lost, he took his education as it came. He recog- nized that there was much to be learned outside the classroom, and that the best teachers did not always work in schools. Johnson's education gave him considerable factual information, strengthened his intellectual discipline, and helped to sharpen those writing skills evident very early on, but just as impor- tant, it helped him open his eyes to the world around him.

As he grew, he became aware of race. "My own childhood," he recalled,

---

1. Lois Johnson, interview by author, tape recording, Southern Pines, N.C., August 15, 1989; Mary Rebecca Watson Powers et al., *Our Clan of Johnsons* (Kinston, N.C.: 1940), 73–75.

"was . . . racially and religiously dominant, not dominated. As far as indoctri-nation went, it was anti-racist; when I first heard the word 'nigger' I was informed, with the utmost emphasis, that it was an obscenity, and if I were ever heard uttering it, I was promised a switching laid on with vigor." In the more heterogeneous world of Thomasville, he encountered cruelty that he had not witnessed in Riverton: "Only at ten or twelve did I discover, with genuine astonishment, that there existed a class of white boys who regarded 'rocking (i.e., stoning) niggers' as a legitimate pastime; but I was informed that it was a very low class and a disgrace to the white race." Johnson never forgot such wanton cruelty and, throughout his career, attacked all racial vio-lence. "During my lifetime," Walker Percy has explained, ". . . I cannot re-call a single talented Southern politician (and only the rare writer) who has not been obsessed with the problem of the relation of white people and black people. It was in fact for better or worse the very condition of being South-ern."[2] Johnson may well have quibbled with the sweep of "obsessed," but he would have agreed with the gist of the remark. He would labor, sometimes optimistically and sometimes in near despair, to make sense of the relationship between the races. He would conclude, in general, that their fates are inter-twined—a position that went too far for some and not nearly far enough for others.

He also grew aware of the pitfalls of conservative religion. As a boy, he encountered, outside the home, the specter of Fundamentalism, and he was chilled. At about eight or nine, he witnessed a fire-and-brimstone sermon; "it took me," he would recall, "fifteen years to get over it." He would always wonder how humankind could debase a benevolent God for its own nefari-ous purposes, and he would attack the horrors resulting from what he viewed as an overly literal interpretation of the Bible.[3]

He paid attention to class, but not in the conventional sense of the term. Discussing his boyhood in Thomasville, he explained, "Since nobody, white or black, in my neighborhood gained much more than bare subsistence from his labor, who was poor?" Given his background, it is not surprising that he would care nothing about people's bank accounts and little about their lin-eage. He would care greatly, however, about their intellectual ability. Rather

2. GWJ, *Hod-Carrier: Notes of a Laborer on an Unfinished Cathedral* (New York: William Morrow, 1964), 26; see GWJ to H. L. Mencken, August 31, 1947, HLM Papers; Walker Percy, *Signposts in a Strange Land* (New York: Farrar, Straus and Giroux, 1992), 29–30.

3. GWJ to Katherine Johnson Parham, November 15, 1971, GWJ Papers.

than pay homage to money or blood, he would celebrate the aristocracy of expertise and intellect.[4]

In the end, the education of Gerald Johnson meant considerably more than formal schooling. As a youth, adolescent, and young adult, he struggled to make sense of the world around him. This is, certainly, an old and familiar story, but there was a significant difference. Most people struggle—some making sense of little, others becoming astute—before passing into oblivion, their voices eternally stilled. Johnson was blessed with the gift of the artist— the ability to understand and articulate—and the little boy who followed his father to Thomasville in 1896 would become an author who shaped these experiences and beliefs and then passed them along to posterity.

The Thomasville where Flora and the children joined Archibald then had a population of about a thousand. The town was experiencing the beginnings of the furniture industry, particularly the chair industry, that would later distinguish it. Johnson celebrated its quality of life: "the broad, warm, kindly, cheerful humanity," "the quiet heroisms," and the "golden generosities." He made Thomasville seem a bit like Grover's Corner in Thornton Wilder's *Our Town*. Flora and Archibald found Thomasville a fine place to raise a family. After the initial trauma of the move, Gerald adjusted easily, resilient as always, and Archibald, moving forward into what may be called his public life, experienced considerable success as an editor, writer, and speaker.[5]

The Thomasville Baptist Orphanage (now called the Mills Home) had opened in November 1885. It sheltered boys and girls ages eight to sixteen and offered both academic and vocational training. The home grew rapidly; by 1903, it was the second-largest Baptist orphanage in America. The first issue of *Charity and Children,* a weekly, had appeared on July 4, 1887. Prior to the time that Archibald signed on as editor, its publication had been sporadic.[6]

Archibald had two main duties, to serve as field representative for the orphanage and to edit the periodical, and he achieved fame in both areas. He ascended so many pulpits to raise funds and to explain the mission of the orphanage that half of his mail came addressed to "the Reverend" Archibald Johnson. The Charlotte *Observer* explained that "yes, he constantly speaks

4. GWJ, *Hod-Carrier,* 26.

5. GWJ, foreword, to *Wheels of Faith and Courage: A History of Thomasville, North Carolina,* by Mary Green Matthews and M. Jewell Sink (High Point, N.C.: Hall Printing Co., 1952), vii; GWJ, "Sample City," *BES,* June 8, 1939.

6. Bernard Washington Spilman, *The Mills Home: A History of the Baptist Orphanage Movement in North Carolina, 1885–1932* (Thomasville, N.C.: Mills Home, 1976), 36–103.

from pulpits but he is not a licensed preacher—you might say he is a 'blockade preacher.' " The son of this "blockade preacher" delighted in recounting this story until the end of his days. Under Archibald's editorship, the circulation of *Charity and Children* rose from 2,000 in 1896 to 7,000 in 1900 and finally reached 30,000. It was called the most skillfully edited religious paper in the country. Archibald now had an extensive audience; his editorials were widely reproduced and proved influential throughout the state.[7]

None of this was lost on Gerald. The paper was printed at the orphanage, and he spent so much time in the print ship that he was "sort of brought up there." From this time on, he "never considered entering any line of work other than journalism." Moreover, Archibald always said what he thought— "the paper trod on various toes and howls of scandalized protests began to come in"—and as Gerald grew, he better recognized the costs of candor. Like his father, he would refuse to temper his remarks to placate an audience.[8]

Although Archibald chose not to house his family on the orphanage grounds—he thought that this would make for too much of a closed community—he did send his children to the orphanage school. Here, Gerald met the first of a number of superb teachers who influenced him. Miss Sallie McCracken taught him when he was about ten years old, "with no more judgment than a puppy," and he "hated her" for making him study what did not interest him. Later, he felt differently and remarked that "it was many years before I realized that I had . . . learned what was not in any textbook and never mentioned in any classroom—namely, some inkling of the tremendous power inherent in what we call, vaguely, character." Johnson paid this teacher the greatest possible tribute: he wrote about her and said thank you publicly. Later, when he was in the seventh grade, another teacher gave him a copy of *Bulfinch's Mythology*. He easily memorized the abridged version and had little trouble with the unabridged. "I was hooked," Johnson admitted, and he concluded that "there must be a story here." There were many stories

7. James Walt, "Tale of Another Liberal's Progress," *Maryland English Journal* (fall 1965): 58; GWJ, "A Letter from Gerald Johnson," *LD*, March 15, 1978; Lloyd Dennis, "Gerald Johnson: Man of Many Parts," *GDN*, March 22, 1964; Wingate Johnson to GWJ, March 30, 1933, GWJ papers; see also GWJ, "19th Century Thomasville Recalled," *LD* [1946].

8. Jinny Voris, "According to Mr. Johnson: Some Insights on H. L. Mencken" (unpublished paper based on an interview with Johnson, March 26, 1968), HLM Papers; Mary Johnson Lambeth, "Sketch of the Life of Gerald Johnson by His Sister, Mamie, Mrs. Charles Lambeth of Thomasville, N.C., 1939," 4, GWJ Papers; Mary Rebecca Watson Powers et al., "Archibald Johnson," in *Our Clan of Johnsons,* (Kinston, N.C.: 1940) 72.

indeed, and Johnson would make frequent use of these myths to enrich his writing.[9]

After attending the orphanage school for the first seven grades, he went, apparently for one year only, to the Thomasville Public School. His formal education in Thomasville concluded with tutoring provided by Professor H. W. Reinhart. He taught Johnson Latin and the nuances of English style. Johnson wrote about him as well. In his second novel, he drew Reinhart as Professor Mason and remarked that "he possessed the power to walk familiarly among the shades of the great dead."[10]

What he learned outside the classroom complemented the instruction received within. He read omnivorously. Recalling her brother's childhood, Mary Johnson Lambeth said that "his happiest hours were spend flat on his stomach reading the *Youth's Companion* and everything else that he could get his hands on." A minister in Thomasville was so impressed with the boy's intellectual regimen that he held it up as a model in one of his sermons. Johnson remained open to new experiences, challenged himself intellectually from the beginning, and refused to fear failure. He published early, both poetry and prose, and again had the good fortune to find himself among remarkable teachers.[11]

During a summer visit to Riverton when Johnson was about ten, he saw his cousin Archibald McMillan, a graduate of the University of North Carolina and a veteran of Wheeler's cavalry, come in to dinner after working in the fields. He was literally covered with black dust, and Johnson worked the pump while Archibald washed himself. "He looked at me with a sardonic grin," Johnson recalled, "and broke into the thunderous strophes of the *Geor-*

9. GWJ, "19th Century Thomasville Recalled"; GWJ, "I Hated Miss Sallie," *Charity and Children* 83 (December 2, 1969): 3; Dennis, "Gerald Johnson: Man of Many Parts."

10. In his letter of January 28, 1957, to Adlai Stevenson, Johnson said that he attended the orphanage school for the first seven grades (AES Papers). The records of his schooling here no longer exist, as I discovered when I visited the orphanage in August 1991. Public school education in Thomasville is discussed by M. Jewell Sink and Mary Green Matthews in *Pathfinders Past and Present: A History of Davidson County, North Carolina* (Thomasville, N.C.: 1972), 193. The building where Johnson went to school burned on April 15, 1922, and his records may well have been destroyed then. In any event, they no longer exist (Sharon Lambeth, director of personnel for the Thomasville Public Schools, telephone interview by author, January 19, 1996). *Pathfinders Past and Present* mentions Johnson's studies with Professor Reinhart. He is drawn as Professor Mason in GWJ, *Number Thirty-Six: A Novel* (New York: Minton, Balch, 1933), 113.

11. Lambeth, "Sketch," 2.

gics of Virgil: *'O fortunatos nimium, sua si bona norint agricolas.'* O most happy farmers, if they only knew their good fortune." Johnson was startled at first and then came to recognize that he "had seen something wonderful." He proceeded to explain that while his cousin's "body labored in a land of defeat and poverty, his mind 'could turn to the glory that was Greece, and the grandeur that was Rome.' It was triumph, triumph of time over fate. And there is no greater."[12] Johnson would relate this tale of resiliency, this testament to the redemptive power of art, in a number of forums, and the landscape of the imagination would prove as important for him as it was for his cousin.

About four years later, Johnson received similarly powerful instruction from another cousin, the poet John Charles McNeill. Sixteen years Johnson's senior, McNeill was a journalist and teacher and the author of two volumes of verse (a third would be published posthumously). He and Gerald and some other boys were talking one afternoon when someone described a neighborhood character as a bore. McNeill said that the comment reminded him of something in Ovid, and he went and fetched the book. Johnson recalled that "he was stunned. Ovid, properly translated, made sense, and extremely good sense at that! More than that, here was one of the neighborhood lads, one of the kinfolks, who understood the old Roman and enjoyed him. Forty years later the boy [testifies] that that was the moment when the can-opener pierced the tin and . . . fresh air began whistling through the vacuum."[13] Typically modest—his mind was far from empty—Johnson was using a lively trope to describe his intellectual epiphany.

He repaid his debt to McNeill through the currency of art. On October 17, 1907, McNeill died at thirty-three of undetermined causes. A few days later, a polished quatrain appeared anonymously in the *Charlotte Observer:*

> We saw him start his way with joy and mirth,
> We watched his dizzy flight with straining eyes,
> We marked the moment that he ceased to rise
> And saw with silent pain his fall to earth.

12. GWJ, "The Cadets of New Market," in *America-Watching: Perspectives on the Course of an Incredible Century* (Owings Mills, Md.: Stemmer House, 1976), 27–37; GWJ "To Live and Die in Dixie," in *South-Watching South-Watching: Selected Essays by Gerald W. Johnson,* ed. Fred Hobson (Chapel Hill: University of North Carolina Press, 1983), 146–57; GWJ, "The South: How May It Obtain Virtue and Wisdom?" *GDN,* May 8, 1960.

13. GWJ, "The Lumbee River," 4–5, GWJ Papers.

The poet, who wrote impeccable iambic pentameter, clearly recalled the Icarus myth. The family wondered who had written the poem and decided that it was Mr. Kesler, the head of the orphanage. Johnson finally owned up: "I wrote it. I was chopping wood and it just came to me." He proved just as proficient as a writer of prose in the aforementioned story about Riverton that had appeared in the *Biblical Recorder* two years before. Moreover, in 1907, in addition to eulogizing McNeill, Johnson covered, for *Charity and Children,* the Jamestown Ter-Centennial Exposition in Norfolk. By the age of seventeen, then, Johnson had published both verse and essays and had covered his first story as a reporter.[14]

The year 1907 marked a watershed of sorts. With the exception of an extended period during 1915, when he was sick with tuberculosis, Johnson would from this time on live in Thomasville only periodically—during summers as he continued his education, on weekends after he took his first journalism job, and during various brief trips thereafter. With Thomasville, as he had done with his teachers, he would acknowledge his debt in print. The town would be drawn as Rodgersville in *Number Thirty-Six: A Novel,* a *Bildungsroman* chronicling the protagonist's journey from innocence to experience. This journey would be detailed again, albeit more obliquely, through Johnson's power of association. Much later, in 1953, when the sixty-three-year-old-man was doing television commentary, he would winsomely recall the period right near the end of his Thomasville days. He thought of Peter Pan: "It was a world that had room for Sir James Barrie and a lovely princess of the realm of illusion; and when they made us weep floods of tears and swear to believe in fairies, it was not a complete fraud." Once one of the Lost Boys, Johnson had grown up.[15]

He left Thomasville to spend the 1907–1908 academic year at Mars Hill College. This two-year Baptist institution was located eight miles north of Asheville, in the mountains, and its enrollment was then 364. Johnson's academic records there have not survived. Decades later, he would use the *Baltimore Evening Sun* to celebrate Aunt Kate, a local woman who offered conversation and Sunday dinner at her home, as "the greatest animal tamer I have ever encountered." With no official connection to the school, she was "the best teacher in the place." An agent of civilization, she taught her young guests to look past appearances, and "her boys and girls have always been a

14. Lambeth, "Sketch," 3.
15. GWJ, *HTLFBS,* aired on July 19, 1953, *HTLFBS* Papers.

bit more skeptical than they were before, much less impressed by money, and social position, and political power." Such attitudes were clearly Johnson's. Whether he distinguished himself academically during this year may never be known, but more than four decades later, in May 1955, Mars Hill would honor its famous graduate as Alumnus of the Year.[16]

In the fall of 1908, Johnson matriculated to Wake Forest College, then located in the village of the same name seventeen miles north of Raleigh. He stayed three years; the school's influence stayed with him for the rest of his life. To say the least, there had been a strong family presence there. Among others, there had been John Charles McNeill, who had graduated in 1898, and Dr. Wingate Memory Johnson, later a professor at Bowman Gray Medical School and the editor of the *North Carolina Medical Journal,* who had graduated seven years later. It would have been unthinkable for Johnson to go elsewhere. " I didn't select [Wake Forest]," he remarked waggishly; "I was drafted."[17]

He was drafted into a small school that had few physical amenities. The enrollment during his final year was only 402. There were no paved roads and few automobiles. Only the gymnasium had indoor plumbing, and the dormitories were only then being wired for electric light. Such spartan conditions, however, gave all the more emphasis to the life of the mind, and the college's small size enhanced the interaction between students and faculty, who emphasized teaching rather than research. Professor John Bethune Carlyle—"Johnny B.," as Johnson fondly dubbed him—convinced the young man of the contemporaneity Cicero. Professor Benjamin Sledd—Johnson would nickname him "Old Slick"—"succeeded in making the study of English for his students an adventure." More important, he taught them "some sense." Dr. William Louis Poteat, that remarkable figure whom Johnson would colorfully capture for posterity as "Billy with the Red Necktie," was a professor of biology as well as president of the college since 1905. In Dr.

16. John Angus McLeod, *From These Stones: Mars Hill College, 1865–1967* (Mars Hill, N.C.: Mars Hill College, 1968), appendix V; Edith L. Whitt, registrar of Mars Hill College, to author, April 18, 1995; GWJ, "An Old Woman Passes," *BES,* July 17, 1941; "Mars Hill to Honor Gerald W. Johnson," *Raleigh News and Observer,* May 28, 1955.

17. G. W. Paschal, *History of Wake Forest College,* vol. 1, *1834–1865* (Wake Forest, N.C.: Wake Forest College, 1935), 3. For a discussion of the family presence at Wake Forest, see Jasper L. Memory, "Robert LeRoy McMillan," GWJ Papers; Elaine Westarp, "School Says Thanks for the Memorys and Kin," *Raleigh News and Observer,* March 2, 1985; and GWJ, "The Battle of Ideas," GWJ Papers.

Poteat, Bruce Clayton has observed, Wake Forest "had a courageous exemplar of New South liberalism—that idealistic, perhaps even sentimental notion that social change could be effected by moderate middle-class reformers (college professors and the like) who embraced the basic assumptions of industrial capitalism, education, and white supremacy." Besides engaging in many heated intellectual battles—he kept his head while many of those around him seemed to be losing theirs—he profoundly influenced those students who sat before him. Every year, Johnson observed, Dr. Poteat received "a horde of backwoods boys with not a glimmer of an idea. . . . To them, his dictum, reiterated constantly, that 'no man has a right to an opinion until he has examined the facts' was nothing short of revolutionary. The way of the passionate South was to form an opinion first and then seek facts to support it." Johnson listened attentively.[18]

He was also drafted into a school with an established literary tradition. Johnson lived in the room occupied previously by both Thomas Dixon (1883), author of *The Clansman,* the source for the controversial film *The Birth of a Nation,* and John Charles McNeill. Johnson would continue this tradition, as would Laurence Stallings (1915) and Wilbur J. Cash (1922). Wake Forest obviously spurred creativity. While Johnson was challenged intellectually, he felt comfortable socially. He fell in love, apparently for the first time. After being jilted by a young woman named Gretchen, he howled embarrassingly. Later, when he got older and got more sense, he would laugh loudly at the grotesquely humorous efforts of men and women to deal with one another.[19]

During Johnson's stay, Wake Forest had no Department of Journalism, and he majored in English. His other courses suggest his wide range of interests: French, German, and Latin among the languages; mathematics, biology, chemistry, and physics among the natural sciences; and government, history, and political economy among the social sciences. This course of studies

18. GWJ, "There Are Those Who Love Her," *Raleigh News and Observer,* 28 September 1958; Jesse Glasgow, interview by author, tape recording, Baltimore, July 10, 1990; GWJ, "On Greatness in Teaching," *BES,* July 21, 1946; GWJ, "1876—The Hopkins—1926," *BES,* October 22, 1926; GWJ, "Death of a Teacher," *BES,* January 19, 1940; GWJ, "Old Slick," in *South-Watching,* 200–207; Bruce Clayton, *W. J. Cash: A Life* (Baton Rouge: Louisiana State University Press, 1991), 27; GWJ, "Death Takes a Tar Heel," *BES,* March 16, 1938; and GWJ, "Billy with the Red Necktie," in *South-Watching,* 191–99.

19. GWJ, "There Are Those Who Love Her"; GWJ to Gretchen [last name not identified], September 17, 1911, GWJ Papers.

would prove eminently suitable for a writer who would function best as a generalist. Johnson recalled that "never a spark of ambition to be a scholar stuck in [my] breast, but [I] collected a huge and astonishing amount of *curiosa*." He graduated cum laude—an admirable enough performance, but one suspects that he spent a great deal of time reading outside the syllabi. He definitely spent considerable time and effort on his literary endeavors.[20]

Johnson received a number of honors and awards, among them a fiction medal given at the end of his first year and the editorship of the *Wake Forest Student,* the literary magazine, during his last. The author of Johnson's biographical blurb in his senior yearbook emphasized literary matters: "He is socially endowed with a love for literature; not only is he an admirer of the classics, but he has excelled among his classmates as a producer of fiction." In a letter to Archibald written during Gerald's first year, Professor J. H. Gorrell went considerably further. He praised the style in Gerald's short stories and proceeded to remark that, as a writer, the young man might well surpass his father. Archibald had to be delighted.[21]

Actually, Johnson wrote not only short stories but also poetry and prose fiction that was both expository and polemical. (He wrote no journalism, since the student newspaper, *Old Gold and Black,* was not established until 1916.)[22] He was in a fortunate position at Wake Forest. With the yearbook (*The Howler*) and the student literary magazine, he had convenient forums for his writing. Moreover, he faced no hostile audience.

During his first semester, using the old pseudonym of "Ian M'Ian," Johnson published three short stories in the literary magazine. The second, "Peter," is named after its protagonist. A lawyer homely and poor, Peter proves thoroughly dependable (the religious symbolism is patent) as he competes with a rich lawyer for the affection of Miss Alice Boynton. Resorting to melodrama, Johnson concocts a sledding accident, and Peter risks his life to save Alice's. At the end of this moral tale, she recognizes the virtues of the wounded hero, rejects money, and marries for love. "On Christmas Eve," the longest of these three stories, proves the most ambitious. Johnson the humorist populates this tall tale with a pastor, fond of drink, who likes to steal

20. Glasgow; Hallie Arrington, associate registrar, Wake Forest University, to author, September 6, 1991; GWJ, *Number-Thirty Six,* 180.

21. *The Howler, 1911* 36; Professor J. H. Gorrell to Archibald Johnson, September 13, 1908, GWJ Papers.

22. G. W. Paschal, *History of Wake Forest College,* vol. 3, *1905–1943* (Wake Forest, N.C.: Wake Forest College, 1943), 417.

chickens; with a goat named Mrs. Micawber (Johnson never forgot his Dickens); and with two heated lovers from feuding families. This farce generates a few chuckles as the lovers, protected by the goat, are finally able to marry.[23]

He wrote considerably less poetry than prose fiction. Some verse was serious—"The Seeker," for example, a Shakespearean sonnet. On the other hand, he waxed humorous in "To Peggy in Church," three quatrains culminating in the discovery of a fly on a deacon's nose. In "Mother Goose Up-to-Date," he concocted a series of fractured fairy tales, some slightly amusing. None of these poems rivaled the quatrain about John Charles McNeill.[24]

Johnson spoke at greater length and most confidently in his prose nonfiction. When he became editor of the *Wake Forest Student,* he used his monthly forum to range widely. Offering praise and censure, at times laughing and at times enraged, he covered a variety of topics. He stressed the importance of keeping college athletics in perspective and spoke of the need for protecting the environment. He praised Woodrow Wilson, who was beginning his campaign for the election of 1912. Scorning worldly things, he acknowledged that Wake Forest had little money but was wealthy in other ways, for "if loyalty, a spirit of self-sacrifice and devotion, that does not count the cost, may be considered wealth, then we are rich indeed." He raged at racial prejudice: the attitude of the "Morally Stunted" who referred to the study of African American life as "Niggerism."[25]

In these early forums, Johnson was clearly searching for his authentic voice by experimenting with a number of literary forms. Later, his use of analogy and allusion, irony and humor, would grow more effective, and he would improve his ability to carry a narrative. A number of ideas present in this early work would, of course, manifest themselves later. Unlike a number

23. Ian M'Ian, "A Fishy Story," *Wake Forest Student* 28 (October 1908): 62–68; Ian M'Ian, "Peter," *Wake Forest Student* 28 (November 1908): 99–105; Ian M'Ian, "On Christmas Eve," *Wake Forest Student* 28 (December 1908): 185–87. Johnson published another story, "Where Billy Made His Mistake" under his own name (*The Howler, 1909,* 190–93).

24. Ian M'Ian, "The Seeker," *Wake Forest Student* 30 (April 1910): 3; Ian M'Ian, "To Peggy in Church," *Wake Forest Student* 30 (March 1910): 543; GWJ, "Mother Goose Up-to-Date," *The Howler, 1911,* 189–92.

25. In October and November 1911 issues of the *Wake Forest Student,* Johnson discussed college athletics; he discussed the need to save the trees on campus. He praised Woodrow Wilson and laughed about asinine academics in the December 1910 issue. The next month, he offered the quoted material about Wake Forest's wealth. In the April 1911 issue, he attacked racial prejudice. GWJ, "Why Does a Man Decide He'd Like to Stay Alive?" *Charlotte News,* June 10, 1958.

of other authors, Johnson proved rather objective about his own work, for he recognized early that his strength lay primarily with prose nonfiction. He wrote no more poetry or short stories after this time.

The writing life was tugging at him, and it was time to move on. However, his graduation from Wake Forest in the spring of 1911 meant no final break with the institution. It meant, rather, that he was done only with his role as a student, for he would return to play a variety of parts. He would speak in 1938 at the memorial service for Dr. Poteat and deliver the commencement address in 1944. Five years later, after Dr. Thurman D. Kitchin's retirement as president, Johnson would serve on the search committee for his successor. In 1951, he would bring President Harry S. Truman (a fellow Baptist) to the ground-breaking ceremony in Winston-Salem; in 1964, Johnson would be appointed to the Board of Visitors. The college, in turn, would honor this loyal alumnus with several awards. In 1927, Wake Forest would give him the first of his numerous honorary doctoral degrees. In 1941, he would be appointed to the Wake Forest chapter of Phi Beta Kappa. In 1959, on its 125th anniversary, the school would salute Johnson as a Distinguished Alumnus.[26]

While he was grateful for these honors, Johnson valued far more what he carried away with him intellectually. "When I entered Wake Forest at the age of 17," he recalled, "I knew everything. When I graduated I had already begun to discover that I knew nothing, and the discovery of that great truth is a gift for which I hold the college in grateful memory." His B.A., he would remark several times, was "his license to go hunting for an education." It was an education that would continue until the end of his days. Professor Sledd had taught Johnson "to respect men of ideas and scorn frauds." He proved, understandably, most grateful to Dr. Poteat, the "apostle of discontent" who fought a "Homeric battle for freedom of the mind." Shortly after Dr. Poteat's death, Johnson explained that "the finest thing I ever heard said of him was not intended as a compliment at all. An unfriendly critic complained, 'He unsettles the boys' minds.' It is true, splendidly, gloriously true. He unsettled boys' minds and men's minds and women's minds, too. He unsettled them so thoroughly that they would never settle back into the old complacencies,

---

26. Johnson's roles and awards are discussed in Paschal, *History of Wake Forest College,* vol. 3, and in Bynum Shaw, *The History of Wake Forest College,* vol. 4, *1943–1967* Winston-Salem, N.C.: Wake Forest University, 1988). Lois Johnson, Charles Lambeth and Catharine Carlton, interviews by author, tape recording, Southern Pines, N.C., August 15, 1989; Glasgow, interview.

the old prejudices, the old rules of ignorance and partisanry."[27] This was precisely what Johnson would take great pleasure in and do with considerable skill for decades—this business of unsettling people's minds.

It was time, at the age of twenty-one, to begin his literary apprenticeship, to move from his position of some prominence on campus to the lowly post of "unlicked cub" in the newspaper world.[28] Any portrait of Johnson as a young man should begin by remarking that he was very fortunate to have been born when he had been, rather than five or six years later. He would have three years before World War I began and then another thirty-two months before America entered the fray—almost six years to learn his trade. He would be twenty-seven before he left North Carolina to witness in France a carnage that he could not have imagined, destruction so vast that it profoundly affected the course of Western civilization. This was an education far removed from the classroom, utterly divorced from the tranquillity of a young boy lying on his stomach and reading a book. It was an education by shock, but he would be fortunate enough to survive it. Millions of others were not so lucky.

27. GWJ, "There Are Those Who Love Her;" GWJ, "Why Does a Man Decide He'd Like To Stay Alive?"; GWJ, "As of 1958—Tensions and Stereotypes," text of lecture delivered at East Carolina College, Greenville, on November 11, 1958, GWJ Papers; GWJ, "Death of a Teacher"; GWJ, foreword to *William Louis Poteat: Prophet of Progress,* by Susanne Cameron Linder (Chapel Hill: University of North Carolina Press, 1966), viii; GWJ, "The Future and Dr. Poteat," *Biblical Recorder,* June 29, 1938.

28. GWJ, "Editor-Turned-Author Writes of Lexington," *LD,* [October 1972]. This article first appeared, probably under a different title, on May 5, 1921.

3 Cub
1911-1917

> I went to Lexington almost simultaneously with P. V. Critcher, both with the
> ink scarcely dry on our diplomas from Wake Forest. . . . To Critch and me
> Lexington might be called a way-station, for it was understood that he was
> on his way to the Supreme Court of the United States, and I to the editorship
> of the *New York Times*. Somewhere along the line we were diverted, but,
> considering the present state of the nation, perhaps it is just as well. At least
> nobody can hold us responsible.
>
> —*Gerald Johnson, "19th Century Thomasville Recalled,"* Lexington (N.C.)
> Dispatch, *1946*

It's a familiar scene in American letters—the young man with
the desire to write taking those first steps up the ladder of journalism. Mark
Twain and Stephen Crane and Dreiser and Hemingway climbed the ladder
before finding fame with their fiction. Mencken and Johnson climbed as well
and went on to achieve distinction in this and other fields, but always continued to think of themselves primarily as journalists. During this period from
1911 to 1917, Johnson was associated with three newspapers, each carrying
him higher in his ascent. He proved, as he had at Wake Forest, a young man
willing to listen, and older journalists took the time to teach him his trade.
He worked hard and saw the beginnings of a style that would be fully articulated later. He was young and unattached and full of energy; he made little
money—$10.00 a week in Lexington and $12.50 in Greensboro—but that
didn't matter. In retrospect, he proved very grateful for all the fun. These
were good times, the years before he turned away from the typewriter to put
on a military uniform.

Soon after he left Wake Forest, Johnson joined the *Thomasville Davidson-
ian*. This four-page weekly had been established on June 3, 1910, "to promote the development of Thomasville." It was published at the orphanage.
Johnson took over as editor with the issue of May 26, 1911, and served in
that capacity until September of that year, when he left for the *Lexington Dis-*

patch. Typically self-effacing, he looked back thirty years later and spoke of his "brief and rather lamentable effort to run a newspaper in Thomasville." Actually, the editorial experience proved invaluable for a man so young.[1]

In going from Thomasville to Lexington Johnson did not travel far; these sister cities were only a short distance apart in Davidson County. The *Dispatch* had been established on May 3, 1882. This eight-page weekly had a circulation of about 40,000; Lexington's population was then only about 6,000. In 1911, the *Dispatch* boasted that "it is considered the best weekly in the state and has the largest circulation of any local weekly in the United States." The newspaper was, not surprisingly, solidly Democratic and pro-Temperance. It tried to show allegiance to both the Old South and the New. It celebrated industry, whose "steadily rising hum . . . foretells an era of prosperity the like of which we have never dreamed." On the other hand, the newspaper acknowledged the importance of the agrarian way of life by remarking that "great as are our manufacturing industries . . . North Carolina is now and for many years must remain an agricultural state."[2] Colossus-like, the *Dispatch* was standing with one foot in either world, but the two worlds were growing increasingly divergent. The difficulty of such a policy was hardly lost on Johnson; later, this conflict would prove pivotal in his commentary on his native region.

When Johnson signed on, nobody told the young man: "I greet you at the beginning of a great career." His first day on the job was actually far more prosaic. Johnson recalled laughingly that the editor, A. L. Fletcher, was unaware that an "unlicked cub" had been hired. He "got up from his desk amazed, almost agape." Johnson was given a typewriter that "had come out of Noah's ark" and with considerable banging produced copy that "could [be turned] into English." A staff of one, he played a variety of roles. Besides writing editorials, he synthesized the news. It was his job to read the daily papers and write abstracts of the important regional, national, and international news stories. He boarded during the week with Mr. and Mrs. A. B.

1. M. Jewell Sink and Mary Green Matthews, *Pathfinders Past and Present: A History of Davidson County, North Carolina* (Thomasville, N.C.: 1972), 222; Wint Capel to author, August 19, 1991; Wint Capel, telephone interview by author, from Thomasville, N.C., August 16, 1991; G.B., "Brilliant Baltimore Writer Never Forgets He's a Tar Heel," *GDN*, September 1, 1940; John T. Kneebone, *Southern Liberal Journalists and the Issue of Race, 1920–1944* (Chapel Hill: University of North Carolina Press, 1985), 15.

2. "XXIX," *LD*, May 3, 1911; "Looking Forward," *LD*, August 28, 1912; "What the Dispatch Is," *LD*, December 11, 1912.

Hamner, at whose table a "garrulous old lady" recounted all the town gossip. Resourceful, Johnson suggested a society column and gathered his material "with no work at all." The *Dispatch* as he remembered it was "a place where much honest, hard work was done . . . merrily rather than grouchily." He was grateful not only for the work environment but also for the versatility that he gained. He believed that, just as medical students are trained in every department of a hospital, young journalists should be given "a very thorough tour 'slam through' every phase of newspaper work."[3] Specialization could come later. The versatility that began in Lexington would be supplemented in Greensboro, where he would play an even larger number of roles, and its significance would be stressed when he taught journalism in Chapel Hill.

This was a time, Johnson would recall, "when the world was still blissfully unaware of the raging volcano underneath it." He joined the North Carolina National Guard in 1912. His outfit, Company A, 3rd Infantry, was dubbed the "Lexington Wildcats." During that summer he trained at Camp Pettus in Alabama. The highlight of the train journey there occurred in Austell, Georgia, where the soldiers routed local police after they had arrested a Wildcat for trying to steal a chicken. Playing soldier seemed fun at the time. Later, Johnson would sigh that some of these young soldiers with whom he had cavorted lay "under the weeping sky of France."[4]

Johnson, however, would still have several more years to serve his literary apprenticeship in peace before sham battles in the Alabama sunshine were replaced by the carnage of the Western Front. In early 1913, the *Greensboro Daily News* "snapped its fingers," and "he came running." He ran to a morning daily that had been established on July 18, 1909. The newspaper was "independent in politics." It was also "in a state of collapse." Johnson recalled that "pay-day was conditional; the hired hands got their money on Friday if there was any money. . . . The fabulous part of the story is that nobody thought of quitting." Reminiscing more than fifty years later, he said that "after serving eight newspapers ranging from size from a county weekly to the stateliest of the New York dailies I have never worked in a happier

3. GWJ, "Editor Turned Author Writes of Lexington," *LD*, [October 1972] (this column appeared, probably under a different title, on May 5, 1921); GWJ, "19th Century Thomasville Recalled," *LD*, [1946]; Wint Capel, telephone interview; GWJ, "A Letter from Gerald Johnson," *LD*, March 15, 1978; Victoria Boney, "Gerald Johnson Still Tar Heel Editor," *GDN*, March 29, 1941.

4. GWJ, "Editor Turned Author Writes of Lexington."

shop."[5] The presence of Earle Godbey definitely contributed to Johnson's joy and edification.

Godbey had arrived from Asheville in 1911. Although he did not technically replace W. A. Hildebrand as editor until 1918, Godbey was "in immediate supervision" of the editorial department when Johnson signed on. He called Godbey "brilliant, witty [and] sardonic but courageous and honest." From Godbey, Johnson learned a truth that would stay with him for the rest of his life—that humankind's greatest apprehension is "that fear of taking the next step, however logical and necessary that step may be."[6] In time, Johnson would prod many a politician and many a common citizen to overcome this fear. As he had done with Professors Sledd and Poteat at Wake Forest and with Mr. Fletcher in Lexington, Johnson found in Godbey another mentor to teach him what was important.

Johnson began this phase of his apprenticeship on January 27, 1913, when he joined the city and state news staff. "As the very junior member . . . ," he explained, "I was a very small frog in a large puddle." He wrote news stories and read proofs; he also wrote music criticism, book reviews, and editorials. Of these various roles, the editorial writing proves the most difficult to identify.[7]

During this time, the *Daily News* ran few signed editorials; only the editor initialed those that he wrote; thus, determining which are those written by Johnson is problematic. Some editorials convey ideas that are similar to, in some cases the same as, those that Johnson set forth in his signed pieces. In terms of their use of myth as well as biblical and classical allusion, yet other editorials resemble the Johnsonian style that was evolving at this time. Some editorials carry titles that he would use later in his signed columns. Unfortunately, Johnson's correspondence at this time rarely identifies his editorial work. It finally proves most sensible to set forth the newspaper's editorial positions and compare them to Johnson's own.

The *Daily News* lambasted racial violence, argued that the fates of the races are intertwined, and scoffed at those Yankees who patronizingly told Southerners how to solve their problems. The newspaper argued for racial

---

5. James Walt, "Tale of Another Liberal's Progress," *Maryland English Journal* (fall 1965): 59; R. L. Beall, "Notes on the History of the Greensboro News and Record, *Including the Greensboro Daily News* . . . ," photocopy in the possession of the author; GWJ, "Johnson Recalls Days Here," *GDN*, March 22, 1964.

6. Beall, "Notes"; GWJ, "The Revelations of Fifty Years," *GDN*, November 20, 1966.

7. "Gerald Johnson on the Greensboro News," *LD*, January 29, 1913; GWJ, "The Revelations of Fifty Years."

equality before the law but not for social integration. It attacked anti–Semitism and demagoguery, and it believed that woman's suffrage, while fair and inevitable, would not come without cost. Johnson agreed with all of these positions. He and the *Daily News* differed most about the Temperance movement, and he had to have been embarrassed by the newspaper's remonstrations about "Demon Rum."[8]

During 1913, Johnson wrote infrequently under a by-line, but two of his signed pieces, about industry and race, prove quite revealing. On March 16, he reported that a New York firm manufacturing underwear was to open a cotton mill outside Lexington. The promoter rather than the critic of industry, he celebrated the hundreds of jobs that would be created and praised Lexington's progressivism. Later, he would prove far more skeptical about the supposed advantages of the factory. On June 13, he published the first significant statement about race that ran under his own name. He lamented the death of Dr. Edgar Gardner Murphy, an Alabamian who had been vilified for championing industrial and vocational training for blacks. Discussing the many books about race, Johnson explained that "the vast majority of the writers approach this subject in a more or less controversial spirit, either as critics, whose scorn burns up the good things they might accomplish, or as defenders of the South, more interested in preserving the fair fame of this section than in finding the real solution to the problem." Johnson proceeded to praise Murphy's commonsensical view that both races would benefit as conditions for African Americans improved. Significantly, the young Johnson rejected the polarities of both doomsayer and apologist, and he would maintain this position throughout his career.[9]

8. For the position of the *GDN* on racial violence, see "Lynching at Laurens," August 14, 1913; and "Lynching Cannot Be Gently Removed," July 4, 1916. "The Exodus of Negro Labor," January 28, 1917, speaks of the mutual interest of the races. For attacks upon meddlesome Northerners, see "New York's Anti-Jim-Crow Law," September 20, 1913; "The Negro Exodus," October 15, 1916; and "Julian Street Discovers the Negro," January 24, 1917. The newspaper proposes equality before the law and speaks against social integration in "Still without Form and Void," January 27, 1914; "Science of Segregation," January 4, 1914; and "The Negro Exodus." For attacks upon anti-Semitism, see "Tom Watson Helped," August 18, 1915; and "Georgia and the Assassination of Frank," August 22, 1915. Demagoguery is attacked in "The Defeat of Blease," September 14, 1916. For discussion of woman's suffrage, see "Another Feminist Fad," July 21, 1915; and "The Suffragists and Their Activities," August 17, 1915. For anti-alcohol editorials, see "Jack Johnson's Conviction," May 17, 1913; and "A Losing Game," March 11, 1914.

9. GWJ, "Lexington Disturbs London," *GDN,* March 16, 1913, p. 6; GWJ, "White Man Loses," *GDN,* July 11, 1913, p. 4.

During 1914, Johnson's few signed news stories and columns seemed to energize him less than the opportunity afforded him in late August. With both Hildebrand and Godbey out of town, Johnson reveled in his power. "You are now being addressed," he happily told a correspondent "by the Lord High Executioner. . . . During the past six days I have managed to to start rows with three newspapers, libelled the city of Charlotte . . . and am preparing to enrage the Socialist party of Guilford county." Dr. Poteat would have been proud of his twenty-four-year-old protégé.[10]

The following year was far less happy, for Johnson was sick with tuberculosis for "the better part" of 1915. The newspaper carried no notice of his illness or of his return. His first signed column that year ran on October 3. He remained busy during the rest of the year by covering various denominational state conventions: the Presbyterians in Gastonia, the Methodists in Reidsville, and the Baptists in Charlotte.[11]

Early in 1916, he first encountered the prose of a third-generation agnostic who viewed religion far less favorably than the conventions did. In February, a professor of sociology in Greensboro gave Johnson a copy of the *Baltimore Evening Sun* carrying one of H. L. Mencken's columns about the antics of the preacher Billy Sunday. Mencken thought the average American a moron who was perpetually duped by frauds, and he denounced those demagogues who used their oratory to stoke the mob. Depicted with Mencken's characteristic hyperbole, the meeting of Sunday and his followers became an obscene farce—an "orgy," the writer called it—which alternately delighted and disgusted him. Johnson had never before witnessed such prose; after finishing the column, Johnson believed that he had discovered "a new planet." He also began to read the *Smart Set,* the lively literary monthly edited by Mencken and George Jean Nathan in New York City, and "never missed an issue from that time on." The following year, Mencken would use the *New York Evening Mail* to publish "The Sahara of the Bozart," an indictment of Southern culture that not only would profoundly affect Johnson but would also help to bring about the Southern literary renaissance during the 1920s. In time, Mencken would prove by long odds the most important literary contact of Johnson's career. But in early 1916 Mencken knew nothing

10. GWJ to Louise Futtrell, August 22, 1914, GWJ Papers.

11. Lois Johnson, interview by author, tape recording, Southern Pines, N.C., August 15, 1989. Johnson's three columns on the Presbyterians ran on October 27, 28, and 31; the six columns on the Methodists were published on November 14, 18, 19, 20, 21, and 23; the columns on the Baptists appeared on December 5, 8, 9, and 10.

of Johnson, and these significant events would have to wait—until Johnson returned from the war and established himself as "the best editorial writer in the South."[12]

That volcano which Johnson had mentioned in 1912 finally erupted. His literary apprenticeship ended; his military life began. It had been increasingly difficult for America to remain neutral after the *Lusitania* was sunk on May 8, 1915. On February 1, 1917, Germany declared unrestricted submarine warfare; two days later, the United States severed diplomatic relations. On April 6 America entered the war, and Johnson enlisted immediately. "In my case," he would later explain, "one had to go. Here was the greatest adventure of all time. To participate in [the war] might mean coming to a highly unpleasant end in a muddy trench somewhere in France. But not to participate— what would that mean?" He had no choice. Johnson could no more have avoided military service during World War I than his ancestors could have avoided fighting in the Civil War. His sojourn in France would change him profoundly. He would ship out as a Southerner and return as an American.[13]

12. GWJ, interview with Carl Bode, June 13, 1963, HLM Papers; GWJ, "A Very Great Lady Indeed," in *America-Watching: Perspectives in the Course of an Incredible Century* (Owings Mills, Md.: Stemmer House, 1976), 16. During this time, Mencken wrote three columns about Billy Sunday for the *Baltimore Evening Sun*: "The Impending Orgy," February 17, 1916; "Doctor Seraphidus and Ecstaticus," March 14, 1916; and "The Calliope of Zion," March 27, 1916. Mencken called Johnson "the best editorial writer in the South" in a letter to Emily Clark (Emily Clark, *Innocence Abroad* [New York: Knopf, 1931], 120–21). Later in 1916, Johnson covered the Baptist State convention in Asheville; two columns ran on May 18, and other columns appeared on May 19, 20, 21, and 22. A final column, about Cuba's wanting to cash North Carolina bonds issued in 1869, ran on December 10. Johnson wrote no signed columns during 1917 before he enlisted.

13. GWJ, *Number Thirty-Six: A Novel* (New York: Minton, Balch, 1933), 196. GWJ wrote in "Diary," on December 5, 1918: "In 1916 I regarded a venture over the Mason-Dixon line as a venture into a foreign country. . . . I started the war as a North Carolinian and a Southerner. I am now an American. This is certainly something" (GWJ, "Diary," 24, GWJ Papers).

4　Over There
1917–1919

By God, we were men! Not great men, but highly human and not willing to
fill our bellies with the husks the swine did eat. We had a leader who not
once appealed to national avarice, or national cowardice, but only to the national sense of justice and common decency. And the nation rose like Old
Faithful at the predestined moment.

　　Surely, we presently subsided, guzzling and belching, and farting, and
emitting noxious gasses. But the point is that we rose.

—*Gerald Johnson to Paul Green, December 16, 1967*

Like many soldiers, Johnson saw war as a test of his courage.
Discussing his fictional counterpart in *Number Thirty-Six,* Johnson candidly
remarked that "visions of military glory drifted across his mind, but what he
really hoped and prayed for was that he might not bolt when the first shell
landed within half a mile of him." Johnson's prayer would be answered.[1]

Also, like so many other soldiers from both the Allied and Central Powers, Johnson could hardly have anticipated the nightmare that World War I
would become—a struggle so horrific that writers would labor to find a language to capture it. By the end of the war, a total of eight million soldiers
would lie dead; another twenty-two million would be wounded or diseased,
and civilian casualties would run to an additional twenty-two million. The
war would cost the equivalent of $600 billion, an unassumable debt. About
25,000 miles of trenches, enough to encircle the equator, would be gouged
out of the Western Front. By the time of the Armistice, much of France
would lie in ruins: a pockmarked, corpse-ridden landscape that would savagely mock the aspirations of Western civilization.[2]

1. GWJ, *Number Thirty-Six: A Novel* (New York: Minton, Balch, 1993), 194.
2. Charles L. Mee, Jr., *The End of Order: Versailles, 1919* (New York: E. P. Dutton, 1980),
260; Paul Fussell, *The Great War and Modern Memory* (New York: Oxford University Press,
1975), 37.

Nor could Johnson have anticipated the fate of so much of the optimistic rhetoric of the time, a rhetoric that to posterity seems noble but naive. H. G. Wells wrote *The War That Will End War* (the title became a ghoulish joke), and Woodrow Wilson spoke of "making the world safe for democracy." Actually, after haggling at Versailles, politicians hammered out a vindictive treaty that marked, to borrow Charles Mee's phrase, "the end of order." Hitler would rise to power less than fifteen years later, and the battle would have to be fought all over again, at even great cost. As the British historian Charles F. G. Masterson has remarked, World War I "proved the greatest secular catastrophe which has tormented mankind since the fall of Rome."[3]

Finally, Johnson could not have anticipated the profound change in sensibility that would be generated by the war. "I am saying," Paul Fussell remarks in *The Great War and Modern Memory,* a monumental study that is as moving as it is wise, "that there seems to be one dominating form of modern understanding; that it is essentially ironic; and that it originates largely in the application of mind and memory to the events of the Great War."[4] Of course, Johnson would face his own devils as he looked into the dark nights of the twentieth century, and he would use irony quite effectively as a literary device, but he would never become fundamentally an ironist regarding the human condition. Hence, his own thought would prove an exception to such a modern understanding.

From the time of his enlistment until the summer of the following year, Johnson trained at Fort Jackson, South Carolina. When he traveled by train to his next assignment, Fort Upton on Long Island, he was gratified by the "wild cheers" and "genuine tears" that greeted the soldiers. "The fact that the enterprise on which we are now fairly started is likely to prove both difficult and dangerous," he wrote home, "sinks into insignificance in the joy that it is to serve a people ready in appreciation. . . . [N]obody seemed to give a whoop in hades whether we were roughnecks or gentlemen. . . . We were American soldiers going to war, and that was enough." He shipped out, landed in England on August 16, 1918, and reached Le Havre about four days later.[5]

---

3. Samuel Hynes, *A War Imagined: The First World War and English Culture* (New York: Atheneum, 1991), 37; Charles F. G. Masterman, *England after War* (London: 1922), ix, quoted in Hynes, *A War Imagined,* 315.

4. Fussell, *The Great War and Modern Memory,* 35.

5. Ethel Stephens Arnett, *Greensboro, North Carolina: The County Seat of Guilford* (Chapel Hill: University of North Carolina Press, 1955), 404–405. For reasons of military security, Johnson was not allowed to keep a diary during World War I. He began his diary after the

As a member of Company M, 321ˢᵗ Infantry, 3ʳᵈ Brigade, 81ˢᵗ Division, Johnson moved about a good deal in the Vosges during his first six weeks. He endured insufficient rations, an uncomfortable climate ("the cold was awful to a North Carolinian"), and homesickness. From Le Havre he went by train to Flagny and then spent three weeks "working furiously" at Marolles. He took another train to Bruyere and then marched to Darnfainy. From there he trucked to St. Remy. On September 19, his unit reached Mazenmortier at the front, where he served in "an advance billeting party." He saw no combat in the trenches. At Darnfainy, his unit was strafed one night, and at Mazenmortier it was shelled three times. "No damage," Johnson then remarked laconically.[6]

Thirteen years later, he would recount these experiences at greater length and with considerably more emotion to his readers in *Harper's Magazine:*

> I have experienced the delights of sleeping in the mud and waking up with hoarfrost an eighth of an inch long on my shoes; and of marching under a full pack with flu shaking my bones and my temperature running one hundred three and a half, and thanking God for the privilege of finding a bunk in a cow-stable. I know what a merry jest it is to have your fingers frostbitten until the flesh comes sloughing off. . . . I know how laughable it is to have shells land close enough to jar the ground under your feet, and to dive headfirst for cover at the drone of an airplane motor, and to have your village machine-gunned by an enemy aviator. . . . I have seen burial parties, and hospital trains coming back from the front.

He had been there—three months in a combat zone—and he dared those who had not (those civilians who had never enlisted and those soldiers who had never made it oversees) to dispute with him. He knew only too well, however, that he was one of the fortunate ones. No veteran exaggerating his record, Johnson said candidly that "I didn't win the war. I merely attended it. [N]ary a German soldier did I kill. I never even shot at one. I was one of the lucky dogs who were detailed to duty around the edges of the war."[7]

Armistice. His first entry is dated November 26, 1918; the final entry is dated May 4, 1919. This diary contains a little more than thirty-two pages in cursive and runs to between 10,000 and 15,000 words. The entries differ appreciably in frequency, subject matter, tone, and scope. The dates of his arrival in Manchester and Le Havre are given on p. 3.

6. GWJ, "Diary," 3–4, 8, 9, 11, 15, 16, GWJ Papers.

7. GWJ, "For Ignoble Pacifism," in *America-Watching: Perspectives in the Course of an Incredible Century* (Owings Mills, Md.: Stemmer House, 1976), 53–54.

He proved especially fortunate in his decision, on October 3, 1918, to enter officer candidate school and train for a commission. So many lieutenants had been killed in the Meuse-Argonne offensive that "orders . . . came down to our corps commander to pick out 900 enlisted men who could at least read English" and send them for officers' training. Johnson "jumped at the chance," for it meant "sleeping for ninety days under a roof." Moreover, "considering what was then going on in the Meuse-Argonne, it probably meant living three months longer." He enjoyed the company of his fellow candidates and called them "a light-hearted bunch of scoundrels." He was commissioned on November 9, and the Armistice was signed two days later. Subsequently, Johnson discovered that, among the group commissioned just prior to his own, four officers had been killed and three wounded. Moreover, when he returned to his old unit in January of the following year, he found that it had sustained thirty casualties, including six killed, during the final two days of the war.[8]

The events of Armistice Day both delighted and disgusted this "new-made shavetail." He rejoiced, of course, over the end of the war, and he laughingly recounted how he had received the news. He and a fellow soldier were hauling a fifteen-gallon can filled with raw beef from the supply depot to the kitchen. As they struggled up a hill, a truck roared by, and a soldier leaned out and hollered that the war was over. "That's good," Johnson said. "Well, let's get this damned thing up the hill before the mess sergeant starts having kittens." That night, he discovered that his commission had been canceled "to save expenses." Decades later, Johnson said that this affront "came nearer to turning me into a Communist than anything else in my life."[9]

While the politicians haggled at Versailles, General Pershing and his two million men were ordered to stand by; there was the possibility that negotiations might break down and hostilities resume. Pershing sent about 300,000 men into Germany as part of the army of occupation, but there remained the matter of what to do with more than a million and a half soldiers. "At that point," Johnson explained, "some anonymous but very great man in Washington had an idea—why not let any man who had a college degree and $50 go into detached service for three months at some European university?" Oxford and the Sorbonne could not accommodate all the applicants, and Johnson was

8. GWJ, untitled manuscript, folder 2/212, GWJ Papers; GWJ, "The War Is Over: Armistice Day, 1918," *Long Island (N.Y.) Newsday,* November 11, 1976; GWJ, "Diary," 6, 16, 26.

9. GWJ, untitled manuscript, folder 2/212, GWJ Papers; *HTLFBS,* November 11, 1952, *HTLFBS* Papers. Johnson's pass as the University of Toulouse identifies his rank as sergeant (folder 7/87, GWJ Papers).

assigned to the University of Toulouse. "At the time I was mildly disappointed," he recalled, ". . . but it was one of the finest strokes of luck that I ever had." He would find himself challenged, both inside and outside the classroom, fall in love again, and catch his first glimpse of Woodrow Wilson.[10]

He arrived in Toulouse on February 27, 1919, and stayed until sometime in July. He signed up for a variety of courses at the university: "France and the American War of Independence," the "Geography of France," "French Literature of the Eighteenth Century," "French Art," "Archeology" and the "French Family." He delighted in listening to the lectures and taking notes in French and progressed in all of his courses except "The Political Evolution of France, 1815–1875." He wrote down nothing because he "was unable to understand anything" that the teacher said.[11]

At times, he was puzzled by the more cosmopolitan French perspective. Growing up in North Carolina, Johnson had encountered few Catholics and was uncertain about protocol. He asked a Frenchman if it were possible for him, a Protestant, to enter the cathedral during mass. The Frenchman replied, "Monsieur, no man, not even His Holiness the Pope, has the right to forbid any human being to enter the House of God." Johnson felt "properly squelched." As John Kneebone has remarked, life in Toulouse gave Johnson "an awareness of alternatives to the southern way of life."[12]

Genevieve Dunais was decidedly not Southern, and Johnson fell in love with her "to the consternation of his family." (This was apparently his first serious involvement since his romance with Gretchen at Wake Forest.) Johnson wanted to marry Genevieve but then lacked the funds. He told her that, after returning to America, he would earn enough money to send for her. "Three thousand miles of Atlantic Ocean," Mary Johnson Lambeth has remarked, "evidently cooled their love." Several years later, Lois Johnson would visit Genevieve and find her "charming" but could not "picture her exotic ways fitting in with the Johnson family."[13]

It was especially fitting that, as his time in France was drawing to a close,

10. GWJ, "A Cry for Blood from the Peanut Gallery: The Opera Really Lives," *BES,* April 26, 1972.

11. GWJ, "Diary," 30, 31 GWJ et al., *The Sunpapers of Baltimore, 1837–1937* (New York: Knopf, 1937), 386n; GWJ, notebooks for classes taken at the University of Toulouse, folders 1/86 and 2/15, GWJ Papers.

12. GWJ to Wingate Johnson, October 25, 1957, GWJ Papers; John T. Kneebone, *Southern Liberal Journalists and the Issue of Race, 1920–1944* (Chapel Hill: University of North Carolina Press, 1985), 19.

13. Mary Johnson Lambeth, "Sketch of the Life of Gerald Johnson by His Sister, Mamie, Mrs. Charles Lambeth of Thomasville, N.C., 1939," 5, GWJ Papers.

Johnson attended Memorial Day exercises, the first since the Armistice. He and a friend visited the military cemetery at Suresnes and watched a speaker climb upon a box. When the speaker turned, Johnson recognized with a start that he was looking at Woodrow Wilson, "the Conqueror who had the world at his feet." But the costs of victory were high. The president was "an old man at sixty-three, obviously feeble." (He would be dead in five years.) Johnson was moved by the spectacle. "I know when I am doddering in the chimney corner," he wrote sixteen years later, "and wish to make my grandchildren sit up with a start, and regard the old man curiously . . . I shall say that in 1919 I saw Woodrow Wilson at Suresnes." Out there among the crosses and the ghosts, with those awful realities of the war still very much in mind, Johnson thought of heroes. He could hardly have asked for a more resonant conclusion to his military life.[14]

World War I had changed the United States, the American South, and Gerald Johnson. Unlike Johnson, many Americans grew skeptical of President Wilson's grandiloquence. As Congress refused to ratify the League of Nations, and as the country slid into what Johnson saw as mindless materialism, he argued that the unknown soldier had not died "for a craven fear on the part of a nation that never showed fear before. Most surely not that our great business houses might add untold millions to their staggering wealth." Wilson, Johnson would declare, "[haunts] our minds like a bad conscience." As time passed, and as it became increasingly clear that America could not hide from the rest of the world, Johnson would make no effort to avoid saying, "I told you so."[15]

The American South to which Johnson returned was less insular. The war, he explained, had made Southerners "a newspaper reading public." Moreover, the "call to arms" had generated the South's "martial spirit" and "strengthened the self-confidence of the section and put it in the mind to attempt great things." Later, when he criticized the isolationists, he would take considerable pride in the fact that this movement generated little sympathy in the South.[16]

14. GWJ, "Since Wilson," in *America-Watching: Perspectives in the Course of an Incredible Century* (Owings Mills, Md.: Stemmer House, 1976).

15. GWJ, "The Funeral of an Unknown Soldier," *GDN,* November 11, 1921; GWJ, *Woodrow Wilson: The Unforgettable Figure Who Has Returned to Haunt Us* (New York: Harper and Brothers, 1944), 9.

16. GWJ, *Number Thirty-Six,* 190; GWJ, *The Undefeated* (New York: Minton, Balch, 1927), 58; see John T. Kneebone, *Southern Liberal Journalists and the Issue of Race,* 18–19, 235n.41.

When Johnson returned to the United States in July 1919, it was indeed as an American rather than a Southerner. He explained that his ideas had "changed rapidly" while he was in France. Not surprisingly, his time abroad had given his an even greater appreciation of his native country. He hymned America as "beloved of the sun, land of peace and plenty."[17]

His twenty-seven months in the army did not leave him unscathed, either physically or psychologically. He contracted flu, perhaps during the epidemic of October 1918. Not thoroughly treated at the time, the illness involved a middle-ear infection that ultimately had a toxic effect on the auditory nerve. This resulted in increasing deafness, an especially serious condition for an amateur musician and music critic. By the end of his life, Johnson would find all conversation difficult. Moreover, the memories of the dead and wounded never left him: "Such things every man who has gone to war carries in his mind, and always will. You may have been lucky. You may have come back all in one piece . . . but you didn't escape unscratched. You may have saved your hide, but your memory bears long, red scars."[18]

Finally, however, it was with gratitude that Johnson viewed his military life. He never wrapped himself in the flag, never became a professional patriot. He found both pacifists and jingoists misguided and dangerous. He came to understand that his service in World War I had set him free: "The man who has gone under fire for his country is ever a man apart. He has paid his keep. . . . He can look George Washington in the eye, with respect, yes, but without servility. He is, in the fullest sense, a free man; for he has taken the final test of the free man, and he has passed it." In time, Johnson would regard his months in France as "the springtime of [his] life." He would celebrate that fact that, during desperate times, he and his compatriots had "stood against the sky, white, shining, and draped with rainbows."[19]

17. GWJ, "Diary," 1, 22.

18. Kathryn Hayward Johnson, interview by author, Valparaiso, Ind., June 8, 1989; Lambeth, "Sketch," 5; GWJ, *HTLFBS,* November 11, 1952.

19. GWJ, "From an Old Soldier to the New Ones," *BES,* December 11, 1941; GWJ, "Hurrah for the Children's Crusade," *NR* 157 (April 20, 1968): 12; GWJ to Paul Green, December 16, 1967, Paul Green Papers.

5 "The Best Editorial Writer in the South"
1919–1924

> The South discovered nearly sixty years ago what was revealed to the North
> only when the Eighteenth Amendment gripped it, namely that the law is an
> ass. Therefore, the proposal of the Ku Klux organizers that enforcement of
> the current religious, social and political code be removed from the hands of
> the peace officers and undertaken by a masked secret order was not particu-
> larly shocking to the average barber or cotton mill hand. The soundness of
> the Ku Klux doctrine seemed to him beyond debate, for had not its essentials
> been expounded for years by his pastor, his paper, and his political boss?
>
> —*Gerald Johnson, "Fourteen Equestrian Statues of Colonel Simmons"*

When Johnson returned in July 1919 to the position of associate editor on the *Greensboro Daily News,* he was one month shy of his twenty-
ninth birthday and eager to get on with his life. He had not yet written a
book, and no magazine article had appeared under his name. Grateful for
what he had learned in France, he was still very much aware of time's flight.
It was with a sense of urgency that he set out to make a name for himself, a
name that would transcend purely local celebrity.

This next period of Johnson's life would stretch five years and two
months and conclude with his acceptance of a professorship in Chapel Hill.
During this time, his expanding professional life encompassed the three roles
that marked the rest of his career: book authorship, magazine writing, and
journalism. The appearance of three new periodicals—the *Reviewer* in Richmond, the *Journal of Social Forces* in Chapel Hill, and the *American Mercury* in
New York City—increased his readership. Johnson the regional writer discussed Southern issues for these magazines. As Fred Hobson has remarked,
"During the early twenties [Johnson] was the loudest and clearest voice in
the rising chorus of native Southern criticism." As a journalist, Johnson
would write so skillfully that Mencken called him "the best editorial writer
in the South and one of the best in America." Johnson's writing so incensed
the Klan that they threatened to show up at his house one night. They never

arrived, and Johnson remarked that this episode "fortified" him. He took pride in the fact that he was making the right sort of enemies.[1]

The *Daily News* made no formal announcement when Johnson rejoined the staff. His time in France did become evident, though, in four signed columns about the country.[2] These proved less important than his editorial work, which proved easier to identify than it had been before the war. He wrote more signed editorials and more frequently used his correspondence to identify his writing. Finally, his style, marked by a more skillful use of literary devices and more distinctive cadences, grew more individualistic.

Johnson developed very definite ideas about what a good editorial writer must do. Using a boxing metaphor, he told a fellow journalist that "if you begin to write stuff that counts, stuff that has a wallop in it, it is simply out of the question for you to land every time." He told his friend not to be needlessly complicated or highbrow—"for God's sake avoid deep stuff"—and never to lie. Both the good editorial writer and his editor, Johnson concluded, must never fear censure and never run with the crowd.[3]

Johnson followed his own advice, and he took considerable pride in the growing stature of the newspaper. He called the *Daily News* under Earl Godbey's editorship "one of the sanest, steadiest, and withal most enlightened newspapers to be found in the South." In *Liberalism in the South,* Virginius Dabney has remarked that "when Gerald W. Johnson was on its editorial staff, the *News* held undisputed sway in the state, and was the mouthpiece of North Carolina liberalism."[4]

It is worth noting here exactly what "liberalism" meant for the newspaper and for Johnson. Endorsing First Amendment rights, the *Daily News* defended free speech. This was hardly without its attendant evils, but to attempt

1. Fred C. Hobson, Jr., *Serpent in Eden: H. L. Mencken and the South* (Chapel Hill: University of North Carolina Press, 1974), 100; H. L. Mencken to Emily Clark, 1922, quoted in Emily Clark, *Innocence Abroad* (New York: Knopf, 1931), 120–21; GWJ to Howard W. Odum, September 7, 1951, HWO Papers.

2. GWJ, "In Languedoc: I. President Wilson's Square," *GDN,* September 7, 1919; GWJ, "In Languedoc: II. Of Towers and Troubadours," *GDN,* September 14, 1919; GWJ, "In Languedoc: III. 'Not Made with Hands.' " *GDN,* October 5, 1919; GWJ, "In Languedoc: IV. The Seamless Side," *GDN,* November 16, 1919.

3. GWJ to Lenoir Chambers, September 13, 1924, Lenoir Chambers Papers, Southern Historical Collection, Wilson Library, University of North Carolina at Chapel Hill.

4. GWJ, "Southern Image Breakers," in *South-Watching: Selected Essays by Gerald W. Johnson*, ed. Fred Hobson (Chapel Hill: University of North Carolina Press, 1983), 108; Virginius Dabney, *Liberalism in the South* (Chapel Hill: University of North Carolina Press, 1932), 406.

to do away with them was to create a cure worse than the disease. As the controversy grew more heated between Modernists and Fundamentalists (today's evolutionists and creationists), the newspaper lamented that "the vigor of the effort to suppress freedom of discussion is astonishing." The *Daily News,* as expected, strongly endorsed the separation of church and state.[5]

"Liberalism" meant, as it had before World War I, that the newspaper acknowledged the justice of woman's suffrage. However, the *Daily News* contended that "women must inevitably surrender their claims to special privileges in exchange for the privilege of voting." Rejecting gyneolatry, the newspaper ridiculed "the braying of certain asses who set themselves up as 'protectors of the pure womanhood of the South.' Such protection usually contemplates the use of masks and shotguns." "Liberalism" meant that the newspaper accepted the responsibility of explaining how America, "a rich and cynical nation," had become corrupted by greed and fear and had lost its way. This editorial page, which could be quite moralistic, indeed served as a public conscience.[6]

Regarding race, "liberalism" meant hatred for prejudice and violence. The *Daily News* excoriated members of the Klan as "moral cowards" and likened them to agents of the Inquisition. The newspaper called lynching "a form of social gangrene, that, unless it is cut out, will eventually destroy our civilization." "Liberalism" meant both acknowledging the pride taken by blacks in their heritage and accepting the facts that the fates of the races are intertwined. Race relations, the editorial page argued analogically, are not like the action of a seesaw but instead resemble the relationship "of the members of an Alpine Club. . . . As the front member climbs, he is compelled to haul the others up with him; if he were necessarily fool enough to try to thrust the others down, he would necessarily be jerked from his footing. Both must go up, or both must come down."[7]

5. " 'Jurgen' Unjailed," *GDN,* August 23, 1922. For further commentary on censorship, see the following unsigned editorials: "The 'Immature Mind' Stained," August 14, 1922; "The Most Useless Battle," June 29, 1924; and "Pope Cameron Issues a Decree," June 25, 1924. For further commentary on the religious controversy, see the following unsigned editorials: "Secondhand Gospelers," February 10, 1924; and "A Matter of Fundamental Principles," February 24, 1924.

6. The following are unsigned editorials in the *GDN:* "Growing Pains in the Industrial South," August 16, 1919; "An Incident," July 4, 1920. For further commentary on suffrage, see "Tar Heel Democrats Go on Record," April 10, 1920; "Effects of a Diet of Sweetened Wind," August 15, 1921; and "Ten Years," August 3, 1924.

7. The following are unsigned editorials in the *GDN:* "A Cloak for Terrorism and Anarchy," November 23, 1923; "Valuable Presence," August 18, 1921; and "Easy Is the Descent to Avernus," July 25, 1920; see also "What Lynching Means in the South," February 25, 1922;

"Liberalism," on the other hand, meant no renunciation of racial superiority. For all of its contempt for the Klan, the newspaper announced that "it believes as strongly as any Klucker in White Supremacy." While the *Daily News* supported equality before the law as well as equality of employment, it argued that social integration was unthinkable. Some blacks, the newspaper argued, were as wary of integration as whites were: " 'Social equality' is a term not employed by intelligent white people . . . and the attitude of intelligent negroes is one of resentment to its use. It is a concept of aliens and fools." This editorial writer clearly knew about the horns of a dilemma: his opponents were cast as either meddlesome Yankees or home-grown "fools."[8]

Johnson concurred with the newspaper's views on segregation. Moreover, he was hardly the only prominent Southern journalist to take such a position. As John Kneebone has explained so well, "The journalists' experiences in the 1920s convinced them that liberals could improve race relations without weakening segregation." Johnson was among that group which John Egerton has called "liberal segregationists"; this term, as Mr. Egerton has pointed out, did not become an oxymoron until much later, at the end of World War II. Johnson defended segregation on the grounds that it was an attempt on the part of both races to acknowledge and preserve their heritage. Moreover, he explained, in one of his more curious letters, that the segregationist was not prejudiced: "When I refuse to have a negro at my table, no matter how civilized or how well-bred he may be, I am accused of race prejudice, whereas that is just when I am acting not on prejudice, but on a judgment formed after and not before investigation. . . . [I]f I were to receive W. E. B. Du Bois today, the innate democracy of the Negro race would insure that my cook would be outraged if she were not received on the same footing. In rejecting Du Bois, I am therefore acting not on prejudice but on its antithesis."[9]

That horrific vision of the first Dutch slave ship carrying blacks to the

"North and South, to the Negro," September 30, 1919; and "Two Friendly Criticisms," July 16, 1923.

8. The following are unsigned editorials in the *GDN:* "An Insult to the White Race," December 18, 1922; "The Negro and the Labor Unions," August 23, 1919; "The Black Man's Burden," October 24, 1921; and "Mr. Saunders Takes a Whirl at the Race Question," December 31, 1923.

9. John T. Kneebone, *Southern Liberal Journalists and the Issue of Race, 1920–1944* (Chapel Hill: University of North Carolina Press, 1985), 75; John Egerton, *Speak Now against the Day: The Generation before the Civil Rights Movement in the South* (New York: Knopf, 1994), 549; GWJ to Mencken, May 18, 1924, HLM Papers.

New World never left Johnson. He took dangerous stands to defend the civil liberties of all Americans, and he never doubted that change is the fundamental law of life. However, Johnson the segregationist refused, at this time and later, to transcend the customs of his ancestors. One sees here the incongruous picture of Johnson the traditionalist who, like the neighboring farmer in Robert Frost's "Mending Wall," rebuilds needless barriers every spring by piling stones where they are not meant to go and do not want to stay. That Johnson began his career as a segregationist is hardly surprising; that he would end as one is surprising indeed.

During 1920, Johnson's first full year as a journalist since his return from the war, none of his news stories or signed editorials dealt with racial issues. The issue that affected him most was the republication of "The Sahara of the Bozart," Mencken's scathing indictment of Southern culture. This piece, as we have seen, had first appeared in the *New York Evening Mail* in late 1917, when Johnson was in the army. Mencken revised and expanded "Sahara," and it was published in essay form under the same title in *Prejudices: Second Series,* a volume issued by Knopf in November. His *Prejudices* series (it ran to six volumes and a collected edition) gave him the space to frolic as he pleased—to regale and admonish, to shock and sigh—and he showed little interest in presenting both sides of an issue. With his penchant for the absurd and his skill with neologism, he coined "bozart" as the preposterous Southern rendition of *beaux arts.* He had much fun detailing, with characteristic hyperbole, the philistinism of the region.[10]

Calling the South a cultural "vacuity," he proclaims that "it is almost as sterile, artistically, intellectually, culturally, as the Sahara desert." The South embarrasses itself as a "gargantuan paradise of the fourth-rate," a benighted region where "there is not a single picture gallery worth going into, or a single orchestra capable of playing the nine symphonies of Beethoven, or a single theater devoted to decent plays." With the single exception of the Richmond novelist James Branch Cabell, there is not "a single southern prose writer who can actually write." The modern South has so deteriorated, Mencken complains, that "a Washington or a Jefferson, dumped there by some act of God, would be denounced as a scoundrel and jailed overnight."[11]

The sweep and force of Mencken's condemnation caused some people to

10. Mencken, "The Sahara of the Bozart," in *Prejudices: Second Series* (New York: Knopf, 1920), 136–40.

11. *Ibid.*, 138.

conclude, quite wrongly, that he hated the South. Actually, the antebellum South, he remarks appreciatively, "was a civilization of manifold excellences— perhaps the best the Western hemisphere has ever seen—undoubtedly the best These States have ever seen." He proceeds to assert that the South prior to the Civil War was populated by "superior men." Mencken prods the South to return to its former place of prominence. The Baltimorean functioned, to borrow Fred Hobson's apt analogy, as a "serpent in Eden," and this devil did an immense amount of good for Southern literature in general and Johnson in particular. In the end, "Sahara" proved the single most influential essay that Johnson ever read.[12]

Years later, Johnson would recall that he had "gasped [and] grinned" after his first exposure to "Sahara," and he would dub Mencken an "intellectual bombardier." When the men began to correspond later during the 1920s, Johnson would remark appreciatively that "you said so many things I felt, but had not the wit to think out nor the guts to utter." Johnson also correctly perceived that Mencken did not hate the South; his "real sentiments . . . are indistinguishable from those of a cavalry captain seven times wounded in the service of the Confederacy." It would not be until 1923, however, that Johnson responded at length to "Sahara" in a public forum, one that Mencken acquired for him.[13]

Johnson closed out 1920 by writing on a topic that made irony and Southern culture seem far away indeed. In late December, he paused to reflect upon the meaning of the Nativity. This first Christmas column began a tradition that would continue, with some gaps, for over fifty years. Moved by the sanctity of childhood, he celebrated "the childish heart [that] can still thrill to the rapture of the day's beginnings," and he spoke of the mother who "can laugh with delight at her secret midnight work by the chimney." He concluded by speaking of the lasting happiness of those "who have known the divinity of childhood, even for a little while."[14] He managed here to capture much sentiment without stooping to sentimentality. He was setting forth a credo of sorts—an attitude that would allow him to cherish uncorrupted goodness—and he was also hymning those lamb-white days of his

12. *Ibid.*, 137.

13. GWJ, "Guess Work," *Menckeniana* 1 (spring 1962): no pagination; GWJ, foreword to *Serpent in Eden: H. L. Mencken and the South,* by Fred Hobson (Chapel Hill: University of North Carolina Press, 1974), ix; GWJ to Mencken, December 26, 1922, HLM Papers; GWJ to Mencken, January 15, 1925, quoted in Hobson, *Serpent in Eden,* 153.

14. "The Message It Brings," *GDN,* December 25, 1920.

own lost youth. Moreover, he was implicitly lamenting the wife he had not yet met and the children whom he had not yet fathered. Although he could not know it at the time, he would spend only one more Christmas without his own family.

During the following year, Johnson found love and fought a battle that proved portentous. In late July, the *Daily News* ran a four-part series that anticipated Johnson's combat with the Southern Agrarians. The occasion was President Harding's criticism of the South as a "famine-stricken" and "pestilence-stricken" land. Johnson argued that it was time for Southerners "to quit making excuses and begin making good." ("No More Excuses" would be the title of his most vitriolic review of *I'll Take My Stand*.) He scoffed at the South as "the national cry-baby" and criticized its leaders for their refusal to face unattractive truths. His use of antithesis could hardly have been more effective:

> From stump and press alike the south is hearing too much about Cold Harbor and the Hindenburg line, and too little about pellagra and cattle ticks. We need to pay less attention to the gratifying number of great men in our past and more attention to the astounding number of idiots in our present. We need to reduce somewhat the admiration that we lavish upon a great orator, and transfer some of it to a great dairyman. If we are not to produce to earn the lasting contempt of the world, we need to produce more beef and less bull.[15]

As always, he scorned the South's tendency to retreat into its storied past, and his exhortation was clear: "Look ahead, Dixie land."

In the first magazine article that ran under his name, Johnson proved equally combative about the costs of industrialism in the New South. "The Cotton Strike," which appeared in *Survey Graphic,* details the inherent battle between capital and labor. After wages had been cut by as much as 50 percent in some of the North Carolina mills, the United Textile Workers of America called a strike in June at four different plants. On August 11, the Locke mills

15. GWJ, "The Most Successful Failure in Greensboro," *GDN,* July 3, 1921, p. 5. "Remedy Must Be Assigned from Top to Bottom," *GDN,* July 29, 1921. The other unsigned editorials in this series were "Starving in a Fat Land," July 27, 1921; "Denying Allegations That Have Not Been Made," July 28, 1921; and "The President Sticks to His Purpose," July 31, 1921.

in Concord reopened with between 100 and 125 of the former 450 opera-
tors. Governor Cameron Morrison sent in troops four days later, and "the
backbone of the strike was broken." Arguing that "the strike never really had
a chance of success," Johnson explains that "the overwhelming nature of the
owners' mill victory can hardly be overstated. Quietly, efficiently, ruthlessly,
the union has been blotted out." Johnson's word choice clearly depicts his
sympathy for the workers. The article closes by speaking of the possibility of
future strife. Johnson proved oracular.[16]

During the following year, Johnson would begin to correspond with both
Howard W. Odum and H. L. Mencken and find his writing praised in the
Baltimore Evening Sun, but the most momentous event of 1922 was personal
rather than literary: his marriage to Kathryn Dulsinea Hayward that July.
Nine years Johnson's junior, Kathryn was the daughter of Minnie Roberta
Duls and William Richard Hayward. Born in Charlotte in 1875, Minnie
Hayward was a first-generation American (both parents had emigrated from
Germany) and a graduate of the Charlotte Seminary; she was also a teacher
and musician. Born in 1870 in Benton, Iowa, William Richard Hayward
graduated from Valparaiso College in 1892 and became an educator. After
Kathryn, an only child, was born in Atlanta in 1899, the family moved to
Charlotte, Philadelphia, Greensboro, Passaic (New Jersey), and New York
City, where Mr. Hayward served as principal of Theodore Roosevelt High
School in the Bronx. Kathryn graduated from Curtis High School in Staten
Island and won a scholarship to Vassar. She entered in 1915, at age sixteen,
and graduated four years later.[17]

From the fall of 1920 until the fall of 1921, she lived in Greensboro to
help her uncle, Joseph J. Stone, a merchant whose wife had died. She and
Johnson met during the fall of 1921, and they married on April 22, 1922.
Johnson wrote the wedding service, and the ceremony was performed by Dr.
Milne at Kellwood, Mr. Stone's home. The couple took their honeymoon
in the mountains. Catharine Lambeth Carlton, Johnson's niece and the
flower girl, has recalled that the day of the wedding was "freezing cold." The
marriage, however, could hardly have been warmer or happier. The couple's
first child, Kathryn Hayward, would be born on February 6, 1923, and be
given the Scottish nickname "Wee." The second daughter, Dorothy Hayward, would be born on April 23, 1924. Johnson was blessed, and he knew

16. GWJ, "The Cotton Strike," *Survey Graphic* 46 (November 1921): 646–47.
17. Folders 230–237, GWJ Papers.

it. Decades later, he would explain that "the terrible vulnerability of the father consists in the fact that his need of his children is so much greater than their need for him."[18]

Johnson's decision to marry Kathryn says a good deal about him. He did not insist upon a Southern bride; although born in Georgia, Kathryn had spent the better part of her life outside the South. Her formal education equaled his. She was an independent woman with strong convictions who was inclined to express them. For her as for Johnson, material things were never of primary importance. She and her husband agreed upon the need for culture; she played the cello, danced, and made certain that her daughters were thoroughly educated in the fine arts. She ran the home that gave Johnson the tranquillity to write. Later, when he became a freelance writer, she founded her own business to help with the finances.[19] In choosing this intelligent, attractive, and highly capable woman, Johnson married wisely and well.

In late February 1922, Professor Howard W. Odum began corresponding with Johnson about the forthcoming first issue of his bimonthly *Journal of Social Forces*. A native Georgian six years Johnson's senior, Odum had graduated from Emory University in 1904, taken a master's degree two years later at the University of Mississippi, and proceeded to earn doctorates from both Clark University and Columbia University. After teaching at the University of Georgia and serving as dean of Emory College, he came to Chapel Hill, where he chaired the Department of Sociology and served as the dean of the School of Social Welfare. A prolific writer with varied interests, Odum became "the South's best-known social scientist in the first half of the 20th century."[20]

Having learned of Johnson through his editorials, Odum asked the North Carolinian to serve on the magazine's editorial board. Johnson was flattered but replied candidly that he knew little about social science. Given Johnson's writing ability, his wide interests, and his courage, however, his lack of experience in this field mattered little. The men were soon corresponding regularly, and Johnson assumed a variety of roles; he evaluated manuscripts, offered editorial advice, and suggested both contributors and potential sub-

---

18. Catharine Lambeth Carlton, interview by author, Riverton, N.C., August 17, 1989; GWJ, "Letters from the Head of the Family," *NYHTB*, April 24, 1960, 10.

19. Kathryn Hayward Johnson, interview by author, Valparaiso, Ind., June 8, 1989.

20. Wayne D. Brazil, "Howard W. Odum," in *Encyclopedia of Southern Culture,* ed. Charles Reagan Wilson and William Ferris (Chapel Hill: University of North Carolina Press, 1989), 296.

scribers. Odum solicited Johnson's prose as well. In November, the month that the magazine's first issue appeared, Johnson submitted a manuscript that would appear the following year under the title "Mr. Babbitt Arrives at Erzerum," and Odum thought it one of the best essays that he had ever read.[21]

Soon after the magazine's first issue, the *Daily News* saluted it in two editorials. The second offered a typically Johnsonian idea, the need the change with the times: "We are realizing that with a great industrial state growing up on our hands we cannot go on doing as our fathers did with respect to social problems." In time, Johnson became, in Fred Hobson's phrase, *Social Forces'* "boldest spokesman."[22] Johnson and Odum proved simpatico intellectually—they would collaborate on a book the following decade—and became close personal friends. In all, this proved to be one of the most significant relationships in Johnson's career.

Mencken's influence became increasingly evident throughout the year, and the men began to correspond in late 1922. Like Odum, Mencken found his ideas and writing defended in the *Daily News*. Discussing both poetry and drama, Johnson called, as Mencken had, for an indigenous Southern literature. Johnson praised both Sinclair Lewis and Joseph Hergesheimer, novelists whom Mencken was applauding in the *Smart Set*. On June 1, Johnson wrote his first signed review of a book by the Baltimorean. The reviewer could hardly have chosen a livelier and more controversial volume than *In Defense of Women,* a book that guffaws about the bumpy passage of men and women down the road of life and continues to this day to delight some and outrage others. Johnson called the volume "a brilliant and corrosive book" by "the great Khan of Baltimore" and admitted to "a marked partiality for Mencken taken moderately." Johnson also sometimes misinterpreted the book. He argued that "Mencken's defense is really the most diabolically clever assault." Actually, *In Defense* praises women for their superior intelligence, their realism and lack of hypocrisy, and their willingness to revolt against convention more frequently than men do. Mencken asserts that "the average woman, whatever her deficiencies, is greatly superior to the average man." The typi-

21. Howard W. Odum to GWJ, February 28, 1922; GWJ to Howard W. Odum, March 1, 1922; Howard W. Odum to GWJ, February 20, 1923; GWJ to Howard W. Odum, February 17, 1923, February 28, 1923, and October 26, 1923; GWJ to Howard W. Odum, November 12, 1922 and October 21, 1922; Howard W. Odum, November 28, 1922, HWO Papers.

22. "A Journal of Social Forces," *GDN,* November 7, 1922 and December 27, 1922; Fred Hobson, introduction to *South-Watching: Selected Essays by Gerald W. Johnson,* ed. Fred Hobson (Chapel Hill: University of North Carolina, 1983), xiii.

cal married man, Mencken remarks memorably, "is weary when he gets home, and asks only the dull peace of a hog in a comfortable sty." In the end, the book's title proves ironic, for women, as Mencken well knew, need no defense at all. Later that year, Johnson reviewed *Prejudices: Third Series* as a "shocking, infuriating, and uproariously funny" volume by "the wild man of Baltimore."[23]

Imitation proved the sincerest form of flattery, and the wild man found his prose aped on the newspaper's editorial page: "The *Daily News* is the possessor of a compilation of alleged Southern literature. . . . And for arrogant piffle, for unendurable twaddle, for ineffable bosh we back that collection against anything else of the sort." Mencken also discovered that "he was one of the most important critics in the country" and that his assault had done some good, for there was "the promise of an oasis in the Sahara of the Bozart." Late in 1922, another editorial explained that five articles in the December issue of *Carolina Magazine* had responded to Mencken's blast in *Prejudices*. The editorial did not mention that Johnson contributed to the magazine and that Mencken's prose was imitated once more.[24]

Having been asked to comment on the possible formation of a North Carolina Poetry Society, Johnson declared that its "first business" must be "the extermination of the maundering imbecility, the sniffling puerility, the sloppy sentimental, the bunk, bosh and tommyrot that pass for poetry in North Carolina." Mencken praised Johnson's commentary in the *Baltimore Evening Sun* on December 26 as "an admirable manifesto of the New South." Mencken also wrote to Johnson, who replied that he was "gratified beyond

---

23. GWJ, "Drama of the Plain People," review of *Carolina Folk Plays*, ed. Frederick H. Koch, *GDN*, December 17, 1922; GWJ, "Southern Poetry That Is Real," review of *Carolina Chansons*, by DuBose Heyward and Hervey Allen, *GDN*, December 31, 1922; GWJ, "Easement for Tired Hearts," review of *Songs Merry and Sad* and *Lyrics from Cotton Land* by John Charles McNeill and *Idle Comment* by Isaac Erwin Avery, *GDN*, December 24, 1922; GWJ, "Main Street in an Urban Setting," review of *Babbitt*, by Sinclair Lewis, *GDN*, September 24, 1922; GWJ, "Hergesheimer's New Novel," review of *Cytherea* by Joseph Hergesheimer, *GDN*, March 5, 1922; GWJ, "Magnificent Entertainment," review of *Bright Shawl*, by Joseph Hergesheimer, *GDN*, September 19, 1922; GWJ, "Women Defended by the Enemy," *GDN*, June 1, 1922; Mencken, *In Defense of Women* (New York: Knopf, 1922), 125, 114; GWJ, "Mencken Submits a Few Remarks," *GDN*, November 5, 1922.

24. The following are unsigned editorials in the *GDN*: "The Trouble with Southern Literature," June 25, 1922; "Mild Deprecation for Mencken's Blast," December 15, 1922; for further references to "The Sahara of the Bozart," see "An Impulse That Deserves Respect," February 7, 1922; and "One of the Greatest Civilizing Influences," September 4, 1922.

measure." Johnson proceeded to explain that he had "gained a lamentable reputation among certain of the orthodox as a backslider from grace . . . hardened to sin." This religious trope is revealing, for Johnson saw Mencken and himself as fellow heretics. This entire episode—Mencken's first exposure to a magazine article by Johnson, the Baltimorean's first mention of Johnson in print, and the beginning of their correspondence—proved quite significant. At the time, they were kindred spirits, and Johnson would serve, as Fred Hobson explains, as Mencken's "lieutenant in the Southern war of liberation."[25]

Upon Mencken's recommendation, J. Edwin Murphy, managing editor of the *Evening Sun,* wrote to Johnson in January 1923 and asked him to interview for the position of associate editor. Johnson traveled to Baltimore later that month, made a favorable impression, and was offered the job. The parties could not agree about salary, however, and Johnson rejected the offer of seventy-five dollars a week. However, the newspaper's editor, Hamilton Owens, asked Johnson to write occasionally about Southern issues, something in which the *Evening Sun* was especially interested.[26]

The newspaper was not disappointed. The *Evening Sun* ardently opposed Prohibition and with the colorfully entitled "Onward Volstead Soldiers" received a column thoroughly in keeping with its editorial policy. Johnson criticized North Carolina's Turlington Law, which gave automatic immunity to a state's witness in a Prohibition case. His next contribution, on the highly topical gender issue, proved just as lively. He compared the living conditions of a working woman in Moscow with those of "Carolina Sal," who worked in a Southern cotton mill. Johnson's columns, Owens remarked, generated much attention, and he thought that the North Carolinian "wrote like an angel." That fall, Owens traveled to Greensboro to make Johnson another job offer. By this time, however, President Harry W. Chase of the University

25. GWJ, "Why Not a Poetry Society for North Carolina?" *Carolina Magazine* 53 (December 1922): 2, quoted in Hobson, introduction to *South-Watching*, x–xi; Mencken, "Confederate Notes," *BES*, November 26, 1922; GWJ to Mencken, December 26, 1922, HLM Papers; Hobson, *Tell About the South: The Southern Rage to Explain* (Baton Rouge: Louisiana State University Press, 1983), 188. Mencken's first letter to Johnson is in private hands. For further discussion of Mencken's response to Johnson's article, see Hobson, *Serpent in Eden*, 88–89.

26. J. Edwin Murphy to GWJ, January 19, 1923, GWJ Papers; GWJ to Mencken, January 15, 1923, HLM Papers; J. Hamilton Owens to GWJ, January 22, 1923, January 31, 1923, and February 9, 1923, GWJ Papers; H. L. Mencken to GWJ, March 2, 1923, HLM Papers. Johnson recounts his interview with Murphy in "A Help and Ornament," *BES*, April 1, 1943.

of North Carolina at Chapel Hill had other plans for Johnson, plans that would postpone for several years the possibility of a permanent move to Baltimore.[27]

He wrote just as boldly on the home front. The civil libertarian used the *Daily News* to attack the censors suppressing *The "Genius,"* Theodore Dreiser's controversial novel. Reviewing *Nigger,* another controversial novel by the Alabamian Clement Wood, Johnson argued that as a social indictment the book was "too sweeping" but asserted that "it is worth the attention of every thoughtful Southerner." With "Sahara" very much in mind, he praised the establishment of *The Fugitive* magazine in Nashville. On the other hand, the *Yearbook* of the Poetry Society of South Carolina felt his wrath. Calling again for an indigenous Southern literature telling the truth about the region, he called for "something more virile . . . than [its] wax-like creations." The gadfly called for a "rigid re-examination" of Southern attitudes and argued that "we are already exhibiting symptoms of spiritual diabetes, and a reduction in sugar in our diet is urgently needed." Dr. Johnson prescribed "more gall and wormwood."[28]

Johnson's diagnoses so appealed to Mencken that he used the September *Smart Set* to assert: "There is no other newspaper in the South so intelligent as the Greensboro *Daily News,* and few editorial writers so shrewd and courageous as . . . Gerald Johnson." Johnson wrote gratefully that "our efforts to turn out a newspaper that analyzes slightly above the Volstead ration of truth not infrequently encounters a hostility of amazing bitterness. . . . Consequently, intelligent praise is a sweet morsel indeed." He also wrote that he was going to throw the *Smart Set* on the desk of the business manager and demand a raise.[29]

27. GWJ, "Onward Volstead Soldiers," *BES,* October 30, 1923; GWJ, "Natasha of Moscow and Carolina Sal," *BES,* November 23, 1923; Hamilton Owens to GWJ, October 31, 1923, GWJ Papers; Lloyd Dennis, "Gerald Johnson: Man of Many Parts," *GDN,* March 22, 1964.

28. GWJ, "The Elephant Now Goes Round," *GDN,* December 16, 1923; GWJ, "A Bitter Tonic for the South," *GDN,* February 4, 1923. "Two Southern Magazines," *GDN,* June 18, 1923; "Sectional Literature," *GDN,* December 7, 1923; "Further Consideration of Sectional Literature," *GDN,* December 14, 1923. See Hobson, *Serpent in Eden,* 70; "For Instance, Lexington," *GDN,* September 28, 1923; "Battling for American Idealism," *GDN,* 21 September 1923; Johnson acknowledged authorship of "Battling" in his letter of September 21, 1923 to Howard W. Odum, HWO Papers.

29. Mencken and George Jean Nathan, "Repetition Generale," *SS* 36 (September 1923): 62; GWJ to Mencken, September 18, 1923, HLM Papers.

Johnson was happy as well when he was given the opportunity to write for the *American Mercury,* Mencken's next magazine venture. From the time that he and George Jean Nathan had begun to co-edit the *Smart Set,* Mencken was dissatisfied with its cover, title, readership, and budget. Unable to shape the magazine as he wished, he grew increasingly exasperated. During the summer of 1923, Mencken announced that "I am making plans to start a serious review—the gaudiest and damnedest ever seen in the Republic." Having been asked to contribute, Johnson replied that he appreciated this "chance of a lifetime."[30] He was not exaggerating.

Johnson also proved grateful because Mencken introduced him to Emily Clark, editor of the *Reviewer,* whose first issue had appeared in February 1921. Clark, whom Johnson later celebrated as "the de Sévigné of the James river Valley," presided over a journal that paid "in fame and not in specie" and "had no policy beyond a fixed standard of good writing, and a determination to make articulate the new Southern consciousness." Mencken himself wrote for the magazine, as did such prominent Southern authors as Paul Green and Frances Newman, Donald Davidson and Allen Tate.[31]

Clark contacted Johnson in February 1923, and Johnson replied that he would be "delighted to lend a hand in any effort to stimulate better writing in the South." With considerable humility, he submitted "The Congo, Mr. Mencken," which ran in the July issue. Johnson argues that Mencken's image of dessication for the South is inappropriate: "The South is not sterile. On the contrary, it is altogether too luxuriant. It is not the Sahara, but the Congo of the Bozart." He invites Mencken "to plunge into the trackless waste of the Library of Southern Literature, where a man might wander for years, encountering such a profusion of strange and incredible growths as could proceed from none but an enormously rich soil." As a result, Johnson concludes, Southern literature "may be gorgeously barbaric, but it will not be monotonous."[32]

30. Mencken to Sara Haardt, June 10, 1923, in *Mencken and Sara, a Life in Letters: The Private Correspondence of H. L. Mencken and Sara Haardt,* ed. Marion Elizabeth Rodgers (New York: McGraw-Hill, 1987), 84; Mencken's letter to Johnson is in private hands and hence unavailable; GWJ to Mencken, July 11, 1923, HLM Papers.

31. GWJ, "Heroic, Amusing, Startlingly Indiscreet," *BS,* April 18, 1965; Emily Clark, *Innocence Abroad,* 8, 6, 112.

32. Clark, *Innocence Abroad,* 120–21, 253–55; GWJ, "The Congo, Mr. Mencken," in *South-Watching: Selected Essays by Gerald W. Johnson,* ed. Fred Hobson (Chapel Hill: University of North Carolina, 1983), 3–8.

Johnson knew that "Congo" could have been "somewhat smoother" but was pleased when Mencken complimented him on the essay. Emily Clark was pleased as well; looking back in 1931, she called "Congo" the "best article that [Johnson] has yet written and undeniably one of the best that [the *Reviewer*] ever published." DuBose Heyward wrote from South Carolina to praise "the suicidal, but ecstatic spirit that has entered into our fellow rebel Gerald Johnson." And an editorial in the *New York Times* spoke of Johnson "amusing himself and looking for trouble."[33] It was right on both counts.

Johnson continued to look for trouble in "Fourteen Equestrian Statues of Colonel Simmons," which ran in the *Reviewer* three months later. In this mock encomium for the founder of the Klan, Johnson criticizes the region's "spiritual bondage," "the amazing docility of [its] masses," and its "lack of keen and reflective self-criticism." To attack corruption wrought by journalists, the clergy, and politicians, the honest Southerner must "burst all bonds of conservative tradition, break with the past and defy the present with the bald, unequivocal, and conclusive assertion that lying is wrong." In a lively prose replete with Menckenese—"editorial belchings," "poltroonery," "heights of imbecility," and "empty gabble"—Johnson functions as a Southern image breaker.[34]

He stirred up more controversy in the essays for *Social Forces*. "Mr. Babbitt Arrives at Erzerum" laments the fact that North Carolina is "intellectually inert, disliking exceedingly to be pestered by new men or ideas." Johnson insists that social legislation, both rural and urban, must adapt to the changing times. The "Mr. Babbitt" in Johnson's title refers of course to Sinclair Lewis's philistine businessman. Erzerum was a supposedly impregnable fortress in Turkey which fell to Grand Duke Nicholas of Russia during the nineteenth century. Through the literary allusion and the historical reference, Johnson suggests that the reflective life is superior to mindless materialism and that change is inevitable.[35]

"Issichar Is a Strong Ass," the lead essay in the November issue, generated

33. GWJ to Mencken, July 30, 1923, HLM Papers; Mencken's earlier letter praising "Congo" is in private hands and hence unavailable; DuBose Heyward to Emily Clark, August 1923, in Clark, *Innocence Abroad*, 242; "Is The South Purple?" *New York Times*, August 6, 1923; Clark, *Innocents Abroad*, 258.

34. GWJ, "Fourteen Equestrian Statues of Colonel Simmons," in *South-Watching: Selected Essays by Gerald W. Johnson*, ed. Fred Hobson (Chapel Hill: University of North Carolina, 1983), 9–14.

35. GWJ, "Mr. Babbitt Arrives at Erzerum," *JSF* 1 (March 1923): 206–209.

more contention. In this piece, whose title alludes to the forty-ninth chapter of *Genesis,* Johnson laments North Carolina's brain drain and points out that the state ignores its artists but deifies those who deal "with material things." He scoffs at the variety of villains who profane the state: "every business pirate who has ground up the bodies and souls of his workmen," "every vacant-minded editor who hears his master's voice from the counting-room," "every dry-as-dust professor who warps the mind of . . . unfortunate students," and "every cleric of the diabolist persuasion who steals the humanism from the intensely human doctrine of the gentle Nazarene." He took pride, Johnson told Odum, that the essay "goes not one step out of its way to avoid treading on anybody's corns." Johnson was attacked in the Asheville and Wilmington newspapers, and he expressed surprise that he was not vilified even more. "There is neither pleasure nor profit in being the official hard guy," he told Odum, "but if the state is ever to quit lotus-eating somebody's got to be rough; and since I have nothing particular to lose by it, might as well be my job."[36]

It had been an extremely productive and combative year. By the end of 1923, Johnson was understandably tired. In December he took his first vacation in twelve years. His family set out on its own odyssey, a trip to New York City (Johnson's first visit) to see the Haywards.[37]

In his thirty-fourth year, Johnson was becoming better known all across the country. Bobbs-Merrill asked him to submit a book manuscript, and *Scribner's Magazine* asked for a contribution. Both the *Norfolk Ledger-Dispatch* and the *St. Louis Post-Dispatch* asked him to consider taking editorial positions on their staffs. A career change would, in fact, be effected in 1924. Long dead, the British naturalist Charles Darwin would exert considerable influence from the grave.[38]

When Johnson returned to North Carolina in early January 1924, the big news was the appearance of the first issue of the *American Mercury.* "It is the only genuinely new thing that has appeared in the magazine world in my

36. GWJ, "Issachar Is a Strong Ass," *JSF* 2 (November 1923): 5–9; GWJ to Howard W. Odum, January 10, 1924, and September 27, 1923; GWJ to Howard W. Odum, January 10, January 27, 1923, HWO Papers.

37. GWJ to Mencken, December 21, 1923, HLM Papers.

38. Hewitt W. Howland (editor, Bobbs-Merrill) to GWJ, July 22, 1924; Alfred S. Dashiell (Editorial Department, *Scribner's Magazine*) to GWJ, August 8, 1924; S. L. Slaver (president, *Norfolk Ledger-Dispatch)* to GWJ, May 27, 1924; George S. Johns (editor, *St. Louis Post-Dispatch)* to GWJ, May 27, 1924, GWJ Papers.

time," Johnson wrote to Mencken. "I congratulate you, wonderingly and admiringly." Congratulations were indeed in order, for Mencken showed unerring good sense regarding the magazine's title, appearance, and editorial policy. Theodore Dreiser had suggested several flashy titles. "What we need," Mencken explained laughingly to his friend, "is something that looks highly respectable outwardly. The American Mercury is almost perfect for that purpose. What will go on inside the tent is another story. You will recall that P. T. Barnum got away with burlesque shows by calling them moral lectures." The times were good; many Americans were ready to guffaw, and about one-third of the magazine's essays tended to be satirical. Some of the land's more vulnerable targets were assaulted repeatedly: misguided pedagogy, chiropractic, homeopathy, Christian Science, Puritanism, and the sad credulity of rural America. The *Mercury*'s first issue had an initial printing of five thousand; a second was necessary, then a third. By the end of the year, circulation had soared past 42,000, a figure that far surpassed even the most optimistic expectations.[39]

Mencken was fascinated by the literary opportunities provided by the American South. During its first eighteen months, the magazine ran fifty-five contributions by twenty-three Southerners. Johnson's essays graced three of the *Mercury*'s first seven issues. He discussed the Klan, the South's attitudes toward the Yankees, and the destructive effect of Southern evangelists.[40] His readers were never bored.

"The Ku Kluxer" was scheduled to appear in the *Mercury*'s prestigious first issue but was bumped to February because of lack of space. Johnson wrote agreeably that he understood Mencken's space problems and was pleased to have received payment. (This was apparently his first check from

39. GWJ to Mencken, January 3, 1924, HLM Papers; Theodore Dreiser to H. L. Mencken, September 9, 1923, in *Dreiser-Mencken Letters: The Correspondence of Theodore Dreiser and H. L. Mencken, 1907–1945,* ed. Thomas P. Riggio (Philadelphia: University of Pennsylvania Press, 1986), 2:501–502; Vincent Fitzpatrick, *H. L. Mencken* (New York: Continuum, 1989), 65–68; Vincent Fitzpatrick, "H. L. Mencken," in *Dictionary of Literary Biography,* vol. 137), *American Magazine Journalists, 1900–1960,* (2nd series) (Detroit: Gale Research, 1994), 193–95. For the most detailed history of the magazine, see M. K. Singleton, *H. L. Mencken and the American Mercury Adventure* (Durham, NC: Duke University Press, 1962), especially 55–110. George Jean Nathan co-edited the *American Mercury* from January 1924 until August 1925.

40. Mencken to Howard W. Odum, September 10, 1923, HWO Papers; Hobson, *Serpent in Eden,* 108. For further discussion of the *Mercury* and the American South, see Hobson, *Serpent in Eden,* 99–101, and Kneebone, *Southern Liberal Journalists,* 33.

a magazine.) Decades later, though, he would remark that this failure to appear in the first *Mercury* was one of the great disappointments of his career.[41]

Sketching a portrait of a hypothetical Klansman, an exalted Cyclops named Chill Burton, Johnson the revisionist argues that "the lurid imaginings of many writers on the Klan, particularly in the North, may be dismissed at once." Chill is a "pillar of the church" and an "exemplary husband" but also an "incurable romantic" who is manipulated by demagogues. Chill fears Catholics, Jews, blacks, and strangers—anyone, in short, who threatens his frosty and insular world. As he had done in "Fourteen Equestrian Statues," Johnson drubs the corrupt pastor and politician, and he proceeds to remark that the Klan profanes Christianity and chivalry. No white knight, Chill is instead a "thug," a "'racial bully,'" and a "spiritual bushwhacker."[42] Nobody misconstrued Johnson's ideas.

Three months later, the *Mercury* ran "The South Takes the Offensive." Its thesis, Johnson facetiously wrote to Mencken, is that "the Southerner finds nothing really objectionable about the North except its morals, its manners, its politics, its religion, its cuisine, its business code, its domiciles, its sports, its dialect and its gait." The essay's title announces Johnson's technique. He attacks "Yankee squatters" and their messianic delusions about preaching the gospel in a heathen land and proceeds to scoff at Yankee politicians. He laments the encroachment of Northern customs and criticizes the Yankees for "their abominable treatment of the Negro." Johnson concludes by depicting the South as "the saving remnant of sanity in a nation threatened mentally with total eclipse." Although he was praised in the *Daily News* for carrying the war into enemy territory, Johnson boasted that the essay was "much deprecated" in Durham and Chapel Hill. "I am much relieved," he told Mencken. "The thing must have had some life in it after all."[43]

The alliterative and ironic "Saving Souls" had a good deal of life in it as well. Johnson lampoons rural evangelists and their tent revivals. With their

41. GWJ to Mencken, November 29, 1923, HLM Papers; Jinny Voris, "According to Mr. Johnson: Some Insights on Mr. Mencken," HLM Papers.

42. GWJ, "The Ku Kluxer," in *South-Watching: Selected Essays by Gerald W. Johnson,* ed. Fred Hobson (Chapel Hill: University of North Carolina, 1983), 15–21.

43. GWJ to Mencken, July 30, 1923, HLM Papers; GWJ, "The South Takes the Offensive, in *South-Watching: Selected Essays by Gerald W. Johnson,* ed. Fred Hobson (Chapel Hill: University of North Carolina, 1983), 93–105; Archibald Henderson, "A New Type of Criticism," *GDN,* May 14, 1924; Walter F. Coxe (managing editor, *Southern Magazine* to GWJ, April 24, 1924, GWJ Papers; GWJ to Mencken, May 3, 1924, HLM Papers.

assent to ignorance and superstition, their fear of learning and intelligence, such agents of darkness pander to the base prejudices of the mob. They are moral men without honor—like Judas, they will sell out their friends—and they hate Catholics and Jews. Johnson likens these evangelists to witch doctors and medicine men and circus barkers, and he explains that these revivals have something in common with sexual orgies. In brief, the proceedings mark a throwback to a more barbaric time. Exactly a year later, Mencken would use some of the same analogies and reach similar conclusions as he pondered the proceedings in the hills of Tennessee.[44]

Johnson's pervasive interest in the condition-of-the-South question also affected his writing for his old magazine markets. Versatile, he played a variety of parts. For *Social Forces,* he assumed the role of sober explicator. "Critical Attitudes North and South" acknowledges the South's increasing importance in the nation's affairs and addresses the issue of who speaks best for the South. It must be the Southerner, Johnson concludes, but this spokesperson must be an honest commentator rather than a press agent. For Emily Clark, Johnson frolicked as a satirist. "In Greensboro, or What You Will," Johnson laments the encroachment of false religion: "There is not God but advertising, and Atlanta is his prophet." Echoing "Sahara," Johnson draws Greensboro as "well fed but musicless, dramaless, destitute of painting and sculpture and scantily endowed with architecture meriting a second glance."[45]

Johnson's readers in the *Evening Sun* glanced at Greensboro when the newspaper ran an abbreviated version of the essay. They also witnessed the iconoclast attacking the Southern Democratic Party as an organization that "has degenerated into the vessel of religious hatreds." Using a metaphor that would prove prescient, Johnson complained that with William Jennings Bryan the party has "repudiated evolution, but it is demonstrating devolution. Already it has reverted to the lowest form of animate nature, and four

44. GWJ, "Saving Souls," in *South-Watching: Selected Essays by Gerald W. Johnson,* ed. Fred Hobson (Chapel Hill: University of North Carolina, 1983), 22–28; Mencken, "Yearning Mountaineers' Souls Need Reconversion Nightly, Mencken Finds," in *The Impossible H. L. Mencken: A Selection of His Best Newspaper Stories,* ed. Marion Elizabeth Rodgers (New York: Doubleday, 1991), 576–82.

45. GWJ, "Critical Attitudes North and South," in *South-Watching: Selected Essays by Gerald W. Johnson,* ed. Fred Hobson (Chapel Hill: University of North Carolina, 1983), 85–92; GWJ to Howard W. Odum, January 14, 1924, HWO Papers; GWJ, "Greensboro, Or What You Will," in *South-Watching: Selected Essays by Gerald W. Johnson,* ed. Fred Hobson (Chapel Hill: University of North Carolina, 1983), 45–50; Clark, *Innocence Abroad,* 256.

years hence will have been absorbed in the primordial slime." In a column entitled "Fundamentalism by Fiat," Johnson attacked North Carolina governor Cameron Morrison: "His Excellency . . . has announced that the evolutionary hypothesis of the origin of man shall not henceforth be applied to Tarheels." The governor was also skewered in the *Daily News,* and he was not pleased.[46]

On May 31, 1924, after the Thomasville newspaper released the news of Johnson's appointment in Chapel Hill, Governor Morrison objected strongly and questioned Johnson's character and standards. University president Harry W. Chase refused to back down; he defended Johnson's reputation and said that the University of Virginia was ready to offer him a similar position. When Johnson learned of the governor's objection, he offered to resign, but Chase refused the offer. Another controversy overcome, Johnson had a new job—professor of journalism and head of the newly created Department of Journalism—and a salary of $4,000.[47]

A number of matters affected this decision to change careers. President Chase knew that the battle over evolution would grow more heated and that a courageous and articulate supporter such as Johnson on the faculty would prove invaluable.[48] Johnson, for his part, had to be flattered by the prestige and the new position and the university's willingness to resist pressure from above in order to hire him.

There were also, however, more practical considerations. First, Johnson felt that such a move would better his financial situation. He never handled money well (he told a relative that he was a "financial illiterate"), and he faced pressing familial expenses with his two young children. He candidly admitted to Odum that he was in debt. Also, because of the low journalistic salaries in the state, he questioned the wisdom of a long-term commitment to this profession in North Carolina, and at this time he was not ready to move else-

46. GWJ, "Come to Greensboro, N.C." *BES,* June 19, 1924; GWJ, "Diskivered," *BES,* July 9, 1924; "GWJ, "Fundamentalism by Fiat," *BES,* January 20, 1924. The following unsigned editorials ran in the *GDN:* "Pope Cameron Issues a Decree," January 25, 1924; "Secondhand Gospelers," February 10, 1924; and "The Most Useless Battle," June 20, 1924.

47. President Harry W. Chase to GWJ, November 9, 1923, February 5, June 13, 1924, GWJ Papers; President Harry W. Chase to Governor Cameron Morrison, June 5, 13, 1924, University of North Carolina at Chapel Hill Archives and Records Services, Wilson Library; "Board of Trustees, 1879–1932," vol. 2; "University Papers," vol. 6; "Faculty Affairs," vol. 16; "University of North Carolina Trustee Minutes, 1924–1930."

48. Dennis, "Gerald Johnson: Man of Many Parts."

where. After he received a letter praising his journalism and questioning the career change, Johnson bluntly told the correspondent: "I am quitting the newspaper business simply because I cannot afford to hang on any longer; if I did my wife and children would pay the price 15 or 20 years hence."[49]

Second, he had to adjust to his changing stature as a writer. The man who began this phase of his career as a relatively unknown author hustling his wares was now in the enviable but difficult position of having too much to write. Feeling besieged, he complained to Odum that even a weeklong bout with the flu caused work to pile up alarmingly. At times, he grew weary of the daily grind of journalism and surely anticipated that, with fewer deadlines, his time would be more his own.[50]

He left the *Daily News* on the best of terms and contributed to it periodically throughout the rest of his career. Announcing his departure, the newspaper said that Johnson was "without peer in North Carolina," praised his "catholic sympathy," and lauded his ability to reach both scholars and the common reader. His students in Chapel Hill, the paper predicted, "would find him an astonishing compendium of things they should know—which is to say, something about everything in the world, and much about many things in it."[51] The best editorial writer in the South was to become a mentor himself, thereby continuing the tradition of Professors Poteat and Sledd for which he had proven so grateful.

Johnson could hardly anticipate that this new career, begun with the best of intentions, would prove abortive—that in less than two years he would be heading north to Baltimore for another position in daily journalism. Nor could he anticipate the direction that the inevitable battle over evolution would take. After the conflict was settled in Chapel Hill, he would cast his eyes west over the mountains to a little town on the Tennessee River north of Chattanooga. The town was called Dayton, and as Edward J. Larson has explained so well in *Summer for the Gods,* what happened there would pass into legend.

49. GWJ to Charles Lambeth, August 14, 1974, in possession of Mr. Lambeth, Thomasville, N.C.; GWJ to Howard W. Odum, October 3, 1924 and November 22, 1924, HWO Papers; GWJ to Alexander Worth McAlister, June 4, 1924, AWM Papers.

50. GWJ to Howard W. Odum, March 20, 1924, HWO Papers.

51. "To a Wider Field of Service," *GDN,* September 10, 1924; "Announcement," *GDN,* September 12, 1924.

6   Professor Johnson
1924–1926

I ain't got no learnin' and never had none. Glory be to the Lamb! Some folks work their hands off up to the elbows to give their young-uns education, and all they do is send their young-uns to Hell. . . . I ain't let no newspaper into my cabin for nigh unto year since the Lord bathed me in his blood. . . . I never sinned enough to look on one of these here almanacs. . . . I've eight young-uns in the cabin and three in glory, and I know they're in glory because I never learned 'em nothin'.

—*Joe Lefew preaching in 1925 in Dayton, Tennessee*

It was a noble idea, this passing along one's expertise to a younger generation. However, Johnson would come to discover, as some other educators have, that the responsibility for developing someone else's mind can have its attendant frustrations. In time, he came to question his role as a professor, and he moved on after four semesters. To call this a failed experiment, however, would be unfair, for Johnson did considerable good for both his students and the university.

In early September 1924, the Johnsons moved from Greensboro to 311 Pittsboro Street in Chapel Hill. Showing considerable concern for this new faculty member, the university had built this house largely to the family's specifications, and Odum had spent many hours overseeing the project. Johnson was moving to the oldest state university in America. At the time, Chapel Hill was, as Fred Hobson had described it, "a center of the Southern awakening." Among other notable figures, the university boasted Odum and his *Social Forces*; Frederick Koch and his Carolina Playmakers; Addison Hibbard and his "Literary Lantern," a newspaper column that appeared throughout the South; and the multitalented Paul Green. Johnson joined an impressive group. The campus, he remarked, "was swarming with people full of energy and ideas." He told Mencken that "the most hopeful characteristic of this institution is the fact that it has neither conscience nor patriotism. It will hire a damyankee any time for any sort of job. A good third of the faculty, including the President, came from the wrong side of the Potomac, to the scandal of all 100% Tar Heels."[1]

He was not the first teacher of journalism in Chapel Hill. Fifteen years before, Edward Kidder Graham, later president of the university, had taught the first journalism course under the auspices of the English Department. He was succeeded by James F. Royster in 1910 and Richard H. Thornton in 1914. After World War I, Lenoir Chambers headed a news bureau, and in 1921 Louis Graves was appointed professor of journalism, once more under the aegis of the English Department. The university's decision to create a Department of Journalism and hire Johnson generated favorable publicity. The *Wilmington (N.C.) News-Dispatch* said that "the brightest light of North Carolina journalism" was now in Chapel Hill, and the *Danville (Va.) News* noted the good fortune of the prospective students of this man "with a distinctive editorial style, a fearlessness of expression, and an independence of thought that has won him a high place among the writers of the South."[2]

Johnson carried out some of his professorial duties expertly. He was expected to lecture outside the classroom and during his first semester gave an address that was covered by the press. Journalism is an important trade, he explained, because "the power of the press . . . is rapidly increasing." Although many journalists work long hours for low pay, they are rewarded instead with power, profitable contacts, and considerable amusement. No other worker, Johnson remarked, "is thrown so constantly into the company of the great. He is also thrown constantly into contact with the foolish and the wicked. The great drama of human existence is played out before him." Detailing the influence of the journalist, Johnson said that "he gives safety to the state, no less" and that "he gives light to groping minds." Defending his trade

1. Fred Hobson, *Serpent in Eden: H. L. Mencken and the South* (Chapel Hill: University of North Carolina Press, 1974), 86; John T. Kneebone, *Southern Liberal Journalists and the Issue of Race, 1920–1944* (Chapel Hill: University of North Carolina Press, 1985), 28–29; Virginius Dabney, *Liberalism in the South* (Chapel Hill: University of North Carolina Press, 1932), 305; GWJ, "The Old North State," *BES*, October 14, 1937; GWJ to H. L. Mencken, December 10, 1924, quoted in Hobson, *Serpent in Eden*, 86.

2. William D. Snider, *Light on the Hill: A History of the University of North Carolina at Chapel Hill* (Chapel Hill: University of North Carolina Press, 1992), 176; "Looking Back—The Deans," *JAFA News* 14 (spring 1994): 4–5; "Journalism Is Taught along Practical Lines at Carolina," *GDN* December 21, 1924; "Johnson," *Wilmington (N.C.) News-Dispatch,* reprinted in *GDN,* September 14, 1924; "Gerald Johnson," *Danville (Va.) News,* June 2, 1924. The School of Journalism of the University of North Carolina at Chapel Hill was founded in 1950.

and the subject that he taught, Johnson proved an articulate representative of the university in general and the department in particular.[3]

Moreover, he put his considerable expertise to good use in the classroom, and he showed a good deal of common sense and adaptability. His department's accommodations could have been more stately. He was given three rooms, an office and two classrooms, in a building constructed in 1857; he taught beneath the area where the wrestling team practiced. Each student was given a secondhand typewriter. He explained to Mencken that "everything we do here is based on North Carolina conditions, that is to say, on country newspaper work, which requires no great technical skill, but cries aloud for men a little less ignorant, bigoted and degraded than many who are now engaged in it." Turning out such students, he told his friend, is "a noble endeavor but a devilishly hard job," and he facetiously asked for the Baltimorean's prayers.[4]

Johnson emphasized practice rather than theory and taught "at point-blank range." Trying to recreate actual working conditions, he set up one classroom to resemble the city room of a newspaper. His Elementary Journalism class met six days a week and covered news stories, copy reading, headlines, and make-up. The Advanced Journalism class, which met three days a week, concentrated on feature writing. He focused on those aspects of newspaper work most likely to be encountered by the beginning journalist. He ordered not only textbooks but also a number of morning and afternoon newspapers to serve as models. He wanted to teach his students "how to write clear, accurate English rapidly" and understood that "the best way to train writers is to let them write and then show them where they are wrong." During his first semester, Johnson remarked that his students' work exceeded his expectations, and the students reported that they were "highly pleased with the new department and its chief."[5]

While he was an impressive public spokesman and an effective teacher,

3. "Johnson Says Power of the Press Increasing," *Durham Morning Herald,* November 11, 1924.

4. "Journalism Is Taught along Practical Lines at Carolina"; GWJ to H. L. Mencken, September 28, 1924, HLM Papers.

5. GWJ to Lenoir Chambers, September 13, 1924, Lenoir Chambers Papers, Southern Historical Collection, Wilson Library, University of North Carolina at Chapel Hill; "Journalism Is Taught Along Practical Lines at Carolina"; GWJ to Business Manager, University of North Carolina, Chapel Hill, September 16, 1924, GWJ Papers; GWJ to Mencken, September 28, 1924; "Newspaper Training in Carolina," *GDN,* December 21, 1924.

Johnson had trouble with academic procedure and made the administration unhappy. Dorothy Johnson van den Honert spoke of this decades later when her father was being honored by the university:

> I find it broadminded of this particular university to so honor my father. If he was their first professor of journalism, he swore that he was also their worst. The administrative details of teaching—taking attendance, ordering textbooks, and the like—were foreign to his nature. Keeping attendance records, for example, he found nonsensical, since "he only wanted to talk to people who wanted to listen, anyhow." So he simply . . . marked everybody present every day. This blithe approach to administrative detail occasionally got him in the soup. A certain inconsiderate Mr. Smith, for instance, once blew Gerald's cover by being in the infirmary with pneumonia—a fact which had been duly noted by all the other professors.

When Johnson decided to return to daily journalism, it was, she said, "to the great relief of the Dean, I'm sure."[6]

Explaining his decision to leave teaching, Johnson typically shunned excuses. He called himself "incompetent" and said that he "was not cut out to be a teacher." Showing once again the refreshing ability to laugh at himself, he spoke of his sojourn in Chapel Hill as his "[going] to college for the second time" and remarked that he got out of the university "while the gettin' was good." Actually, the university proved very grateful for his presence. In 1956, six years after the founding of the School of Journalism, a scholarship was established in Johnson's name.[7]

Finally, Johnson's decision to leave seems to have been influenced by matters besides his administrative foibles, matters that his self-humor about his exaggerated ineptitude does not address. Daily journalism was in his blood, and he missed that "great drama of human existence" played out in the newspaper world. Moreover, his wife "longed . . . to set foot in a big city once again." In any event, looking back in laughter many years later, he said

6. Photocopy in the possession of the author; Kathryn Hayward Johnson, interview by author, Valparaiso, Ind., June 8, 1989.

7. GWJ, "The Old North State"; Mrs. J. A. Yarbrough, "Interesting Carolina People," *Charlotte Observer,* [1946], clipping in GWJ Papers; GWJ, "What Does the University Think?" *Century Magazine* 114 (June 1927): 111; Victoria Boney, "Gerald Johnson Still Tar Heel Editor," *GDN,* March 29, 1941; "Scholarships to Honor Graves, Johnson, and Coffin," *Chapel Hill Weekly,* February 7, 1956.

that he had "on one lamentable occasion made a two-year excursion into the groves of Academe, since when he has cherished a terrific admiration for school teachers, as performers of a noble and indispensable task which they, please God, can keep."[8] Actually, during his sixth decade, he would walk in the groves once more.

Johnson's work ethic at the typewriter accompanied him to Chapel Hill. During the fall of 1924, he continued to write lively columns about a variety of Southern issues for the *Baltimore Evening Sun*. Once more scorning demagogues, he lamented the election of South Carolinian Cole L. Blease to the United States Senate and attacked the "illiterates, morons, [and] criminals" who supported him. Looking farther south, he snorted that "the approaches to Georgia are hedged with spears." Bemoaning the encroachment of religion upon education (a recurrent theme at this time), he complained that a teacher at Mercer University had been fired because he "failed to convince the Grand Inquisitor that his method of teaching is designed to strengthen the faith of his students." Looking closer to home, Johnson lambasted James Buchanan Duke, the deceased tobacco magnate. Johnson scoffed at Duke's business practices—his "crew . . . includes many of the fieriest cut-throats that ever appeared among the buccaneers of commerce"—and criticized his philistinism.[9] The following summer, Johnson would speak far more respectfully of another dead man, William Jennings Bryan.

A variety of events would transpire during 1925, however, before Johnson pondered the implications of the Scopes trial. He would see his first book published, contribute his first essay to a collection, broaden his magazine market, help to edit the *Reviewer,* and, during the summer, move to Baltimore to write for the *Evening Sun*. Following the uproar in Dayton, he would travel to Norfolk to write for the *Ledger-Dispatch*. By long odds, 1925 would prove the most eventful year of his career up to this time.

Completed while he was in Greensboro, *The Story of Man's Work,* coauthored with his father-in-law, was published by Minton, Balch and Company of New York City. While the authors speak in both first- and third-person plural, the cadences of the prose are clearly Johnson's. This book is

---

8. GWJ, "Freedom: The Right and Duty," *NYHTB,* August 3, 1947, p. 4; GWJ to Katherine Johnson Parham, July 2, 1925, GWJ Papers; GWJ, "Artists Whose Clay Is the Human Soul," *NYHTB,* September 24, 1950, p. 8.

9. GWJ, "Blease Will Give a Good Show and Tarheels Will Rage," *BES,* September 16, 1924; GWJ, "Georgia Stands Firm," *BES,* October 22, 1924; GWJ, "The Sanctification of 'Buck' Duke," *BES,* December 16, 1924.

long out of print, and few, if any, contemporary readers first come to Johnson through this volume. However, the book proves significant because it says as much about Johnson as it does about its subject. Moreover, it shows the strengths and weaknesses (the tendency to oversimplify material, for example) that would mark the more than forty books to come.

The book's purpose, the preface announces, is "to give the reader a working knowledge of the economic system under which he lives. It has no claim to be called a work on economics; it is really an attempt to show the reader that the subject is worth studying." This volume, then, offers a popularization of economic theory. Structurally, the book falls into two parts, with the pivotal event predictably being the invention of the steam engine resulting in the industrial revolution. The volume's 241-page narrative moves chronologically from primitive man to the twentieth century.[10]

The volume employs methodologies that Johnson would continue to use and develops ideas that would appear later. The comparative historian draws history as a drama with villains (Adam Smith, whose theory of laissez-faire capitalism helps the strong and hurts the weak) and heroes (the humanitarian Robert Owen) slithering and striding across the the stage. Johnson the civil libertarian defends free speech; the egalitarian speaks of "the intelligence of the masses" and insists upon the need for equal opportunity. He sympathizes with the working man rather than with capital and, like Thomas Carlyle, extols the dignity of labor. Significantly, this volume published five years before *I'll Take My Stand* shows marked reservations about industrialism.[11]

This first book is marked by Johnson's considerable range as a stylist. Portions are written in spare journalese. On other occasions he uses those colorful extended analogies that he loved to concoct. Moreover, he shows his concern for life's unfortunates by shifting to the second-person for increased immediacy and employing the cadences of the pulpit:

> Now when a man works hard all his life and gets nothing out of it but a
> bare living, and a miserable one at that, so that when he is too old to work
> he has to be taken care of by the government; when in exchange for his
> labor he receives barely enough food to keep him alive . . . ; when he lives
> in a wretched hovel, and has never a cent to spend for luxuries or amuse-

10. William R. Hayward and GWJ, *The Story of Man's Work* (New York: Minton, Balch, 1925), viii.

11. *Ibid.,* 182, 224, 208, 115, 93, 114, 150, 127, 175, 157–58, 140–41.

ments; when he can never educate his children, but must see them doomed to the same sort of life; you can call that man a freeman, or what you please, but the practical difference between him and a slave is hardly worth mentioning.[12]

In this, the volume's coda, Johnson the homiletic humanitarian writes with power and grace.

Change is inevitable, Johnson asserts in the book's conclusion. He scoffs at the notion of the good old days, a myth that he always found galling: "As far back as written history goes, men were talking about the good old days, the Golden Age that is gone forever. . . . But . . . we can now pick out any point in the long rise of man from savagery and see that, contrary to the belief of men of the time, better days were ahead than any that were in the past."[13] He would never retreat from this position. While it is flawed, *The Story of Man's Work* is not dull. Johnson could have written a far worse first book.

Throughout the year, he used a variety of magazines to continue his commentary upon Southern issues. Significantly, he took a stand on the relationship between the Old South and the New. With "Sahara" still very much in mind, Johnson again imitated Mencken's prose and called for a more manly school of Southern poetry.[14] He surely made some readers cackle and others rage.

This year after Woodrow Wilson's death, Johnson's provocative assessment, appearing in both *Social Forces* and Odum's book *Southern Pioneers in Social Interpretation,* calls for his native region to assess Wilson not as an internationalist but as a Southerner. Having lamented the region's propensity for violence against the helpless and its interest in the automobile rather than education, he combines a nursery rhyme and skillful juxtaposition to observe that "it is no virtue for us to proclaim vociferously that [Robert E.] Lee is good enough for us. Simple Simon can see that. What would puzzle Socrates to decide is, are we good enough for Lee?" Calling for a spirit of "intellectual pioneering" in keeping with the late president's attitudes, Johnson blasts the Southern "theologue" and laments the presence of "many formidable rulers, especially in the ecclesiastical realm, who frankly and openly advocate shackling the reason in the presence of what they deem sacred subjects." A liberator, Johnson challenges his readers to burst these shackles.[15]

12. *Ibid.,* v, 138, 214.
13. *Ibid.,* 240.
14. GWJ, "Call for a Custom-Built Poet," *Southwest Review* 2 (April 1925): 26–30.
15. GWJ, "Southern Pioneers in Social Interpretation (VI. Woodrow Wilson: A Chal-

Pleased with both *Social Forces* and Johnson, Mencken received two contributions in 1925 for the *American Mercury.* The second, "Service in the Cotton Mills," proved the more significant. Johnson uses both this essay and his correspondence to acknowledge his debt to *The Rise of the Cotton Mills* by Broadus Mitchell, a professor at the Johns Hopkins University. Johnson begins "Service" by attacking an old enemy, sanctimonious Yankees fond of criticizing all things Southern, in this case particularly Southern mill owners. Johnson argues that the first wave of owners, who created "a new industrial order" between 1879 and 1881, were less concerned with profit than with the "salvation of the decaying community." Significantly, Johnson likens these men to the antebellum plantation owners: "The founding of the textile industry . . . may therefore fairly be regarded as the last great effort of the old order, the final gesture of the slave-owning aristocrat before he left the stage forever."[16]

The second wave, on the other hand, "swooped in from all quarters" and were more concerned with profit than the common good. Johnson laments that "the ancient aristocracy had relinquished the helm and the industry was manned by a crew hard-boiled enough to hold its own with the blood-thirstiest pirates of Lowell and Providence." He explains that, despite the difference in motivation between the two groups, "it is certainly human for the Southern cotton mill man of today to regard himself as in all respects the heir of his distinguished predecessor." In spite of his energy and good intentions, however, "the man of commerce is as ill at ease in this realm as the man of the master class was in commerce" and consequently "falls a ready victim to astounding frauds." In "Mill Men Who Were Statesmen," which ran the following month in *Cotton and Its Products,* Johnson offers the same conclusion about the relationship between the Old South and the New. There was, in short, a decided affinity between the first wave of mill owners and the

---

lenge to the Fighting South)," *JSF* 3 (January 1925): 231–36; GWJ, "Woodrow Wilson," in *Southern Pioneers in Social Interpretation,* ed. Howard W. Odum (Chapel Hill: University of North Carolina Press, 1925), 29–49; Kneebone, *Southern Liberal Journalists,* 21.

16. GWJ, "The Curve of Sin," *AM* 5 (July 1925): 363–67; GWJ to H. L. Mencken, December 23, 1924, HLM Papers; GWJ, "Service in the Cotton Mills," in *South-Watching: Selected Essays by Gerald W. Johnson,* ed. Fred Hobson (Chapel Hill: University of North Carolina Press, 1983), 64–71. In his December 23, 1924, letter to Mencken, GWJ wrote, "As for the cotton mill article . . . it ought to be easy to put together. All that is necessary is to purloin it from Broadus Mitchell's dissertation. I believe that burglarizing a doctor's thesis, far from being legally or morally criminal, is in the very spirit of Service; and jimmy and skeleton keys are at hand."

aristocracy that preceded them; the affinity that the second wave claimed was, in part, imaginary.[17]

At this time, Johnson had never heard of Wilbur J. Cash. Cash, on the other hand, was quite familiar with Johnson. Ten years Johnson's junior and a fellow Wake Forest graduate, Cash was a struggling writer in 1925. He read the *American Mercury* attentively (and would later contribute) and was influenced by Johnson's essays. Cash, like Johnson, was also influenced by Broadus Mitchell. As Fred Hobson has remarked, "Service in the Cotton Mills" sets forth a thesis that "anticipates . . . Cash." Sixteen years later, when Alfred A. Knopf published the monumental *The Mind of the South,* Cash would argue that Southern history is (to use the conventional critical terminology) continuous rather than discontinuous, that there is a salient affinity between the plantation owners and the mill barons. "Service in the Cotton Mills" would prove, in part because of Cash, one of Johnson's most significant statements about Southern history, his own contribution to the debate that continues to this day.[18]

Continuing the tradition begun two years earlier with "The Congo, Mr. Mencken," Johnson chose to criticize and cavort in "Onion Salt," his final essay in the *Reviewer.* Wondering whether the South will become assimilated by an America rapidly becoming standardized, Johnson likens his native region to the distinctive spice that "is rapidly absorbed, but rarely lost." As long as it retains its pride, patriotism, and "incandescent" religion, the South will continue to produce a colorful array of characters: "prophets and martyrs, demagogues, heroes, fakirs, and religious, social, and political whirling dervishes." Johnson remarks more somberly that the South "will continue to stand ready to die at the stake for its ideals and equally ready to burn negroes and other nonconformists."[19] Unfortunately, it was not such barbarism that died but rather the magazine, despite Johnson's efforts to save it.

17. GWJ, "Mill Men Who Were Statesmen," *Cotton and Its Products* 3 (July 1925): 72–73.

18. Bruce Clayton, *W. J. Cash: A Life* (Baton Rouge: Louisiana State University Press, 1991), 217; Fred Hobson, introduction to "Service in the Cotton Mills," by Gerald Johnson, in *South-Watching: Selected Essays by Gerald W. Johnson,* ed. Fred Hobson (Chapel Hill: University of North Carolina, 1983), 64. For a very valuable discussion of Cash's book and that debate that it has caused, see Louis D. Rubin, Jr., "W. J. Cash after Fifty Years," *VQR* 67 (spring 1991): 214–28.

19. GWJ, "Onion Salt," in *South-Watching: Selected Essays by Gerald W. Johnson,* ed. Fred Hobson (Chapel Hill: University of North Carolina, 1983), 51–54. GWJ's final contribution to the *Reviewer* was "Shaw and Henderson," a review that appeared in the October 1925 issue.

From its inception, the *Reviewer* had operated on a small budget and had been forced to reduce the frequency of its publication. In October 1924, the final issue published in Richmond had appeared. Two months later, Paul Green went to Virginia and bought the magazine for two dollars. "Of course," Johnson told Mencken, "Hibbard and I and two or three others will do what we can to help out, but I am afraid that the boy will break his heart over this thing." The first issue published in Chapel Hill appeared in January 1925, with Paul Green as editor and Johnson as a member of the board of directors. "The South needs the *Reviewer,*" Johnson told the Associated Press, "and its loss would be nothing short of tragic." Despite the heroic efforts of all involved—Paul Green said that the magazine "was walking over [his] back with spiked shoes"—the *Reviewer* ceased publication in October.[20]

Fortunately, for both Johnson and Southern letters, the *Virginia Quarterly Review* was born in Charlottesville the year that the *Reviewer* died. Johnson's first essay for this new forum, "A Tilt with Southern Windmills," alludes to *Don Quixote* in detailing the futile efforts of the Democratic Party in the South. Bemoaning the region's descent into single-party politics, he remarks that "in the choosing of candidates we do not count; and in subsequent elections we are already counted." "Do we not," he proceeds to wonder, "incessantly walk past slaughter houses to open graves behind the banner of the Democratic party?" This voting pattern, he explains, proves racial to a considerable extent; in order to maintain a "white man's government," the South "has traded in [its] political principles" and fallen into a "state of bondage." The South must make an honest effort to rectify its racial problems, for "every unnecessary hardship inflicted on the black South postpones the day when the white South can resume its full membership, political, moral, and intellectual, in this union." Although Johnson insists that blacks be afforded "equality of economic opportunity and equality before the law," he again asserts the need for social segregation. One of Johnson's most significant essays about race, "A Tilt with Southern Windmills" sets forth a number of the ideas developed earlier in those editorials in the *Greensboro Daily News.*[21]

20. Emily Clark, *Innocence Abroad* (New York: Knopf, 1931), 22, 25, 26, 264; GWJ to Mencken, December 10, 1924.

21. GWJ, "A Tilt with Southern Windmills," in *South-Watching: Selected Essays by Gerald W. Johnson,* ed. Fred Hobson (Chapel Hill: University of North Carolina, 1983), 139–45. Discussing Johnson's attitudes on race, Fred Hobson says, "A representative Southern liberal of the 1920s, Johnson insists that the Negro should receive equal treatment before the law but not social equality. He manifests a paternalism in race relations that he, to some extent, always retained." Fred Hobson, introduction to "A Tilt with Southern Windmills," by Gerald John-

In July 1925, the same month that "Southern Windmills" appeared, *Scribner's Magazine,* a prestigious monthly published in New York City, carried Johnson's "The Dead Vote of the South." As its title suggests, it covers much of the same ground. Four months before, Johnson had used *Scribner's* to speak more optimistically about his native land. "The Battling South" shows him concerned less with mortuary matters than with fighting the region's detractors.[22]

Using that ubiquitous theater metaphor, Johnson explains that "the South went into shadow in 1865. It is unaccustomed to occupying the center of the stage. In the sudden and unflattering prominence which Klansmen have achieved for it, it shows to little advantage. It has forgotten the art of make-up, and in consequence all of its warts stand out terrifically." While acknowledging the region's blemishes, Johnson also celebrates, for his national audience here, "the long line of illustrious Southerners from Washington to Robert E. Lee." He argues that, if this illustrious civilization is dead, then "the South is dead, and its material activity is . . . the horrible activity of a cadaver stimulated by electricity." His rousing conclusion serves as both a celebration and a call to arms: "The social order that produced . . . [the] Ku Klux Klan . . . that lynched fifty-two negroes in 1922, and that persecutes scientists who repudiate the medieval theology of hedge-priests, is challenged every year with increasing sharpness and vigor by the civilization that produced the Declaration of Independence, the Bill of Rights, and Robert Edward Lee." In *The Advancing South,* Edwin Mims extolled Johnson's essay as "a veritable trumpet-blast in the war for Southern liberation." There were other blasts as well, blasts in which the hedge-priests figured prominently.[23]

The war in North Carolina over evolution was growing more heated. In 1924, President Harry Chase had been confronted by a bill drafted by Representative David Scott Poole, a Presbyterian elder, publisher, and educator from Raeford. This Poole Bill, as it was called, declared that "it is injurious to the welfare of the people of the State of North Carolina for any official or teacher . . . paid wholly or in part by taxation, to teach or permit to be taught

son, in *South-Watching: Selected Essays by Gerald W. Johnson,* ed. Fred Hobson (Chapel Hill: University of North Carolina, 1983), 139.

22. GWJ, "The Dead Vote of the South," *Scribner's Magazine* 78 (July 1925): 38–43; GWJ, "The Battling South," in *South-Watching: Selected Essays by Gerald W. Johnson,* ed. Fred Hobson (Chapel Hill: University of North Carolina, 1983), 55–63.

23. Edwin Mims, *The Advancing South* (Garden City, N.Y.: Doubleday, Page, 1926), 125, quoted by Kneebone, *Southern Liberal Journalists,* 238 n. 32.

as a fact either Darwinism or any other evolutionary hypothesis that links man in blood relationship with any form of lower life." At the beginning of the fall 1924 semester, President Chase addressed the student body and said that the university opposed the bill as a violation of free speech. Provocatively, he placed the bill in the contexts of the Inquisition and America's embarrassing witch hunts. Johnson wrote to Mencken that he was very proud of Chase's courage.[24]

Addressing the state legislature in early 1925, Chase said that he was "not here to discuss evolution as a biologist but to speak in behalf of human liberty." After being reminded that the state had yet to make final the university's appropriations, Chase replied that "if the university doesn't stand for anything but appropriations, I, for one, don't care to be connected with it." This man of courage feared that he did not have sufficient votes to defeat the bill. Dr. William Louis Poteat told Odum that the passage of the bill would be humiliating. Seventeen of the Wake Forest graduates in the General Assembly—they came to be known as "Poteat's boys"—supported Chase, and the bill was defeated on February 19, 1925, by a vote of 67 to 42. Another anti-evolution bill drafted by Poole would be defeated two years later. Johnson was immensely proud—of his current president, of his old college, and of his former biology teacher. He proclaimed that "the tide was turned by men . . . who have a profound belief in the liberty of conscience."[25]

As Hamilton Owens tells the story, President Chase wrote to him after the defeat of the Poole Bill and "said that he didn't need Johnson any longer and I could have him." Owens wrote to Johnson on May 16, 1925, and asked him to work in Baltimore that summer as a guest editor on the *Evening Sun.* He would write editorials and an occasional signed column for a salary of one hundred dollars a week, and he and the newspaper's management could get to know one another. Johnson replied that he had already accepted a position for the month of August with the *Norfolk Ledger-Dispatch,* but, say-

24. Snider, *Light on the Hill,* 188; Harry Chase, draft of speech, 1924 (dated "1925?"), HWO Papers; Suzanne Cameron Linder, *William Louis Poteat: Prophet of Progress* (Chapel Hill: University of North Carolina Press, 1966), 130–31; GWJ to H. L. Mencken, October 23, 1924, HLM Papers.

25. Snider, *Light on the Hill,* 190–92; Dr. William Louis Poteat to Howard W. Odum, February 16, 1925, HWO Papers; GWJ to John Webb, July 23, 1975, in the possession of Mr. Charles Lambeth, Thomasville, N.C.; GWJ to John C. Masten, April 5, 1978, GWJ Papers; GWJ, "The Battle of Raleigh," *BES,* February 26, 1925.

ing that the offer in Baltimore was more attractive, asked if he could come in July. Owens agreed.[26]

Johnson went to Baltimore alone and served on the editorial staff of the *Evening Sun* from July 1, 1925, until August 15. He contributed numerous editorials, several signed columns, and one book review. Managing Editor J. Edwin Murphy told Johnson, the North Carolinian wrote home, that "a position as editorial writer is open . . . and suggested that I take it under consideration with the understanding, of course, that I finish out my year in Chapel Hill. I was flattered, for the Evening Sun really does stand right among the first American newspapers." Johnson saw his work that summer as by long odds the greatest test so far of his abilities as a journalist.[27]

Unaware that Johnson was considering summer employment in Baltimore, Mencken had told Odum on May 31 that he was going to cover the Scopes trial, and he invited the editor to come along and to bring Johnson. On March 21 of that year, the Tennessee legislature had passed the Butler Bill, which made it unlawful for any instructor in a school publicly funded "to teach any theory that denies the story of Divine creation as taught in the Bible, and to teach instead that man has descended from a lower order of the animals." John Scopes, a high school science teacher and football coach, volunteered to test the law and was subsequently arrested. After William Jennings Bryan agreed to serve as prosecuting attorney, Mencken sensed the chance to have a good deal of fun and to give his newspaper immense notoriety. He suggested that the prominent defense attorney Clarence Darrow be engaged for the defense. "Nobody gives a damn about that yap schoolteacher," Mencken told Darrow. "The thing to do is make a fool out of Bryan." The Scopes trial, as Paul K. Conkin has remarked, "proved one of the first great media extravaganzas of the twentieth century, with over two thousand newspapers . . . and direct radio broadcasts by a Chicago station." The trial showcased two prominent opponents who could hardly have dis-

26. Lloyd Dennis, "Gerald W. Johnson: Man of Many Parts," *GDN,* March 22, 1964; Hamilton Owens to GWJ, May 16, 21, 1925; GWJ to Hamilton Owens, May 18, 1925, GWJ Papers.

27. Vivian Kramer, payroll manager, *Baltimore Sun,* telephone interview by author, August 16, 1995; GWJ, "The Tarheel Renaissance," *BES,* July 29, 30, 1925; GWJ, "Latest and One of the Best Rinehart Detective Stories," *BES,* August 15, 1925. On July 31, 1925, Johnson wrote four of the nine editorials in the *Evening Sun.* GWJ to Katherine Johnson Parham, July 31, 1925, GWJ Papers.

agreed more. Bryan believed that "we must win if the world is to be saved." Darrow, on the other hand, believed that "we have the purpose of preventing bigots and ignoramuses from controlling the education of the United States." The Sunpapers posted Scopes's bond and sent five men, a cartoonist and four columnists including Mencken, to cover this highly publicized battle between science and religion, this age-old struggle, as Mencken saw things, between knowledge and superstition. Johnson watched this "Tennessee circus" from Baltimore.[28]

Mencken's coverage of this circus marked the zenith of his career as a journalist. He could not have been more controversial. Some deified him as the defender of enlightenment and free speech; others vilified him as the devil incarnate. The events of the trial both disgusted and delighted him. He was appalled that such an event could take place in a supposedly civilized country during the twentieth century. On the other hand, he was amused by Judge John T. Raulston and the court that opened each day with a prayer. Mencken laughed at the atheist parading a mangy chimpanzee through the town, at the spurious messiahs who descended upon Dayton, and at the meeting of Fundamentalist Christians in the hills beyond that culminated in the speaking of tongues and a writhing heap of flesh.[29]

He did not, however, laugh at Bryan. "Once he had one leg in the White House," Mencken scoffed, "and the nation trembled under his roars. Now he is a tin-pot pope in the coca-cola belt." Mencken returned to Baltimore after the judge refused to admit the testimony of expert witnesses called by

28. Mencken to Howard W. Odum, May 31, 1925, quoted in Arthur Garfield Hays, *Let Freedom Ring* (New York: Bone, 1928), 125; Mencken, quoted in William Manchester, *Disturber of the Peace: The Life of H. L. Mencken* (New York: Harper and Brothers, 1950), 164; Paul K. Conkin, *When All the Gods Trembled: Darwinism, Scopes, and American Intellectuals* (Lanham, Md.: Rowman and Littlefield, 1998), 84; Edward J. Larson, *Summer for the Gods: The Scopes Trial and America's Continuing Debate over Science and Religion* (New York: Basic Books, 1997), 128, 6; Mencken, "The Tennessee Circus," *BES,* June 15, 1925. For an informative discussion of Mencken's motivation and the role of the Sunpapers in this trial, see S. L. Harrison, "Anatomy of the Scopes Trial: Mencken's Media Event," *Menckeniana* 135 (fall 1995): 1–6.

29. Mencken, "Yearning Mountaineers' Souls Need Reconversion Nightly, Mencken Finds," in *The Impossible H. L. Mencken: A Selection of His Best Newspaper Stories,* ed. Marion Elizabeth Rodgers (New York: McGraw-Hill, 1991), 576–82; Vincent Fitzpatrick, *H. L. Mencken* (New York: Continuum, 1989), 60–63; Vincent Fitzpatrick, "H. L. Mencken," in *Dictionary of Literary Biography,* vol. 137, *American Magazine Journalists, 1900–1960,* 2nd series, ed. Sam G. Riley (Detroit: Gale Research, 1994), 196–97. For Mencken's commentary after the fact, see *Thirty-five Years of Newspaper Work: A Memoir by H. L. Mencken,* ed. Fred Hobson, Vincent Fitzpatrick, and Bradford Jacobs (Baltimore: Johns Hopkins University Press, 1994), 136–49.

the defense; consequently, he was absent when Darrow called Bryan to the stand and the Great Commoner thundered that man is not a mammal. Bryan died of a stroke on July 26. Tennessee governor Austin Peay said that Bryan had died "a martyr to the faith of our fathers" and proclaimed a state holiday to honor the funeral. Mencken felt differently. His "Bryan" ran as a signed column in the *Evening Sun* the day after Bryan's death, and it was the cruelest thing he ever wrote. Mencken became needlessly personal in his attack: "There was a vague, unpleasant manginess about [Bryan's] appearance." He likened the deceased to a "dog with rabies" that "bit right and left" and rebuked him as "one of the most tragic asses in American history." This man who had come into life as "a hero, a Galahad, in bright and shining armor" was now "passing out a pathetic fool." To conclude this column, which was as much an indictment of rural America as a scathing assessment of a man whom Mencken despised, the Baltimorean scoffed that "he seemed only a poor clod like those around him, deluded by a childish theology, full of almost pathological hatred of all learning, all human dignity, all beauty. He was a peasant come home to the dung-pile." Reducing Bryan to images of sweat, dirt, and excrement, Mencken in this column made his adversary seem scarcely human.[30]

Johnson was appalled. Mencken's attack was so violent, he wrote home, that it had unnerved the managing editor. Baltimore, Johnson explained, "has risen with wild howls for Mencken's head . . . but that is an occurrence here too common to deserve remark. Baltimore hates Mencken more violently than the South hates him. But the trouble is, everybody buys a paper when he has an article in it, so the circulation manager grins when the howls begin."[31] Johnson's comment was atypically hyperbolic; while some Baltimoreans did indeed loathe Mencken, others lionized him. It is significant, though, that Johnson used his correspondence to distance himself from the Baltimorean.

Johnson also distanced himself in print. On the same day that Mencken's "Bryan" appeared, Johnson contributed an unsigned editorial that ran under the same title and offered a far more humane commentary. This is not to say

---

30. H. L. Mencken, "Malone the Victor, Even Though the Court Sides with Opponents," in *The Impossible H. L. Mencken: A Selection of His Best Newspaper Stories,* ed. Marion Elizabeth Rodgers (New York, McGraw-Hill, 1991), 593–97; Larson, *Summer for the Gods,* 203; H. L. Mencken, "Bryan," in *The Impossible H. L. Mencken: A Selection of His Best Newspaper Stories,* ed. Marion Elizabeth Rodgers (New York: McGraw-Hill, 1991), 604–608.

31. GWJ to Katherine Johnson Parham, July 28, 1925, GWJ Papers.

that he wrote hagiography. "William Jennings Bryan died as he lived," Johnson began, "far removed from actuality, fighting in a world of his own. . . .
He lived in his dreams; it is fitting that he should die in his sleep." Johnson
declared that "Bryan's followers never left him completely. Romance never
fails to enthrall the masses. The knight in armor he remained to hundreds of
thousands, and the knight in armor he died. *De mortuis nil nisi bonum.* . . .
[H]e tried to do good as he saw it. May he rest in peace." Although Mencken
and Johnson both used the chivalric image, they reached contrary conclusions. While contempt fueled Mencken's commentary, Johnson's editorial
was shaped by his characteristic compassion. While Mencken's irony was ce-
rebral, Johnson's empathy for another living creature, flawed but struggling
to do his best, came from the heart. Johnson's editorial, as Harold A. Williams, the historian of the newspaper, has remarked, "caused no comment"
among the readers. Mencken, however, was impressed, and Johnson triumphantly wrote home that "the great Khan of Baltimore . . . pronounced it an
excellent editorial, and [made] the pronouncement in the presence of one of
the owners of the newspaper."[32]

In their assessment of the watershed in Dayton, Mencken and Johnson
both agreed and disagreed. Both abhorred this infringement upon free
speech. The "fundamentalist outbreak" led Johnson to recall a darker, more
barbaric time, and he said portentously that "there is here all the will in the
world for the resurrection of the thumbscrew and the rack." The men did
not, however, concur about religion. Unlike Mencken, Johnson did not see
science and religion as irreconcilable, nor did he view religion as a haven for
weaklings in the battle of life. Johnson argued that the person suffering most
in the battle between Modernists and Fundamentalists was the quiet man
concerned not with disputation but rather with good works. "Nobody pays
any attention to his appeals . . . ," Johnson remarked, "because the crescendo
thundering of the guns drowns his voice completely." Looking at Dayton,
Mencken found an objective correlative of the American mentality that he
found so patently offensive: its lust for cheap theatrics, its provincial fear of
learning, and its assent to ignorance and superstition. Johnson's vision was less
expansive but more perceptive. In his view, what happened at Dayton was
only part of the Southern experience. The month after the trial, Johnson

32. [GWJ], "Bryan," *BES,* July 27, 1925; Harold A. Williams, *The Baltimore Sun, 1837–
1987* (Baltimore: Johns Hopkins University Press, 1987), 182; GWJ to Katherine Johnson Parham, July 28, 1925.

urged his readers to "climb the mountains behind Dayton" and look east to another battlefield where "the fight has gone unnoticed by the outside world." The enemy was strong, and for the forces of enlightenment it was a "matter of hanging on like grim death." But they persevered, and the enemy was beaten, at least for a time. "Dayton told only one side of the story of the South," Johnson declared. "In justice to Dixie, the other side, the side typified by the career of William Louis Poteat, should be publicized abroad."[33] Johnson was such a publicist. While his commentary was less colorful than Mencken's, and while it would prove far less famous, it was finally more just.

Johnson could not then know that the Butler Bill would remain on the books until May 16, 1967, when he was seventy-six and Mencken had been in his grave for more than eleven years. Johnson did recognize, though, that what happened in Dayton was no anomaly. He likened the anti-evolution laws to a pestilence, and he knew far too much about the American mentality to believe that such a plague would ever disappear entirely. Rather, it would lie dormant for a while, tucked away in the darker corner of people's minds, before becoming active again to spread its infection of self-righteous certitude.[34]

Johnson's six weeks in Baltimore had proven well-spent. There were costs, of course. Living alone in the Altamont Hotel, Johnson missed his wife and children. He did, however, find himself a new job that would begin the following summer. He would never again question his abilities as a journalist. While he had not traveled to Tennessee, he had taken the opportunity to go on the record about an event whose import can hardly be exaggerated. "Powerful social forces," Edward J. Larson has explained, "converged on Dayton that summer: populist majoritarianism and traditional evangelical faith versus scientific secularism and modern concepts of individual liberty.

33. GWJ, "The Funeral of Uncle Bob," *BES,* July 12, 1925. Johnson offers such commentary on religion in "The Greater Reason," *GDN,* March 26, 1922; GWJ, "The Religious Refugee," *Century Magazine* 111 (February 1926): 399–404; GWJ, "Religious Thought in the South, but Unlike That of Dayton," *BES,* August 1, 1925. For more of Johnson's commentary on the implications of the events in Dayton, see "Meade Minnegrode a Deft Painter of Feminine Portraits," *BES,* May 22, 1926; "Death to Professors," *BES,* January 27, 1927; and "Making a Monkey of Judicature," *Chicago Sun-Times,* January 7, 1968.

34. Fred Hobson, *Tell About the South: The Southern Rage to Explain* (Baton Rouge: Louisiana State University Press, 1983), 186; *The Impossible H. L. Mencken,* 562; GWJ, "An Excuse for Universities," in *America-Watching: Perspectives in the Course of an Incredible Century* (Owings Mills, Md.: Stemmer House, 1976), 96.

America would never be the same again."[35] Moreover, Johnson had gone head-to-head with Mencken and held his own. This would happen again.

Johnson left Baltimore on Saturday, August 16, and traveled to Norfolk to write editorials for the *Ledger-Dispatch*. He wrote to Paul Green three days later: "I have really been driven furiously all summer, and the pressure continues." Johnson remained in Norfolk until September 6. He met Louis Jaffé, the editor of the *Virginian-Pilot* who would later win two Pulitzer Prizes and whom Johnson would celebrate in the tradition of "Southern image breakers." Obviously impressed with Johnson's work, Jaffé asked him to contribute two or three editorials each day from Chapel Hill. Between September 21 and October 21, the *Virginian-Pilot* ran 142 inches of Johnson's copy (1 inch equals about forty words), and he contributed an additional 90 inches between December 1 and December 13.[36]

On September 25, the Johnsons moved to 414 Park Place, their residence during Gerald's final year at the university. In addition to his teaching duties and the editorials written for the *Virginian-Pilot,* he continued to write a variety of pieces about Southern issues for the *Evening Sun.* He applauded Professor Koch and his Carolina Playmakers. He praised "the prominent place given Booker T. Washington" in Odum's *Southern Pioneers in Social Interpretation,* and he remarked with pride that the *Norfolk Journal and Guide,* an African American newspaper, had praised North Carolina for its enlightened racial attitudes. Johnson pointed out that the state had gone four years without a lynching and scoffed at "the ebullient gentry who practice murder as an outdoor sport."[37]

By the end of the year, Johnson was more than ready for the vacation he had not taken that summer. In late December, the Johnsons traveled to New

35. James H. Bready, interview by author, tape recording, Baltimore, May 29, 1990; Larson, *Summer for the Gods,* 83.

36. GWJ to Paul Green, August 13, 19, 1925, Paul Green Papers, Southern Historical Collection, Wilson Library, University of North Carolina at Chapel Hill; Louis I. Jaffé to GWJ, September 15, October 22, 1925, Louis I. Jaffé Papers, Special Collections, Alderman Library, University of Virginia, Charlottesville, Va.; Kneebone, *Southern Liberal Journalists,* 19, 28, 35; Joseph E. Shank and Lenoir Chambers, *Salt Water and Printer's Ink* (Chapel Hill: University of North Carolina Press, 1967), 312–14, 321; GWJ, "Southern Image Breakers," in *South-Watching: Selected Essays by Gerald W. Johnson,* ed. Fred Hobson (Chapel Hill: University of North Carolina, 1983), 106–14.

37. GWJ, "Drama in the Sticks," *BES,* December 29, 1925; GWJ, "Social Forces in the South," *BS,* September 19, 1925; GWJ, "North Carolina Is Kicked Out of the South," *BES,* November 20, 1925.

York City to visit the Haywards. Making the literary rounds, he had lunch with Mr. and Mrs. Laurence Stallings as well as with Walter Lippmann ("the biggest man in American journalism today") and the novelist James M. Cain. He broke bread with W. W. Howland, editor of *Century Magazine,* to which Johnson would contribute the following year. He also visited the *American Mercury* office and remarked, as many others did, upon the pronounced difference between Mencken's public and private personas: "It is curious how the wild man of Baltimore always appears to me in the guise of a kindly, good-humored and courteous gentleman, eager to help and enviously tolerant."[38]

In early 1926, newspapers carried the announcement that Johnson would resign at the end of the academic year to return to daily journalism. His final semester saw the same work ethic that distinguished the previous three. He continued to write for the *Evening Sun.* He worked on *What Is News?,* a volume that Knopf would publish that fall. He was finishing out his career at a university that had boldly defended free speech during the uproar over the Poole Bill, and it was fitting that the final essay published while Johnson headed the Department of Journalism was a ringing defense of free speech.[39]

So ended another stage of his journey. The road had carried him thus far from Riverton to Thomasville, from Mars Hill to Wake Forest, from Lexington to Greensboro, from the red fields of France back to Greensboro and then on to Chapel Hill. Hereafter, it would take him up to Baltimore, where he would spend his final fifty-four years. This man who had expressed dismay over the exodus of Southern intellectuals surely perceived some irony in his own move. He would not be going to London like Walter Hines Page, or to New York City like Thomas Wolfe. Johnson would travel only about 350 miles and, yes, he would be working south of the Mason-Dixon line. But far more important in the eyes of Southerners, he would be setting up shop north of the Potomac.

Moving to Baltimore, Johnson increased his salary to $6,000 and joined the staff of an editorial page that was one of the most highly regarded in the United States. In time, he would witness the publication of more than forty of his books. Louis Jaffé congratulated Johnson but remarked that what was

38. GWJ to Katherine Johnson Parham, December 23, 1925, GWJ Papers.

39. "Will Resume Editorial Work," *Kinston (N.C.) Free Press,* February 10, 1926; "Gerald Johnson Reported Going to the Baltimore Evening Sun," *LD,* February 11, 1926; GWJ, " 'The New Negro' Recommended to Southern Students," *BES,* January 30, 1926; GWJ, "Duke University to Adopt Hopkins' Plan," *BES,* March 19, 1926; GWJ, "An Unfortunate Necessity," *Century Magazine* 112 (May 1926): 41–47.

good for him was not necessarily good for North Carolina. There was a marked sense of loss among Johnson's colleagues in Chapel Hill. Louis Graves, whom Johnson had succeeded at the university, ran a poignant column that pictured Johnson walking among his boxed possessions and concluded: "And so, having . . . sent their daughters with a nurse in a Pullman car to visit their grandparents in New York, Gerald Johnson and Mrs. Johnson enter their Ford sedan to leave the village. I do not like it." Johnson generated loyalty and affection, and endings were never easy, either for him or his friends. Later, when he looked back on his stay in Chapel Hill, Johnson gave thanks: "In many ways the two years . . . were the happiest of my life, and I still count my association with such men as Chase [and] Odum . . . as one of my life's great good fortunes." While he was leaving in body, he would remain in spirit, for he stressed that "no matter how long I live anywhere else, 'when I die I'll be a Tar Heel dead.' "[40]

40. Louis I. Jaffé to GWJ, February 10, 1926, Jaffé Papers; Louis Graves, "Deserting Academic Shades for Free State," *Chapel Hill Weekly,* June 21, 1926; G. B., "Brilliant Baltimore Writer Never Forgets He's a Tar Heel," *GDN,* September 1, 1940; Yarbrough, "Interesting Carolina People."

7 Heading North
1926–1930

> Baltimore city is in some respects the great lady. She has her habits which she
> disdains to alter merely to avoid being run over by a deplorably hasty and
> noisy world. . . . Does the nation adopt an Eighteenth Amendment to the
> Constitution, contrary to Baltimore's notion of what is fitting and proper?
> She does not explode into vituperation; she merely shrugs and instructs her
> police officers to attend strictly to enforcing the laws of the city and of Mary-
> land, letting Prohibition severely alone.
>
> —*Gerald Johnson, "Baltimore"*

While the trip from Riverton to Thomasville surely proved
wrenching for the boy of six, the transition from North Carolina to Baltimore proved easy for this man approaching his thirty-sixth birthday. Johnson
came to a city where life was so comfortable that indolence was easy, but
with his work ethic he never fell prey to sloth. He arrived at a place whose
distinctive accent—natives called their city "Bawlamer" in the state of "Mer-
lin"—surely startled someone accustomed to the more euphonious patterns
of North Carolina speech. However, he never complained, and decades later
as a television commentator, he made himself thoroughly intelligible to a
local audience. He arrived in a city that had a "downright fabulous ugliness,"
but he found such homeliness "more fascinating than spick-and-span tidiness
could ever be."[1]

He came to a city that understood the danger as well as the futility of
trying to make its citizens virtuous. The average Baltimorean, the tolerant
Johnson remarked delightedly, is a "mild cynic . . . who finds endless quiet
amusement in the reflection that its minor vices contribute enormously to
Baltimore's charm." He was pleased that this city proved decidedly more
Southern than Northern in its ambiance; in fact, one neighborhood where

---

1. GWJ, "The Ideal Marylander," *BES*, September 9, 1933.

he lived for forty-three years was known as "Little Virginia." He extolled Baltimore's serenity, amiability, and lack of overt materialism. Incorporated in 1797, Baltimore was old by American standards, and he appreciated its strong sense of the past. His road had taken him, he concluded, to "a better place of residence for a civilized man than any other big city in the country."[2]

One aspect of residency in Baltimore that Johnson found especially enjoyable and enlightening was his membership in the Hamilton Street Club, which had been founded the previous year in downtown Baltimore. Hamilton Owens of the Sunpapers brought Johnson to the club not long after his arrival in the city, and he happily remained a member until death more than five decades later. Walker Lewis, the club's historian, has explained that its founder, James Carey 3d, "wanted to create on a local scale something along the lines of the Century Association in New York, an intellectual elite drawn primarily from professional fields." Johnson happily broke bread and swapped conversation with judges and fellow journalists, lawyers and physicians, professors and businessmen, architects and librarians and musicians. During Johnson's tenure, the club's membership included such notable figures—to offer a very short list from a long and highly distinguished roster—as John Dos Passos, Milton Eisenhower, William Manchester, and C. Vann Woodward. "We are opinionated men with a very low tolerance of fools, especially pompous fools," Johnson engagingly described the ambiance of the club, "and we are keenly aware that the member sitting next to us, stubbornly wrongheaded as he may be in his opposition to some of our pet idols, evidently knows *something,* or he wouldn't be in this room. . . . thus, when we touch treacherous ground, we back off lightly. So the evening, or the Saturday lunch, or whatever, passes off in a glow that never turns into blistering heat." He proceeded to explain that "every member of this club [knows] how to laugh and usually to laugh at himself." Outside of his family and the newspaper, the Hamilton Street Club proved Johnson's most important association in Baltimore. Dr. Thomas B. Turner, the distinguished physician who spent more than four decades at the club with Johnson, has called Johnson "one of [its] most stimulating members."[3]

2. GWJ, "The Veiled City," *BES,* November 14, 1929; GWJ to Cass Canfield (Harper and Brothers), November 10, 1949, Selected Records of Harper and Brothers, Publisher, Firestone Library, Princeton University, Princeton, N.J.; GWJ, "White House Hopes in Maryland," *North American Review* 229 (June 1930): 642–46; "A Proud Tower in the Town," *Peabody Bulletin* 33 (May 1937): 7–13; Frank Shivers, interview by author, Baltimore, August 13, 1996.

3. Walker Lewis, "The 14 West Hamilton Street Club: A History of Sorts," in *Fifty Years*

The Johnsons moved to 7101 Bristol Road near what is now Towson University, and the daughters began their formal education at a nearby elementary school. As their father had done decades before, they learned much outside the classroom. "Every night after supper," Dorothy Johnson van den Honert has recalled, "Daddy would sit on the couch, one little girl on each side, light up a cigar and read us stories. We went through all the fairy stories, *Tom Sawyer, Treasure Island,* and I don't know what else. . . . It was the nicest moment of the day." And Kathryn, on her part, had gotten her wish to return to a big city. In short, all of the Johnsons had a new home in which they felt eminently comfortable. He explained that he was "not merely a citizen, but an addict of Baltimore." Along with Mencken, Johnson was one of the city's most eloquent celebrants; Baltimore, in turn, celebrated Johnson until the end of his days.[4]

This initial phase of Johnson's residence in Baltimore lasted from June 28, 1926 (his first day as a full-time member of the staff of the *Evening Sun*), until November 1930, when *I'll Take My Stand* was published and Johnson took on once again the role of "official hard guy." The newspaper that Johnson joined was "the gaudiest journalistic show in the United States." Decades later, he would reminisce warmly that

> the office bristled with salient personalities. The late J. Ed. Murphy, as managing editor, ruled the premises with thunder and lightning; the late H. L. Mencken came in every afternoon to drop a bomb; the late Harry C. Black strolled through the place daily, and the flash of his rapier-wit nearly always left some ruined pomposity behind. It was a turbulent and clamorous organization, over which the late Paul Patterson presided, shaking his head ruefully at the uproar, but admitting that we got out a paper in which the nobility and gentry of Baltimore rejoiced with great joy.

Six years before Johnson signed on as an associate editor, there had been a "divorce" between the evening newspaper and its morning counterpart.

---

of the 14 West Hamilton Street Club (Baltimore: 14 West Hamilton Street Club, 1975), 4, 7, 9, 12–13, 49–54; GWJ, "Fifty Years, Almost, in Hamilton Street," in *Fifty Years of the 14 West Hamilton Street Club* (Baltimore: 14 West Hamilton Street Club, 1975), 47–48; Dr. Thomas B. Turner, interview by author, tape recording, September 20, 2000, Baltimore. For further discussion of the Hamilton Street Club, see Thomas Bourne Turner, *Part of Medicine, Part of Me: Musings of a Johns Hopkins Dean* (Baltimore: Johns Hopkins Medical School, 1981), 196–201.

4. GWJ, "Query for Ladies," *BES,* January 28, 1932; Kathryn Hayward Johnson, interview by author, Valparaiso, Ind., June 8, 1989; Dorothy Johnson van den Honert to author, July 5, 1991; GWJ, "Fifty Years, Almost, in Hamilton Street," 45.

Each was assigned a separate staff, and a "friendly rivalry" was encouraged.[5] The *Sun* and the *Evening Sun* proved rivals indeed. While the morning paper was stately and far more studied in its pronouncements, the afternoon paper was rowdy and forever interested, to borrow one of Mencken's favorite phrases, in "stirring up the animals."

Johnson fully understood that Mencken, who had helped to found the newspaper on April 18, 1910, was its most storied attraction. Mencken cavorted in center ring—that is, on the *Evening Sun*'s editorial page. Today's op-ed page did not yet exist, and his "Monday Articles" ran for eighteen years alongside the editorials. His first, "A Carnival of Buncombe," assailed the presidential aspirants, and he dubbed the United States House of Representatives "The Asses' Carnival." After being forced to endure Warren Harding's inaugural address, Mencken entitled a column "Gamalielese" (a spoof on the president's middle name) and proclaimed that "setting aside a college professor or two and half a dozen dipsomaniacal newspaper reporters, he writes the worst English I have ever encountered. It reminds me . . . of dogs barking idiotically through endless nights." It was difficult to follow such a virtuoso performance, but Johnson relished the challenge. For twelve years, his column on Thursday would follow Mencken's on Monday. Baltimore's newspaper public thoroughly enjoyed the show.[6]

The seven or eight editorials (often only two or three paragraphs long) that appeared on this page were similarly iconoclastic and deftly written. They were, in the words of Harold A. Williams, "rambunctious, breezy, imaginative [and] mischievous." Stanley Walker, city editor of the *New York Herald Tribune,* began his day by reading the *Evening Sun*'s editorial page. It

5. Vivian Kramer, payroll manager of the *Baltimore Sun,* telephone interview by author, August 16, 1995; Kathryn Hayward Johnson, interview; GWJ, "Gilbert Kanour," letter to the editor, *BES,* March 23, 1960; GWJ et al., *The Sunpapers of Baltimore, 1837–1937* (New York: Knopf, 1937), 409–36; Harold A. Williams, *The Baltimore Sun, 1837–1987* (Baltimore: Johns Hopkins University Press, 1987), 169. Harry C. Black was Chairman of the A. S. Abell Company, then owner of the newspaper; Paul Patterson was the newspaper's president and publisher. For further discussion of the differences between the two newspapers, see Williams, *The Baltimore Sun,* 215, 220.

6. Fred Hobson, Vincent Fitzpatrick, and Bradford Jacobs, introduction to *Thirty-Five Years of Newspaper Work: A Memoir by H. L. Mencken,* ed. Fred Hobson, Vincent Fitzpatrick, and Bradford Jacobs (Baltimore: Johns Hopkins University Press, 1994), xxx. Mencken's three "Monday Articles" mentioned here ran in the *Evening Sun* on February 9, 1920, January 31, 1921, and March 7, 1921.

was, as R. P. Harriss has explained, "perhaps the most quoted and quotable editorial page in America," and Johnson's copy, "at once tart and mellow, counted in no small part for its spicy flavor."[7]

Editorial writers gathered at eight each morning, and suggestions poured in from a variety of sources. Assignments were made (Johnson was often given the more difficult ones), and he retired to his office in "brain alley"—an office with books and papers covering the desk and only one chair, his own. He wrote quickly, following Johnson's law of editorial writing: "The fewer facts—and the more ideas." Hamilton Owens observed that "he never knew anyone else to go farther on a gallon of gas." The breadth of knowledge distinguishing Johnson's copy became legendary throughout the newspaper. "Go ask Gerald" became a common expression when colleagues had questions about myth, the Bible, history, and classical literature. Two months after Johnson signed on, Mencken called him "the best editorial writer the South has yet produced in my time."[8]

To his benefit, Johnson was joining a newspaper that continued to be especially interested in Southern issues and a paper that over the years served as a forum for many accomplished Southern journalists—among them Virginius Dabney, Louis Graves, Louis Jaffé, and Grover C. Hall. Looking south from Baltimore, Johnson discussed the growth of industrialism in his native region and criticized the paternalism of the factory owners. He deplored the fanaticism of the Reverend J. Frank Norris of Texas, who tried to "reintroduce into America the demoniacal religion of Jonathan Edwards," but extolled the enlightenment of Dr. William Louis Poteat. Never shy, he took on miscegenation, a topic considered taboo by many, by remarking sensibly that "it is conceivable that miscegenation may be encouraged by being mentioned, but that possibility is remote, because it is certain that it has not been prevented by being ignored." Lampooning the stereotype of the Southern aristocrat be-

7. Williams, *The Baltimore Sun,* 229, 215; R. P. Harriss, "Remembering a Great Editorial Page," *BES,* April 29, 1980; R. P. Harriss, "Gerald W. Johnson: Journalist and Author," *Gardens, Houses, and People* 22 (September 1947): 10–12; see also Gwinn Owens, "Reflections on the Legendary Years," *BES,* April 18, 1995.

8. R. P. Harriss, interview with Harold A. Williams, Baltimore, April 12, 1984, in the possession of Mr. Williams, Baltimore; Jesse Glasgow, interview by author, tape recording, Baltimore, June 19, 1990; James H. Bready, interview by author, tape recording, Baltimore, May 29, 1990; Lloyd Dennis, "Gerald Johnson: Man of Many Parts," *GDN,* March 22, 1964; Mencken, "The South Looks Ahead," *AM* 8 (August 1926): 507.

fore the Civil War, he snorted that such men possessed only a "discriminating taste in whiskey and a good eye for horse flesh."[9]

In "Journalism below the Potomac," his sixth essay for the *American Mercury,* Johnson proved just as provocative. He had, of course, previously commented on Southern journalism while he was a part of it, but this was the first assessment offered from the shop north of the Potomac. "The average Southern newspaper publisher today," he quips in his lead paragraph, "is more respectable than a merchant[;] some are even more so than a banker, and a few are almost as holy as the owner of a cotton mill." Failing to grasp their responsibility to afflict the comfortable and comfort the afflicted, many Southern newspapers have been seduced by Babbittry, have acquiesced to philistinism, and have allowed their policies to be guided by the local Chamber of Commerce. Not all Southern journalists, however, have so lost their way. Johnson praises, among others, Julian Harris of the *Columbus (Ga.) Enquirer-Sun;* Grover C. Hall of the *Montgomery Advertiser;* his old boss Earle Godbey, whose *Daily News* "is the radiant delight of the wrongheaded"; and the celebrated Josephus Daniels of the *Raleigh News and Observer,* a newspaper that "cannot be bought . . . and cannot be bullied," a publication that "is too honest and too bold to qualify as an acolyte in the temple of modern business." With its stultifying effect upon Southern attitudes, this profane amalgam of money and religion must be fought, and the hortatory Johnson closes by calling for "the hard battle of ideas, the hard, vigorous clash of contending intelligences in the great world beyond the county line." The good journalist, Johnson stressed, could never be timid or insular in his thought.[10]

He also made this observation, among a number of others, in *What Is News?: A Tentative Outline.* This brief volume (eight chapters, between 20,000 and 25,000 words) was published in late 1926 by Alfred A. Knopf as

9. GWJ et al., *The Sunpapers of Baltimore,* 385; James H. Bready, "Gerald W. Johnson: Looking Back over 30 Years," *BS,* March 30, 1980. For discussion of the newspaper's interest in Southern issues, see John T. Kneebone, *Southern Liberal Journalists and the Issue of Race, 1920–1944* (Chapel Hill: University of North Carolina Press, 1985), 33–34; GWJ, "Rural Industrialism," *BES,* July 15, 1926; GWJ, "Norris and His Cults," *BES,* June 29, 1926; "Portrait of a Heretic," *BES,* November 22, 1926; GWJ, "Mentioning the Unmentionable," *BES,* November 28, 1926; GWJ, "The Southern Aristocrat," *BES,* September 17, 1926.

10. GWJ, "Journalism Below the Potomac," in *South-Watching: Selected Essays by Gerald W. Johnson,* ed. Fred Hobson (Chapel Hill: University of North Carolina Press, 1983), 72–81. See Kneebone, *Southern Liberal Journalists,* 31–32.

the third volume of a four-part series called the Borzoi Journalism Handbooks. Johnson's portrait of a journalist illuminates both his motivation and his character. He must value the life of the mind rather than material things. Again using a theater metaphor and alluding to *As You Like It,* Johnson observes that the journalist "must have a profound interest in the human comedy; he must note its significant exits and entrances; he must also mark and appreciate its dramatic climaxes." In addition to being curious and observant, he must be honest and responsible and sufficiently articulate to make his writing intelligible to the masses."[11]

Significantly, *What Is News?* sets forth, more clearly than anything else in his canon, Johnson's views on "popularization" and "clarification." He admits that scholars "regard 'popularization' with holy horror" but proceeds to explain that such an aversion is "due to the fact that genuine popularization is rare—as rare as first-rate newspapermen. What often passes for popularization is the muddle-headed work of incompetent journalists." Johnson contrasts such ineptitude with skillful popularization, which he describes as "principally clarification [whose] difficulty lies in the fact that no man is capable of clarifying a subject until he understands it himself." In time, this technique of popularization would become increasingly attractive to Johnson the author of books, and he would become quite skillful in making a subject intelligible to the common reader without vulgarizing it. In time, he would prove capable of doing with biography and history what Mencken does with philology in *The American Language* and what Edmund Wilson does with history in *To the Finland Station* and with literary Modernism in *Axel's Castle.* *What Is News?* was translated into Japanese, and one South Carolina reviewer praised it as "a keen, biting, stinging" book that "[strips] from the press the glittering incrustation that hides its decay from puffed and obedient owners."[12] Dr. Poteat's disciple had to be pleased with the review.

Johnson's next book, *The Undefeated,* definitely unsettled a number of people. His first book about the South since he had headed north, this vol-

11. Eleanor Carlucci (archivist, Random House), telephone interview by author, October 18, 1995; GWJ, *What Is News?: A Tentative Outline,* Borzoi Handbooks of Journalism (New York: Knopf, 1926), 7, 21, 41.

12. GWJ, *What Is News?* 30–31; Michael Kirkhorn, "Gerald W. Johnson (6 August 1890–22 March 1980)," in *Dictionary of Literary Biography,* vol. 29, *American Newspaper Journalist, 1926–1980,* ed. Perry J. Ashley (Detroit: Gale Research, 1984), 133; "Writers and Books," *Columbia (S.C.) State,* December 5, 1926.

ume about the Confederate memorial carved on Stone Mountain, Georgia was banned in parts of the state, and irate citizens demanded that a copy be removed from a library window in Greensboro. Johnson uses this book, an amalgam of narration and exposition, to comment upon those figures whom Charles Reagan Wilson has referred to so appropriately as "the Lost Cause Trinity." Johnson also celebrates the bravery and skill of Gutzon Borglum, the Idahoan who began the sculpting of the memorial. Finally, Johnson takes this opportunity to discuss what true art must be.[13]

Not surprisingly, Johnson begins his analysis, as Borglum began his sculpture, with Robert E. Lee. Johnson likens Lee's story to that told by Sophocles in *Oedipus at Colonus,* where Oedipus, despite his infirmities, "is a king to the end." While Lee personifies the courage of the Confederacy, Stonewall Jackson exemplifies its faith. "Not since Cromwell," Johnson writes, "has any commander so impressed his army with his religious fervor. . . . Yet, while [Jackson] never doubted that his cause was the cause of the God of battles, never did he regard himself as anything but the Lord's most unworthy servant." Unlike Lee and Jackson, Jefferson Davis, who personifies statecraft, "was broken by his fall." Confederate statecraft, Johnson remarks somberly (and surely heretically to some of his readers), "can by no means be raised into the sublime. . . . Its very inflexibility sent it diving into sheer ruin. The protagonists of the South took their stand on the Constitution. . . . They could not, or would not, see that the Constitution belonged to the country, not the country to the Constitution." The eloquence of the parallelism in the final sentence aside, Johnson shows himself to be far less concerned here here with polemics than with celebrating heroism and the "indomitable" Southern spirit.[14]

Gutzon Borglum proves indomitable as well. His audacity leads him to take on a project that many thought impossible—"carving the world's largest mass of exposed granite"— and he manages, despite the huge danger, to protect his own life as well as those of his workers. The sculpting of Stone Mountain, Johnson remarks, has "no rules, no precedents," and Borglum manages a "minor miracle." This adventurous artist, never fearing to take

13. GWJ to Howard W. Odum, March 21, 1927, HWO Papers; Charles Reagan Wilson, "Stone Mountain," in *The Encyclopedia of Southern Culture,* ed. Charles Reagan Wilson and William Ferris (Chapel Hill: University of North Carolina Press, 1989), 703.

14. GWJ, *The Undefeated* (New York: Minton, Balch, 1927), 94, 97, 101, 103, 105.

that proverbial next step from which so many shrink, prevails as the typical Johnsonian hero. Borglum's heroic efforts lead Johnson to consider the true artist's responsibility: "[A] work of art is masterly only in proportion as its spirit is comprehensible to men other than the artist. . . . [I]f the artist can not express his dreams in such terms that others can comprehend at least part of them, his art is futile in so far as affecting the spiritual life of mankind is concerned." Johnson, of course, was always accessible, and always concerned with the life of the spirit rather than material concerns. One reviewer of *The Undefeated* remarked that Johnson is "generally considered the ablest critic of the South," and Professor Sledd wrote to his former pupil that the book was making a triumphal passage through Wake Forest.[15]

Johnson triumphed to a far greater degree with *Andrew Jackson: An Epic in Homespun.* Another author had been writing a biography of Jackson for Minton, Balch and Company but suffered an accident and could not continue. Johnson took on the project and worked very quickly. He signed a contract on April 15, 1927, which called for the delivery of the manuscript on August 1; the book was published that October. Johnson produced here a volume of a bit more than three hundred pages that proved his most ambitious undertaking so far. "I can't make up my mind," he wrote to Odum, "whether [*Jackson*] is pretty good or inconceivably rotten, but I maintain that it is not at all a conventional biography." It proved both very good and unconventional.[16]

As a biographer, Johnson understood quite well what he himself was not and what he was. He was not a researcher. "I revel in polemics and hate research," he told an editor. Nor, he asserted repeatedly, was he a scholar. "I will not go [into the field of scholarship]," he told Henry Steele Commager, "because there I should be only ridiculous. I am not a scholar; I am a propagandist—I prefer to say 'advocate.' " He was, on the other hand, a synthesizer who knew that his "forte [was] explaining or popularizing the original sources." He believed that the biographer must above all else explain causality. He believed that the good biographer makes value judgments rather than

15. Wilson, "Stone Mountain," 703; GWJ, *The Undefeated,* 15, 24, 16, 80; H.O. [Hamilton Owens], "The Heroic Epic of Gutzon Borglum," *BES,* February 19, 1927; Benjamin Sledd to GWJ, March 17, 1927, GWJ Papers.

16. James Walt, "Tale of Another Liberal's Progress," *Maryland English Journal* 4 (fall 1965): 56–62; *Jackson* contract, GWJ Papers; GWJ to Howard W. Odum, September 11, 1927, HWO Papers.

hiding behind a wall of facts, and he believed that the field of biography had room for a "character study" as well as for an exhaustive account of a life. He explained to Paul Green that the field of American biography had witnessed three phases, all of which were inherently limited: "the hero-worshipping phase," the "debunking phase," and "the fact-finding phase, the meticulous balancing of this inference against that probability, which is a necessary part of historiography, but a dreary one." Johnson called instead for an "esthetic approach," which he defined as "the artistic treatment that assimilates a hero into the very tissues of the nation."[17] This is precisely what he achieves in *Jackson.*

Johnson's title, a clever oxymoron, places his subject very much in the American grain. Johnson's epic recounts the story of no classical hero—no Achilles on the windy plains of Troy, no Ulysses wandering the Mediterranean, no Aeneas courting Dido and founding Rome. In this life of "Old Hickory," Johnson instead democratizes the epic to include this hero garbed in the humble cloth of rural America. Raised in the proverbial school of hard knocks, Jackson is captured and imprisoned as a youth during the Revolutionary War and orphaned at fifteen. "This penniless immigrant's son," Johnson explains, "started life as as a nobody determined to become a Somebody, and from that ideal he never swerved but . . . pursued his aim until he had become the most considerable Somebody in the western hemisphere."[18] This Southerner fought and beat the Indians, was twice elected president of the United States, opened the White House to the common folks, and trounced South Carolina's Order of Nullification. This is the story of a man so strong as to seem mythic, a story with huge resonances, a story that a bold biographer tells with considerable skill.

Johnson offers here a biography for the common reader. Providing neither notes nor a bibliography, he proves far more concerned with his story than with his sources. The opening chapter's first two paragraphs trumpet that what follows will prove neither conventional nor dull:

17. GWJ to Eugene Saxon, January 4, 1941, Selected Records of Harper and Brothers, Publisher, Firestone Library, Princeton University, Princeton, N.J.; GWJ to Henry Steele Commager, February 5, 1951, GWJ Papers; Lawrence Freeny, "Gerald Johnson: The Needle Gets Sharper," *Baltimore Magazine* 61 (October 1968): 24; GWJ, " 'Old Bullion' in All His Many-Sided Grandeur," *NYHTB,* January 26, 1958, pp. 1, 9; GWJ to Lois Johnson, August 6, 1966, GWJ Papers; GWJ, "Enigmatic Catherine," *BES,* September 14, 1936; GWJ to Paul Green, October 31, 1947, Paul Green Papers, Southern Historical Collection, Wilson Library University of North Carolina at Chapel Hill.

18. GWJ, *Andrew Jackson: An Epic in Homespun* (New York: Minton, Balch, 1927), 119.

Tradition relates of Rachel Jackson that she explained a family epidemic once by saying, "The General kicked the covers off and we all cotch cold."

Historians and biographers have written many estimates of of Andrew Jackson's career that might fairly be summed up in Rachel's words. The General kicked right lustily. He kicked off many of the warm wrappings that swathed the young republic from the bitter blasts of democracy. He kicked away the existing political system and substituted one more to his liking. He was the most uncomfortable of political bedfellows.

Johnson liked to remark that he was no historian but rather a journalist writing history. His first paragraph, only one sentence long, functions as the typical journalist lead, brief and arresting. In this case, the dramatic quotation is made even more effective by the colorful colloquialism. In the next paragraph, Johnson skillfully develops the metaphor provided by Rachel's remark. To anyone interested in Johnson's intent, these first two paragraphs say a good deal more. The first sentence of the second paragraph wryly criticizes the windiness of previous assessments. He is saying, in effect, "I'm going to try something new here." As Robert Frost remarks at the beginning of "The Pasture," the spring must be cleaned and the leaves raked away before the water becomes clear. Johnson captures his readers right away, and they stay caught until the end of the tale.[19]

As *Jackson* proceeds, it shows Johnson's considerable facility with the narrative. This Southerner, like his ancestors, is eminently comfortable spinning out a tale, and the volume maintains its sense of drama throughout. To Johnson's credit, Jackson does not come off as a wooden hero on the stage. The biographer details his subject's immense temper, his dueling, and his checkered career in business. To borrow an expression that Johnson himself used as a reviewer, he makes his hero "stand up and walk." This is not to say that the book is flawless. Some of the chapter titles are elephantine. Moreover, Johnson sometimes tries too hard to be literary; he seems determined to show that he remembers his Shakespeare, and the book is overly allusive. Such flaws, though, finally prove inconsequential in the face of Johnson's compelling story of this "great man," this "hero of the people."[20] The biographer offers here a tale emblematic of the huge possibilities of this immense and violent and democratic country.

19. *Ibid.,* 3; GWJ to Fanny Memory, February 18, 1948, GWJ Papers.
20. GWJ, "Colonial New England Clergymen," *BES,* July 9, 1952; GWJ, *Jackson,* 133, 4.

Jackson was a popular and critical success. The book went through six cloth editions and was later reissued in paperback. It was included among the "Forty Notable American Books of 1927" and was one of the first hundred volumes suggested by American booksellers for a "home library" in the White House. Emily Clark and Mencken praised the biography. The *Saturday Review of Literature* lauded Johnson's "artistry," and the *New York Times* praised "his extraordinarily dramatic and convincing character study" and called the book "memorable." At the age of thirty-seven, Johnson had achieved national acclaim.[21]

Returning to time present and looking over the American scene during 1927, he decried the decline in personal freedom and ridiculed religious quackery. He continued to deplore the fact that freedom meant less to his contemporaries than it had to the country's bold founding fathers. Decrying the lingering effects of Puritanism, he attacked Anthony Comstock and Prohibition and scoffed at "the terrible solemnity of America." He lampooned a plan to build religious tabernacles in all cities with a population over 100,000. These were to be serviced by a troupe of traveling evangelists, with the enterprise being overseen by the controversial Aimee Semple McPherson. Disgusted with the profanation of true religion, he likened these tabernacles to burlesque shows.[22]

Johnson's stature had greatly increased in Howard Odum's eyes. In early 1928, he called his friend one of the most promising authors in America. Odum also suggested another project: a book comparing the Old South and the New. Johnson had no time; he was already researching a biography of John Randolph, which would appear the following year. Moreover, he doubted his credentials for such a project. "What," he asked Odum, "do I know about the Old South?" Had he undertaken this project, it would have

21. "Johnson Paperback," *BS,* August 26, 1956; GWJ to Eugene Saxton, December 28, 1939, Selected Records of Harper and Brothers; "Jackson Biography Praised to League," *BES,* August 1, 1928, "Mencken, Gerald Johnson Books Put in White House," *BES,* April 28, 1930; Emily Clark, *Innocence Abroad* (New York: Knopf, 1931), 261; Mencken, "The Library," *AM* 13 (March 1928): 382–83; James Truslow Adams, "Biography as an Art," *Saturday Review of Literature* 4 (November 12, 1927): 299; Charles Willis Thompson, " 'Old Hickory,' Frontier Hero," *New York Times Book Review,* October 30, 1927; R. P. Harriss, "Gerald Johnson: Journalist and Author," 12.

22. GWJ, "On Civil Liberty," *BES,* May 27, 1927; GWJ, "Anthony Comstock, the 'World's Most Celebrated Clown,' " *BES,* March 19, 1927; GWJ, "The Same Old Story," *BES,* September 29, 1927; GWJ, "Thanksgiving Meditation," *BES,* November 24, 1927; GWJ, "Discourse on an Ecclesiastical Theme," *BES,* March 17, 1927.

been the closest volume that Johnson wrote to Cash's *The Mind of the South*.[23]

Obviously happy with Johnson's writing, the *Evening Sun* raised his salary to $6,500. On his part, however, less than two years after signing on with the newspaper, Johnson complained that his journalism took too much time and energy that he wanted to devote to other projects. He wrote to Odum about "the need of time, time, time!" This dilemma would become more pronounced. Journalism paid better, but he was growing increasingly interested in magazine and book writing, far more tenuous sources of income. Despite the press of time, he and Kathryn managed to get away for about a month during the summer of 1928 to visit Paris, with the expenses paid by the royalties from *Jackson*. After his return, he noted that, as the tenth anniversary of the Armistice approached, Paris showed strong anti-American sentiment.[24]

"The Third Republic—And After," which appeared in *Harper's Magazine,* proved by considerable odds Johnson's most consequential essay during 1928. Setting forth the various phases of the American experience, he explains that this country, "when it became the habitat of white men, really began as a theocracy which gradually merged into an autocracy." America's First Republic began in 1789 with the ratification of the Constitution and continued until Andrew Jackson's election in 1828. The "Gentleman," Johnson explains, "was the master of the First Republic." The Second Republic lasted until the Armistice in 1918, and its "master [was] the man of the people." He proceeds to denigrate the plutocrat of the Third Republic and argues that such plutocracy "cannot possibly last." He asserts that "the great movements that have agitated the public since 1922 are Prohibition, fundamentalism, and Ku Kluxism, all three of which purport to be divinely inspired." These are, Johnson scoffs, "not an appeal to men's interests, but the embodiment of a moral principle." He expresses no surprise over this, for "it is simply a revival of the philosophy of theocracy." Seeing history as cyclical, he predicts that the Fourth Republic will itself be theocratic. Subsequent events did not prove him wrong.[25]

---

23. Howard W. Odum to D. L. Chambers, January 14, 1928, Howard W. Odum to GWJ, January 19, 1928, GWJ to Howard W. Odum, January 27, 1928, HWO Papers.

24. Kramer, telephone interview; GWJ to Odum, January 27, 1928; Dorothy Johnson van den Honert to author, June 8, 1995; GWJ, "Paris Ten Years After," *BES,* October 11, 1928.

25. GWJ, "The Third Republic—And After," in *American-Watching: Speculations in the Course of an Incredible Century* (Owings Mills, Md.: Stemmer House, 1976), 7–14.

The specific occasion for "The Third Republic—And After" was the impending presidential election of 1928, which Johnson speculated about with some frequency and whose import, especially for Southerners, he assessed afterwards. He was very interested in finding out whether the Democratic nomination of Al Smith—a Catholic, a New Yorker, and an opponent of Prohibition—would break the voting pattern of the "Solid South." Johnson knew full well that Smith's religion, domicile, and platform would prove bugaboos below the Potomac.

Prior to the Democratic National Convention, Johnson argued that the South would accept Smith. In early June, still prior to Smith's nomination in Houston later that month, Johnson predicted that Smith's Catholicism would hurt him more than his stand on Prohibition. In July, lamenting the effect of racial prejudice in his native land, Johnson complained that "already in the South, dry, Protestant rustics are being reminded that if the South goes Republican the Negroes will demand, and receive, a share of the patronage; and the mental picture of raids conducted by Negro prohibition agents . . . [stampedes] the very Ku Klux into Al Smith's camp." That fall, Johnson widened his vision and spoke less somberly. Using the carnival trope that Mencken so loved to apply to American politics, Johnson proclaimed that "Al in his own person is a good show. He is a three-ringed circus in a bored land." Johnson voted for Smith with "real enthusiasm."[26]

Johnson, however, celebrated no Smith victory. Besides winning the election, Herbert Hoover carried five Southern states: Florida, Virginia, Texas, Tennessee, and North Carolina. He won in Johnson's home state by about 63,000 votes. Rather than lament Smith's defeat, Johnson extolled the Democrat as a liberating force. "It is already respectable to be a Republican in the South today," Johnson rejoiced soon after the election. "Probably the next election will reveal that it has become respectable to be a wet in the South. It is not beyond imagination that another four-year period will mark such an advance that one may adhere to the Roman communion without being suspected of . . . collecting machine guns in the basement of churches."

26. GWJ, "Al Wasn't Raised on a Farm," *BES,* April 14, 1927; GWJ, "Smith's Friends Get an Issue," *BES,* December 29, 1927; GWJ, "Who's Against Al and Why," *BES,* May 12, 1928; GWJ, "The Battle in Tarheelia," *BES,* June 7, 1928; GWJ, "Making Al into St. Andrew," *BES,* June 28, 1928; GWJ, "What Is a City?" *BES,* July 26, 1928; GWJ, "On Voting Democratic: Confession of a Party-Liner," *NR* 170 (June 22, 1974): 16–18; GWJ, "Too Much Al," *BES,* October 28, 1928. For an illuminating discussion of the response of Southern liberals to the presidential election of 1928, see Kneebone, *Southern Liberal Journalists,* 36–55.

Johnson speculated that Smith's birthday might someday be celebrated as "Southern emancipation day."[27]

Johnson would change his mind about Smith and remark decades later that he and Hoover "were opposite sides of the same coin . . . a plugged nickel." However, Johnson exhibited no such cynicism during 1928, that final year of innocence before the stock market crash. Times were good, and Johnson offered rollicking commentary on the American scene. His fellow countrymen were a credulous lot, and the land was "the happy hunting ground for all merchants of panaceas." Johnson wondered whether "any other great nation [has] confidence more sublime in priests, conjurers and medicine men." He waggishly entitled a column "On Behalf of Idiots" and proclaimed that "nothing adds more to the amusement of life in the great republic than the absurdities which are characteristically American." However, the crash on October 29, 1929, would make the conjurers and medicine men seem villains rather than clowns and would make the America of amusements and absurdities seem far away indeed.[28]

It was indicative of Johnson's growing stature in 1929 that he was invited to be a guest at Yaddo, the prestigious retreat for writers and artists in Saratoga, New York. (Though he declined, he was sufficiently distinguished to be invited again the following year.) Continuing to be impressed by Johnson's writing, Odum suggested another project, a book on "liberalism in the South." Johnson wrote no such book, but three years later, Virginius Dabney published a distinguished volume under this title. Johnson's second biography appeared, and he began his first novel. The number of magazines soliciting his material increased, and he used his journalism to assess industrial violence in the South and to ponder the implications of America's financial catastrophe. Things grew curiouser and curiouser across the land: a woman was brutally murdered in a region that valued the chivalric tradition, and Americans confronted want in a land of plenty. Johnson was challenged to come to terms with a republic that seemed to be turning upside down.[29]

27. Kneebone, *Southern Liberal Journalists,* 49; Bruce Clayton, *W. J. Cash: A Life* (Baton Rouge: Louisiana State University Press, 1991), 9, 76; GWJ, "The Liberator," *BES,* November 22, 1928.

28. GWJ, "On Voting Democratic"; GWJ, "The Little Eohippus," *BES,* January 12, 1928; GWJ, "Powwow," *BES,* December 6, 1928; GWJ, "On Behalf of Idiots," *BES,* April 5, 1928.

29. GWJ to Katherine Johnson Parharm, January 26, 1930, GWJ Papers; Howard W. Odum to GWJ, July 24, 1929, GWJ Papers; GWJ, "A Tar Heel Looks at Virginia," *North American Review* 228 (August 1929): 238–43.

Randolph of Roanoke: A Political Fantastic was published by Minton, Balch and Company on April 12, 1929. Once again, Johnson took the opportunity to say thank you in print; he dedicated the book to Professor Benjamin Sledd, "a gentleman of Virginia." This biography, like Johnson's first, assesses a controversial Southern politician. Unlike Andrew Jackson, John Randolph never attained the presidency, but this thorny figure with "one of the most terrible reputations ever attached to an American politician" was elected to Congress in 1799 at age twenty-six and was voted into the United States Senate twenty-six years later. Johnson states early on that "it has been difficult in the extreme for the generations that have succeeded [Randolph] to descry the man under the mime."[30] Johnson succeeds in getting beneath appearances and offers here another biography where the subject "gets up and walks."

As he had with Jackson, Johnson finds in Randolph much to admire. The biographer praises his subject's fearlessness, sense of duty, and insistence upon personal honor. Like Johnson, Randolph had "an insatiable thirst for learning" and recognized the virtues of the plain style. As an orator, "his diction was so simple that in that day of the ornate it seemed positively austere; and his delivery was still simpler." Johnson extols Randolph's humanitarianism in taking responsibility for six fatherless children. There was, the biographer explains, "something profoundly moving in Randolph's laborious and endless efforts in behalf of other men's sons." Like both Archibald and Gerald Johnson, Randolph befriended life's unfortunates.[31]

On the other hand, Johnson finds himself, more frequently than in the previous biography, philosophically at odds with his subject. A staunch proponent of democracy, Johnson draws Randolph as "the great aristocrat . . . the advocate of the government of the masses by the classes." An optimist, Johnson depicts Randolph as "the national Cassandra, a gloomy prophet of wrath to come." A forward looker, Johnson portrays Randolph as a man of the past whose lack of vision had chilling consequences: "Upon the bounding life of the new country, he strove to fix the dead hand of the colonial revolutionists, and the prospect that he might wreck the union deterred him not at all; nor did it deter those who continued to work after him. . . . [T]he harvest of his labor was found in his Virginia fields in windrows of corpses."[32]

30. GWJ, *Randolph of Roanoke: A Political Fantastic,* Biographies of Unusual Americans Series (New York: Minton, Balch, 1929), 25.
31. *Ibid.,* 45, 221, 171.
32. *Ibid.,* 254, 183, 225.

Despite Johnson's censure, however, the volume never degenerates into debunking.

In all, Johnson offers here a rounded portrait of a complicated figure. Like all good biographers, Johnson knows precisely when to quote his subject; too little quoting leads to a string of unsupported generalizations, while too much clots the narrative. He passes along Randolph's famous derogation of Thomas Jefferson as "St. Thomas of Cantingbury" and provides Randolph's reaction after he was informed that someone had denounced him: "Denouncing me? That is strange. I never did him a favor."[33] This vibrant volume remains thoroughly accessible to the common reader whom it addresses.

Randolph of Roanoke did not achieve the national acclaim of the *Jackson,* but this second biography was warmly received. The *New York Herald Tribune* applauded the book, and the *Boston Evening Transcript* called Johnson "one of the most able of American biographers." The *New York Times Book Review,* which found *Randolph* superior to its predecessor, remarked that Johnson "has done the thinking for the more extensive research biographers" and explained, quite correctly, that "his work is among ideas, not manuscripts." On the other hand, an anonymous review in the *Raleigh News and Observer* flayed Johnson for not being a scholar. He learned of the review by word of mouth and made certain to acquire a copy. He was impressed. The reviewer, Johnson candidly told a correspondent, "has landed squarely on the fact that I am devoid of scholarship. . . . I am compelled to applaud his cunning." Johnson also said that "a really good roast is worth having."[34]

Mencken read an early review copy, found the biography superior to its predecessor, and requested excerpts to run in the *Mercury.* His request came too late to be honored, but the magazine did run two essays by Johnson in 1929. The second, "Chase of North Carolina," appeared in June. Johnson relished the opportunity to applaud this man of immense courage who had stood by him in the face of Governor Morrison's objections and who had treated him so well.[35]

33. *Ibid.,* 62, 236.

34. Gamaliel Bradford, "A Memorable Figure," *NYHTB,* April 21, 1929, 5; Sherwin Lawrence Cook, "John Randolph, the Man from Roanoke," *Boston Evening Transcript,* April 20, 1929; Allen Sinclair Will, "John Randolph of Roanoke, Master of Invective," *New York Times Book Review,* April 21, 1929; GWJ to Harriet Herring, June 12, 18, 1929, Harriet L. Herring Papers, Southern Historical Collection, Wilson Library, University of North Carolina at Chapel. Hill.

35. H. L. Mencken to GWJ, March 4, 1929, HLM Papers; GWJ, "Why Men Work for Newspapers," *AM* 17 (May 1929): 83–88; GWJ, "Chase of North Carolina," in *South-Watch-*

Offering no tame encomium, Johnson begins by detailing Chase's difficulties as the president of a state university in the South. He is "the target for
all the bricks, bottles, and dead cats which the enemies of intelligence and
civilization are able to hurl." However, because of Chase's pluck and persis-
tence, the university has developed so greatly during his ten years as president
that "today . . . it is recognized as the most aggressive and vigorous university
in the South, and among the most aggressive and vigorous in the country."
Johnson applauds Chase's defense of free speech for his instructors and his
refusal to cave in when Odum's *Journal of Social Forces* was attacked by clerics.
Not mentioning his own role in the battle, Johnson details the defeat of the
Poole Bill. "Without the magic of a highly magnetic personality," Johnson
remarks, "without the aid of Bryanesque eloquence, without strong political,
or social, or financial backing, with nothing in the world save courage, a level
head and common decency, he has won the confidence of his State to an
extent that is matched by few of his colleagues." Johnson was pleased when
Chase praised the essay. There was, unfortunately, the sense of an ending here
that Johnson could not then foresee. President Chase would resign on February 20, 1930, and this would prove Johnson's final essay for *Mercury*.[36]

While Johnson the old soldier took pride in the battle that he had fought
and helped to win in North Carolina, he also glanced further back in Southern military history to those desperate times after the defeats at Vicksburg and
Gettysburg in July 1863. In the spring of 1864, Confederate major general
John C. Breckinridge, formerly vice-president of the United States, launched
an attack at New Market in Virginia's Shenandoah Valley. Federal artillery
created a gap in his line. Lacking manpower, he debated what to do with the
cadets from the Virginia Military Institute. "They are only children," Breckinridge protested at first, but then he relented to necessity: "Put the boys in,
and may God forgive me for my order." Ten cadets were killed, and forty-
seven were wounded, but they held their position and even captured a Federal battery. Johnson was stirred by this heroism on the battlefield; he was
stirred even more by what the survivors of this generation were able to accomplish after Appomattox.[37]

---

ing: Selected Essays by Gerald W. Johnson, ed. Fred Hobson (Chapel Hill: University of North
Carolina, 1983), 115–27.

36. H. W. Chase to GWJ, May 29, 1929, GWJ Papers; William D. Snider, *Light on the
Hill: A History of the University of North Carolina at Chapel Hill* (Chapel Hill: University of North
Carolina Press, 1992), 200.

37. *Brother against Brother: Time-Life Books History of the Civil War* (New York: Prentice
Hall, 1990), 354; GWJ, "The Cadets of New Market: A Reminder to the Critics of the South,"

In "The Cadets of New Market: A Reminder to the Critics of the South," Johnson explains that these survivors became the South's "lost generation." They returned home "to find the old civilization wrecked" and spent the rest of their lives fighting foes more dangerous than the Yankees. Discussing Reconstruction and its aftermath, Johnson writes of "a policy . . . of which one is at a loss to say whether its stupidity or its viciousness was the more conspicuous." While Johnson could still grow angry about this controversial period in Southern history, he was not an irreconcilable. Typically, he suggests the need to look ahead rather than dwell upon a nettlesome past. "Cadets," much to its benefit, proves far more a celebration of the strength of the Southern character than it does a polemic about Reconstruction. Johnson hymns the stalwart figures of these difficult times: the farmer, "a manful man," who "could smile ironically over the ruin of his own aspirations"; the physician who worked himself to death by carrying on for "forty years . . . a practice so immense and widely scattered that it would drive three modern medicos into nervous prostration in six months"; the newspaper editor who "against every outside obstacle . . . maintained a standard of decency and intelligence"; and the mill owner who worked not for profit but rather "to drag his native land from the morass." Johnson remarks pointedly that "the members of the new generation are very fine fellows . . . but I cherish serious doubts that, with all their admitted brilliance, they are quite the men their fathers were." The appeal of "Cadets" is finally to the heart rather than to the head, and the reader is moved emotionally rather than bedazzled. The poet DuBose Heyward wrote from South Carolina to applaud Johnson, and William Alexander Percy said that "Cadets" "left a lump in my throat."[38] At age thirty-nine, this highly skilled essayist wrote what may well be his finest essay.

As Johnson assessed the ills of the contemporary South, he spoke in a far different tone. In 1921, it will be recalled, he had discussed the clash between management and labor in the cotton mills and had predicted further strife.

---

in *South-Watching: Selected Essays by Gerald W. Johnson,* ed. Fred Hobson (Chapel Hill: University of North Carolina, 1983), 115–27.

38. For an informative discussion of different Southern responses to the loss of the Civil War and Reconstruction, see Gaines M. Foster, *Ghosts of the Confederacy: Defeat, the Lost Cause, and the Emergence of the New South, 1865–1913* (New York: Oxford University Press, 1987); DuBose Heyward to GWJ, December 5, 1929, GWJ Papers; William Alexander Percy to Donald Davidson, [December 1929], quoted in Fred Hobson, *Tell About the South: The Southern Rage to Explain* (Baton Rouge: Louisiana State University Press, 1983), 277.

The strikes and violence in Marion and Gastonia, North Carolina, among other places, confirmed his premonition. During 1929, he deplored the Communists' efforts to use the workers' plight to further their own power. Once again, his sympathies lay not with capital but rather with those forlorn souls struggling against huge odds to make a decent living. "The cynical denial of all human rights to cotton mill hands," he remarked, "goes further than anything the country has produced elsewhere."[39]

In Gastonia, North Carolina, the chief of police was killed when the strikers' "tent city" was stormed. Considerable violence against the strikers ensued when the case against the sixteen accused unionists resulted in a mistrial. Assessing the uproar, Johnson remained very much aware of how his native state would be viewed elsewhere, and he tried to be temperate. "The lesson of the Gastonia trials," he said, "has been the melancholy information that the rest of the world has yet to be convinced that North Carolina is incorruptibly virtuous."[40]

He wrote with far less restraint, however, after Ella May Wiggins was murdered on September 14, 1929. A social activist and mother of five, she was shot in the back on a public highway outside Gastonia. Her assailants were tried and acquitted. In the scathingly entitled "Outside the Law," Johnson scorned the Communists, expressed outrage over the acquittal, and showed sympathy for the strikers who were beaten by police and had their headquarters raided. Johnson declared that "this is a condition of the most serious import. The more the cotton mill hands consider their condition, the deeper must become their sense of injustice, and the fiercer their resentment. Eventually, this resentment is bound to find an outlet. It is as certain as daybreak that there will be more trouble in the North Carolina cotton mills." He pondered what action should be taken. He explained to Odum that he was "an individualist" against "social control" but went on to say that he felt trapped between the forces of greed and corruption: "Between the brutality and arrogance of capitalists and the venality and asininity of politicians there is small choice." While his refusal to believe in panaceas enhanced his credibility as a writer, it did nothing to alleviate the pain that human suffering brought to Johnson the man.[41]

39. GWJ to Lenoir Chambers, October 11, 1929, Lenoir Chambers Papers, Southern Historical Collections, Wilson Library, University of North Carolina at Chapel Hill; see also GWJ to Paul Green, August 9, 1929, Paul Green Papers.

40. Clayton, *W. J. Cash,* 88–89; GWJ, "The Education of Tarheelia," *BES,* August 29, 1929; see also GWJ, "Eagles above the Street," *BES,* September 12, 1929.

41. Clayton, *W. J. Cash,* 89; Bill C. Malone, "Protest," in *The Encyclopedia of Southern*

Black Tuesday brought pain to millions and did nothing to diminish Johnson's contempt for capitalistic arrogance. As the cataclysm neared, Johnson was one of those who anticipated trouble. In early October he spoke of "the economic machinery which is whirling us toward we know not which fate." Three days after the crash, he lambasted "the priests of the Church of Holy Dividends." Exactly two weeks after Black Tuesday, he wrote to Odum that "the Wall Street crash is but the fore-runner of trouble to come." Personally, Johnson was one of the fortunate ones: he lost nothing because he had no money invested.[42]

In print Johnson tried to be optimistic; perhaps he reasoned that public reassurance was needed at this bleak time. In any event, he called his Thanksgiving column "Count Your Blessings" and argued that "most of us are in the position to return thanks that it was no worse. . . . [R]elatively few of us have been caught in such a jam that the only alternatives are suicide or the penitentiary." The didactic Johnson lectured that the crash taught a valuable lesson: Americans should beware of false prophets. As time passed, Johnson's columns on the Depression would grow increasingly moralistic. One suspects that at least some of his readers, confronting the very real problem of filling an empty stomach, grew rather tired of being lectured to about the error of their ways during boom times.[43]

That Thanksgiving, the Johnsons supped with Gerald's parents in Thomasville. Johnson felt that his daughters needed to see their paternal grandparents more frequently. In early December, the family traveled to Charleston, where Gerald, always interested in his heritage, attended a meeting of the St. Andrew's Society. Charleston was "bitterly cold in temperature, but warm in hospitality," and his daughters found it charming. Johnson thought more about his heritage when he began his first novel, *By Reason of Strength,* just prior to Christmas. This celebration of his ancestors would progress quickly, be well received, and make him some money. On December 29, the *Evening Sun* gave him another raise, to $7,000. Things could have been considerably worse for the Johnsons at the end of 1929.[44]

Culture, ed. Charles Reagan Wilson and William Ferris (Chapel Hill: University of North Carolina Press, 1989), 1023; GWJ, "Outside the Law," *BES,* October 24, 1929; see alwo GWJ, "Comedy in a Churchyard," *BES,* September 19, 1929; see Kneebone, *Southern Liberal Journalists,* 64; GWJ to Howard W. Odum, November 7, 1929, HWO Papers.

42. GWJ, "A Nice Man, But . . . ," *BES,* October 10, 1929; GWJ to Howard W. Odum, October 26, November 12, 1929, HWO Papers; Kathryn Hayward Johnson, interview.

43. GWJ, "Count Your Blessings," *BES,* November 28, 1929.

44. GWJ to Harriet L. Herring, November 9, 1929, Herring Papers; GWJ to Katherine

The following year, the Johnsons moved several miles to the southwest to Wildey Avenue (now Mossway) in what is now the neighborhood of Pinehurst. In print, Johnson remained upbeat about America's economic condition. He called his first column "Unhappy New Year" but argued that "it would be preposterous to suppose that . . . calamity impends." He proceeded to assert that "the great bulk of business will go on as usual" and, in a startling analogy, announced that "our cake is all right, but the icing bids fair to be appreciatively thinner." Eleven months later, in his Thanksgiving column, he still believed that "a relatively slight readjustment of our scale of production and consumption can restore business to a solid and reasonably profitable basis."[45]

Looking south, he also took the opportunity to speak optimistically. "After Gastonia," he admitted, "the more pessimistic among the brethren gave up North Carolina as a completely bad job. She had gone for Hoover with hymns of prayer and praise on her lips in 1928; in 1929, she went for the textile workers with blood in her eye." However, he was reassured by the nomination of J. W. Bailey for the United States Senate, the appointment of Frank Porter Graham as President Chase's successor in Chapel Hill, and the appointment of Thurman D. Kitchin as the president of Wake Forest. These men, Johnson explained, "were enthusiastically elected to important offices without the advice and consent of political parson and medieval textile barons. None of the three is given to bigotry, religious, political, or economic."[46] In both his national and regional commentary, Johnson was clearly striving to avoid playing the doomsayer.

The year's longest discussion of the South dealt with time past rather than time present. Standing at a crossroads of sorts during his fortieth year, Johnson felt compelled, as many other writers have, to find out if he actually had a novel in him. As he told the story, the book forced itself upon him. "Somehow or other," he wrote to fellow author Lenoir Chambers, "I have got to write a novel. It will probably be the worst novel conceived in the minds of men, but until it is written I shall never be able to go whole-heartedly after anything else." He wrote quickly and finished the manuscript in two months.

Johnson Parham, December 10, 1929, GWJ Papers; GWJ, "The Frozen South," *BES,* December 5, 1929; GWJ to Howard W. Odum, December 15, 1930, HWO Papers; Kramer, telephone interview.

45. GWJ, "Unhappy New Year," *BES,* January 2, 1930; GWJ, "Shower of Blessings," *BES,* November 27, 1930.

46. GWJ, "Tarheelia Begins to Emerge," *BES,* July 17, 1930.

Typically self-effacing, he told Odum that "I fear it is damned bad, but it is the best I can do, so I am submitting it to the publishers, regardless." Minton, Balch and Company felt differently and offered a contract on March 27. The following month, Johnson sold the serial rights to *Household Magazine* for one thousand dollars, no mean sum during these Depression days. *By Reason of Strength* appeared in book form in November 1930.[47]

In this first foray into fiction, Johnson returns to his roots. Prior to the beginning of the novel, he offers a conventional disclaimer: "This story is entirely fictitious, and no character depicted in it is intended to be a representation of any historical personage." Like Mark Twain, Johnson told the truth mainly, but this disclaimer, to crib from Huck, is a "stretcher." Actually, Johnson narrates the story of Daniel Whyte and Catharine Campbell and their offspring—from their birth in late eighteenth-century Scotland through their emigration and their struggles to tame the Southern wilderness. The tale carries up to 1867, the year of death for the novel's heroine (and for Johnson's own great-great-grandmother). He assesses these ancestors and their household gods and discovers the values that helped to shape him.[48]

Trying his hand at this new genre, Johnson wisely makes use of his detailed knowledge of history. In fact, several of the major events of nineteenth-century American history—the War of 1812, the Nullification Crisis, the Mexican War, and the Civil War—help to shape the novel's plot. Johnson also uses the book to set forth his views on such salient historical issues as slavery. Catharine remarks, "I have never been too well satisfied that we have a right to hold the Negroes, anyhow. Suppose the Yankees did sell them to us in the first place? My husband always was a little uneasy about slavery, and if this war [the Civil War] should result in wiping it out, I don't know but what it would be a good thing for everybody concerned."[49] In terms of the proficiency of its attack upon slavery, *By Reason of Strength* falls somewhere between *The Adventures of Huckleberry Finn* and *Uncle Tom's Cabin,* two far more highly publicized novels. Johnson proves capable of nothing so powerful as the moral center of Mark Twain's masterpiece, where Huck bravely

47. GWJ to Lenoir Chambers, October 11, 1929, Chambers Papers; GWJ to Howard W. Odum, February 21, April 5, 13, July 24, 1930, HWO Papers.

48. GWJ, *By Reason of Strength* (New York: Minton, Balch, 1930), unnumbered page opposite the table of contents; Vincent Fitzpatrick, introduction to *By Reason of Strength,* by GWJ (Laurinburg, N.C.: St. Andrews College Press, 1994), i–xiii.

49. GWJ, *By Reason of Strength,* 192.

ignores church and state, abstractions both, to opt for his friendship with Jim. On the other hand, Johnson avoids the smugness and pamphleteering that mar Harriet Beecher Stowe's book.

Once again the moralist, and once again seeing history as theater, Johnson offers here a type of morality play with clear villains and heroes moving across the stage. The villains, such odious figures as MacLeod the drunken blasphemer and Peterson the cruel slave owner, prove stock characters. Even such a representative of good as Daniel Whyte functions more as a religious symbol than a human being. Besides resorting to stereotypes, Johnson also shifts his point of view, offers some wooden dialogue, and lets his narrator grow overly discursive. As one would expect, Johnson's first novel is hardly flawless.

With his heroine, on the other hand, Johnson offers a fully conceived character who stands as the center of the tale. Intelligent as well as beautiful, Catharine stresses the importance of the life of the mind, and she could hardly be more altruistic in her dealings with others. To Johnson's credit, this "doctor, nurse, confessor and lawgiver to half the county" is no saccharine saint.[50] *By Reason of Strength* engrossingly chronicles the pilgrim's progress of its heroine—from youth to age and from the Old World to the New. She surrenders her destiny to the Lord, is guided to North Carolina's Cape Fear Valley, and manages to prevail. She can be placed in the tradition of such strong Southern heroines as Dilsey in Faulkner's *The Sound and the Fury,* published the year before, and Scarlett O'Hara, whose name would captivate Depression America when Margaret Mitchell's *Gone with the Wind* appeared six years later.

With *By Reason of Strength,* Johnson proved that he was a competent novelist. The *Baltimore Evening Sun* praised the book, and the *Confederate Veteran* ran a long and laudatory review. The *New York Times* applauded Johnson's "portrait of a grand old lady." Capturing the novelist's attitude toward his material, Jonathan Daniels called the book Johnson's "almost homesick novel about the beginnings of his own North Carolina people."[51]

---

50. *Ibid.,* 142.

51. Frederic Nelson, "Gerald W. Johnson's First Novel Depicting a Forgotten Phase of the Old South," *BES,* October 18, 1930; Mrs. Cabell Smith, " 'By Reason of Strength': A Recent Contribution to the Confederate Literature of North Carolina," *Confederate Veteran* (February 1932): 52–54; "Carolina Generations," *New York Times Book Review,* November 2, 1930, p. 7; Jonathan Daniels, *Tar Heels: A Portrait of North Carolina* (New York: Dodd, Meade, 1941), 68, quoted in Kneebone, *Southern Liberal Journalists,* 243 n.13.

With this hymn of praise to a Southern past worthy of it, Johnson wrote—as Fred Hobson has remarked—a book that should have been appreciated by the Southern Agrarians who contributed to *I'll Take My Stand*.[52] Coincidentally, the Agrarian manifesto appeared the same month that *By Reason of Strength* was published. Johnson would find much in *I'll Take My Stand* offensive, and the Agrarians would, in turn, be offended by his caustic commentary. As we have seen, the opposing forces had been in the field for some time, and the publication of the manifesto merely provided the occasion for a pitched battle. It did not prove decisive—literary combat rarely does—and the skirmishing would continue long thereafter.

After he read *By Reason of Strength*, William Allen White, the distinguished Kansas author and editor, praised the book, wished Johnson success and a kind fate, and remarked that now, in late 1930, Johnson was entering his career. At first glance, White's observation seems an odd thing to say about a forty-year-old author who had already distinguished himself in daily journalism, written masterful essays in regional and national magazines, and seen the publication of six books. White's observation was astute, however. At the end of 1930, Johnson stood at the beginning of what would prove, by long odds, his greatest decade so far.[53]

Various tropes have been used to capture the American experience during the 1930s: the departure from the garden after the fall from grace, for example, and the long hangover after a raucous and very wet party. Whether religious or secular, the analogies acknowledged that there had been a profound upheaval in the American experience. Some disagreed, of course, Mencken among them, and many people came to view the Baltimorean as a walking anachronism. As unemployment swelled past 25 percent, Johnson would reconsider that startling analogy about the cake and the icing. In 1930, he remarked that Franklin Delano Roosevelt's health problems would undermine any candidacy. In time, Johnson would become a fervid New Dealer who saw FDR as America's savior. Much to Johnson's benefit, he would be writing at the height of his power during a decade that was temperamentally suited to what he had to say.[54]

During 1926, when times were good, Johnson had traveled from North

52. Fred Hobson, introduction to *South-Watching: Selected Essays by Gerald W. Johnson,* ed. Fred Hobson (Chapel Hill: University of North Carolina, 1983), xxii.

53. William Allen White to GWJ, December 29, 1930, GWJ Papers.

54. GWJ, "White House Hopes in Maryland," *North American Review* 229 (June 1930): 642.

Carolina to Baltimore to begin this new phase of his career. During the 1930s, desperate times for many, Johnson's journey would prove an intellectual one, a journey that would gain him considerably more national renown than he had experienced before. Before he looked out over the American scene, however, he had to look south and fight yet another battle over the land which had shaped him, the land that, no matter what his detractors might claim, he never ceased loving.

8   Who Speaks for the South?
Johnson and the Agrarians

To avoid the dire consequences and to maintain a farming life in an industrial imperialism, there seems to be only one thing left for the farmer to do. . . . [H]e must deny himself the articles the industrialists have for sale. . . . Do what we did after the war and Reconstruction: return to our looms, our handcrafts, our reproducing stock. Throw out the radio and take down the fiddle from the wall.

—*Andrew Nelson Lytle, "The Hind Tit"*

At first blush, it seems incredible that twelve men, all born and raised in the South, all literate, and all of legal age, could preach such a doctrine without once thrusting the tongue in cheek or winking the other eye.

—*Gerald Johnson, "No More Excuses"*

Johnson went to his grave believing that the Civil War could have been avoided. However, he never doubted that his battle with the Southern Agrarians needed to be fought. This war of words stretched on for decades and showed considerable acrimony. In Johnson's published assessments, the Agrarians had a flawed vision of Southern history; they gloried in a storybook past that existed only in their own minds. Moreover, he thought them sheltered from the more unattractive aspects of contemporary Southern life. He recognized that they were highly literate, patriotic, and well-intentioned, but he found them a dangerous foe that needed to be vanquished. The Agrarians, in turn, saw Johnson as a flaming liberal, a Menckenite, and a turncoat, now living with the enemy, whose criticism profaned his native land.

The Agrarians believed that hostile critics, both Yankees and traitorous Southerners, had embarrassed the South and that a counterattack was very much in order. Donald Davidson, for example, likened the decision to publish *I'll Take My Stand* to General Lee's decision to carry the war into Pennsylvania.[1] Johnson, on his part, thought that the South had already done a remarkable job of embarrassing itself and that the publication of this volume embarrassed it even more. Although these foes were implacable and made much of their differences, there were actually significant affinities between them. Both Johnson and the Agrarians deeply loved their native land, and it was the fervor of this love that convinced the contending forces that each was best suited to speak for the South.

As I have tried to suggest, the dispute generated by the publication of *I'll Take My Stand* was hardly unexpected. It would be erroneous, though, to regard the events and commentaries of the first portion of the 1920s as a direct progression toward conflict. It will be recalled that, back in 1921, while Johnson was writing editorials for the *Greensboro Daily News,* he had portentously used the phrase "no more excuses" to criticize those Southerners who chose to explain away President Harding's pointed criticism of the region. The following year, he mocked what he perceived to be the saccharine view of the antebellum South presented in the fiction of Thomas Nelson Page. Calling it an "idealization," Johnson complained that "we see its dignity without its pomposity, its patriotism without its provincialism, its statecraft without its demagogy, its splendid, open-handed hospitality to strange visitors without its fanatical and poisonous hatred of strange ideas." In 1923, he used *Survey Graphic* to comment on the plight of the impoverished Southern farmer during the first wave of industrialism: "Working conditions in the mills might be bad, but anything was better than the terrible fight for a bare existence that they had been waging on their rocky, barren farms." On the other hand, Johnson celebrated the primacy of the life of the mind, a major Agrarian tenet, when he praised the establishment of *The Fugitive* magazine in Nashville. We know now what he could not anticipate then: four of the magazine's major figures—John Crowe Ransom, Donald Davidson, Allen Tate, and Robert Penn Warren—would figure prominently in the Agrarian manifesto, and Johnson and Davidson would become adversarial. Moreover, it is significant that in these years prior to the Scopes trial both Tate and Davidson saw fit to praise Johnson's writing.[2]

1. Donald Davidson, *Southern Writers in the Modern World* (Athens, Ga.: University of Georgia Press, 1958), 51.

2. "Remedy Must Be Applied from Top to Bottom," *GDN,* July 19, 1921; "Of the Past's Highest Type," *GDN,* November 3, 1922; GWJ, "Behind the Monster's Mask," *Survey Graphic* 50 (April 1923): 20–22; "Two Southern Magazines," *GDN,* June 19, 1923; Donald Davidson, "Spyglass," *Nashville Tennessean,* March 1, 1925, cited by Fred Hobson, *Serpent in Eden: H. L. Mencken and the South* (Chapel Hill: University of North Carolina Press, 1974),

Such approbation changed, however, after the events in Dayton. David-son explained that the Yankee mockery of the South "broke in upon our literary concerns like a midnight alarm." *The Fugitive* ceased publication in December 1925. There were now more pressing concerns than poetry, a more threatening enemy than philistinism.[3]

As we have seen, Johnson was far more humane than Mencken in his assessment of Bryan. While Johnson found the proceedings in Tennessee em-inently regrettable, he pointedly remarked that there were forces of enlight-enment elsewhere in the South. Unlike Mencken, Johnson refused to draw the South as some sort of national joke, alternately amusing and pathetic. There was, however, more to this matter than what Johnson actually wrote, for the proceedings in Dayton caused the future Agrarians to view him far more censoriously. As they initiated their counterattack, Johnson was per-ceived as a prominent member of the enemy.[4] He was thus embroiled in a controversy not entirely of his own making. The irony is clear, at least to posterity: had Mencken written less devastatingly about Dayton, then John-son's commentary would have seemed more palatable.

Over the next three years, Davidson used several forums for his censure. He criticized Johnson in his "Spyglass" column in the *Nashville Tennessean* as well as in his essay "First Fruits of Dayton: The Intellectual Evolution in Dixie." In the *Saturday Review of Literature,* Davidson argued that Johnson had lost touch with his Southern environment and rebuked him for his "tart essays."[5]

In early 1929, however, the Agrarians asked this tart essayist to contribute to their manifesto. They had begun to plan *I'll Take My Stand* back in March 1927. Two years later, they were still discussing possible contributors. Several men were considered—among them Louis Jaffé, Grover Hall, and Julian Harris, all progressive Southern journalists whom Johnson had praised—but

---

149; Allen Tate, "Last Days of the Charming Lady," *Nation* 121 (October 28, 1925): 486, cited by Fred Hobson, introduction to *South-Watching: Selected Essays by Gerald W. Johnson,* ed. Fred Hobson (Chapel Hill: University of North Carolina Press, 1983), xix.

3. Paul K. Conkin, *The Southern Agrarians* (Knoxville, Tenn.: University of Tennessee Press, 1988), 33, 18; Davidson, *Southern Writers in the Modern World,* 30.

4. Hobson, *Serpent in Eden,* 156.

5. Davidson's "Spyglass" columns are cited by Fred Hobson, *Tell About the South: The Southern Rage to Explain* (Baton Rouge: Louisiana State University Press, 1983), 210; Davidson, "First Fruits of Dayton: The Intellectual Evolution in Dixie," *Forum* 79 (June 1928): 896–907; Davidson, "The Artist as Southerner," *Saturday Review of Literature* 2 (15 May 1926): 1–3, dis-cussed by Hobson, *Serpent in Eden,* 160–61, and in his introduction to *South-Watching,* viii.

only Johnson and Stringfellow Barr, editor of the *Virginia Quarterly Review,* were actually asked. Barr was receptive, but the manifesto carried none of his writing. On the other hand, Johnson turned down the offer, as Davidson recounts the episode, "with a curt jocular quip." Why, one wonders, was Johnson asked to contribute, and why did he decline? Neither question can be answered with certitude.[6]

In retrospect, Davidson explained that, although *I'll Take My Stand* was intended "to emphasize trans-Appalachian thought," the names of possible contributors from the Atlantic states demonstrated "how catholic [was] our intention, or how great our innocence of mind." Thus, there seemed to have been room, at least in one stage of the planning process, for a Southern liberal who had been raised in North Carolina and who then had moved to Baltimore. Perhaps the motive was more practical. As Paul K. Conkin has remarked, the Agrarians needed to find a publisher, and a writer of Johnson's regional and national reputation would greatly enhance the prospects. The twelve men who finally contributed were in all a most worthy group, but Johnson the celebrated journalist, essayist, and successful biographer was unarguably then better known than all but a few of them.[7]

It is uncertain exactly what Johnson was told about the specifics of the project, so any discussion of his motive for declining proves speculative at best. As always, he was extremely busy with a variety of projects; perhaps he felt that he did not have the time to take on another one. Such a motive, though, would have been out of character, for he rarely declined an opportunity to write. Perhaps he was annoyed by Davidson's attacks and hence declined to contribute. This would also have been out of character, for Johnson always understood that others had the right to discuss his work as they pleased. As always, Johnson needed money; perhaps he declined because he did not wish to get involved in a project that did not look lucrative financially. (If this were indeed his premonition, then it proved correct.) With few

6. Conkin, *The Southern Agrarians,* 46–47; Davidson, " 'I'll Take My Stand': A History," *American Review* 5 (summer 1935): 301–21; John T. Kneebone, *Southern Liberal Journalists and the Issue of Race, 1920–1944* (Chapel Hill: University of North Carolina Press, 1985), 58–59; Hobson, *Serpent in Eden,* 166. I have found no evidence of correspondence between Johnson and Davidson. Among Johnson's papers at Wake Forest, I have found no invitation asking him to contribute to *I'll Take My Stand.* Perhaps Johnson's "curt jocular quip" indicates that the invitation was offered orally.

7. Davidson, " 'I'll Take My Stand,' " 313; Kneebone, *Southern Liberal Journalists,* 59; Conkin, *The Southern Agrarians,* 69.

exceptions, Johnson throughout his career was an individualist rather than a joiner, someone who hesitated to ally himself with the methodology or philosophy of a particular group or cause; perhaps this made him decline. Perhaps he had been told enough about the volume to suspect that there would be a conflict between his views and those of some of the other contributors. Finally, perhaps it was as much to these people (or to some of these people) as it was to their principles that he refused to connect himself. In any event, he declined, a decision that would prove fateful. The book would have to proceed without Gerald Johnson. At the end of 1929, as the volume neared its publication with Harper and Brothers, Allen Tate told Davidson that Johnson was a man of character who wrote well; Tate, however, also questioned the quality of Johnson's mind.[8] In time, Johnson would wonder about the Agrarians' sanity.

Johnson's bellicose and wrongheaded response to Stringfellow Barr the following September foreshadowed his response to the Agrarian manifesto. Without a forum in *I'll Take My Stand,* Barr used the *Virginia Quarterly Review* to set forth his views on the conflict between the industrialists and those he called "traditionalists." Temperately, Barr called for the opposing forces to use less rhetoric and more common sense. "A mill is not a divine institution," he remarked, "nor was cotton pickin' time. . . . It is time for the traditionalists to cease romanticizing about the Old's South unessential economic characteristics and it is time for the progressive individualist to cease romanticizing about the whistles that blow people to barren places." Barr saw industrialism as a fait accompli and argued optimistically that "the South faces a brilliant chance for a new industrial experiment that will rehabilitate her economically without wrecking her spiritually." Arguing that the traditionalists and industrialists could prove complementary rather than adversarial, suggesting the possibility of compromise between heart and head, Barr offered a lively, incisive essay that was fair to both positions. It should have appealed to all but the extremists on both sides.[9]

Significantly, it did not appeal to Johnson. Later that month, he responded at length in "Dixie and Babbittry," an *Evening Sun* column. He erroneously accused Barr of defending the traditionalists and, in misconstruing Barr's po-

8. Allen Tate to Donald Davidson, December 11, 1929, in *The Literary Correspondence of Donald Davidson and Allen Tate,* ed. John Tyree Fain and Thomas Daniel Young (Athens, Ga.: University of Georgia Press, 1974), 242.

9. Stringfellow Barr, "Shall Slavery Come South?" *VQR* 6 (October 1930): 481–94.

sition, conveniently set up the traditionalist as the proverbial straw man whom he took obvious delight in toppling:

> I doubt that the attitude described by Mr. Barr—namely a revolt against industrialism—is common to any considerable number. Most Southerners have eyes and ears and memories that go back a dozen years or two dozen. And any Southerner so equipped, unless he is an especially moony fellow, cannot revolt against industrialism. He remembers, with a shudder, that it was no pleasant pit from which he was digged. It was the industrial spade that brought it out, and if he calls it a spade he names it with a very sincere respect.[10]

Like Barr, Johnson viewed industrialism as a fait accompli, and he would make this point repeatedly when he reviewed the manifesto. But Johnson was not, as his language suggests here, any unequivocal defender of industrialism. He was spoiling for a fight, and in time he would call the Agrarians far worse things than "moony" fellows.

Review copies of *I'll Take My Stand* went out in early November. The book's main title is taken from the song "Dixie," and the volume is subtitled *The South and the Agrarian Tradition*. Ten of the twelve contributors, all except the Mississippian Stark Young and the Arkansan John Gould Fletcher, had been or were then associated in some way with Vanderbilt University.[11] Offering a mix of the traditional literary modes, the essays range in tone from the angry to the elegiac. The distinguished list of contributors write about a variety of topics: Robert Penn Warren on race and Allen Tate on religion, Herman Clarence Nixon on economics and John Gould Fletcher on education, Donald Davidson on literature and Frank Lawrence Owsley on history, Andrew Nelson Lytle on Southern farm life and Lyle H. Lanier on philosophy. John Donald Wade's dramatic account of "The Life and Death of Cousin Lucius" chronicles, among other things, his successful struggle to live a humane, reflective life during the difficult times of Reconstruction. With the single exception of Henry Blue Kline's awkward "William Remington: A Study in Individualism," the essays are, in their various voices and modes, uniformly well written, sometimes strikingly eloquent.

This provocative volume very much demands to be taken on its own

10. GWJ, "Dixie and Babbittry," *BES,* September 18, 1930.
11. Conkin, *The Southern Agrarians,* 69; Davidson, " 'I'll Take My Stand,' " 307.

terms. In his introductory "Statement of Principles," John Crowe Ransom, the book's editor, explains the collection's unity in the face of so much seeming diversity. He says that the essays "all tend to support a Southern way of life against what may be called the American or prevailing way; and all as much agree that the best terms in which to represent the distinction are contained in the phrase, Agrarian *versus* Industrial." Ransom asserts (an assertion that would infuriate Johnson) that Agrarianism is a concept that "does not stand in particular need of definition." While he remarks that "the culture of the soil is the best and most sensitive of vocations, and . . . therefore . . . should have the economic preference and enlist the maximum number of workers," Ransom also notes that "these principles do not intend to be very specific in proposing any practical measures.[12] In the end, *I'll Take My Stand* is visionary rather than prescriptive.

These highly literate essayists use a variety of literary devices to attack industrialism. Ransom metaphorically depicts it as a malignancy; for Davidson, it is a malaise. Owsley draws industrialism as a destructive "Juggernaut," and for Wade it is a "motor-car" proceeding wildly in the wrong direction. Lanier scorns industrialism as a "public anaesthetic," and Lytle likens it to poison. Moreover, the essayists use allusion and resonance to attack their foe. Drawing upon the Bible, Davidson scorns industrialism as a false messiah. Perhaps thinking of Circe, Nixon speaks of industrialism casting its "spell"; moreover, he compares the acceptance of industrialism to a pact with the devil. Agrarianism, on the other hand, is depicted as a barrier blocking a destructive force, a type of brake that will slow down a civilization hurtling out of control. Clearly, *I'll Take My Stand* is not directed at the literal-minded.[13]

Its appeal lies elsewhere. As Louis D. Rubin, Jr., has explained so well, the volume is "best . . . considered as an extended metaphor." *I'll Take My Stand* is not, he remarks, "a treatise on economics; it is not a guide to political

12. John Crowe Ransom, "Introduction: A Statement of Principles," in *I'll Take My Stand: The South and the Agrarian Tradition,* by Twelve Southerners (New York: Harper Torchbooks, 1962), xix, xxviii, xxix.

13. All references in this note pertain to the Harper Torchbook edition of *I'll Take My Stand*. John Crowe Ransom, "Reconstructed, but Unregenerate," 15; Donald Davidson, "A Mirror for Artists," 58; Frank Lawrence Owsley, "The Irrepressible Conflict," 91; John Donald Wade, "The Life and Death of Cousin Lucius," 294; Lyle H. Lanier, "A Critique of the Philosophy of Progress," 123; Andrew Lytle, "The Hind Tit," 203; Davidson, "A Mirror for Artists," 35; Herman Clarence Nixon, "Whither Southern Economy?" 192, 199; Ransom, "Reconstructed, But Unregenerate," 22; Nixon, "Whither Southern Economy?" 198.

action; it is not a sociological blueprint. It is a vision of what the good life can be." It is also, as Donald Davidson has pointed out, "an experiment in 'insubordination.' "[14] Twelve Southern essayists proclaim "I accuse" and question the direction and quality of life in their native land. *I'll Take My Stand* pleads for sanity and decorum and the life of the mind. It spins out a modern morality play between the forces of good and evil.

In January 1931, the *Virginia Quarterly Review* published "The South Faces Itself," Johnson's composite review of not only *I'll Take My Stand* but also *An American Epoch* by Howard W. Odum, *King Cotton Is Sick* by Claudius T. Murchison, and *The Industrial Revolution in the South* by Broadus Mitchell and George Sinclair Mitchell. Johnson says that the four volumes are "charming" but far from "light." He labels *An American Epoch* the most "striking" of the four and *I'll Take My Stand* the most "curious." Closing the review with six paragraphs about the Agrarian manifesto, the longest discussion of any of the four books, Johnson points to the relative youth of the contributors and says that "for that reason what they have to say is worth particular attention, as it might be expected to echo the voice of the South for the next twenty years." Although he does not say so outright, the thought of this appalls him.

Johnson acknowledges the sickness that industrialism has brought to Marion and Gastonia but rejects Agrarianism as the cure. That these twelve writers, he observes, "should turn to agrarianism as a remedy would seem to indicate their sole knowledge of the South has been gleaned from the pages of Joel Chandler Harris and Thomas Nelson Page. Have they never been in the modern South . . . ? Have they never been told that the obscenities and depravities of the most degenerate hole of a cotton-mill town are but pale reflections of the lurid obscenities and depravities of Southern backwoods communities?" He proceeds to assert that "no purely agrarian policy can maintain a fine civilization for any length of time" and concludes by arguing that "the bogy of industrialism in the South is a figment of the imagination."[15] In the review that followed the next month, Johnson would make a

14. Louis D. Rubin, Jr., "Introduction to the Torchbook Edition," in *I'll Take My Stand: The South and the Agrarian Tradition,* by Twelve Southerners (New York: Harper Torchbooks, 1962), xi, xv; Davidson, *Southern Writers in the Modern World,* x; see Hobson, introduction to *South-Watching,* xxi; and Virginia Rock, "The Twelve Southerners: Biographical Essays," in *I'll Take My Stand: The South and the Agrarian Tradition,* by Twelve Southerners (New York: Harper Torchbooks, 1962), 360.

15. GWJ, "The South Faces Itself," *VQR* 6 (January 1930): 152–57.

number of the same points—especially about the bookishness of the contributors and their refusal to face the harsh realities of the contemporary South—but he would also use *Harper's Magazine* to take a far stronger stand concerning what he saw as the embarrassment of the South by men who, in his opinion, should have known better.

"No More Excuses: A Southerner to Southerners" appeared in February 1931, three months after the Agrarian manifesto. Johnson's bellicosity is evident in the first part of the title, a phrase that, as we have seen, he had already used scathingly in that *Greensboro Daily News* editorial. The subtitle announces that, even after residing in Baltimore for over four years, he speaks here as a Southerner. He may well have anticipated criticism that he was now only a Yankee who could not understand the import of the book. "No More Excuses" proves one of the longest and most impressionistic reviews that Johnson ever wrote. In this piece of between four thousand and five thousand words, he does not speak directly of *I'll Take My Stand* until paragraph ten. He does not discuss any of the individual essays, and he quotes only three times, with all three quotations taken from Ransom's "Statement of Principles."[16]

With bludgeoning irony, Johnson opens with an olfactory image to denigrate those "professional Southerners" who have damaged their native land:

> The appalling stenches that have come out of the cotton-mill towns of Dixie within the last year . . . may serve, in the end, a more useful purpose than all the essences of magnolia and cape jasmine that all the professional Southerners have scattered over the South since the Civil War. For these are frank, undisguised, forthright stinks, not, like many odors which have emanated from the South in the past, compounded of the breath of the honeysuckle with just a faint suspicion of putrescence.

Turning to the events in Marion and Gastonia, he argues that they cannot be explained away by complaints about slavery and Appomattox and Reconstruction, "the old excuses which we Southerners have been using for sixty years." He complains that Southerners have used excuses to lynch blacks, to "regard the Constitution . . . as a scrap of paper," and "to manipulate the electorate." After considerable preliminary discussion, he arrives at "the latest

16. GWJ, "No More Excuses: A Southerner to Southerners," in *South-Watching: Selected Essays by Gerald W. Johnson,* ed. Fred Hobson (Chapel Hill: University of North Carolina, 1983), 128–36. Subsequent quotations are from this edition.

dodge," the excuse of blaming the South's problems upon "the invasion of industrialism."

Turning more specifically to *I'll Take My Stand,* he calls Agrarianism "the latest cult of Dixie" and expresses astonishment that twelve Southerners, "all literate and of legal age," could put forth such a doctrine without being facetious. Scorning Agrarianism as a distortion of reality conceived by isolated men laboring in the proverbial ivory tower, he complains that "it smells horribly of the lamp, [and] that it was library-born and library-bred." After quoting Ransom's assertion that Agrarianism "does not stand in particular need of definition," Johnson bristles that "perhaps a philosopher could detect in this one line a great part of the tragedy of the South since the Civil War. We have never thought much of precise definitions, of precision of thought in any sense. Facts are inconvenient things; let us stick, rather, to emotions." Waxing metaphorical, he suggests that the Agrarians are not physicians healing the South but rather dangerous quacks, whose "medicine" is only a "draught compounded of the essences of civic disease, of communal madness, of moral and physical death." The man who had previously called for "more beef and less bull" scoffs at the Agrarians for their "gaseous rhetoric."

Casting a cold eye on the Old South, one of the Agrarians' icons, Johnson denigrates "the ruinous agricultural system" in the region prior to the Civil War. The notion that "before the war we possessed a civilization which was one of the ornaments of the world" is for Johnson only "sentimental tommyrot." Actually, Southern civilization was then "economically rotten" because it was based on slavery. "It was so rotten," he continues, "that it was swiftly crumbling into ruin long before the blast of war struck it."

Speaking about the results of industrialism in the South since 1900, this editorial writer skilled in polemics admits several issues. Industrialism has marred the countryside, brought with it "a horde of parvenus," generated too much worship of the almighty dollar, and speeded up the pace of life. On the other hand, Johnson points out that industrialism has also "created Chapel Hill and that neighboring hill on which Duke University is now rising." Moreover, money from industrialism has helped to reduce illiteracy, improve public health and public education, and hasten prison and child-labor reform.

At the beginning of the review's final section, after restating his belief that industrialism is a fait accompli, Johnson proclaims that "I am enough of a Southerner to be a little arrogant in my demands of the South." After listing the region's distinguished ancestors, Johnson challenges the South "to take industrialism and with it fashion a civilization in which such men as these could live." Face the future squarely, Johnson exhorts; don't retreat once more into the past. Looking forward proves the South's only viable option, for "sniveling and excuse-hunting on the part of intelligent Southerners are a worse betrayal of their ancestors than are Gastonia, lynching, demagoguery and fanaticism combined." It is doubtful that any reader put down this essay-review in boredom or had any confusion about Johnson's position.

In all, "No More Excuses" proves an uneven performance—lively and eloquent and flawed. As critics have pointed out, the Agrarians obviously made Johnson angry. Such ire affects this piece whose structure occasionally wobbles and whose irony is unnecessarily heavy-handed. As Fred Hobson has remarked, Johnson's "distress" about industrial violence in the South created a sense of urgency that led him to be literal-minded in response to a volume that begs to be interpreted as metaphor.[17] In this review for a national periodical, far more so than in his first assessment for the more regional *Virginia Quarterly Review,* Johnson labored to distance himself from what he saw as a destructive force in his native land. His ardor to do so, however, generated a review with too much invective and too little reasoned analysis. He had the space here, had he chosen to use it, to analyze at least several of the individual essays, to comment upon their specific strengths and weaknesses. This, however, was not his agenda. While Johnson vented his displeasure, sometimes brilliantly, he may well have frustrated those readers who picked up "No More Excuses" to find out what *I'll Take My Stand* actually said.

Johnson himself may well have been bothered by aspects of the volume that he chose not to discuss. The fact that Archibald Johnson had been an unsuccessful farmer precluded any romantic notion of life on the land by his son. Johnson had to be skeptical when literary people, most of whom had little or no experience with farm life, hymned the sacred joys of husbandry. More specifically, he disagreed with Owsley's defense of states' rights and his argument that the Civil War was inevitable. Davidson believed that art flourishes best in "stable, religious, and agrarian" societies. (Decades later, Johnson would explode in rage over this.) Johnson the egalitarian had to be disturbed by the patently elitist slant of Fletcher's essay on education. So conversant

---

17. Kneebone, *Southern Liberal Journalists,* 59; Fred Hobson, introduction to "No More Excuses: A Southerner to Southerners," in *South-Watching: Selected Essays by Gerald W. Johnson,* ed. Fred Hobson (Chapel Hill: University of North Carolina, 1983), 128; Hobson, introduction to *South-Watching,* xxi. For further discussion of Johnson's reviews, see Kneebone, *Southern Liberal Journalists,* 65–66; Hobson, *Tell About the South,* 216–17; and Hobson, *Serpent in Eden,* 169–70.

with the pitfalls of organized religion, Johnson had to be skeptical about Tate's discussion of its benefits. In brief, there were significant biographical and ideological differences between Johnson and the Agrarians that were never fully articulated in this review.[18]

The affinities, however, outnumbered the differences. Like Ransom, Johnson recognized the dangers of deracination and the fact that the "good life" is not based upon material possessions but rather upon "the free activity of the mind." Like Owsley, Johnson despised the Abolitionists. Like Fletcher, Johnson recognized the South's huge achievement in surviving Reconstruction—"perhaps the most heroic fact in all American history," Fletcher calls it. Both Lanier and Johnson acknowledged the significance of the decline of the family. Like Stark Young, Johnson celebrated an aristocracy of intellect rather than money; both men believed that the true aristocrat has "a certain long responsibility for others." Johnson and Robert Penn Warren both defended social segregation and equality before the law; both held that the fates of the races are intertwined. John Donald Wade's "The Life and Death of Cousin Lucius" is arguably the volume's most moving essay; in subject matter and tone, it is unarguably the closest to "The Cadets of New Market." Cousin Lucius, like those resolute souls in Johnson's essay, manages to endure the hard times of Reconstruction, the period that both essayists compare to the biblical wandering in the desert. These essays, highly evocative both, attest to the huge import of seemingly small lives.[19]

Finally, Johnson and the Agrarians proved kindred spirits in several ways. They were moralists who despised the triumph of evil. Like the Agrarians, Johnson decried materialism, senseless hurry, and the worship of false gods

18. Davidson, *Southern Writers in the Modern World,* 54; GWJ to Howard W. Odum, September 24, 1952, HWO Papers. Davisdon counters GWJ's argment that the Agrarians had no experience with farm life by pointing out that, at the time *I'll Take My Stand* was published, Owsley, Lytle, Lanier and Wade "either owned farm property themselves or were directly involved in the management of farm land." Owsley, "The Irrepressible Conflict," 87; Davidson, "A Mirror for Artists," 29; Allen Tate, "Remarks on Southern Religion," in *I'll Take My Stand: The South and the Agrarian Tradition,* by Twelve Southerners (New York: Harper Torchbooks, 1962), 174–75.

19. Ransom, "Reconstructed, but Unregenerate," 10; John Gould Fletcher, "Education, Past and Present," in *I'll Take My Stand: The South and the Agrarian Tradition,* by Twelve Southerners (New York: Harper Torchbooks, 1962), 114; Stark Young, "Not In Memoriam, but in Defense," in *I'll Take My Stand: The South and the Agrarian Tradition,* by Twelve Southerners (New York: Harper Torchbooks, 1962), 350; Wade, "The Life and Death of Cousin Lucius," 286–87.

and championed civility, the life of the mind, and a respect for the past. Had he wanted it, there was indeed a place for Johnson in *I'll Take My Stand*—a place, that is, for the poignant elegist of "Cadets," not for the belligerent polemicist. And had the times not been so out of joint, had Johnson felt less urgency about the South's industrial problems, he might well have written a more temperate review, an assessment that better explained this volume that would, in time, prove a required text for any serious study of Southern intellectual history.

In the years after its publication, *I'll Take My Stand* sold poorly—a little more than 2,000 copies before it went out of print in 1941. Few reviewers gave the book unqualified praise; many, like Johnson, argued that industrialism was a fact of life and its opponents were vain dreamers. In "Uprising in the Confederacy," a substantial review that ran in the *Mercury* in March 1931, Mencken proved just as splenetic as Johnson had been. Significantly, he praised Johnson at the expense of the Agrarians. He proclaimed that "what the South needs is not fashioners of utopias, but leaders who are competent and ready to grapple with things as they are." He mocked the Agrarians as "sufferers from nostalgic vapors" and declared that the South's "deliverance lies in the hands of such realistic and indomitable fellows as, say, Julian Harris, Gerald W. Johnson, and Grover C. Hall." Echoing Johnson, Mencken said that the air of "the professional pedagogue" hung about the volume. Knowing exactly what old wound to reopen, the Baltimorean concluded that "one Scopes trial did more damage to Tennessee than all the cotton-mills in it—more damage immediately, and far more damage in the long run. The Anti-Evolution Act is still on the books there, an insult and a disgrace to every self-respecting citizen of the State. I'll begin to believe that educated Southerners should let it stand unchallenged, the while they spin lavender fancies under a fig-tree, when I am convinced that Thomas Jefferson, if he were alive today, would tolerate it." Both flayed and burlesqued, the Agrarians were most unhappy with the Baltimorean and his North Carolina cohort who had attacked them and then been praised in their stead. Later that month, Davidson wrote to Fletcher that Johnson "badly needed to be exposed" and that it was "up to one of us to hit him good and hard."[20] They did hit him, but he drubbed them in return.

20. John Egerton, *Speak Now against the Day: The Generation before the Civil Rights Movement in the South* (New York: Knopf, 1994), 68; Conkin, *The Southern Agrarians,* 87; H. L. Mencken, "Uprising in the Confederacy," *AM* 22 (March 1931): 379–81; Donald Davidson to

The battle proved especially heated during the remainder of the decade, as the opposing forces used both public and private forums for their attacks. After reading "No More Excuses," Owsley acknowledged to Davidson that *I'll Take My Stand* "smells of the cloister" but argued that Johnson had "little ground . . . to stand on." To Edwin Mims, Davidson explained that his "The Dilemma of Southern Liberals" was an attack on "younger liberals—Gerald Johnson & Co.," because they "have had an opportunity that [Walter Hines] Page did not have for making a frank estimate of the social and political history of the South." Although he referred to Johnson only once by name, Davidson criticized the Southern liberals, the group with which Johnson was prominently associated, as "prophets whose miracle has not worked." These liberals, Davidson complained, abolish "the evils of chain-gangs by proposing to put everybody in chains." He accused them of "opportunism" and argued that, for all their criticism, they did not really know what sort of society they wanted.[21]

Mencken's "The South Astir," which appeared in early 1935, further inflamed Davidson and helped to precipitate further denunciation of Johnson. Again reopening an old wound, Mencken referred to the Scopes trial as "the Dayton clown-show." He denounced the Agrarians as utopians dreaming of a "New Jerusalem." Employing that rollicking Menckenese that could make his adversaries seem preposterous, the Baltimorean proclaimed that "even the Agrarian Habakkuks themselves are the clients of industrialism, which supplies them generously with the canned goods, haberdashery, and library facilities that are so necessary for the free ebullition of the human intellect. Left to the farmers of Tennessee, they would be clad in linsey-woolsey and fed on sidemeat, and the only books they could read would be the excessively orthodox." Stung by Mencken's pen, Davidson, like his Old Testament predecessor, grew indignant indeed.[22]

In " 'I'll Take My Stand': A History," his response to Mencken's ridicule,

---

John Gould Fletcher, March 23, 1931, quoted in Hobson, *Tell About the South*, 219. Mencken's "Uprising in the Confederacy" is discussed by Hobson, *Serpent in Eden*, 170–71.

21. Frank Owsley to Donald Davidson, April 8, 1931, quoted in Hobson, introduction to *South-Watching*, xxi; Donald Davidson to Edwin Mims, January 24, 1934, quoted in Michael O'Brien, *The Idea of the American South, 1920–1941* (Baltimore: Johns Hopkins University Press, 1979), 201, and in Hobson, introduction to *South-Watching*, xxii; Davidson, "The Dilemma of Southern Liberals," *AM* 31 (February 1934): 227–35. The Davidson article is discussed in Hobson, *Tell About the South*, 223.

22. Mencken, "The South Astir," *VQR* 11 (January 1935): 47–60. The article is discussed in Hobson, *Serpent in Eden*, 179–83.

Davidson, among other things, scoffed at the critics of the volume. He listed Johnson first, quoted from "No More Excuses," and remarked scathingly that "it is easy to imagine the pictures in his mind of a wealthy, urbanized South, plentifully equipped with machines, hospitals, universities, and newspaper literates as alert as he is." Johnson, of course, was as skeptical about financial wealth as the Agrarians were. Denouncing those who denounced the book, Davidson argued that "when we championed agrarianism, they were amused and incredulous, if not disgusted, and therefore the tone of their discussion was often one of scornful levity."[23] Actually, Johnson showed much scorn and incredulity but little levity or amusement.

On his part, Johnson used both his correspondence and his writing for publication to continue to denounce the Agrarians. It is worth pointing out, though, that he could have been, publicly at least, even more bellicose than he was. He declined an invitation to participate in the Southern Writers' Convention held in Charlottesville in October 1931, a convention to which Davidson, Fletcher, and Tate were also invited. Moreover, Johnson declined to respond in May 1933 to the first issue of the *American Review,* a periodical that served as a forum for the Agrarians. Nor did he review *Who Owns America?,* a book that appeared three years later carrying essays by eight of the contributors to *I'll Take My Stand.* In 1935, the *Virginia Quarterly Review* requested another commentary on the Agrarians. Johnson declined but showed his disgust in his correspondence with the magazine: "What credit is there to be gained by beating up a blind man?" He called Agrarianism one of the "phantasies" plaguing the South and complained that "the Southern gentleman simply doesn't fight; his gonads are atrophied; he is either a cynic or an agrarian."[24]

Throughout the decade, Johnson used the *Evening Sun* to discuss agrarian life in general and the foibles of the Agrarians in particular. He debunked the supposed sanctity of the life of the soil. He likened the Agrarian philosophy to that of Mohandas Gandhi, whom he found preposterous, and complained that the Agrarians, instead of responding to the very real problems of the South, "spend all their time praising the excellencies of a system as dead as Jefferson Davis and beyond resuscitation." In 1939, Johnson admitted that

23. Conkin, *The Southern Agrarians,* 119; Davidson, " 'I'll Take My Stand,' " 301–21.

24. GWJ to James Southall Wilson, February 7, 1931, James Southall Wilson Papers, Special Collections, Alderman Library, University of Virginia, Charlottesville, Va.; Conkin, *The Southern Agrarians,* 109, 123; GWJ to Lambert Davis, March 25, 1935, quoted by Kneebone, *Southern Liberal Journalists,* 71, 111. See also GWJ to Howard W. Odum, April 25, 1935, HWO Papers.

the Agrarians were correct in their argument that "the South should look into its own past and its own present to find trustworthy guides for the future." He complained, however, that the Agrarians "exhibit the tendency to imagine that the Golden Age belongs to the past, and so they drift toward senility."[25] So ended the battle of the 1930s.

Never again would either party devote so much time and energy to denouncing the other. This is not to say, however, that the attacks ceased or became any less caustic. During the next decade, Davidson again denounced Johnson in an essay about W. J. Cash. On his part, Johnson tried to be civil and fair in his 1948 review of Davidson's book on the Tennessee River. He praised Davidson's scholarship and style but could not resist returning to the hot summer of 1925 and the uproar that proved so significant for *I'll Take My Stand:* "Mr. Davidson is resentful of the way Tennessee was trampled in the ensuing contest between two great showmen, Clarence Darrow and William Jennings Bryan, but he does not even suggest that Tennessee had long been subjected to the domination of a singularly ignorant and superstitious priesthood, and so had brought the trouble upon herself."[26] For both men, this past was always present.

During the following decade, Davidson proved most uncivil indeed. In November 1957, he delivered a series of lectures at Mercer University in Georgia; these talks were published the following year under the title *Southern Writers in the Modern World.* Explaining the genesis of *I'll Take My Stand* and its critical reception, Davidson took the opportunity to vilify an enemy of long standing. He called Johnson "a typically loud and persistent voice" of misguided Southern liberal criticism and scoffed that "this fire-eating Southern liberal found nothing good either in the traditional South or in the Agrarian proposals." Actually, Johnson found much to value in the traditional South. Such censure, though, paled in comparison with Davidson's remark that the Agrarians "were rejecting the defeatism of Walter Hines Page and Henry Grady and the servile collaborationism of modern Southern liberals."[27] Given the historical moment, with the horrors of World War II and the Nazi atrocities and the Vichy government still very much on everyone's mind, Da-

25. GWJ, "Abolishing the Farmer," *BES,* September 7, 1933; GWJ, "Ingredients of Aristocracy," *BES,* March 26, 1936; GWJ, "Pulmotor Squad," *BES,* January 19, 1939. The last-mentioned article is discussed in Kneebone, *Southern Liberal Journalists,* 71.

26. Donald Davidson, "Mr. Cash and the Proto-Dorian South," *Southern Review* 7 (summer 1941): 1–20, quoted in Hobson, introduction to *South-Watching,* viii; GWJ, "A River Runs through Our History," *NYHTB,* January 25, 1948, pp. 1–2.

27. Davidson, *Southern Writers in the Modern World,* 38, 47, 51.

vidson could hardly have chosen a more highly charged phrase than "servile collaborationism." The import of the remark seems undeniable: Southern liberals like Johnson sold out the South to the Yankees just as French collaborationists betrayed their country to the Nazis. If Johnson read this caustic remark, he chose not to respond.

Four years later, six years before Davidson's death in 1968, *I'll Take My Stand* was reissued as a Harper Torchbook with an illuminating introduction by Louis D. Rubin, Jr. Far more available, the volume in time became a staple in many Southern literature and history courses and continued to generate a sizable amount of commentary. One can argue that *I'll Take My Stand* and Cash's *The Mind of the South* have proven the two most significant books written by Southerners about the South during the twentieth century. Thus, it is accurate to say that the judgment of posterity has differed markedly from Johnson's assessment in early 1931, but it is not altogether fair. More often than not, reviewers are concerned with more immediate matters than how their judgments will be perceived by posterity.

It is tempting to speculate what might have happened had Johnson chosen to contribute to *I'll Take My Stand*. The volume has stood the test of time far better than any of the more than forty books that Johnson wrote or to which he contributed. Would his participation in this project have enhanced his reputation? It is, apparently, a question that never troubled Johnson, for there is no evidence that he ever regretted his decision to decline. Beyond argument, Johnson's response to the Agrarian manifesto and the war of words that followed marked one of the most significant episodes in his career as a regional writer.

The story told here transpired over a lengthy period of time. Hoover was president when Johnson was asked to contribute. The opposing forces battled throughout the New Deal years, and Eisenhower was in his second term when Davidson scoffed at Johnson as a collaborationist. While America changed greatly, the men's fundamental beliefs about the South, and each other, changed not at all. In Johnson's view, Davidson remained behind in Tennessee chasing ghosts. As Davidson saw it, Johnson first abandoned the land of his fathers and then profaned it. Both men were wrong. There were no ghosts, no profanation. Both Davidson and Johnson were Southerners with long memories, thoroughly incapable of forgetting about old times there. Both men were highly literate and loyal, proud and stubborn, wrongly convinced that someone else who saw the South so differently could ever love it as well. Both men spoke for the South, albeit in a profoundly different way. And it was to the credit of this much-maligned region, this problematic land of sunshine and shadow, that the South was large enough for both of them.

9   The World Theater
1931–1936

> All over the country, people are accepting as Americanism ideas that are perfectly acceptable to Hitler, Mussolini, and Stalin. It is one of the ironies of the age that people who are bawling loudest against Communism are offering, as an antidote, the very ingredient that is the active poison in Communism itself. It is also the active poison in Fascism and Naziism, too; for in their central principle all are identical. This poisonous idea is the notion that the people belong to the government, not the government to the people.
>
> —Gerald Johnson, "A Third Question" Baltimore Evening Sun, November 7, 1935

While Johnson publicly remained very much an infidel regarding the dogmas in *I'll Take My Stand,* he would in time become an eager convert to the New Deal. While he vilified Donald Davidson for refusing to take that proverbial next step, he would deify Franklin Delano Roosevelt for taking bold measures to combat the Depression. This next portion of Johnson's career stretched from early 1931, soon after the publication of the Agrarian manifesto, until late 1936, after the presidential election. During this time, Johnson paid increasing attention to the world theater. The ghost of Woodrow Wilson hovered overhead and reminded everyone, as Johnson loved to point out, of the huge ramifications of the botched Treaty of Versailles and the subsequent failure of the League of Nations. A variety of villains—totalitarians such as Hitler, Mussolini, and Stalin—slithered across the boards. As the archetypal hero, Roosevelt held center stage. To the side, Johnson played a lesser role, but it was hardly insignificant. Defending civil liberty, he reminded his readers that the disturbing events happening elsewhere could indeed happen here.[1]

During this time, Johnson received considerable acclaim. He found himself praised in books by such Southern authors as Virginius Dabney and Clar-

---

1. GWJ, "Salute to the Flag," *BES,* October 24, 1935.

ence Cason. Mencken called Johnson "one of the most competent newspaper men in America," whose "work has been characterized by unfailing excellence." The College of Charleston awarded Johnson an honorary doctorate, as did the University of North Carolina, Chapel Hill, and the University of the South. In bad times, Johnson's career prospered.[2]

Harper's Magazine played a significant part in the growth of Johnson's reputation. This monthly served him as well as the *Mercury* had during the previous decade. Throughout 1931, Johnson used *Harper's* to discuss a variety of topics besides the foibles of the Agrarians. He decried the effects of Puritanism, criticized both jingoists and pacifists, and criticized what he saw as the country's lack of political leadership.[3]

He wrote just as aggressively in the *Evening Sun* about some of the same issues. The civil libertarian decried the shameful war upon blacks in the South. Insisting upon equal protection under the law for all Americans, he used a column scathingly entitled "Dixie's Outdoor Sport" to excoriate the lynching of eighteen African Americans the previous year. This was a symptom, he argued, of "thoroughly rotten social conditions" and "rotting minds." Attacking blue laws and Prohibition, he declared that "people are rarely made good by being made miserable; and they are never made good by being forbidden and forcibly prevented from being bad." This inveterate defender of free speech pointed out that "no American who really believes in Jeffersonian theories can approve the forceful suppression of an idea."[4]

Growing increasingly disenchanted with Herbert Hoover, Johnson scoffed at the president's inability to respond forcefully to the Depression. On the other hand, Johnson argued, as he had earlier, that the Depression was not as serious as the doomsayers claimed. He predicted that the stock market

2. Virginius Dabney, *Liberalism in the South* (Chapel Hill: University of North Carolina Press, 1932), 390; Clarence Cason, *90° in the Shade* (Chapel Hill: University of North Carolina Press, 1935), 49; H. L. Mencken to Mrs. F. N. Gibson, November 7, 1932, HLM Papers.

3. GWJ, "The Policeman's Bed of Roses," in *America-Watching: Perspectives in the Course of an Incredible Century* (Owings Mills, Md.: Stemmer House, 1976), 735–39; GWJ, "For Ignoble Pacifism," in *America-Watching: Perspectives in the Course of an Incredible Century* (Owings Mills, Md.: Stemmer House, 1976), 53–58; GWJ, "Bryan, Thou Shouldst Be Living at This Hour," in *America-Watching: Perspectives in the Course of an Incredible Century* (Owings Mills, Md.: Stemmer House, 1976), 46–53.

4. GWJ, "Dixie's Outdoor Sport," *BES,* December 3, 1931; GWJ, "Good Opinion of the Law," *BES,* January 29, 1931; GWJ, "Perjured Scoundrels," *BES,* October 1, 1931; GWJ, "The Human Touch," *BES,* April 2, 1931; GWJ, "Faint-Hearted Americans," *BES,* April 23, 1931.

would rise and pointed out that, in comparison with other world powers, America was still "in excellent condition." He bemoaned the fact that his fellow citizens were "harried and worried, anxious and blue." He thought that public charity was not a reasonable strategy (he acknowledged the psychological effects of the "dole") and called instead for generosity from the private sector. Hence, Johnson in 1931 still underestimated the effects of the Depression—he was hardly alone in this—and was obviously determined to resist playing Jeremiah.[5]

He closed the year with another evocative Christmas column, entitled "Magicians," in which he skillfully combined his lament for the passing of youth and innocence with his concern for those affected by hard times. His daughters were then eight and seven, still young enough to believe in magic. Like all parents, he wanted this sacred time to last forever: "We acquire the melancholy wisdom of the world soon enough." But he knew all too well that "in a few swift years . . . the magic will be forever beyond our capacity." As he looked over the American scene, he remarked that "it is impossible to estimate the number of men who have been prevented from suicide because their children have not given them time to realize how miserable they are." Unfortunately, as the Depression worsened during 1932, such misery would increase appreciably. [6]

Unemployment reached thirteen million, and the show *Americana* featured the haunting lyrics and plaintive melody of "Brother, Can You Spare a Dime?" The Bonus Army camped in Washington that summer, and Johnson expressed sympathy for the plight of these veterans who had fought in World War I. He criticized President Hoover's hesitancy to leave the White House: "So the country was presented with the edifying spectacle of the President of the United States treed by his army!"[7]

For a time, Johnson still tried to be upbeat about the economy. In early May, he used a nautical trope to insist that America was relatively well off: "Europe is struggling to keep the Ship of State afloat. We have no more to do than scrape off a few barnacles." He moralistically decried the bad habits of the 1920s and spoke of the toning effects of adversity. As the year wore

5. GWJ, "The Grand Almoner," *BES,* August 27, 1931; GWJ, "New Humanism in the White House," *BES,* February 5, 1931; GWJ, "The Coming Bedlamite," *BES,* January 15, 1931; GWJ, "The Poor Rich Country," *BES,* March 26, 1931; GWJ, "The Scotch Litany," *BES,* November 26, 1931.

6. GWJ, "Magicians," *BES,* December 24, 1931.

7. GWJ, "Treed!" *BES* July 21, 1932.

on, however, Johnson finally admitted that America's economic machinery needed to be "overhauled," and his Christmas column acknowledged that "not within the memory of this generation have we needed Christmas worse." Significantly, the election that November did not cause Johnson to see President Roosevelt as the answer to America's problems. The writer's conversion would come later, after the Hundred Days began.[8]

During 1932, Johnson proved far more certain about Southern "poor white trash" and the racial situation than he did about Roosevelt. A response to the recent report of the Southern Commission on the Study of Lynching, "Note on Race Prejudice" turned out to be one of Johnson's more provocative essays on the issue of color, for it offers the startling opinion that race prejudice has its benefits. "To say a word in behalf of race prejudice . . . ," the opponent of Prohibition and the devil's advocate opens this essay, "is almost as outlandish a thing as to express a desire for the return of the old-fashioned saloon."

Paradoxically, he points to "the need of revivifying and strengthening the race prejudice" of the South. Prosperous Southerners, he observes, do not lynch. The smaller the economic differences are between the races, the more the "poor white trash" and "Crackers" are prone to violence against blacks. The white man rules the world, Johnson explains without approbation, because "in his combination of strength, cunning, and ferocity he is superior to any other race. He is, if you choose, the wickedest man alive." Given this, the "sermons and soda-water" of the well-intentioned prove far less effective than "a pass book in every white man's pocket." Only then, Johnson explains, is his "race prejudice so inflated that he can, with tolerant scorn, leave the Negro criminal to the police."[9]

This essay is marked by Johnson's typical love of paradox. So often the moralist, he eschews the moral argument here in favor of the economic one.

8. GWJ, "No Better Than Foreigners," *BES,* May 5, 1932; GWJ, "Aunt Clarcy," *BES,* May 26, 1932; GWJ, "Of Dictators," *BES,* June 9, 1932; GWJ, "A Lad with Ideas," *BES,* September 16, 1932; GWJ, "And None Too Soon," *BES,* December 22, 1932; GWJ, "The Patient Runs Amok," *BES,* November 10, 1932. The last-mentioned article is discussed in John T. Kneebone, *Southern Liberal Journalists and the Issue of Race, 1920–1944* (Chapel Hill: University of North Carolina Press, 1985), 117–18.

9. GWJ, "Note on Race Prejudice," *North American Review* 233 (March 1932): 226–33. See Michael Kirkhorn, "Gerald W. Johnson (6 August 1980–22 August 1980)," in *Dictionary of Literary Biography,* vol. 29: *American Newspaper Journalists, 1926–1980,* ed. Perry J. Ashley (Detroit: Gale Research, 1984), 134.

A liberal and egalitarian, Johnson ignores the more conventional liberal position to stress racial differences rather than similarities. "Note on Race Prejudice" was surely not what some of his readers expected. As John T. Kneebone has explained, Will W. Alexander, the executive director of the Commission on Interracial Cooperation, had planned to ask Johnson to write a book on the findings of the Southern Commission on the Study of Lynching. Alexander, though, read "Note on Race Prejudice" with "consternation" and decided that Johnson "would not do."[10] While Johnson had criticized racial violence, he had done so in an unconventional, irreverent manner.

As always, controversy failed to bother him. In fact, during the following year, Johnson would scoff once more at "sermons and soda-water." He would use this phrase ironically as the title of his final chapter in *The Secession of the Southern States,* a volume whose conclusion many Southerners and Yankees surely found heretical: the Civil War could have been avoided and was not worth the cost. Indeed, both books published during 1933, *Secession* and *Number Thirty-Six,* an autobiographical novel, demonstrated Johnson's concern with the past—his country's, his region's, and his own.

Johnson had very definite ideas about the historian's job. Not all historical writing need be exhaustive; there was a place for an impressionistic chronicling of events and attitudes. The historian should never fear disputation; there was a need, Johnson argued, for "more well-supported controversy in American historical writing." Stressing the importance of style, he remarked waggishly that "maybe it would be no bad idea for scholars to withdraw and leave the business of writing history to poets. After all, Hesiod and Homer made a fairly lasting impression." Good historical writing, he proclaimed, makes "first-rate reading."[11] All of these tenets—the selective chronicling of what interested Johnson particularly, the generation of controversy, and the spinning out of a highly readable tale—are evident throughout *Secession,* a brief volume of 145 pages that remains accessible to the common reader.

Regarding the causes of the war, Johnson begins his foreword disputatiously. After quoting Charles Francis Adams—"Everybody, in short, was

10. Kneebone, *Southern Liberal Journalists,* 84–85.

11. GWJ, "Thomas Lamont—Who Was Usually Right There When Big Things Happened," *NYHTB,* August 26, 1951, p. 5; GWJ, "Did a 'Grey Eminence' Stand Behind Most Strong Presidents?" *NYHTB,* February 2, 1960, p. 3; GWJ, "A Child of the Times Looks at the 30s," *NYHTB,* May 26, 1963, pp. 4, 15; GWJ, "This Is What We Mean by America," *NYHTB,* May 28, 1944, p. 3.

·

right; no one was wrong"—Johnson argues that "the truth is just the reverse of this statement. Everybody, in short, was wrong; no one was right." Secession, in Johnson's view, was essentially "a bawdy farce." With his penchant for ironic reversal, he draws upon *Macbeth* to argue that "it was a day of delirium, when small men sat in the seats of the mighty and madmen thrust the wise from the councils. It was a tragedy, certainly, but it was also filled with grisly humor. For the bloodiest-minded among those who fired the witches' cauldron were intensely pious!" Angered by so much needless slaughter, Johnson uses *Secession* to explain what happens when self-righteous individuals try to play God, when stubborn men refuse to believe that they can be wrong.[12]

Chapter 1, "The Event," begins with the Constitutional Convention in 1787 and ends with the withdrawal of the eleven Confederate States in 1861. Johnson calls the Constitution a "patchwork compromise" that is "full of flaws and weaknesses" and complains that men "insisted upon viewing it by the doctrine of verbal inspiration." Discussing the causes of Secession, he acknowledges that slavery, the tariff, and industrialism were "contributing" factors but argues that "the architect and builder was a statesmanship that had lost contact with the realities of the world." In criticizing Southern statesmanship, he echoes what he had said previously in *The Undefeated*. Moreover, in designating slavery as a "contributing" factor rather than a primary cause of the Civil War, he once again takes a position that exposes him to attack. While Johnson found slavery to be wrong as well as economically ruinous for the South, he would never conclude that the South fought the Civil War primarily to defend this institution. Johnson closes by arguing that, given the huge differences between North and South in manpower and industrial capacity, it was a "miracle" that the Confederacy lasted as long as it did. It is here, in some of the volume's more cogent prose, that the polemicist steps aside and the eulogist enters. Johnson memorializes the immense achievement of the Confederate forces, "a story written by officers who were masters of their trade and troops whose courage and devotion have never been surpassed since armed men first drew up in the order for battle." Broadening his vision, he asserts that "this much, at least, can be said of the Civil War—at the first touch of the flame of that fiery furnace, the clowns, charlatans, and frauds, the men of paper and paste, shriveled and vanished, and the men who

---

12. GWJ, *The Secession of the Southern States,* Great Occasions Series (New York: G. P. Putnam's Sons, 1933), 13, 15, 18, 19; see Kneebone, *Southern Liberal Journalists,* 102.

marched through and came out the other side were the iron men." The soldiers, not the statesmen, were the heroes.[13]

Synthesizing American history, Johnson explains that "what happened, in brief, was that the North and the South contrived to effect an unnatural and vicious cleavage between the law and the prophets. The South had the law and the North the prophets." This cleavage provides the structure and the titles for Chapters 2 and 3. Both vilify the plethora of well-intentioned but dangerous individuals. Among Southern politicians, Johnson chastises John Calhoun for his "rigid legalism," for understanding "everything about the Constitution except what made it work." Johnson observes that Nat Turner, the leader of that storied slave revolt, " 'cultivated fasting and prayer and reading of the Bible' when he was not actively engaged in the gentle pastime of splitting the skulls of school children with an axe." (One reader found this the book's most memorable sentence.) The Yankees responsible for the carnage are drawn with similar flair. Loathing abolitionists, Johnson says that William Lloyd Garrison "never doubted for a moment that his was the right, and duty, to instruct God how to rearrange the universe." Johnson remarks pointedly that "human bondage was not confined to the South," and that Harriet Beecher Stowe, the author of *Uncle Tom's Cabin* and, in the words of Abraham Lincoln, "the little lady who made this great war," was herself a slave to the puritanical attitudes of her father, Lyman Beecher. She had never, Johnson wryly observes, "seen a cabin belonging to Uncle Tom or any other slave," and he regards her pious pronouncement that "God wrote" the novel as the proclamation of a lunatic.[14]

In *Secession*'s conclusion, Johnson assesses the damage done to both North and South. "It is now almost seventy years," he explains, "since the fighting stopped; but the solution of many of the problems it created is not yet in sight." However, he concludes this engrossing story not as a dirge but as a cautionary tale. Beware of "holy men," Johnson warns his readers, for they are "poor guides for a nation of sinners." The *New York Herald Tribune* called *Secession* "a masterpiece of historical interpretation" and announced that "it should be studied by every intelligent American citizen and explained to those who are not so intelligent."[15]

13. GWJ, *Secession*, 25, 27, 46–47.
14. *Ibid.*, 53, 57, 59, 66, 100, 124–25, 81; Wingate Johnson to GWJ, December 2, 1933, GWJ Papers.
15. GWJ, *Secession*, 131; Avery Craven, "Merchants of Hate," *NYHTB*, December 3, 1933.

Johnson used *Number Thirty-Six* to reflect not upon the causes of the war but rather upon himself and the South that helped to make him what he was. With few exceptions, the novel follows the pattern of Johnson's life. The fictional Rogersville is modeled on Thomasville, and the novel takes its title from the train that so enthralled the young Johnson. Traveling from Atlanta to Washington, this was "the crack train of the whole system, as modern as the new century," and it serves as an obvious symbol of escape throughout the book. This novel can be grouped with what Fred Hobson has called the "literature of self-exploration," in which "the talented, sensitive Southerner, who left home, or even remained, wrote his own obligatory self-study." Almost inevitably, Johnson's second novel was compared to Thomas Wolfe's *Look Homeward, Angel,* which had appeared four years before and created such an uproar in Asheville.[16]

Johnson, at forty-three, uses the novel to give thanks and to reflect upon what has been lost. He is grateful for the family that loved him unconditionally and so valued education. Looking back from middle age, he glories in his youth—the romance of the train, the pure joy of the swimming hole, and "the idyll of the countryside"—a time that, like many people, he failed to appreciate until it had fled. "We walked in Eden," he has one character say portentously to Donald Whyte Watson, the protagonist modeled upon the author, ". . . and never suspected where we were."[17]

Johnson also uses the novel to contemplate a number of subjects discussed in his journalism and his essays. Throughout, he critiques the South's failings: its "burden of respectability," its tendency toward philistinism, its refusal to face facts, and its xenophobia. Decrying the perverse effects of Fundamentalism, Johnson lampoons the "Reverend Thunderbolt Sims," very simian in appearance, and suggests that the Fundamentalists attract only those followers of arrested evolutionary development.[18] Moreover, he portrays the differences between the Old South and the New. Finally, this Southerner who chose to head north ponders the implications of emigration.

Johnson's treatment of the Old South climaxes fittingly with a funeral. Wounded fighting with Jeb Stuart, Major Marshall is regarded as "the biggest man in Rogersville." His service, held in the midst of "flying mist and rain,"

16. GWJ, *Number Thirty-Six: A Novel* (New York: Minton, Balch, 1933), 6; Fred Hobson, *Tell About the South: The Southern Rage to Explain* (Baton Rouge: Louisiana State University Press, 1983), 306; "Gerald Johnson Pictures Local Life in New Novel," *LD,* April 13, 1933.

17. GWJ, *Number Thirty-Six,* 40, 266.

18. *Ibid.,* 144, 218–19, 76, 82–84.

is marked by the inevitable tolling of a bell. Literally the funeral for an individual, the service figuratively represents the end of an era, of another way of life. Moved, as Johnson was, by the heroism of the Confederate soldiers, Donald knows that it is time to look ahead, past this gathering of old people around a wet grave: "The Army of the Confederate States of America. Back in the mists of the past it loomed, gigantic. But it belonged to the mist, it belonged to the past, and in the present it was but a wreath of fog blown across the world by every wind."[19] More experienced novelists have written worse scenes.

While the passing of the Old South is inevitable, neither Donald nor his creator is enthralled by the New South that follows. Cotton mills come to Rogersville, the brainchild of Sam Hoover, a telegraph operator who is drawn as both a Babbitt and a Judas figure. Industrialism exacts a heavy toll. Nature is destroyed; the region is homogenized, and the pace of life speeds up uncomfortably. The daughters of a poor and disgraced family are driven into prostitution. After the poorly paid textile workers go on strike, the owners employ scabs, and violence ensues. Maria Whitsett, a labor sympathizer, is publicly shot down, and the reader thinks here of Ella May Wiggins. (The similarity in the names' initials hardly seems coincidental.) In his journalism, Johnson scoffed at industrialism as a profanation of true religion, and here he has Judge Neale, the book's iconoclast, liken industrialism to the "Golden Calf" and snort about "dividends and holiness." Significantly, Johnson criticizes industrialism more stridently in this novel than he does anywhere in his debate with the Agrarians. While it is a fait accompli, it is no panacea for the ills of the South.[20]

Margie Blair, an actress who has left Rogersville for the stage in New York City, exhorts Donald to leave and test himself in the North. Tempted, he decides to remain, convinced that he can do more good for his region from nearby than from afar. Johnson is Ulysses the voyager; his protagonist is Telemachus, the dutiful son of the South who stays behind to show his people the useful and the good.[21]

This, however, proves no easy task. The novel concludes symbolically on a "dreary, drizzly day." Donald the journalist ponders his dilemma: backing the industrialists will "pay handsomely in blood money," while backing the

19. *Ibid.,* 138, 140.
20. *Ibid.,* 163, 69, 263, 247, 243, 308, 93–94.
21. *Ibid.,* 208.

strikers will cause the political radicals to heap acclaim upon him. He wants neither and explains his difficulties to Judge Neale. The wise old man remarks that Donald has "at last . . . grown up" and benevolently instructs him: "Come in out of the wet, son." Resisting the easy, upbeat conclusion, Johnson shows that there is no safe harbor, no place of grace, and that the truth which can set one free does not always bring comfort. The novel received considerable, and very positive, coverage in the North Carolina press and was later reissued in a British edition.[22]

Throughout 1933, Johnson the daily journalist was confronted by events considerably more pressing than the factors underlying Secession and the fictional universe of Donald Whyte Watson. Racial violence recurred, and Johnson decried lynching on Maryland's Eastern Shore. This man who had surely bothered some of his readers with "Note on Race Prejudice" now found himself extolled in the *Evening Sun*'s editorial mail, where a correspondent remarked that "the Negro public deeply appreciates Mr. Johnson's article."[23] The year offered other opportunities for shame as well as for amazement. With Adolf Hitler's rise to power and the inauguration of Franklin Delano Roosevelt, 1933 was marked by immense change on the American scene and immense hatred in Germany, the beginning, as we know now, of that horrific "Final Solution" in Europe. Johnson struggled, as did his fellow writers, to make sense of these momentous events. In general, he wrote more sensibly about America than he did about Germany.

Hitler was appointed chancellor on January 30 and gained dictatorial power on March 23. He excluded Jews from public service and the universities and, on April 1, instituted a national boycott of shops owned by Jews. Johnson responded quickly; while he attacked the criminal, he could have shown more sympathy for the victim. On April 6, he likened Hitler's philosophy to that of the Klan (a comparison that would be made repeatedly) and argued that it was "a silly and brutish negation of civilization, a stride backward toward the mentality of the ape." However, Johnson also remarked that "it is hard to believe that any rational American seriously advocates any sort

22. *Ibid.,* 314–15; Beth Chambers Holt, "North Carolina Town Is Locale of Gerald Johnson's New Novel," *Charlotte Observer,* May 26, 1933; "Gerald Johnson's New Novel Has Thomasville as New Setting," *High Point (N.C.) Enterprise,* April 30, 1933; "Gerald Johnson's 'Number Thirty-Six,' " *Greensboro Record,* May 8, 1933; GWJ to Charles Lambeth, May 25, 1979, in the possession of Mr. Lambeth, Thomasville, N.C.

23. GWJ, "Lynching as an Art," *BES,* October 26, 1933; Sarah I. Sampson, "An Appreciation of Mr. Johnson's Article on Lynching," *BES,* October 31, 1933.

of official intervention in behalf of the Jews. After all, they are Hitler's Jews, and if he is fool enough to destroy a valuable element of the citizenship in his country, so much the worse for him. It is not our affair." On October 5, Johnson asserted that "the Jew-baiting in Germany is only an incident. . . . The campaign against the Jews is Hitler's method of rabble-rousing. Had the Jews not been available, he would have chosen someone else." This column also made two huge errors in prognostication. First, Johnson claimed that "once the Nazi government is thoroughly intrenched, it will probably quit bedeviling the Jews." Second, although he recognized long before most Americans did that this country could well end up fighting another war with Germany, he badly underestimated the opponent: "It is impossible to believe that the Germans would hold out as long under Hitler as they did under the Kaiser."[24] He miscalculated by seventeen months, a period of immense cost in both military casualties and civilian deaths.

Lest it need saying, Johnson was no anti-Semite, either personally or professionally. It can be said in his defense that he was hardly alone in underestimating the destructive power of anti-Semitism in Germany and counseling against what he then saw as unwarranted intervention.[25] However, this matter finally transcends such an historical defense. Reading these columns today, especially a proclamation such as "it is not our affair," one feels chilled. Subsequent history, the all-but-unspeakable results of that power of darkness, has freighted Johnson's remarks with an import that he could not then anticipate. He was wrong about Germany and the Jews, as wrong as he would ever be as a journalist about a major issue. To his credit, he did not stay wrong.

As he had done with Hitler's rise to power, Johnson responded quickly to President Roosevelt's strategies to resuscitate the economy. Johnson admitted that, on the Monday morning following the inauguration on Saturday, March 4, "the country awoke to find the air so full of dust and feathers that ordinary citizens were completely befogged." However, he praised the Bank Holiday and the president's willingness to "take a chance." The next month, Johnson acknowledged that Roosevelt had been given "dictatorial powers." However, with his fondness for paradox, he argued that the granting of such powers "furnishes the best evidence that democracy in this country is likely

24. William Shirer, *The Rise and Fall of the Third Reich* (New York: Fawcett, 1966), 283; GWJ, "Pseudo-Mussolini," *BES,* April 6, 1933, quoted in Kneebone, *Southern Liberal Journalists,* 168; GWJ, "Beloved Chains," *BES,* October 5, 1933, quoted in Kneebone, *Southern Liberal Journalists,* 177. See also GWJ, "The University in Exile," *BES,* July 27, 1933.

25. Kneebone, *Southern Liberal Journalists,* 176–81.

to survive for such a long time." Seeking precedents for Roosevelt's activities, Johnson pointed to Andrew Jackson's quelling of Nullification in 1832, Lincoln's decisive response to the hostilities in 1861, and Woodrow Wilson's decision to enter World War I. Less than six weeks after Roosevelt's inauguration, Johnson proclaimed that he "will take his place with Grover Cleveland and Andrew Jackson in the national Valhalla," just a step below Washington, Lincoln, and Wilson.[26] Henceforth, Johnson would never seriously question the president. In fact, as Johnson's hagiography increased, Roosevelt would ascend to the highest platform in the American pantheon. Johnson's commentary would play well to a reading public that, as the voting records suggest, overwhelmingly embraced Roosevelt's programs, but it would also exasperate fiscal conservatives, anger those who embraced the traditional American doctrine of self-reliance, and conflict with the editorial policy of his employer.

Given the tenor of the times, it is hardly surprising that most of Johnson's writing during 1934 was marked by utter seriousness. Surveying the effects of the Depression, he spoke sadly about the "derelicts and drifters," the "flotsam and jetsam"; citing the tale of the Good Samaritan, he urged his readers to show compassion. Looking homeward, Johnson again excoriated lynching, "the repudiation of brains and the enthronement of the empty skull"; he implored intelligent Southerners to take responsibility for their communities. As he surveyed Europe, Johnson vilified National Socialism: "All liberty ground into the mud under hobnailed boots. All intelligence publicly mocked by uniformed morons. All science, art, literature subverted to the political purposes of a house painter." He decried the "filthy business of arms manufacturing." And on the twentieth anniversary of the assassination at Sarajevo, he lamented that the current world situation was "sickeningly similar" and said that "there is not a responsible statesman in Europe who isn't well persuaded that [another first-class war] is coming."[27]

26. GWJ, "Psalms CXLVII:10," *BES,* March 10, 1933; GWJ, "Resilient Democracy," *BES,* April 13, 1933. For more of Johnson's commentary in the *Evening Sun* during this first year of the New Deal, see "Contemporary Ancestors," May 18; "Citizens Have Mercy," May 25, quoted in Kneebone, *Southern Liberal Journalists,* 121; "No More Blah," June 22; "The Master of the Ship," July 6, quoted in Kneebone, *Southern Liberal Journalists,* 118; "Variation on an Old Theme," August 3, discussed in Kneebone, *Southern Liberal Journalists,* 130.

27. GWJ, "We Have to Do It," *BES,* October 25, 1934; GWJ, "Red-Letter Day," *BES*; GWJ, "Speaking of Lynchers," *BES,* February 22, 1934; GWJ, "In Germany—and Here," *BES,* July 6, 1934,; GWJ, "International Jack Ketch," *BES,* September 20, 1934; GWJ, "Incident on a Dull Night," *BES,* June 28, 1934.

The major exception to such seriousness was "What an Old Girl Should Know," Johnson's romp through the issue of gender. He concerns himself here with the status and the foibles of the American woman past forty. Foreigners, he explains, have failed to comment intelligently on this matter, and most Americans have chosen (prudently, he admits) to avoid the issue. Recalling his Alexander Pope, Johnson waggishly proclaims that "while the angels quake in their sandals," he "is going to rush in where it is too hot for them."[28]

The typical American woman past forty, Johnson explains laughingly, must learn that "she owes society some reasonable excuse for cluttering up the world and occupying space that might better be devoted to some object of value—a petunia plant, say, or a jimson weed." After mocking her lack of manners, Johnson scoffs at her mindless social climbing and lampoons "the vast armies of incessant bridge-players, tea-drinkers, and gabblers of the suburbs." The "old girl" must learn, in this year after Repeal, "how to drink or how to refuse a drink gracefully." She must learn how to tell the poseurs and the dilettantes from the artists of merit and "give the bum's rush" to the quacks. She must learn "a great deal more than she does [about] sex education," and the answer lies in "less Freud and more Rabelais." Relishing the absurd, Johnson suggests that the best response to the age-old battle of the sexes is to guffaw rather than to accuse or complain. Willing to don the garb of a clown, that wise fool without fear, Johnson was determined, it seems, to have some fun and to stir up his readers. One editorial writer in Alabama called him "extremely brave."[29]

Unfortunately, the final week of 1934 gave Johnson cause to grieve rather than to jest. Archibald Johnson's health had been failing for several years, and Gerald had been assisting his father by contributing unsigned editorials to *Charity and Children*. Archibald died, at age seventy-five, in the early morning of December 27, and Gerald made the somber journey down from Baltimore on the train. The funeral service was held the next day at the First Baptist Church in Thomasville, and Archibald was buried that afternoon in the Spring Hill Cemetery outside Riverton.[30]

28. GWJ, "What an Old Girl Should Know," in *America-Watching: Perspectives in the Course of an Incredible Century* (Owings Mills, Md.: Stemmer House, 1976), 68–76.

29. "Only the Brave Would Say It," *Montgomery (Ala.) Independent,* April 4, 1934.

30. Lois Johnson, interview by author, tape recording, Southern Pines, N.C., August 15, 1989; W. R. Cullom, "Archibald Johnson, 1859–1934," GWJ Papers; Kathryn Johnson Sliger, telephone interview by author, from Valparaiso, Ind., February 4, 1997.

Way back in 1896, as a boy of six with all of his life ahead of him, Johnson had journeyed from Riverton to Thomasville, following Archibald to his new job at the Baptist Orphanage and its newspaper. Now a writer of national renown at forty-four, Johnson made the journey in reverse, taking that ghastly trip to the cemetery behind the coffin of a parent. Surely, this awful symmetry was not lost upon him. Theirs had been an exemplary father-son relationship. They had agreed far more often than they had differed. There had been no strife; rather, there had been love and a mutual respect, with each taking pride in the other's considerable achievements. When he joined his ancestors, Archibald left behind a legacy of consequence—not in worldly goods, which never really interested either father or son, but rather in that mission which marked each man's career: the need to speak for those incapable of speaking for themselves. Gerald paid Archibald the son's ultimate compliment of modeling the father's values.

As Johnson assessed the land of his ancestors during the year after his father's death, he found a number of values, in both literature and politics, that disturbed him. He was bothered by what he saw as the gory sensationalism of some of the South's most celebrated novelists. At the beginning of "The Horrible South," 1935's most significant essay, Johnson quotes from "The Congo, Mr. Mencken" and wonders if, twelve years later, Southern literature still has "the pulse of tom-toms in its veins." Delighted with his prophetic skills, he finds barbaric qualities in the fiction of T. S. Stribling, Thomas Wolfe, William Faulkner, and Erskine Caldwell. Johnson dubs these novelists "the merchants of death, hell, and the grave" and the "horror-mongers in chief." However, he proceeds to admire the novelists' bravery in "[grappling] courageously and vigorously with the problems of the modern South." Yoking olfactory images to motifs of death and fertility, Johnson remarks that, while the South's recent literature "stinks . . . with the odors of the barnyard," its "pretty literature of thirty years ago had a different smell; it reeked of . . . funeral flowers. An undertaker's parlor, banked with floral designs, smells sweeter than a compost heap, but death is in the midst of one, and the promise of a golden harvest in the other."[31] "The Horrible South" proves as significant a statement about literature as "Note on Race Prejudice" and "What an Old Girl Should Know" do about color and gender. Iconoclastic performances all, they show Johnson's refusal to opt for the safety of the fold.

31. GWJ, "The Horrible South," in *South-Watching: Selected Essays by Gerald W. Johnson,* ed. Fred Hobson (Chapel Hill: University of North Carolina, 1983), 29–42.

Looking at the Deep South, Johnson was bothered by the values of Huey P. Long, former governor of Louisiana and, since 1932, a United States senator. In April, Johnson called Long a "serious menace to the democratic system." On the other hand, Johnson acknowledged Long's considerable achievement in the field of public works and said that he had done more for his constituents than had any other Louisiana senator since the Civil War. Long's assassination on September 8 led Johnson to reassess the career. While he questioned both Long's integrity and his methods, Johnson remarked that Long "has the distinction of having injected more realism into Southern politics than any other man of his generation. Huey made millions of Southerners think of the political problems of 1935 as something quite different from those of 1865. Huey really counted."[32]

While he was disturbed by aspects of contemporary Southern fiction, Johnson resisted the easy but erroneous conclusion that the depiction of the violent and perverse has no redeeming qualities. While he found some aspects of Long's career odious, Johnson refused to caricature him as nothing more than a gaudy demagogue, presiding over an unruly kingdom, who met his inevitable demise. In brief, both the controversial novelists and the controversial politician effected some good. Lynching, on the other hand, continued to generate Johnson's unqualified contempt. He again censured those respectable citizens who refused to participate but declined to intervene, and he likened the violence against blacks in the South to the anti-Jewish activities in Germany.[33] Johnson was outraged as well by the abuse heaped upon President Roosevelt by his Southern detractors. They were, in Johnson's view, blind men filled with hate, and he scorned them in one of his most clever and cogent columns, a piece which showed once more that the events in Tennessee the previous decade remained very much on Johnson's mind.

In "A New Dayton," Johnson complained that "in the South something approaching the virulence released by the Scopes trial . . . has been evoked by the New Deal." Scopes's "real offense" lay not in teaching forbidden material but rather in "upsetting the accepted beliefs of the community and threatening it with the necessity of finding a new set of dogma and tradition."

32. GWJ, "How Many Louisianas?" *BES,* April 25, 1935; GWJ, "An Evaluation of Huey," *BES,* April 27, 1939; GWJ, "Waste in Louisiana," *BES,* September 19, 1935; GWJ, "Live Demagogue or Dead Gentleman?" *VQR* 12 (January 1936): 1–15, discussed in Kneebone, *Southern Liberal Journalists,* 111–12.

33. GWJ, "Comment on Lynching," *BES,* April 4, 1935. For further criticism by Johnson of Hitler's treatment of the Jews, see "Diminishing Error," *BES,* August 15, 1935.

A decade later, President Roosevelt engaged in a similar enterprise. Johnson explained that the New Dealers, "while stealing no money, have stolen something which is infinitely more valuable, to wit, the South's implicit faith in the verbal inspiration of of the gospel as it was delivered to Adam Smith in 1776. What Scopes did to Genesis, the New Deal has done to 'The Wealth of Nations.' " Scorning the "political Fundamentalists," Johnson skillfully divided the South into two opposing camps. On the one side were the reactionaries, who obstinately endorsed Fundamentalism and laissez-faire economics. On the other were those people of sense and foresight who refused to interpret the Bible literally and who acknowledged that New Deal economics superseded the old economics of scarcity. Johnson had to be pleased with "A New Dayton," but he could not then anticipate that, in the fall of 1936, the very newspaper that printed this clever copy would respond to the New Deal in a way that he would find exasperating. For a variety of reasons, 1936 would prove especially eventful.[34]

The international scene did not make Johnson sanguine. When the Spanish Civil War broke out that summer, Johnson predictably supported the Republicans and attacked the forces of General Franco as "the heel of military despotism." The extensive coverage of the Berlin Olympics showed beyond argument the scope of German militarism. In September, he argued that "steadily the evidence increases that the long-predicted war is already on. It was, he explained, "a triangular war of fascism against communism and both against democracy. Democracy, so far, is the worst hit of the combatants." In late December, he offered the melancholy conjecture that this could well prove the last Christmas of peace.[35]

Throughout 1936, he warned that the totalitarianism afflicting Europe could well happen in America. He scorned a New Jersey judge who denied child custody to a mother who admitted that she was a Communist and praised "the old American ideal which guarantees every man the right to bray like a jackass if he is fool enough to do so." He denounced the proposition that teachers be made to submit to loyalty oaths and repeatedly argued that no American has the right to inflict his views upon another. "The core of

34. GWJ, "A New Dayton," *BES,* May 25, 1935.

35. GWJ, "Cervantes on His Galley," *BES,* August 13, 1936, cited by Kneebone, *Southern Liberal Journalists,* 268; GWJ, "The War Is On," *BES,* September 24, 1936, quoted in Kneebone, *Southern Liberal Journalist,* 182; GWJ, "At Christmas Unashamed," *BES,* December 24, 1936.

Americanism," he explained, lay in Cromwell's advice to the Scotch Presbyterians: "Pray God to show you that it is possible for you to be mistaken."[36]

Johnson was not mistaken, he remained convinced, about "the dead doctrine of States' Rights" and the need for a strong federal government. Quoting Jefferson's famous remark that "the mass of mankind has not been born with saddles on their backs, nor a favorite few booted and spurred," Johnson argued that Roosevelt did not break with Jefferson's theories about democracy and continued to praise the bold measures of the New Deal. During that spring, Herbert Hoover was being considered as the Republican presidential candidate, and Johnson scoffed that "even in the midst of the plunge into the abyss he was able to make the country yawn."[37]

The *Evening Sun* was hardly attracted to the soporific Hoover. In general, its editorial policy was more favorable to Roosevelt than was that of its morning counterpart. However, on July 28 the *Evening Sun* reprinted an earlier editorial (published before Johnson had joined the staff) whose implications surely seemed ominous to him. "Of all the evils threatening this country today," the editorial argued, "the greatest is the constant inflation of government." The *Evening Sun,* the editorial argued, "is a firm believer in old-fashioned economics. It has an abiding faith in the law of supply and demand, and it resents any interference by the Government with that law." Traditionally, both papers endorsed Jeffersonian liberalism and were skeptical of all reformers.[38]

Among the *Evening Sun*'s columnists, Mencken set forth this position most forcefully. He, Walter Lippmann, and Dorothy Thompson were among the most recognized national critics of the New Deal. From the inception of the Hundred Days, Mencken spoke repeatedly about the futility of robbing Peter to pay Paul. He insisted that any bill, no matter how adeptly postponed, must ultimately fall due and be paid. Mencken also undertook a larger accounting, and the dispute with the president transcended the issue of deficit spending. Mencken never doubted that, once the mentality of the dole was established, continued expectations of public assistance would erode the

36. GWJ, "Uzzah in New Jersey," *BES,* January 30, 1936; GWJ, "Away from Americanism," *BES,* February 13, 1936; GWJ, "Holy Traitors," *BES,* April 2, 1936.

37. GWJ, "Fading States," *BES,* December 3, 1936; GWJ, "Hamiltonian Consistency," *BES,* June 18, 1936; GWJ, "He May Know Best—But," *BES,* April 16, 1936.

38. Harold A. Williams, *The Baltimore Sun, 1837–1987* (Baltimore: Johns Hopkins University Press, 1987), 241–44; editorial, *BES,* July 28, 1936, quoted in Johnson et al., *The Sunpapers of Baltimore, 1837–1937* (New York: Knopf, 1937), 390–91.

American work ethic. Believing above all in self-reliance, he concluded that the New Deal robbed people of their self-respect, and he called it "a complete repudiation of the traditional American moral system." Mencken never questioned that the strong person's gain marks the weak person's loss, and that to destroy the threat of failure is also to destroy incentive. With his fundamental pessimism, he regarded the New Deal as an abomination. He shook his head vigorously and responded to Roosevelt as he responded to all visionaries. Your efforts to improve the scheme of things are futile, was always the gist of Mencken's rejoinder. Divide the wealth; deal the cards anew, again and again. But you will find, if you let the game naturally run its course, that the intelligent person will play proficiently and leave the table with more money than was brought, and that the incompetent player will be a chronic loser. You mean well, but you are naive and dangerous. Your efforts to restructure American society are doomed because you cannot change the nature of man. So roared Mencken in his columns on Monday night.[39]

On Thursday, Johnson spoke more quietly, but no less compellingly, for the opposition. The situation, as he saw it, was not complicated. If people submit to be governed, then the government has the responsibility to take care of them. Millions of people were out of work. Families were shattered. Breadlines were growing. Some former executives, now ruined, jumped off buildings. Others were selling pencils and apples on the street. People were sleeping out in the cold, wrapped in newspapers and huddled over heating grates. This was a chilling turn to that American experiment begun with such great expectations. The optimistic Johnson believed that something could be done, indeed had to be done, to rescue a country that had so badly lost its way. And all of the arguments about self-reliance and the work ethic and free enterprise were mere posturing, the antiquated pronouncements of misguided individuals who retreated into the past rather than face the difficulties of the present.

They were both remarkable men, this conservative Baltimorean and this liberal Tar Heel standing together at a crossroads in American history, looking in opposite directions. Neither man could have presented his position much more eloquently. For all that America has changed since then, their remarks

39. Mencken, "Utopia Eat Utopia," *BES,* August 20, 1934; Fitzpatrick, *H. L. Mencken* (New York: Continuum, 1989), 86–88; Fred Hobson, Vincent Fitzpatrick, and Bradford Jacobs, introduction to *Thirty-Five Years of Newspaper Work: A Memoir by H. L. Mencken* (Baltimore: Johns Hopkins University Press, 1994), xv.

are as relevant today as when they appeared. With Mencken and Johnson, a stunning confluence of talent at a critical time, the *Evening Sun* was glorious.

As the election of 1936 neared, Paul Patterson, the president of the *Sun* and the *Evening Sun,* grew increasingly bothered by complaints about the differences between the papers' editorial pages. On September 10, he called a meeting of the editorial staffs and showed them a copy of the editorial that would run the next day. It said that the newspaper could not endorse Roosevelt's candidacy and spoke of "the fundamental errors in [his] policies." (This broke with the tradition that had seen the newspaper endorsing the last six Democratic candidates; the next month, the paper would decline as well to support Governor Alf Landon of Kansas, the Republican candidate.) At first, Patterson's announcement met with silence. Then, as fellow North Carolinian, novelist, and *Evening Sun* writer R. P. Harriss tells the story,

> Gerald Johnson got up and said he realized this was a fait accompli but added that he thought it was the wrong decision and that he was for Roosevelt's reelection. It was a careful, reasoned statement, done in a quiet way. Then I stood up and said I associated myself with Gerald's view. No one else said a word in rebuttal, but most looked sort of sheepish. Everyone felt that Gerald had acted beautifully. Nothing dramatic, but he had made a reasoned case for the papers to support Roosevelt. Hamilton [Owens] stayed to suggest some mechanical changes in the editorial. The rest of us went back to our desks, trying to do some routine work, but felt like we had been kicked in the ass.[40]

Johnson's response was typical for him; he spurned histrionics, which he always found in bad taste, but confronted authority to say in plain language what he thought.

Although at odds with his friend philosophically, Mencken believed that Johnson should have the chance to dissent. Consequently, Mencken gave up his first "Monday Article" after the appearance of the anti-Roosevelt editorial (a noble gesture that Johnson never forgot), and in its place appeared John-

40. Williams, *The Baltimore Sun,* 241–42; Johnson et. al., *The Sunpapers of Baltimore,* 204, 430. Shortly thereafter, Johnson joined Mencken to cover Governor Landon's campaign and wrote three news stories for the *Evening Sun*: "Likeness of Jefferson Greets Landon at N.Y." (September 12), "Governor Landon Greeted by Muggy, Soggy Night" (September 13), and "Johnson Finds Landon Put in Mistaken Role in Maine" (September 14). Mencken was not impressed by the quality of Johnson's work (*Thirty-Five Years of Newspaper Work,* 296).

son's "One for Roosevelt." He thanked Mencken and the newspaper—
"They may be against Roosevelt, but they are for free speech"—and offered
a lengthy defense of the president focusing upon his courage in responding
to new conditions. Johnson argued that "the greatest service that Roosevelt
has rendered to this country [is] the introduction of intelligence into the conduct of the country's affairs." In Johnson's view, America's economic problems could not be solved "by simply relying on precept, precedent, and
tradition." Johnson also offered a few stretchers, and his anti-Roosevelt readers surely chuckled or howled when they came across the proclamations that
Roosevelt was "the great bulwark of capitalism, conservatism and democracy" and that his administration was "libertarian." Jonathan Daniels reprinted this column in the *Raleigh News and Observer,* and Johnson received
several highly laudatory letters from North Carolina. Roosevelt liked the column so much that he quoted from it in a speech that he gave in Syracuse
later that month.[41]

Although he felt gagged as an editorial writer, Johnson continued to use
his columns to support the president. In early October, Johnson called himself "a congenital Democrat and a convinced New Dealer." While he never
doubted that Roosevelt would win, Johnson was elated when the president
carried all but two states, the largest margin up to that time in the history of
American presidential elections. On election night, Johnson openly gloated
in a letter to Odum. And in the bludgeoning "Since We Are Ruined," the
column that ran the next day, Johnson's lead paragraph declared, "Well, the
end of the world has come, the republic has fallen, the Constitution is a
wreck, the judges of the Supreme Court were laid by the heels yesterday
morning, all surviving honest men are on their way to the concentration
camps in Siberia."[42] Johnson's temper had gotten in the way of his prose. It
is not hard to imagine how the newspaper's executives felt when they read
Johnson's copy. On this occasion, he was not a gracious winner.

Johnson never forgot the election of 1936 and remained disgusted by

41. Williams, *The Baltimore Sun,* 242; Jinny W. Voris, "According to Mr. Johnson: Some
Insights on H. L. Mencken," 5–6, HLM Papers; GWJ, "One for Roosevelt," *BES,* September
14, 1936; Jonathan Daniels to GWJ, September 21, 1936, GWJ Papers; Frank Hancock to
GWJ, September 15, 1936, GWJ Papers; LeGette Blythe to GWJ, September 18, 1936, GWJ
Papers; "Compliment, or Something, for Gerald," *BES,* September 30, 1936.

42. GWJ, "It Can Happen Here," *BES,* October 1, 1936; GWJ to Howard W. Odum,
November 4, 1936, GWJ Papers; GWJ, "Since We Are Ruined," *BES,* November 5, 1936.
See also GWJ, "Why Blame Al?" *BES,* October 15, 1936, *BES.*

what he saw as the newspaper's blindness about the president. In fact, as late as 1972, he would tell a correspondent that "in 1936 the *Sun* made the most ghastly mistake, journalistically, of which I have knowledge. In that year FDR was absolutely without support in any big city. A newspaper that would have come to his aid, even half-heartedly, would have been for the next 12 years *the* authoritative paper in American journalism."[43]

Johnson had left his professorship at the University of North Carolina ten and one-half years earlier to head north to Baltimore. He had been eminently successful on the *Evening Sun*. In 1936, he was earning $7,200, no mean sum during those dark days. But the money, as always, meant far less than the writing, and he was never a man who could be accused of complacency. Growing restless, he began to feel that another change was in order, and he wrote a friend that "I am quietly looking for another place to light."[44]

43. GWJ to Charles Flowers, July 25, 1972, quoted in Williams, *The Baltimore Sun,* 242.

44. Vivian Kramer, payroll manager of the *Baltimore Sun,* telephone interview by author, August 16, 1995; GWJ to Lenoir Chambers, February 20, 1937, Lenoir Chambers Papers, Southern Historical Collection, Wilson Library, University of North Carolina at Chapel Hill.

"The House That Jack Built," Riverton, N.C.
Photograph by Emerson Humphrey, Southern Pines, N.C. Courtesy Wake Forest University

Archibald Johnson
Courtesy Wake Forest University

Flora McNeill Johnson
Courtesy Wake Forest University

Gerald W. Johnson at Wake Forest College, 1909
Courtesy Wake Forest University

Sergeant Johnson, Toulouse, France, 1919

Photograph by Jean Jaures.
Courtesy Wake Forest University

Wedding of Kathryn Hayward and Gerald White
Johnson, April 22, 1922, Greensboro, N.C.

Courtesy Wake Forest University

Family scene, Thomasville, N.C., 1923: Kathryn and Gerald Johnson with daughter Kathryn and collie King's Klinker VIII

Courtesy Wake Forest University

Johnson the Baltimore journalist, 1935

Courtesy Wake Forest University

Eminent gentlemen gather for the farewell dinner given for James Bone of the *Manchester Guardian* at Hamilton Street Club, Baltimore in November 1940. *Top row (left to right):* J. Fred Essary, J. Harry Scharf, Newton Aiken, Edmund Duffy, Paul Patterson. *Middle row:* Philip M. Wagner, A. D. Emmart, Frederic Nelson, Paul Ward, Hulbert Footner, Maclean Patterson. *Bottom row:* Hamilton Owens, August Mencken, J. Edwin Murphy, Vice-Consul Mulvaney (British vice-consul at Baltimore), James Bone, Gerald W. Johnson, H. L. Mencken, John W. Owens.

Courtesy Enoch Pratt Free Library, Baltimore

Gerald Johnson's daughter
Kathryn Hayward Johnson
at age seventeen, 1940

Photo by Olan Mills.
Courtesy Wake Forest University

Johnson's younger daughter,
Dorothy Hayward Johnson,
at age seventeen, 1941

Photo by Majestic.
Courtesy Wake Forest University

The Johnson siblings at the wedding of Dorothy Hayward Johnson and Leonard van den Honert, June 12, 1948, in Baltimore. *Left to right:* Mrs. William (Ella) Webb of Wilson, N.C.; Miss Lois Johnson; Gerald W. Johnson; Mrs. Charles (Mary) Lambeth of Thomasville, N.C.; and Mrs. B. W. (Katherine) Parham of Oxford, N.C.

Courtesy Wake Forest University

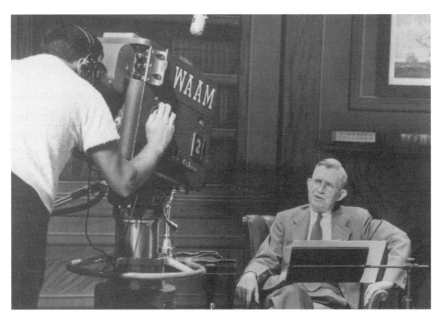

Johnson the television commentator in the studio of WAAM television, Baltimore, 1952

Courtesy Wake Forest University

Adlai Stevenson speaks at Johnson's seventieth birthday party in October 1960 at the Enoch Pratt Free Library, Baltimore.

Photo by Jack Engeman. Courtesy Wake Forest University

10 Shelter from the Storm
1937–1943

For the first time since it became a great power, this country is being tried by fire. The war of 1917–1918 was a mere holiday jaunt; it was over before we really had to extend ourselves, with the result that we learned nothing from it and permitted the same conditions to rise again—for Nazism is only Prussian militarism coarsened.

We shall hardly escape so lightly this time. What, then, will be the result of the battering? One thing will be a greatly increased respect for the prowess of our enemies, and this will generate a determination to fortify against them.

[This will] involve expansion of the United States into the greatest empire in history.

—*Gerald Johnson to Archibald Shepperson, March 14, 1942*

It was sad but inevitable. From 1937 to 1943, Johnson experienced, far more strongly than before, intimations of his own mortality. He lost Dr. William Louis Poteat, his mother, and his mother-in-law. His hearing deteriorated to the point that, in 1940, he adopted a hearing aid, a device that would accompany him for the remainder of his days. His little girls had grown up, and he and Kathryn now faced an empty nest as both daughters departed for college—Kathryn to Oberlin and Dorothy to Vassar, her mother's old school. "Senility is coming upon me rapidly," Johnson joked ruefully with a correspondent during his fiftieth year. "I look back with a sort of stupefaction on the days when I could write 'Andrew Jackson' [and] run the Evening Sun almost single-handed . . . at the same time. I wouldn't last 48 hours on that schedule now."[1] Perhaps not, but his intellectual regimen still put many a younger writer to shame.

During these seven years, he wrote or contributed to nine books, a remarkable achievement even for someone writing books full time. He was, of

1. GWJ to Harriet Herring, February 7, 1940, Harriet H. Herring Papers, Southern Historical Collection, Wilson Library, University of North Carolina at Chapel Hill.

course, still writing daily editorials and a weekly column for the newspaper. He was also publishing essays in magazines all across the land. He proved so prolific, in fact, that he saw fit to hire his first literary agent.[2]

These were not easy years, for he experienced not only time's onslaught but also an increasingly difficult situation with his employer. For five years, America continued to struggle under the pall of the Depression, and the world situation worsened. Exasperated, Johnson scoffed at those Americans who, determined to avoid involvement, dove under the bed when they heard alarming noises.[3]

As the storms swirled outside, Johnson found that proverbial room of his own, a place in which he felt particularly comfortable to watch and analyze and write. In October 1937, the Johnsons moved to a three-story, red-brick row house at 1310 Bolton Street. This neighborhood of Bolton Hill was located just northwest of the downtown commercial district, within walking distance of the newspaper and the museums and the concert hall and the Enoch Pratt Free Library. It proved a fitting home for a family that so valued culture, and Johnson would remain in this house for twenty-eight years, by far his longest residence in one location. Calling Bolton Hill "a gentleman in reduced circumstances," he explained sportively that

> half a century ago, he was the glass of fashion and the mould of form, but the advent of the horseless carriage ruined him. It took all the merchant princes and their elegant ladies out to the suburbs, and the old red-brick houses with their white-marble were, at best, turned over to a younger son, or to a brother, or an uncle, who never did so well in business. Then by degrees they fell into the hands of dubious persons, not felons, but the kind at whom a sound business man must look a little askance—doctors, Johns Hopkins professors, newspaper writers, musicians from the Peabody Conservatory, even, God save the mark, a librarian [and] a portrait painter.[4]

The neighborhood matched the man, and Johnson reveled in the camaraderie of these "dubious persons" whose values, like his own, lay outside the mainstream of mercantile America.

2. Johnson hired George T. Bye of New York City as his literary agent in 1941, and the relationship prospered until Bye's death in 1957.

3. GWJ, "Democracies Are Unstable," *BES,* August 30, 1940.

4. GWJ to Richard G. Walser, March 3, 1952, Richard Gaither Walser Papers, Southern Historical Collection, Wilson Library, University of North Carolina at Chapel Hill.

The Johnsons' social life flourished during their decades in Bolton Hill. They continued their annual holiday party begun in 1930 when they had resided on Wildey Avenue. For nineteen years, Gerald and Kathryn hosted a gathering on Christmas night that was enjoyed by a diverse and distinguished group. H. L. Mencken and his brother, August, an engineer and author, attended, as did the writer Hulbert Footner. Raymond Pearl, the renowned biologist and statistician at the Johns Hopkins University, came to Bolton Street, as did Gilbert Chinard, a much-honored Johns Hopkins professor of French and comparative literature. Curt Richter, a professor of psychobiology at the Johns Hopkins University School of Medicine, was joined by Dr. and Mrs. Thomas B. Turner. Dr. Turner would become the School of Medicine's dean. One of the most colorful guests was William Woollcott, whom everybody called "Willie." The older brother of the New York critic Alexander Woollcott, Willie was a member of the Hamilton Street Club as well as Mencken's musical group, the Saturday Night Club. Woollcott had an administrative position at an adhesives company and liked to introduce himself by remarking, "I make glue. What do you do?" "Where Willie is," one observer remarked, "there is laughter." These parties were marked by laughter and camaraderie and were remembered warmly long after they had ceased. "[T]he food was too plentiful," Dr. Turner has recalled, "the wine superior, and the company excellent." The quality of their friendships said a good deal about Kathryn and Gerald Johnson.[5]

Johnson set up shop in the room at the rear of the second floor at 1310. Books filled the shelves and spilled out into the hall. A locust tree in the backyard, which stretched 150 feet (half a city block) in length, sheltered him from the sun. There was a fireplace to warm him in winter. His typewriter clacked incessantly, disturbing the peace of the smug and championing the causes of the unfortunate. One block to the east lay 1307 Park Avenue, the house inhabited earlier in the decade by Scott and Zelda Fitzgerald. Several

5. GWJ to H. L. Mencken, December 1, 1949, HLM Papers; "Raymond Pearl, Hopkins Biologist, Dies Suddenly at Hershey, Pa.," *BS,* November 18, 1940; "William Woollcott, Raconteur and Convention-Breaker, Dies," *BS,* March 1, 1949; Fred Hobson, *Mencken: A Life* (New York: Random House, 1994), 117; Walker Lewis, "The 14 West Hamilton Street Club: A History of Sorts," in Lewis, *Fifty Years of the 14 West Hamilton Street Club* (Baltimore: 14 West Hamilton Street Club, 1975), 15–19; Thomas Bourne Turner, *Part of Medicine, Part of Me: The Musings of a Johns Hopkins Dean* (Baltimore: Johns Hopkins Medical School, 1981), 205–206; Thomas B. Turner, interview by author, tape recording, Baltimore, September 20, 2000.

miles to the southwest lay 1524 Hollins Street, the residence of H. L. Mencken and one of the most famous literary addresses in America. While 1310 Bolton Street never gained such immense celebrity, Johnson did come to be extolled as the "Sage of Bolton Hill" and "Baltimore's Second Sage." This study proved the single most significant place where this writer practiced his trade. It marked, as James H. Bready has pointed out, "the scene of [Johnson's] great stands."[6]

This year of the family's change of residence proved, as Johnson remarked with considerable understatement, "a big year for me." With *The Wasted Land,* Johnson offered both a précis of and a commentary upon Odum's *Southern Regions of the United States.*[7] With Mencken, Frank R. Kent, and Hamilton Owens, Johnson collaborated on *The Sunpapers of Baltimore,* a centennial history. Harper and Brothers published the firm's first volume by Johnson, the highly impressionistic *A Little Night Music.* Moreover, he began to contribute to the *New York Herald Tribune Books,* a highly regarded forum that would, for decades, carry his finest reviews. This marked the only year during which three books appeared under Johnson's name; 1937 attested not only to his productiveness but also to his versatility. Moving back and forth among books and essays and newspaper columns, with their differences in diction and attribution, in sentence and paragraph length, is always challenging, sometimes exasperating. Johnson made it seem easy.

Howard W. Odum's volume had appeared during the spring of 1936, and Johnson began his commentary that summer. The title, he explained, was a "left-handed allusion" to T. S. Eliot's *The Waste Land.* Modestly, Johnson told Odum that this project was "far out of my line," but his skills as a synthesizer are evident throughout this volume of 107 pages broken into four chapters. In Chapter 1, "Question and Challenge," Johnson ponders whether the South can be saved and answers in the affirmative. Not surprisingly, he calls for a "radical overhauling" of its present agricultural economy. Discussing "The Waste of the Land," Chapter 2 argues that both industry and agriculture have become too specialized and laments that "we are perpetually treat-

6. R. P. Harriss, "Will the Real Sage of Baltimore Stand Up and Take a Bow?" *Baltimore News American,* August 4, 1985; James H. Bready, interview by author, tape recording, Baltimore, May 29, 1990. I visited 1310 Bolton Street on June 3, 1991, and the visit proved especially informative because of the kindness of Frank Shivers, the historian of Bolton Hill, and current resident Laurence Roberts.

7. GWJ to Howard W. Odum, April 12, 1937, HWO Papers; GWJ, *The Wasted Land* (Chapel Hill: University of North Carolina Press, 1937), vi.

ing symptoms, but seldom the disease." In Chapter 3, "The Waste of the People," Johnson discusses both the costs of emigration and the strained relationship between capital and labor. These problems, he asserts, are "avoidable and remediable." In his conclusion, "The Direction of the Answer," Johnson calls for better educational opportunities and argues, again not surprisingly, that the answers to the South's problems lie neither with states' rights nor with the myth of rugged individualism. Optimistically, he proclaims that the Southeast, if managed proficiently, can become the "Eden of America" and "the garden of the world." The volume was well-received, and it was suggested that it be published serially in Southern newspapers. Johnson hastened to point out that the author of the volume, not its synthesizer, deserved the credit. He told Odum that "I am merely playing Huxley to your Darwin."[8]

The Sunpapers of Baltimore proved a different sort of collaboration. This project had been started prior to all the unpleasantness generated by the 1936 presidential election. Mencken had originally thought that Johnson would write the entire history; he and Frank Kent would provide the facts and suggest ideas. Johnson demurred, arguing that such "a collaboration among the three of us would be swill and nothing else." It was then decided that Mencken would serve as general editor, and that he, Johnson, Kent, and Owens would contribute separate chapters to the narrative. This initial misunderstanding resolved, the project proceeded smoothly.[9]

Johnson's contribution, the volume's first six chapters, covers the period from 1837 to 1888, from the establishment of the *Sun* to the death of its founder, A. S. Abell. His interest clearly piqued by the project, Johnson tells his story with honesty and flair: "It is not to be inferred that THE SUN in 1837 was a good newspaper. On the contrary, judged by modern standards it was almost fabulously bad. But in the realm of the blind, a one-eyed man is king and American journalism, in the early days of the Nineteenth Century, was a realm of the blind." Capturing the colorful journalistic ambiance of

8. GWJ to Howard W. Odum, July 26, October 30, 1936, Howard W. Odum to GWJ, July 30, 1936, HWO Papers; GWJ, *The Wasted Land,* 16, 35, 32, 58, 77, 83, 102, 99, 101; John T. Kneebone, *Southern Liberal Journalists and the Issue of Race, 1920–1944* (Chapel Hill: University of North Carolina Press, 1985), 147–48; GWJ to Howard W. Odum, December 29, 4, 1937, HWO Papers. Johnson also discussed Odum's book in "States into Regions: One Man's Formula," *BES,* February 24, 1938.

9. H. L. Mencken to GWJ, October 1, 1935, GWJ to H. L. Mencken, October 2, 1935, HLM Papers; Hamilton Owens, "The Sunpapers' History," *Menckeniana* 12 (winter 1964): 3–10.

that day, Johnson draws James Watson Webb, editor of the *New York Courier and Enquirer,* as "a sort of ten-cent Cyrano, swaggering around with pistols and a horsewhip, perpetually thrashing people or being thrashed, shooting people or being shot, and making a nuisance of himself generally." Mencken told Paul Patterson that Johnson had written better than ever. Johnson had high hopes for the book, hopes that were realized after its publication by Alfred A. Knopf in May. In the wrong hands, *The Sunpapers of Baltimore* could have been a book of puffery generating only local interest. Placed in the right hands, it proved a vibrant volume that was widely reviewed in out-of-town newspapers. The book, Johnson wrote home triumphantly, "has made an astonishing hit . . . because it has been widely accepted as a genuine contribution to the history of the American press." This volume would remain his only collaboration with Mencken.[10]

Richard Q. "Moco" Yardley, who had joined the *Evening Sun* in 1923 and later became the *Sun*'s celebrated editorial cartoonist, illustrated *A Little Night Music,* and his charming drawings proved fitting complements to Johnson's delightful prose. An amateur chamber-music group met twice a month in Johnson's home; Gerald played the flute, Kathryn the cello. *A Little Night Music* (the title is a translation of Mozart's *Eine Kleine Nachtmusik*) celebrates those who make music for the sheer joy of it. "I sing the ruthless amateur," Johnson exults with a tip of the cap to Walt Whitman, "the loud and unabashed amateur, the irresponsible and irreverent amateur, who plays music for no good purpose, but solely to the base and sordid end of having a good time."[11] In the end, though, Johnson sings a good deal more, and this short book of 125 pages stands as one of his most endearing volumes.

Much of this volume is written in a playful style that cloaks Johnson's serious purpose. He finds space in this monograph to range as he pleases, to address those issues that he considers important for a volume that could well

10. GWJ et al., *The Sunpapers of Baltimore, 1837–1937* (New York: Knopf, 1937), 37, 38; Mencken to Paul Patterson, December 26, 1935, in "Letters and Documents Relating to the Baltimore *Sunpapers,*" no pagination, HLM Papers; GWJ to Katherine Johnson Parham, Thanksgiving 1937, GWJ Papers; Gwinn Owens, "When Baltimore Was a Swell Town," *BES,* April 29, 1991; GWJ to Howard W. Odum, June 20, 1937, HWO Papers.

11. Harold A. Williams, *The Baltimore Sun, 1837–1987* (Baltimore: Johns Hopkins University Press, 1987), 202, 301; Kathryn Hayward Johnson, interview by author, Valparaiso, Ind., June 8, 1989; Dorothy Johnson van den Honert to author, June 8, 1995; "Night Music," *Time* 30 (September 20, 1937): 40–41; GWJ, *A Little Night Music: Discoveries in the Exploitation of an Art* (New York: Harper and Brothers, 1937), x.

have been entitled *In Defense of Culture*. With America suffering an economic crisis and the world ready to explode, Johnson asks and answers a question that was surely on the mind of many of his readers: What possible value can the arts have now? In Chapter 1, with the self-deprecating title of "On Playing the Flute Badly," he explains that "I can think of nothing that American life needs more than suave intelligence, coupled with good humor, and a real, but not solemn, appreciation of excellence in the arts." Music, in his view, "must be included in any life that is to be . . . gracious, spacious, and well-ordered." In Chapter 3, "The Art of Coming In," Johnson uses music to offer a parable about the need for good timing in all phases of life. Ever the civil libertarian, he returns to the events in Dayton twelve years before to criticize William Jennings Bryan for "playing a rather hideous fantasia on the theme of government suppression of free opinion."[12]

The volume's final, most impressionistic and most poignant chapter, "A Piano with Dirty Keys," discusses a good deal more than teaching music to children. Speaking of his legacy to his daughters, Johnson says that "in so far as I have the power, I propose to transmit to my children my own belief in unrestricted liberty wherever it is consistent with social safety." Life is short, but art is long, and he counsels his readers not to place their faith in ephemeral political princes: "Already the Eroica means more in the lives of men than Napoleon the Great does and 'Tristan und Isolde' vastly more than Napoleon the Little." At forty-seven, feeling compelled to assess his own efforts, Johnson discusses what is past for him and what is to come for his daughters:

> Heaven knows, my own life has not been the stuff of which high tragedy is made. As I look back over it, I realize that I have been pretty lucky. If fame and fortune have somehow eluded me, Scottish forebears handed down to me an excellent power of adhesion to some kind of pay-roll through fair weather and foul. Even the three great scourges of the race, disease and poverty and war, when they fell upon me, held their hands and whipped but lightly. It is not within reason to suppose that [my daughters] will have an appreciably easier time of it in this world than their father had.[13]

Finally, this book is no more "about" music than *War and Peace* is about military science. Assessing Johnson and his family and his world, *Night Music* of-

12. GWJ, *Night Music,* 11, 13, 57, 53–54.
13. *Ibid.,* 113, 177, 115.

fers the credo of a highly skilled artist willing to take risks and who celebrates, at a time when many of the established footholds seemed to be disappearing, the value of the civilized, reflective life.

In his review in the *New York Herald Tribune Books,* John Erskine, president of the Juilliard School of Music, looked past Johnson's "light-hearted" manner and explained that his "real intention . . . is writing about music . . . as a necessary ingredient for the good life, and his concern is not merely to spread the habit of self-amusement in the home, but to put us in possession of spiritual powers and durable satisfactions." The United States Army distributed over 150,000 copies during World War II, books on which this patriotic author accepted very limited royalties. Moreover, the volume went through multiple commercial printings, and over 10,000 copies were sold by 1950. With good reason, Johnson's readers proved as enthusiastic as the distinguished reviewer did. Soon after the book's publication, NBC radio asked Johnson to appear—not to play the flute but rather to celebrate the joy of music.[14]

Five weeks after it carried Professor Erskine's review, the *New York Herald Tribune Books* carried the first of more than five hundred reviews by Johnson that would grace its pages over the next thirty years. He discussed a wide variety of volumes: among them biography and autobiography, history and music, fiction and travel books and collections of correspondence. He wrote here for a more highbrow audience than the readers of the *Greensboro Daily News* and the *Baltimore Evening Sun.* Moreover, he was usually given more space to express himself, space that was invariably put to good use.

Ranging among the genres and through the centuries, Johnson would give his readers both information and delight. Reviewing a biography of Alexander Hamilton, for example, Johnson showed his love of paradox:

> Examine [Hamilton] from whatever angle you choose, the result is the same—you run into a flat contradiction before you are well started. He fought gallantly for the people against the king, but he despised the people and revered the king. He hated Washington and served him well. He hated

14. John Erskine, "This Country Needs Home-Made Music," *NYHTB,* October 31, 1937; James H. Bready, "Books and Authors," *BS,* August 28, 1955; GWJ to Cass Canfield, July 1, 1946, Harper and Brothers Papers, Firestone Library, Princeton University, Princeton, N.J.; Cass Canfield to GWJ, September 12, 1950, Harper and Brothers Papers. Johnson spoke on the NBC "Home Symphony Program" on January 16, 1938 (GWJ Papers).

Jefferson and served him better—made him President, in fact. He regarded
the acquisition of wealth as highly praiseworthy and charged fees so modest
that he was always pinched for money. He was avid of power and dyna-
mited his own party. He loved his wife and was popularly supposed to have
more mistresses than any other American of his time, except, perhaps,
Aaron Burr. Personally, he was rigidly honest, while politically and professionally he was God's gift to rascals.

Some biographers have taken hundreds of pages to paint far less vivid portraits. Disliking Henry Cabot Lodge for his opposition to Woodrow Wilson,
Johnson skewered him as "too much the gentleman to be quite a man, too
superior to attain the heights, too intelligent to be sensible, too learned to be
wise." Reviewing a biography of Robert M. La Follette, Johnson, bothered
by the Wisconsin politician's haughtiness, remarked memorably that "like
most crusaders [La Follette] was humorless and inflexible. Also, he learned
the lesson that every crusade goes to pieces when it succeeds. The story of La
Follette is a highly diverting illustration of how the Pure in Heart, having cast
the aside the Morally Stunted from the seats of power, fall to swindling each
other."[15]

Understanding, as some others have not, that the reviewer is less important than his job, Johnson never allowed a review to become an exercise in
narcissism. He was too decent to use another author's failings to make himself
appear clever. Never timid, he offered clear judgments, praising those books
that merited approbation and torching those that he found dishonest or
pompous. His analogies were inventive, his irony deft. With his keen eye for
the absurd, he made his readers chuckle and guffaw. Many of these reviews
have stood the test of time far better than the volumes that they evaluate.

While Johnson found a new forum with the *New York Herald Tribune,* he
and the *Chicago Times* were unable to come to terms. The newspaper contacted him in the spring of 1937, and he was willing to listen. He told Odum
that "I named a figure that I thought would stop [the editor], but he has
asked me to meet him in New York. . . . However, I don't like Chicago and
I don't like tabloids, so it will take the clinking of a lot of guineas to move
me."[16] Apparently, the *Chicago Times* did not clink enough of them, for he
stayed where he was.

15. GWJ, "The Patron Saint of All Conservatives," *NYHTB,* June 2, 1946, p. 3; GWJ,
"Able Practitioner of the Art of Politics," *NYHTB,* September 10, 1944, p. 3; GWJ, "That
Tireless Crusader from Wisconsin," *NYHTB,* December 6, 1953, p. 5.

16. GWJ to Howard W. Odum, April 12, 1937, HWO Papers.

Writing for the *Evening Sun,* Johnson characteristically showed both compassion and contempt. He used his Thanksgiving column to praise Baltimore's William S. Baer School for the Physically Handicapped. On the other hand, he scorned racial prejudice in the South: "The theory that the Negro is biologically inferior has no known basis in fact, and every educated Southerner knows it. Yet the theory affects the manners and customs, if not the laws, of a third of the country." Looking across the Atlantic, he called the notion of Aryan superiority a "notorious falsehood," and he argued that the spirt of old Germany, one of "vast tolerance" and "amiability" and "good will," was incompatible with the Nazis' ideology. While he wrote caustically about what bothered him both here and abroad, he did not criticize the domestic politics of his employer. Throughout, Johnson's relationship with the *Evening Sun* proved less strained than it had been in 1936 and would be the following year.[17]

In February 1938, Paul Patterson made sweeping changes in the hierarchy of the newspaper. As Harold A. Williams has explained, Patterson "nullified the autonomy of the two editorial-page staffs" by creating the new position of editor-in-chief for John Owens, who was given "full responsibility" for the editorial pages of both the *Sun* and the *Evening Sun.* Hamilton Owens left as editor of the *Evening Sun* and assumed the same position on the morning newspaper. Johnson was not sanguine about his own position or the future of the *Evening Sun.* "Why they want to blow up the paper that is a popular success and is bringing in the money," Johnson wrote incredulously to a friend back South, "is more than we can figure." He suspected, correctly, that Roosevelt played a part in all this: "My own fear is that the opposition to the New Deal has developed into a sort of religious mania against which there is no arguing." Johnson closed the letter by saying that "if you hear of any good openings, let me know. I shall be very much interested."[18]

Hamilton Owens suggested that he be replaced as editor of the *Evening Sun* by Philip Wagner, his "right-hand man." A graduate of the University of Michigan, Wagner was then thirty-four, and he would go on to have a distinguished career in journalism and become a renowned expert on wine. But Mencken argued that Wagner, at this time, was not yet ready to assume

17. GWJ, "Item for Thanksgiving," *BES,* November 25, 1937; GWJ, "Truth in History," *BES,* October 28, 1937, cited by Kneebone, *Southern Liberal Journalists,* 181; GWJ, "German Immigrant," *BES,* December 23, 1937.

18. Williams, *The Baltimore Sun,* 243; GWJ to Lenoir Chambers, February 1, 1938, Lenoir Chambers Papers, Southern Historical Collection, University of North Carolina at Chapel Hill.

the position. To Owens's surprise, Mencken agreed to take on the editorship himself for three months, during which time he would evaluate Wagner and others. This stint as editor exhausted Mencken, but he characteristically had a great deal of fun. Wearing a Princeton beer jacket, he descended upon the composing room to palaver with the printers. In "Object Lesson," a column that remains notorious to this day, he filled an entire page with one million dots, one for each federal jobholder.[19] For Johnson, on the other hand, these three months proved far from pleasant.

As an editorial writer, Johnson was stymied. Burying him in paper, Mencken told him to research one topic after another. As William Manchester tells the story, Johnson "simply read furiously, every obscure publication in the state of Maryland," but he "did no writing at all." As a columnist, Johnson again found himself at odds with the newspaper over the president. On March 4, the fifth anniversary of the president's first inauguration, Mencken ran "Five Years of the New Deal," a scathing, gargantuan editorial (six and one-half columns, the longest ever published in the Sunpapers), written by Wagner and himself. As he had during the fall of 1936, Mencken gave John-son the opportunity to speak for the opposition. Four days later, his lengthy "On the Profit Side" defended the president's policies. Johnson praised the New Deal for "[eliminating] blind terror from hard times." He closed by pointing out the havoc, inhumanity, and waste generated by "rugged indi-vidualism" and proclaimed thankfully that "now, at last, we have a govern-ment that has turned away from dreams and fantasies and ghosts and is dealing with stern, hard facts." Skillfully, Johnson reversed the stereotype of Roose-velt as the impractical and destructive visionary. Johnson's column was re-printed in more newspapers than was the lengthy editorial that had engendered it. Not surprisingly, Mencken remained unconvinced; he scorned "On the Profit Side" as "feeble stuff."[20]

19. Williams, *The Baltimore Sun,* 232; GWJ et al., *The Sunpapers of Baltimore,* 392 n. 1; William Manchester, *Disturber of the Peace: The Life of H. L. Mencken* (New York: Harper and Brothers, 1950), 288; Vincent Fitzpatrick and Frederick N. Rasmussen, "American Letters' Unsettled Debt: Mencken and Printing," *Menckeniana* 75 (fall 1980): 21–29; H. L. Mencken, "Object Lesson," *BES,* February 10, 1938.

20. Manchester, *Disturber of the Peace,* 288; Philip Wagner, interview by author, tape re-cording, Ruxton, Md., July 16, 1990; "Five Years of the New Deal," *BES,* March 4, 1938; GWJ, "On the Profit Side," *BES,* March 8, 1938; "Diary of R. P. Harriss," March 12, 1938, in the possession of Mrs. R. P. Harriss, Baltimore, selected entries in the possession of Vincent Fitzpatrick; *Thirty-Five Years of Newspaper Work: A Memoir by H. L. Mencken,* ed. Fred Hobson,

After Mencken stepped down in early May 1938, Wagner became editor of the *Evening Sun* and found himself at odds with Johnson. The men differed politically; Wagner was a "classic liberal" who became increasingly disenchanted with the growth of the federal government and the redistribution of wealth through taxation. The men also found themselves at cross-purposes regarding the composition of the editorial page. Wagner complained that Johnson's editorials frequently "had nothing to do" with what had been planned during the editorial conference. Johnson's copy, in Wagner's view, too often sacrificed content for style; the North Carolinian was "great on paradox" but "never had the slightest regard for fact." Wagner acknowledged that his working relationship with Johnson made for "a very awkward situation."[21]

Johnson felt awkward as well. Believing that he deserved better, he grew increasingly frustrated and said that he felt "very gloomy." It seemed a good idea to get out of town for a while. In late July, he sailed alone on the *Europa* for a four-week working vacation in England and France. This journey, financed in part by the *Evening Sun,* was his first trip abroad since 1928. Before he left, he told his friends that "when I get back home it will be the beginning of the end. I'll go free-lancing." He was right about the destination but wrong, by more than five years, about the timetable.[22]

Despite his dissatisfaction with his employer, Johnson the columnist, the consummate professional, continued to write with grace and passion about a variety of topics throughout 1938. Sickened by Neville Chamberlain's conduct in Munich, Johnson drew upon the inhumane lawyer in *Bleak House* to scoff that "Mr. Chamberlain is not a villain; like Mr. Tulkinghorn, he is a respectable solicitor whose function in life is to cover up the rottenness . . . and save appearances." Johnson argued that "the great loss is the extinction, not of Czechoslovakia, but of the ideal of democracy, strong and unafraid." Echoing Abraham Lincoln, Johnson declared that the world "cannot permanently exist half slave." Invoking once more the ghost of Woodrow Wilson, Johnson proclaimed, "God knows, it does not lie in the mouth of an American to speak scornfully of betrayals." At this time and later, Johnson scorned

---

Vincent Fitzpatrick, and Bradford Jacobs (Baltimore: Johns Hopkins University Press, 1994), 306–307.

21. Williams, *The Baltimore Sun,* 295, 229, 244; Wagner, interview.

22. GWJ to Katherine Johnson Parham, July 2, [1938], GWJ Papers; Williams, *The Baltimore Sun,* 244; see GWJ, "The Rough Crossing," *BES,* August 25, 1938, and "Unofficial Peace Palace," *BES,* September 1, 1938.

what he saw as the betrayal of humanity practiced by the isolationists. He saw Senator Borah and Charles Lindbergh as misguided and dangerous. "There can be no peace with the dictators," Johnson remarked artfully, "until the dictators desire peace; and they will not desire peace when there is a chance of making successful war." He celebrated the fact that isolationism generated little interest in the South.[23]

The South occupied his thoughts in a variety of ways throughout the year. He returned twice to North Carolina, the first time to Wake Forest in late May to deliver the memorial address for Dr. Poteat. In November, he attended a conference at Duke University on the changing economic base of the South. Once more, he called for his native region to face the problems of the present rather than to retreat into the past. He argued that the South must shed "the inferiority complex with which [it] has been hag-ridden since Appomattox." In an interview with the *Greensboro Daily News,* Johnson called the rehabilitation of the South "his greatest interest in public affairs at the moment." The interviewer said that, despite Johnson's residence in Baltimore, North Carolina has "no better nor more discerningly loyal spokesman."[24]

While his loyalty to the South was evident, so was his contempt for those figures whom he found backward and bestial. Pointing out that Southerners were being born faster and dying more slowly than citizens in other regions, Johnson called the South the "national nursery" and argued that America's future "seems to be inextricably bound up with that of the late Confederacy." After Roosevelt labeled the South "the nation's number one economic problem," Johnson used several lively tropes to scoff at the president's detractors. He bemoaned the South's "predilection for putting jackasses in high office" and argued that such donkeys, "assuming that their constituents are half-witted," have "snorted and brayed and pawed the earth." Changing the image, he called the president's critics "dogs in the manger [that] snap at everybody who comes close to them." Choosing yet another analogy, Johnson argued that the "the nation will suffer if it permits the antics of the simian

23. GWJ, "Rainy Weather," *BES,* September 22, 1938; GWJ, "The Sinister Note," *BES,* January 6, 1938; GWJ, "Boundaries of Neutrality," *BES,* November 9, 1939; GWJ, "Who Spoke Sunday Night?" *BES,* January 2, 1941; GWJ, "The Rebels Are Coming," *BES,* October 3, 1940.

24. GWJ, "The Future and Dr. Poteat," *Biblical Recorder,* June 29, 1938, pp. 4–5; GWJ, "The Changing South Looks at Its Problems," *BES,* November 22, 1938; Robert M. Hodges, "Gerald Johnson Not a Deserter," *GDN,* November 27, 1938.

element to check its interest in the rehabilitation of the South." Thirteen years after Dayton, Johnson thought once again of monkeys and men.[25]

The tragic death of Thomas Wolfe, on the other hand, led Johnson to write with admiration and regret. Wolfe had visited 1310 Bolton Street during the summer of 1938. The author of those gargantuan novels *Look Homeward, Angel* (1929) and *Of Time and the River* (1934) was himself a huge man; he sometimes wrote standing up, using the top of a refrigerator as a desk. He had charmed his hosts. Johnson recalled that Wolfe "sat in an overstuffed armchair two sizes smaller than a box car but barely big enough to hold him and entertained the family magnificently." Later that summer, Wolfe became seriously ill in the Pacific Northwest and was rushed across the country to the Johns Hopkins Hospital. Surgery was performed on September 12, but he died three days later, at age thirty-seven, of tuberculosis of the brain. On September 17, Johnson eulogized his fellow North Carolinian in the *Evening Sun*. Wolfe had "unmistakable genius," and his books "were filled with the sweep of a storm, filled with a power that needed only channel and direction, to become irresistible. He showed signs, too, of obtaining power over his medium; his books grew steadily better." The meteorological analogy is apt; whether Wolfe was actually improving as a writer is debatable. Beyond argument, Johnson was quite generous to this novelist, ten years his junior, who as a craftsman was profoundly different. Wolfe's early death led Johnson to think back to 1907 when another North Carolina writer, John Charles Mc-Neill, had died too soon.[26]

Mortality could hardly have played a more prominent part in Johnson's single book of 1938. He completed *Green Mount Cemetery,* a volume celebrating the centennial of Baltimore's storied graveyard—the final resting place of the infamous (John Wilkes Booth, the actual location of his remains being kept secret), the brave (Confederate general Joseph E. Johnston), the articulate (writers John Pendleton Kennedy and Sidney Lanier), and the magnanimous (philanthropists Moses Sheppard, Johns Hopkins, George Peabody, and Enoch Pratt). This monograph of about eleven thousand words recounts the cemetery's opening ceremony, sketches the lives of the most prominent fig-

25. GWJ, "Preponderant Dixie," *BES,* June 9, 1938; GWJ, "Problem Number One," *BES,* November 22, 1938.

26. David Herbert Donald, *Look Homeward: A Life of Thomas Wolfe* (Boston: Little, Brown, 1987), 454–63; GWJ, " 'Home Sweet Home' in the Middle of Town," *BES,* March 17, 1946; GWJ, "Thomas Wolfe: Loss for North Carolina," *BES,* September 17, 1938; Roy Z. Kemp, "Gerald Johnson and Thomas Wolfe," *Raleigh News and Observer,* September 20, 1959.

ures buried there, and, in a formal prose befitting the subject, captures the ambiance of the place. Johnson could not then anticipate that, forty-two years later, his ashes would themselves become part of this "long and eventful history."[27]

On December 31, he closed out 1938 with a letter to Paul Green. Johnson took this opportunity to criticize those, his employer included, who stubbornly insisted on believing the worst: "Business in Baltimore is good, but nobody believes it. The merchants are selling a lot of goods, the Sunpapers are carrying a lot of advertising, and factories have a lot of orders, but everybody knows there is a catch in it, because with this s.o.b. Roosevelt in the White House, prosperity is impossible. Even if we all get rich, we shan't believe it, because we have made up our minds that the country is ruined, and ruined it's got to be." He said here what he could not have said in the newspaper, and the bludgeoning irony testified to both his anger and his disgust.[28]

Anger and disgust figured not at all in the two books published in 1939, books that could hardly have proven more different. Concerned with the nineteenth century, the sober historian labored over *America's Silver Age: The Statecraft of Clay-Webster-Calhoun* and produced a respectable study. On the other hand, Johnson the novelist frolicked with *Beware of the Dog!*, a gory and sometimes ribald volume. Its title aside, the book concerned no canines but instead was Johnson's only attempt at detective fiction. It gave Dashiell Hammett and Raymond Chandler no cause for alarm.

Begun in June 1938, *America's Silver Age* was completed at considerable cost. Johnson obviously believed strongly in the project. The book, he told a correspondent, "dammed up all other work, with the result that the family finances are in deplorable shape." He sent the substantial manuscript to Harper and Brothers on December 28, and the volume was published the following spring. Its sixteen chapters provide an amalgam of historical narrative and biographical material. Johnson chronicles the major events from 1812 to 1852, "the drama of the making of a new nation, in which three men [Henry Clay, Daniel Webster, and John C. Calhoun] were to play conspicuous and vitally important parts." These parts failed to culminate in the winning of America's highest political office, and the implications of such

27. GWJ, *Green Mount Cemetery: One Hundredth Anniversary, 1838–1938* (Baltimore: Proprietors of the Green Mount Cemetery, 1938), 71–72.

28. GWJ to Paul Green, December 31, 1938, Paul Green Papers, Southern Historical Collection, Wilson Library, University of North Carolina at Chapel Hill.

failure intrigued the historian, himself writing during hard times. While they never became president, Johnson finds these men "extraordinary," for they accepted the challenge of taking the work of their predecessors and applying it "to conditions that did not exist when their predecessors were alive."[29]

Once again, Johnson assumes the roles of comparative historian and moralist to use the events of the past to comment on the present. Praising the boldness of Webster's famous speech delivered at Portsmouth, New Hampshire, on July 4, 1812, Johnson observes that there was a time when Americans were less timid, a time when they valued safety less and freedom more. There was also a time when they had "the capacity for enthusiasm divorced from profit or the hope for profit." Finally, *America's Silver Age* proves upbeat rather then condemnatory, a volume full of modern instances that Johnson surely found appropriate for his readers near the end of a difficult decade during a tumultuous century. The reviewers proved more enthusiastic than did the book buyers. The volume, Johnson told a correspondent, "received the finest reviews I have ever had [but] was a flop with the public."[30] Johnson's detective fiction, on the other hand, generated considerably more interest among the reading public.

Like *I'll Take My Stand, Beware of the Dog!,* one of the true curiosities of Johnson's career, raises questions that cannot be answered with certitude. Why, with the press of so many other literary duties, did he take the time to write a crime novel? Johnson read detective fiction voraciously; never one to avoid a challenge, he perhaps relished the opportunity to experiment with this new form. Perhaps this author who was hardly growing rich from the vast majority of his books saw an opportunity for a larger royalty check. Second, why did he write under a pseudonym? According to his sister Mary, Johnson was embarrassed by this project. Atypically, he never referred to it in his correspondence, nor did he consign to his archives the contract that he signed with William Morrow. The volume offers no biographical information about "Charles North," the supposed author. Surely, the majority of contemporary readers believed that such an author actually existed. However, it seems that Johnson proved a bit sportive with this charade. "Charles North" can be viewed as an approximate reversal of "North Carolina." Like

29. GWJ to Harriet L. Herring, January 13, 1939, Herring Papers; GWJ, *America's Silver Age: The Statecraft of Clay-Webster-Calhoun* (New York: Harper and Brothers, 1939), 78, 118.

30. GWJ, *America's Silver Age,* 76–77, 158; GWJ to Harriet L. Herring, September 9, 1939, Herring Papers.

Johnson, the protagonist of the novel, Gilbert Fellowes, is a veteran of World War I. Like his creator, Fellowes spends time in Toulouse. Johnson, it appears, was playfully dropping clues for those inclined to follow them.[31]

He sets the novel in the present, in the city of Columbia, somewhere in the eastern part of the United States. As its loquacious narrator explains, the story deals with "the old American story of the Triple Alliance between crooked business, greasy politics, and out-and-out crime." Fellowes, the lean and hard-bitten hero who keeps his own counsel, is appointed chief of police and told to clean up the corruption. Drawing upon myth, Johnson compares Fellowes's task to that of Hercules cleaning out the Augean stables. Drawing upon the Bible, Johnson creates a Judas figure: Fellowes's former paramour, Elsa (the "bitch" who gives the novel its title), betrays him but later repents. Fellowes, like Jesus Christ, is wounded in the side; unlike Jesus, Fellowes survives. Johnson, it seems, had some fun writing this book.[32]

Stock characters parade through the volume. Sally Richardson, an attractive, tough, and honest journalist ("no mere piece of fluff," the reader is told) helps to save the hero's life. She is opposed by a variety of criminals (Abe Shovitz is "the boss of the underworld"), crooked politicians, bought judges (one is a "whited sepulcher"), and corrupt newspaper editors. The story offers considerable gore, a variety of twists and turns, and occasional bawdiness. One has to smile at the thought of the decorous Johnson writing a scene which has a prostitute named Ida "wearing a pair of bedroom slippers and a contemptuous smile, and that was all."[33]

Like *By Reason of Strength* and *Number Thirty-Six,* this novel is flawed. Early on, Johnson's narrator is too discursive, a significant problem in a novel meant to be suspenseful. Some of the chapters are so long that they reach their destination long out of breath. In his attempt to capture dialect, Johnson proves no Mark Twain. On the other hand, the novel improves as it goes along; the pace quickens, and the novelist holds the reader's attention entirely. The book was published in a British edition, entitled *Out of the Dog House,* the following year, and Johnson was offered the opportunity to write three more crime novels. He declined. Perhaps he felt, as he had when he

31. Mary Johnson Lambeth, "Sketch of the Life of Gerald Johnson by His Sister, Mamie, Mrs. Charles Lambeth of Thomasville, N.C., 1939," p. 6, GWJ Papers; Lois Johnson, interview by author, tape recording, Southern Pines, N.C., August 15, 1989; Charles North [GWJ], *Beware of the Dog!* (New York: William Morrow, 1939), 2, 20, 96.

32. GWJ, *Beware of the Dog!* 22, 278, 276.

33. *Ibid.,* 206, 225, 10, 195–96.

decided to leave the University of North Carolina, that it was time to get out while the getting was good.[34]

In early January 1939, both Johnson and Philip Wagner escaped from that awkward situation which found them trying to work together on the editorial page of the *Evening Sun*. Johnson was "exchanged" with Frederic Nelson, an editorial writer who moved from the *Sun* to the evening newspaper. Johnson the editorial writer thus rejoined his former boss, Hamilton Owens, on the *Sun;* Johnson kept his column on Thursday in the *Evening Sun*. Yet the relief proved short-lived for the editorial writer: in April he was warned to follow *Sun* policy regarding foreign affairs.[35]

The newspaper, on the other hand, turned out to be far happier with Johnson's prescience. In February, he remarked that "it would not take [Hitler] long to abandon his opposition to Communism, if it were profitable to do so." The next month, Johnson declared that "the interests of Naziism and Communism run parallel in all basically important matters" and suggested that the dictators might unite to fight democracy. After the Nazi-Soviet Pact was signed on August 23, the *Evening Sun* reprinted Johnson's March column and praised his foresight. This was perhaps the most oracular episode of Johnson's journalistic career.[36]

The next month, Johnson found a dolorous personal matter to attend to in that land which had raised him. The health of his mother, Flora, had been declining for some time, and she died in Thomasville at age eighty-two on September 15, 1939. At the beginning of his fiftieth year, Gerald now faced the world as an orphan. As he had after Archibald's death four years and nine months before, Gerald took that melancholy train journey home. Flora was buried next to Archibald in the Spring Hill Cemetery. After long lives full of love and perseverance and rectitude, husband and wife now lay mute together in this quiet churchyard in rural North Carolina. Their values, however, would continue to find expression in the writing of their only son.

Throughout 1940, Johnson wrote repeatedly about the war in Europe and its implications for America. At this time, he thought it possible that American troops might not have to be committed. However, thinking that

34. Lambeth, "Sketch," 6, GWJ Papers.

35. "Diary of R. P. Harriss," January 3, April 14, 1939; Williams, *The Baltimore Sun,* 242; H. L. Mencken, "Thirty-Five Years of Newspaper Work," 1028, HLM Papers.

36. GWJ, "They Begin to Disagree," *BES,* February 9, 1939; GWJ, "Ganging Up," *BES,* March 16, 1939, reprinted August 25, 1939; see also GWJ, "The War Is On," *BES,* August 24, 1939.

America's position was in no way safe, he remarked that "the totalitarian nations have announced without equivocation that it is their purpose to eradicate popular government. . . . Ours is a popular government; therefore, we are in line for eradication." He argued that America should give England as much aid as possible with the understanding that it might never be repaid. He also argued that American troops should be trained immediately for the possibility of combat.[37]

He continued to see the contemporary scene in terms of heroes and villains. He extolled the Royal Air Force that distinguished itself in the Battle of Britain, and he celebrated the bravery of the American captain of an armed merchant ship who, after the Germans attacked his convoy, fought and died so that the other ships might escape. On the other hand, Johnson scoffed at the dictators as agents of darkness who "who have sown the world with Cities of Dreadful Night, not by their bombers alone, but even more effectively by extinguishing the light of true information." He scorned the pacifists who themselves scorned the "military virtues [of] courage, loyalty [and] endurance." Escalating his attack on the isolationists, he called Charles Lindbergh "a very real danger to the continued existence of this government."[38]

Writing about the American scene, Johnson insisted upon the need to preserve civil liberty. While he found Earl Browder, the leader of the American Communist Party, to be "foolish and incompetent," Johnson sensed a hidden agenda and found it reprehensible when Browder was sentenced to four years in jail for passport fraud. He scorned the xenophobia that generated sixty-eight anti-alien bills, and he pointed out that the abrogation of civil rights plaguing Germany had already happened here with A. Mitchell Palmer. Decrying the expulsion of two Pennsylvania schoolchildren for their refusal to salute the flag, he remarked pointedly that "the thing in America most worth defending is the American ideal of equal and exact justice for every man, regardless of his race, nationality, religion, or politics." He urged his readers that it was "time to keep cool," and he kept his head while a number of those about him seemed to be losing theirs.[39]

---

37. GWJ, "Mr. Perlman's Observations," *BES,* December 27, 1940; GWJ, "Fees, Not Gifts, for Britain," *BES,* December 12, 1940; GWJ, "To an Honest Objector," *BES,* August 7, 1940.

38. GWJ, "In Praise of England," *BES,* August 22, 1940; GWJ, "Captain Fegen," *BES,* November 14, 1940; GWJ, "Lights," *BES,* October 31, 1940; GWJ, "War Is Not the Limit," *BES,* March 7, 1940; GWJ, "What a Young Man Should Know," *BES,* June 7, 1940.

39. GWJ, "Four Years of Browder," *BES,* January 25, 1940; GWJ, "Sixty-Eight Anti-

After Roosevelt's victory that November, Johnson made certain to remain temperate in his commentary. The Sunpapers had endorsed Wendell Willkie, but Johnson, this time, chose not to gloat. Noting that the campaign had been "exceptionally bitter," Johnson called for Americans to unite behind their president. Such unity of purpose was essential because the powerful "enemies of democracy" would try to take advantage of any sort of discord in the United States.[40]

The following year, Johnson discussed the president at much greater length. In February 1941, Harper and Brothers suggested that he write a biography of Roosevelt. The White House reviewed Johnson's credentials and agreed to cooperate. "I want a book," he told the president's secretary, "not to benefit Mr. Roosevelt, nor to benefit the party, but to reassure men who are honest, but scared because, like Columbus's sailors, they fear that they are going over the edge of the world." Johnson had "great hopes" for this project; working under an oppressive deadline—he agreed to complete the manuscript in six months—he found the volume "by long odds the hardest I have ever tackled."[41]

By early April, he had written about ten thousand words and felt dissatisfied. He believed that a personal interview would help. On April 12, Kathryn drove him to the White House and asked, upon his return, if another interview would be held. "I'm not coming back," Johnson replied. "That man has so much force of personality that, if I came back, he'd write the book instead of me." (Johnson became known among the White House staff as the only person to decline an invitation to visit.) Thereafter, he posed his questions through correspondence with the president. Johnson completed the manuscript on August 8, and *Roosevelt: Dictator or Democrat?*, a volume a bit more than three hundred pages long, was published in October.[42]

The volume's opening and closing chapters cover some old ground. In

Alien Bills," *BES,* February 26, 1940; GWJ, "Flag-Saluting Law," *BES,* May 2, 1940; GWJ, "Time to Keep Cool," *BES,* April 18, 1940.

40. Williams, *The Baltimore Sun,* 301; GWJ, "Admonition to Ghosts," *BES,* November 7, 1940.

41. Stephen T. Early (secretary to President Roosevelt), Memorandum to the President, February 25, 1941, Stephen T. Early to Franklin D. Roosevelt, March 4, 1941, GWJ to Stephen T. Early, April 11, 1941, Franklin Delano Roosevelt Papers, Franklin D. Roosevelt Library, Hyde Park, N.Y.; GWJ to Harriet L. Herring, May 9, 1941, Herring Papers.

42. GWJ to Early, April 11, 1941; Kathryn Hayward Johnson, interview by author, Valparaiso, Ind., June 8, 1989; Alex Hooke, "Johnson Reflects on Current History," *Baltimore City Dweller,* September 1976, p. 6; GWJ to Miss LeHand (of the White House staff), May 9, 1941,

the first, Johnson locates Roosevelt in the American political tradition and names his precursors: Jefferson, Jackson, and Lincoln. The New Deal, Johnson argues, "is a natural, not to say inevitable, development of the American democratic process" and is "the strongest existing proof that the progression of American political thought has not changed direction." (Such statements surely made Roosevelt's opponents howl.) In the book's conclusion, Johnson points out Roosevelt's superiority to Hitler and democracy's superiority to fascism.[43]

It is in the book's six middle chapters, a narrative chronicling Roosevelt's life, that the biographer writes most effectively. Knowing that he must account for his subject's attitudes, Johnson sets the epiphanic moment during the summer of 1921, when Roosevelt was struck by polio:

> He had never known defeat . . . but now he knew it, for now he was beaten to the ground, beaten flat and left half dead. He had little personal acquaintance with injustice, but what could be more unjust than this assault of malignant fate? He had known not much of pain, but now he learned. He had been a rejoicing athlete, and now he was a cripple. His companions had been the fortunate of the earth, but now he was among earth's disinherited. He had always been accustomed to deference, as a superior man, but now he knew the fathomless bitterness of being pitied.

Echoing Joseph Conrad's *Lord Jim,* the tale of another brave man who stares down a bitter fate, Johnson says that Roosevelt "came out of that fight scarred and maimed forever, but by that same token, he came back one of us." Decades later, explaining this conclusion to a friend who herself had polio, Johnson would remark that when Roosevelt "realized the tragedy of the human condition he became great, and all that followed was inevitable. For anyone who realizes how vulnerable we all are can never again be callous to humanity."[44]

The president admired the volume; no other contemporary writer, he said, could have done a better job. A prominent reviewer praised Johnson's skills but justifiably pointed out that the book was hardly nonpartisan. Know-

---

Franklin D. Roosevelt to GWJ, May 19, 1941, GWJ to Franklin D. Roosevelt, May 27, 1941, GWJ to Early, August 8, 1941, Franklin Delano Roosevelt Papers.

43. GWJ, *Roosevelt: Dictator or Democrat?* (New York: Harper and Brothers, 1941), 8, 32.

44. *Ibid.,* 118–19; GWJ to Betty Adler, December 21, 1967, BA Papers.

ing that he had written with fervor about a controversial subject, Johnson surely anticipated such criticism. He was surprised, however, when the book failed to sell more widely, and he spoke sadly of its commercial "failure."[45]

Earlier that year, Alfred A. Knopf had published *The Mind of the South* by W. J. Cash, a volume considerably more significant than the Roosevelt biography. Taking huge risks, Cash attempts to account not only for the mind of the South but also for its heart and soul. He plays a variety of parts: historian and raconteur, psychologist and sociologist, the celebrant of what ennobles the South and the critic of what profanes it. *The Mind of the South* proves one of those extraordinary books with which one can disagree vigorously but still admire. "No one who reads Wilbur Joseph Cash," remarks his biographer Bruce Clayton without exaggeration, "is ever quite the same again." Johnson's ideas, as we have seen, influenced this volume, and he responded to the book and its author with magnanimity.[46]

It will be recalled that, back in early 1928, Odum had suggested that Johnson write a book comparing the Old South and the New, a suggestion on which Johnson did not act. In October 1929, Cash's essay "The Mind of the South" had run in the *American Mercury,* and the following month he wrote to Odum and outlined his plans for the book. For a variety of reasons, it had a prolonged gestation. During the 1930s, Cash expressed interest several times in joining the Sunpapers, but he never took a position in Baltimore. (Apparently, Johnson and Cash never met.) In 1937, Johnson supported Cash in his unsuccessful application for a Guggenheim Fellowship, and Cash was grateful.[47]

45. Franklin Delano Roosevelt to Cass Canfield, November 14, 1941, reproduced in Cass Canfield, *Up and Down and Around: A Publisher Recollects the Time of His Life* (New York: Harper's Magazine Press, 1971), 86; Simeon Strunsky, "America's Past and the New Deal," *New York Times Book Review,* November 23, 1941; GWJ to Eugene Saxton, May 11, 1942, Harper and Brothers Papers.

46. Bruce Clayton, *W. J. Cash: A Life* (Baton Rouge: Louisiana State University Press, 1991), 222. Johnson's influence upon Cash has been noted by previous scholars. See Clayton, *W. J. Cash,* 50, 207; Fred Hobson, *Serpent in Eden: H. L. Mencken and the South* (Chapel Hill: University of North Carolina Press, 1974), 100; Fred Hobson, introduction to *South-Watching: Selected Essays by Gerald W. Johnson* (Chapel Hill: University of North Carolina Press, 1983), xvii–xviii; and Fred Hobson, *Tell About the South: The Southern Rage to Explain* (Baton Rouge: Louisiana State University Press, 1983), 252, 253, 257–58.

47. W. J. Cash, "The Mind of the South," *AM* 18 (October 1929): 185–92; W. J. Cash to Howard W. Odum, November 13, 1929, HWO Papers; H. L. Mencken to Hamilton Owens, October 5, 1931, November 11, 1933, January 4, 5, 1935, in Mencken, "Letters and

The Mind of the South praises Johnson and reaches a number of conclusions similar to those expressed in Johnson's essays. Cash applauds Johnson for his "unsurpassed knowledge of the country," for being "courageous enough" to attack the Klan, and for being part of the "movement toward intellectual freedom" in the South. As Johnson had, Cash decries lynching and all forms of racial violence and laments the credulity of the average Southerner and his aversion to change. As Johnson had, Cash discusses the negative effects of religious Fundamentalism and the embarrassment of Prohibition. Both men had reservations about the Agrarians. As Johnson had, Cash ponders the relationship between the Old South and the New. In a famous analogy, Cash calls the South "a tree with many age rings, with its limbs and trunk bent and twisted by all the winds of the years, but with its tap root in the Old South."[48]

Johnson's review ran in the *New Republic* on May 12, 1941. "Lovers of the South and haters of the South alike," he begins, "are pretty sure to be outraged by Mr. Cash's analysis of the region—which is good reason to believe that it is not far from the truth." After praising the book's clarity of style and quality of thought, Johnson captures its thesis by remarking that Cash's "argument, in short, is that the distinction between the Old South and the New is largely imaginary." The reviewer concludes by calling the volume "unromantic, unsentimental, cool [and] clear-headed" and declaring that it is "one of the most stimulating efforts at Southern self-criticism that has yet been made."[49]

Cash, unfortunately, proved far from clear-headed on July 1. Having received the Guggenheim Fellowship, he went to Mexico City to work on a novel and there hanged himself. He was forty-one. Moved by this tragedy, Johnson took the opportunity to praise Cash both in print and in his correspondence. Ignoring his own considerable achievements, Johnson called Cash "far and away [Wake Forest's] greatest literary light." Bynum Shaw, Wake Forest's historian, has called Johnson's judgment "absolute altruism."[50]

What would have happened, one invariably speculates, if Johnson had

---

Documents Relating to the Baltimore *Sunpapers*"; Joseph L. Morrison, *W. J. Cash: Southern Prophet* (New York: Knopf, 1967), 72; Hobson, *Serpent in Eden,* 206 n. 189.

48. W. J. Cash, *The Mind of the South* (New York: Knopf, 1941), 182, 348, 385, x.

49. GWJ, "Below the Potomac," *NR* 104 (May 12, 1941): 673. Johnson also referred to *The Mind of the South* in "An Essay on Unplanning," *BES,* March 13, 1941.

50. Clayton, *W. J. Cash,* 177, 187; GWJ, "Dixie, My Dixie," *NR* 139 (September 22, 1958): 20; GWJ to John C. Masten, March 19, 1967, GWJ Papers; Bynum Shaw, interview by author, tape recording, Winston-Salem, N.C., June 14, 1991.

taken Odum's advice and written that comparison of the Old South and the New? He would surely have written a very different book than Cash did. The cadences of their prose were profoundly dissimilar, and Johnson would have spurned the psychological analysis that so intrigued Cash. It is difficult to imagine that Johnson could have written a better book than *The Mind of the South*. But all of this is, of course, mere speculation. The fact remains that, unlike the unfortunate Cash, Johnson was able to stay the course. Blessed with good health and immense equanimity, he would have nearly four more decades to analyze his native land.

In early February, just prior to the publication of *The Mind of the South,* Johnson returned to North Carolina to deliver the Founder's Day Address at Meredith College, the sister school of Wake Forest and the school that his own sisters had attended. Johnson, who praised the virtues of single-sex education for women, typically urged his audience to look ahead and remain optimistic. He argued that the consummate beauty was not outward appearance but rather "a beautiful spirit." Urging his listeners to despise tyranny, he spoke of "the degradation of women implied in totalitarian philosophy."[51]

As 1941 passed its mid-point, Johnson sensed that America's involvement in the war was approaching. After Hitler broke the Nazi-Soviet Pact and invaded Russia that summer, Johnson called a column "We Can't Let Russia Go" and argued that "if Hitler were permitted to conquer and organize Russia, he could subdue Britain, and then would be able to shut of us off completely from the rest of the world." This writer who so valued reason came to acknowledge that reason, as this time, was by itself insufficient. "This is the great disappointment that the twentieth century has inflicted upon the world," Johnson explained, "but there is not time for weeping over it now. We must accept it, and act accordingly." Johnson entitled this column "Tragedy of a Civilized Man," but this Southerner knew that there were worse things than fighting.[52]

After the Japanese attacked Pearl Harbor on December 7, Johnson wrote that "relentless destiny has propelled us into the inferno that we sought so desperately to escape." His first *Evening Sun* column after that shameful day was entitled "From an Old Soldier to the New Ones." This former member

51. GWJ, Founders Day Address, delivered on February 7, 1941, Meredith College, Raleigh, N.C., published as "A Commission from Raleigh," *Meredith College Quarterly Bulletin* 34 (March 1941): 1–14; GWJ, "What Is It We Defend?" *BES,* August 21, 1941.

52. GWJ, "We Can't Let Russia Go," *BES,* June 26, 1941; GWJ, "The Tragedy of a Civilized Man," *BES,* July 3, 1941, quoted in Kneebone, *Southern Liberal Journalists,* 186.

of the AEF predicted "a victory that is worth winning" and explained that "America has survived because, when it was threatened, it was able to produce a tough man with a gun." On the home front, Johnson actively became involved in the war effort as a lecturer and writer, and his wife and daughters engaged in a variety of patriotic activities.[53]

Once again, he found himself involved in controversy. During 1942, Johnson argued, with some frequency and considerable fervor, that the national interest, especially during a time of crisis, transcended minority rights. He complained that "friends of the Negroes, friends of the Jews, friends of all sorts of minorities that are, or think they are, oppressed are demanding instant reformation of their condition, sometimes coupling the demand with a suggestion that unless it is granted they are under no obligation to sustain the national interest." In his view, this was not "moral suasion" but "blackmail." He acknowledged that minorities continued to be oppressed but declared that "a war to be worthwhile must be wider than the liberation of any particular group." He used his Thanksgiving column to lament the loss of focus upon the national interest by those "who would sooner see every form of equality guaranteed than Hitler beaten." Surely, his opponents felt that Johnson misconstrued their position. It was not a question of the first goal taking precedence over the second; rather, it was a matter of the goals not being mutually exclusive. The black soldier taking his turn walking point was understandably outraged when his family back home had to walk to the rear of the bus, or walk to another lunch counter, or suffer some other sort of racial affront. "Negro leaders . . . pointed out," as John Kneebone has explained so well, "that if Nazi racism was evil, so was racism in the South." Significantly, at the end of 1942, Lillian Smith attacked such racism in an open letter "Addressed to Intelligent White Southerners," which appeared in *South Today,* a magazine published by her and Paula Snelling. Smith spoke of the need "to break the taboo of silence . . . the taboo of action . . . [and] bring [about] non-segregation quickly and harmoniously." As John Egerton has explained,

53. GWJ, "The New Deal as Builder," *NYHTB,* January 18, 1942, p. 12; GWJ, "From an Old Soldier to the New Ones," *BES,* December 11, 1941. The day after the attack upon Pearl Harbor, Kathryn Hayward Johnson volunteered to serve on the Aircraft Warning System. Kathryn Johnson (Kathryn Johnson Sliger) tested radios for the Army Arctic Service. Dorothy Johnson (Dorothy Johnson van den Honert) tested weather instruments and wanted to ferry bombers from the West Coast to the East Coast (Kathryn Johnson Sliger, telephone interview by author, from Valparaiso, Ind., February 4, 1996; Dorothy Johnson van den Honert to author, June 8, 1995).

this was a "significant declaration; for the first time, a white Southerner living and working in the South had come out forcefully in public print in favor of abolishing the Jim Crow laws and other racially discriminatory practices." Regarding his racial attitudes, Johnson, on the other hand, remained among that group whom Mr. Egerton has labeled "conservative liberals."[54]

Johnson's position would continue to generate controversy as the war progressed. "There are Negro leaders," he would argue along the same lines as he had before, "trying to use the emergency to accelerate the already swift progress of their race, oblivious to the fact that what they are really doing is creating suspicion about the loyalty of Negroes." To many blacks, the comment about "the already swift progress of their race" surely seemed absurd; to black families whose members had been killed or wounded or captured in the war, the remark about loyalty surely galled. Johnson's position generated a vituperative letter to the editor from a professor at Morgan State College, a historically black institution in Baltimore. The irony of all this was surely not lost on Johnson. This bold civil libertarian who had so infuriated the Klan, this forward looker who always celebrated the virtues of taking that proverbial next step, here found himself in the odd and awkward position of being accused of dragging his feet.[55]

Characteristically, he avoided controversy in his annual Christmas column. He closed 1942 by pointing out that many family circles contained at least one vacant chair, and that there was "hardly a lighted window into which cold fear isn't peeping from the darkness that covers the world." Typically, he spoke of the children, of the need to look ahead to their world and remain optimistic. And he wrote with passion about each generation's obligation to the next: "If our generation stands acquitted before the bar of history, it will be because it fought without much hope of ever getting anything for itself. The profit will go to the child who is too young to do his own fighting. Well, what of it? Didn't our fathers do as much for us?"[56]

Back in early 1941, Johnson had interrupted work on a book in progress

---

54. GWJ, "Reynolds and Other Aberrants," *BES,* August 27, 1942; GWJ, "Call for Ingenuity," *BES,* November 5, 1942; GWJ, "Thanksgiving, 1942," *BES,* November 26, 1942; Kneebone, *Southern Liberal Journalists,* 195; John Egerton, *Speak Now against the Day: The Generation before the Civil Rights Movement in the South* (New York: Alfred A. Knopf, 1994), 262, 289.

55. GWJ, "The Discordant Notes," *BES,* January 28, 1943; Clinton E. Knox, "Gerald W. Johnson 'Represents the Worst Traditions of the South,' Asserts this Writer," letter to the editor, *BES,* February 2, 1943.

56. GWJ, "Christmas Eve," *BES,* December 24, 1942.

to hasten the completion of the Roosevelt biography. Published two years later, *American Heroes and Hero-Worship* offers an engrossing collection of eight essays focusing upon American politicians during the eighteenth, nineteenth, and twentieth centuries. While Johnson is clearly indebted to Thomas Carlyle's *On Heroes, Hero-Worship, and the Heroic in History* for his title, other similarities are patent. Like Carlyle, Johnson writes here in a highly allusive, hortatory, and moralistic style, and *Heroes* proves one of his more highbrow ventures. This is not to say that the volume is either inaccessible or dull.

Johnson's penchant for paradox is evident in the title of Chapter 1, "The Ever-Changing Past," which serves as the book's introduction and sets forth his intent. The past, he explains, "exists only as it is reflected in the mind of the present; and . . . it is not only reflected, but refracted." He also laments man's propensity to believe "whatever he finds pleasant or convenient." Determined to set the record straight, he offers two highly controversial examples. On the one hand, he explains that John Brown, in reality a "homicidal maniac," has been reshaped as a "martyr to truth—and most astonishing of all—to humanitarianism." On the other hand, in a remark guaranteed to enrage most Southerners, Johnson argues that Federal general W. T. Sherman, so often vilified, was actually "as invaders go, a highly civilized and even considerate commander."[57]

His interest in revisionist history is detailed at greater length in "The Changelings," a comparative study of Jefferson and Alexander Hamilton, and "Victor and Vanquished—But Who's Who?," the chapter assessing the careers of the seemingly unlikely duo of Theodore Roosevelt and William Jennings Bryan. In the former, Johnson rejects the stereotypical views of Jefferson as a visionary, with a poetic temperament, full of hope, and Hamilton as a skeptical realist lacking in sentiment. In the latter, Johnson acknowledges that Roosevelt was successful but argues, as he had in his obituary of the Great Commoner, that Bryan was hardly the buffoon caricatured by his detractors. This man who read the Bible literally was actually "a heretic of a deadly type" in his insistence that "the way to promote the general welfare was to let the people rule." And Roosevelt, "the apparent radical" who terrified many a foe, was actually "a true conservative, the greatest the twentieth century has yet produced." Johnson goes so far as to predict that the man who failed three times in his attempt to capture the presidency will prove

57. GWJ, *American Heroes and Hero-Worship* (New York: Harper and Brothers, 1943), 9, 8, 12, 13.

more important to posterity than the popular president feted for his reforms. Johnson's inclusion of Bryan in this volume and his commentary upon the Scopes trial ("a startling burlesque of the judicial process") show once again that the implications of the uproar in Dayton remained very much on his mind.[58]

His continuing interest in Southern affairs is shown in greater detail in the chapter called "The Sons of Hagar." The biblical allusion (Hagar was Abraham's concubine and the mother of Ishmael, both of whom were evicted at Sarah's insistence) deals with the stereotypical view of the South as an unwanted outsider, perhaps even a reprobate, in the American experience. Judiciously, Johnson metes out both praise and blame to the region of his birth. While he acknowledges that a number of demagogues have embarrassed the South, he also argues that "the true Southern gentleman is . . . one of the most admirable types of humanity that the continent has ever produced." The South, Johnson remarks appreciatively, served from 1760 to 1860 as "the hotbed of radicalism" and "the region of ideas," and it was "the function of the rest of the country to apply the brakes." On the other hand, he complains that the contemporary South has applied the brakes to such necessary reforms as the New Deal.[59] With its striking juxtapositions and intellectual combativeness, *Heroes* often proves more engaging than the Roosevelt biography that interrupted its composition.

As Johnson assessed the war in Europe during 1943, he again bludgeoned the Nazis, proved sympathetic to the German people, and spoke of the need to defend civilization. The war in the Pacific, on the other hand, generated a far different response. Never forgetting the infamy at Pearl Harbor, he called for "war to the finish" and announced that "we are not going to be content merely to outbox Japan. We are going to knock her cold—so cold that it will be generations before she collects enough strength to jump us, or anybody else. To stop short of that would be silly." Looking ahead to the end of the war and assessing America's responsibilities, he called for a more sensible treaty than the one hammered out at Versailles. "If we know no better this time," he remarked pointedly, "then we are unteachable."[60]

The racial hostilities that broke out in Alabama and Michigan during

58. *Ibid.,* 93, 228, 237, 243, 249.

59. *Ibid.,* 149, 163, 149–51.

60. GWJ, "We Don't Need Hate," *BES,* March 25, 1943; GWJ, "Bach and Bizerte," *BES,* May 6, 1943; GWJ, "The Down-Hill Gang," *BES,* August 26, 1943; GWJ, "Have We Learned?" *BES,* October 15, 1943.

1943 did not shake Johnson's beliefs that the races could learn to live together peacefully. In early July, he responded at length to "the appalling race riot in Detroit," which he described as "an outbreak of jitters, occasioned, without doubt, by the long strain of war." He argued that "lamentation" was fruitless; acknowledging that there was more than enough blame to be spread around, he urged both races not to waste their time in recrimination. "Suppressing riots," he concluded, "is a police problem, but preventing them is a matter of building up public opinion against any kind of disorder, and the suppression of all disorder within its own ranks is a problem for each race. . . . The whites cannot do it for the Negroes, nor the Negroes for the whites." Despising foremost the needless violence that hurts all people, he called for common sense and mutual trust rather than for incendiary rhetoric.[61]

Four months later, in his final column as a member of the staff of the *Evening Sun,* Johnson wrote not about race but rather about duty and privilege. A mixture of public pronouncement and personal reflection, it proved one of his finest pieces. The column covered Baltimore's Navy Day parade and took its title, "Privilege," from Woodrow Wilson's declaration that "the day has come when America is privileged to spend her blood and treasure in defense of the principles that gave her birth." Johnson praised those who had died for freedom and then, speaking indirectly of himself, wondered what a man looking back over his life treasures the most. What "warms him against the chill of creeping age," Johnson explained, "are the times when the going was cruel, but he stood up to it. To have such memories is a privilege." He, of course, had them. Recalling his own service in France, Johnson spoke of the marble memorial table that he had seen in Marolles: "This parish to her children, dead for France—memory, prayers, tears, love." He called it "the greatest memorial inscription that I have ever seen—not a suggestion of cheers, not a word about glory, no hint even of pride, but memory, prayers, tears, love. The rest goes without saying." This column served as Johnson's farewell to daily journalism, and it was fitting that this moment, surely freighted with huge emotion, led him to think of that memorial—one which had so affected him as a young soldier and continued to affect him as a writer of national renown facing "that chill of creeping age."[62]

That same day, the *Evening Sun* carried a formal announcement of Johnson's resignation. Not surprisingly, it mentioned no political differences but

61. GWJ, "The Lessons of Detroit," *BES,* July 8, 1943.
62. GWJ, "Privilege," *BES,* November 4, 1943.

said that he was resigning because of the demands of his writing for books and magazines. Hoping that he would continue to contribute as a freelancer, the newspaper said that "the best we have been able to do is elicit from him a promise that, when the occasion moves him . . . he may take pen in hand for our benefit and that of his readers. May these occasions be frequent." They would be, and his copy would distinguish both the *Sun* and the *Evening Sun* for thirty-six more years.[63]

Significantly, everyone maintained public amiability. Both newspapers hosted gatherings in Johnson's honor. A week after his resignation, the *Evening Sun,* always open to the opposition, published a letter to the editor which complained that, with Johnson's resignation, the newspaper had "lost its last known vestige of liberalism." Five days later, the *Evening Sun* reprinted a lengthy tribute from the *Richmond Times-Dispatch* that celebrated Johnson as "the weightiest influence in bringing on the Southern [rebirth] in arts and letters" and as "a force for tolerance, enlightenment and progress." The South "salutes him," the piece continued, "as a doughty warrior in the cause of social justice, and a delightful and incisive editorial writer, essayist, and historian." Johnson exited with grace to well-deserved applause.[64]

He offered several explanations for his exit. For publication, he gave the same reason offered by the *Evening Sun*—that he had resigned to "devote full time to magazine and book work." This was true, as far as it went, but there were other matters involved. In his fifty-fourth year, Johnson was growing weary. All of that copy he had been turning out for decades had understandably exacted its toll. A month later, he told his sister Kate that he had quit "because the grind of routine was wrecking me mentally and physically." Finally, there was the cumulative effect of the political differences between himself and his employer. He acknowledged to one correspondent that he found himself "completely out of line" politically, and "it seemed only fair, to the newspaper and myself, to get out." Writing to Odum, Johnson was more specific and more critical. Returning to that watershed, the presidential election of 1936, Johnson said, "I pulled out of the *Sun* organization largely because I was sick of being gagged for seven years." He was referring, of course, to his editorial writing rather than to his Thursday column. All of

63. "Gerald W. Johnson's Last Thursday Article," *BES,* November 4, 1943.
64. "Diary of R. P. Harriss," November 5, 1943; Joseph I. Paper, "Gerald W. Johnson's Thursday Pieces," letter to the editor, *BES,* November 11, 1943; "A Tribute to Gerald W. Johnson," *BES,* November 16, 1943.

these factors—his literary interests beyond the paper, his fatigue, and the political differences—affected his decision to leave, but the final one proved the most powerful motivation. He had grown so disgusted that a change had to be made. While he remained serene on the exterior, he raged within.[65]

During the first three weeks after his resignation, Johnson found himself "perfectly happy." However, he was then offered "a whale of a big job," handling the publicity for the Democratic Party during the 1944 presidential campaign. The pay was twice his highest salary as a journalist. Not wanting the job but hesitating to turn down such a lucrative offer, he told his sister Kate: "I am impaled on the horns of a dilemma."[66] He decided to reject the offer.

This sort of dilemma would be repeated many times during the coming decades as Johnson lived audaciously without the safety net of a regular income. This uncertainty alarmed Kathryn, but she fully supported his decision to resign, as did his two daughters. It was a decision that, for all its obvious perils, he never regretted. "Freelancing," he would observe decades later, "is a very hard sort of existence. It is preferable, though, to the daily grind. And when I've got nothing to say, I don't have to fill space." Few occasions would find him silent.[67]

Johnson never ceased to praise America's bold settlers who had opted for

65. GWJ's response to a questionnaire sent by the Wake Forest University *Alumni News,* August 7, 1953, GWJ Papers; Vivian Kramer, payroll manager of the *Baltimore Sun,* telephone interview by author, August 16, 1995; GWJ to Katherine Johnson Parham, December 8, 1943, GWJ Papers; GWJ to Richard Walser, March 3, 1953, Richard Gaither Walser Papers, Southern Historical Collection, Wilson Library, University of North Carolina at Chapel Hill; GWJ to Howard W. Odum, December 16, 1943, HWO Papers.

Mencken provides a different account of Johnson's departure. According to Mencken, Hamilton Owens believed that Johnson's editorials were suffering because of the demands of his outside writing and offered an ultimatum in mid-October, 1943: Johnson would have to decide whether he was an author of books or a journalist ("The Diary of H. L. Mencken," October 19, 1943, HLM Papers). Philip Wagner has remarked that this scenario was unlikely. It was not Owens' way to offer such an ultimatum; moreover, he would have encouraged Johnson's outside literary interests (Philip Wagner, interview by author, tape recording, Ruxton, Md., July 10, 1990). Moreover, the newspaper was experiencing a manpower shortage during the war, and it would not have wanted, especially during this time, to lose a writer of Johnson's stature (James H. Bready, interview by author, tape recording, Baltimore, Md., May 29, 1990). In the end, Mencken's observations about this matter must, I think, be challenged.

66. GWJ to Katherine Johnson Parham, December 8, 1943.

67. Kathryn Hayward Johnson, interview; Woody West, "Gerald Johnson: Philosopher for Our Time," *Washington Sunday Star Magazine,* January 19, 1969.

freedom over safety. He once more lived what he wrote. His "act of self-liberation," as James H. Bready has called it, proved that for him "freedom" meant far more than abstraction on a typescript. His decision to light out on his own proved his own way of declaring *non serviam*. This writer who so loved paradox found himself rich, not in terms of the material goods that seduced so many other Americans, but rather in terms of what he could afford to leave alone. At an age where most men are storing up, Johnson was casting aside. It was a happy coincidence that his single book of 1943 discussed American heroes, for after November 4 some of his journalistic colleagues saw him as precisely that: a hero who challenged authority in a civilized way and then walked away to face life on his own terms.[68]

68. James H. Bready, interview; Jesse Glasgow, interview by author, tape recording, Baltimore, July 19, 1990.

11   Freedom and Fame
1944–1950

> The average man is indestructible and immortal. Great men come and go, but the average man is always with us. In the long run, he alone can do the work, and if he fails the work fails.
>
> —*Gerald Johnson to Jonathan Daniels, September 6, 1949*

In this new role, Johnson came to learn, as he surely anticipated he would, about a different cost of freedom. Like many free-lance writers, he experienced both fat times and lean. Some months proved abundant—when he received a substantial advance on a book, or a large royalty check, or a sizable fee for a magazine article—but others were less lucrative. No matter what his cash flow, bills for such things as food and housing rolled in with numbing regularity.

His literary agent, George Bye of New York City, proved invaluable in marketing Johnson's writing, and because of Johnson's national reputation and wide range of contacts, he was spared many of the tedious details and indignities that can exasperate a freelancer. Nobody demanded to see his clippings. He did relatively little writing on speculation, and he did not have to pitch stories over the telephone to harried and indifferent editors. His manuscripts tended not to get buried on somebody's desk; he wrote no feature, for example, which sat so long that, by the time it saw print, its subject was dead. Because many editors wanted repeat business with a writer of Johnson's magnitude, he usually got paid on time. Years later, he would speak of "the stony path of the free-lance." Actually, his own path would prove, at least until he grew very old, relatively smooth.[1]

---

1. GWJ, "Mellow Pessimism of Roger Burlingame," *NYHTB*, October 25, 1959, p. 11.

This period from 1944 to 1950, an expansive time for Johnson, validated his bold decision to set out on his own. He wrote or contributed to seven books. The writer who had previously contributed to such specialized periodicals as the *Reviewer* and the *Journal of Social Forces* now saw his articles appear in such large-market magazines as *Vogue, Life,* and *Look.* His old newspaper markets, particularly the Sunpapers and the *Herald Tribune,* continued to run his copy, and he found new forums for his journalism. As Johnson enlarged his audience, he sometimes found himself confronting the absurd. This man who had chastised the Agrarians now found himself discussing the most productive method of raising peas. With self-irony, he told Howard Odum that he was writing "a lot of propaganda" for the International Dairy Exposition in Indianapolis. One article carried the arresting title of "The Book of the Bulls." In brief, Johnson wrote what he had to in order to write what he wanted.[2]

During 1944, Johnson's first full year on his own, American politics, both past and present, continued to intrigue him. The presidential campaign offered a variety of opportunities for commentary. He analyzed it in July for the *New York Times Magazine.* The next month, he wrote a lengthy piece for *Life* about Senator Harry Byrd of Virginia, "the best all-around example of the conservative Southern Democrat now in public life," that lamented Southern antipathy to the president. In November, three days prior to the election, *Life* carried a positive assessment of Harry S. Truman.[3]

Sensibly, Johnson submitted nothing to the Sunpapers about the campaign or the election. The newspaper endorsed Thomas E. Dewey, but as R. P. Harriss has explained this matter, staff members all but unanimously supported Roosevelt, and it was primarily a matter of Paul Patterson supporting Dewey. Even Mencken, who was not writing for the newspaper at this time but was instead serving in an advisory capacity, thought so little of Dewey that he voted for Roosevelt, whose politics he had so colorfully lampooned as quackery.[4]

Johnson, who did some speech writing for Roosevelt, was quoted in the Democratic Committee's national newspaper advertisements, and had his po-

2. GWJ, "Mobilized Farm," *Country Gentleman* 114 (August 1944): 44–47; GWJ to Howard W. Odum, April 20, and June 16, 1949, HWO Papers.

3. GWJ, "This Strange Campaign," *New York Times Magazine,* July 9, 1944, p. 11, 38–39; GWJ, "Senator Byrd of Virginia," *Life* 17 (August 1944): 81–86, 89–91; GWJ, "Truman," *Life* 17 (November 6, 1944): 111–14, 117.

4. "Diary of R. P. Harriss," November 6, 7, 1944, in the possession of Mrs. R. P. Harriss, Baltimore.

litical commentary read over the radio. Johnson proved, as Harriss has explained, "a real force, locally and nationally." Roosevelt's triumph marked another victory of sorts for Johnson over his former employer. He again felt vindicated, and he looked forward to the end of the war and the continuation of what he thought a humane domestic policy. Obviously, he could not anticipate that this American hero, whom he had already elevated to the American Valhalla, would die a little more five months after the election.[5]

Woodrow Wilson, whom Johnson revered even more highly, had been dead for two decades, and it had been twenty-five years since Johnson had been so moved by the sight of Wilson at Suresnes. For his only book devoted entirely to this figure, Johnson collaborated with the editors of *Look* magazine on *Woodrow Wilson*, a pictorial biography. Its subtitle, *The Unforgettable Figure Who Has Returned to Haunt Us,* was most unsubtle but was thoroughly in keeping with sentiments that Johnson had expressed before. *Wilson* proved a timely publication; with the end of World War II approaching, Johnson announced once again that America could not afford to repeat the blunders at Versailles.

This project, different from anything undertaken previously, captured Johnson's interest. He explained to his sister Kate that it "is going to be a new effort in biography. Perhaps it is going to be a bust, too, but at any rate I think it is worth trying." He would write a sketch of Wilson's early life— called "The Boy Becomes a Man," it ran to about 15,000 words—but after Wilson was elected governor of New Jersey, the story would be told "as far as humanly possible . . . in pictures." Johnson would supply only enough text "to maintain the continuity." About 250 photographs would be selected from approximately 30,000.[6]

Carrying off this new venture with skill and flair, Johnson provides a text that does considerably more than bridge the photographs. He offers not mere captions but rather impressionistic commentaries averaging about seventy-five words. His copy brings these pictures to life, moves this volume along smoothly, and shows both his own range as a stylist and the variety of responses generated by this controversial politician.

Sometimes criticized as wooden, Wilson emerges here as a human being capable of laughing at himself. Under a picture of that famous toothy and

5. Lloyd Dennis, "Gerald Johnson: Man of Many Parts," *GDN,* March 22, 1964; "Diary of R. P. Harriss," November 8, 1944.

6. GWJ to Katherine Johnson Parham, December 8, 1943, GWJ Papers.

unattractive Wilson smile, Johnson cleverly runs the limerick that the president liked to turn upon himself:

> For beauty I am not a star,
> There are hundreds more handsome by far,
> But my face I don't mind it,
> For I am behind it,
> It's the people in front that I jar.

While Johnson laughs, he also rages. He scorns those pacifists who, in his eyes, embarrassed the country and made the president's trying task even more difficult. Pathos joins humor and contempt as Johnson describes the president conducting his final cabinet meeting; his health broken by arduous service to his country, he was "a dead man not yet in his grave." At the end of the volume, beneath a picture of Wilson's tomb, Johnson's eulogy is predictably reverential:

> On the tomb of Woodrow Wilson is carved one decoration and one only. Out of the stone is hewn the long, straight blade with a hilt shaped like the Crusader's sword. In a way, it is highly appropriate, for the crusader he was. Yet the sword has little to do with the legend that Wilson has become. In our book of heroes the "sword of the country" is George Washington, as the pen is Thomas Jefferson. Washington is only in part the name of a man, for his name also means war and statecraft, as Jefferson means democracy, and Lincoln means liberty. The word "Wilson" now has new meaning. It means peace.

Johnson clearly welcomed this opportunity to say hail and farewell to a figure he could not have placed in more distinguished company.[7]

Throughout, Johnson applauds Wilson's huge skills as communicator. The president's ideas, he explains, "were stated in such simple language that the dullest man in the crowd could hardly fail to understand." Whenever Wilson spoke, "the common people seemed to hear, stated in chiseled and beautiful English, exactly what they had confusedly been thinking in their

---

7. GWJ and the editors of *Look*, *Woodrow Wilson: The Unforgettable Figure Who Has Returned to Haunt Us*, *Look* Picture Books Series (New York: Harper and Brothers, 1944), 45, 104, 277, 291.

hearts."[8] This mastery of the plain style was, of course, one of Johnson's greatest strengths. Writing here for an audience far from highbrow, Johnson establishes the magnitude of his subject, long dead, and the continuing relevance of his ideas. Finally, *Wilson* proves no "bust" but rather an innovative and engaging volume, accessible to all, that happily joins a daring subject and a bold biographer.

While Johnson wrote with equal skill for the *New York Herald Tribune,* one is perhaps struck even more by his industry. After he left the Sunpapers, Johnson reviewed books more frequently. He had more time for this task that he enjoyed and did very well, and reviewing provided a steady source of income. During 1944, the newspaper's Sunday book section carried twenty-four of Johnson's reviews. As he had done previously, he often assessed Southern issues. Reviewing a biography of Henry Grady, "the spokesman of the New South," Johnson wrote colorfully that "to find a Renaissance man in nineteenth-century Georgia is as unsettling as it might be to find a pterodactyl in a henhouse." Significantly, the critic of the Agrarians again acknowledged the problems caused by industrialism. Johnson praised Odum's *Race and Rumors of Race* and responded at greater length to Gunnar Myrdal's *An American Dilemma: The Negro Problem and Modern Democracy.* After calling the study "extraordinary" and praising Myrdal's honesty and industry, Johnson expressed reservations about the author's psychological analysis and discussed what he saw as a more "empirical basis" for the racial disharmony in the South. As he had done the previous year in discussing the rioting in Detroit, Johnson steered a middle course. He admitted that the South, and America, had racial problems, but he did not find them insoluble.[9]

Beginning in August 1944, Johnson's fans on the *Herald Tribune* read his reviews even more frequently. He took over the daily column called "Books and Things" from Lewis Gannett, who had gone to Europe as a war correspondent. For the first time since he had moved there during the summer of 1926, Johnson left Baltimore on a regular basis. He stayed in New York City, at the Hotel Woodstock, during the week and rode the train back to Baltimore to spend weekends with his family. During this month, he wrote

8. *Ibid.*, 73, 155.

9. GWJ, "The Warwick of Georgia," *NYHTB,* January 2, 1944, p. 2; GWJ, "Volcanic Forces Are Stirring in the South," *NYHTB,* March 5, 1944, p. 3; GWJ, "Problem of the American Negro," *NYHTB,* August 13, 1944, p. 2.

twenty-three reviews, 500 to 600 words each, and edited the Saturday reviews produced by a stable of writers including Maxwell Geismar.[10]

The thought of producing a review a day would make most writers quiver, but Johnson, with his ability to produce clean copy quickly, wrote with his usual grace about a variety of volumes. Discussing Lonnie Coleman's novel *Escape the Thunder,* Johnson lamented that "in large sections of Negro life in the South the writ of the white man's courts does not run" and acknowledged that "even when there is a sincere desire to administer justice the white man is frequently handicapped by a lack of understanding that makes him unjust against his will." Reviewing *The Gravediggers of France,* the story of those Frenchmen who betrayed their country to the Nazis, he portentously warned Americans to pay attention. In his rollicking assessment of *Time Must Have a Stop,* a novel by Aldous Huxley, Johnson showed his typical love of paradox and made his readers guffaw:

> The story concerns Sebastian, an English poet of seventeen, in search of the meaning of life. Sebastian's father is a liberal politician, intent on doing good but accomplishing evil; his uncle is an esthete, intent on doing nothing and accomplishing evil; his aunt is a woman of character, intent on preserving the bourgeois values, and accomplishing evil; his lady-love is a nymphomaniac, intent on accomplishing evil and perhaps doing Sebastian more good than all the rest of them put together.

After carrying out this herculean task with considerable proficiency, Johnson announced at the end of August that "Books and Things" would be written in September by Professor George Whicher of Amherst. Johnson explained that he had "gained an increased respect for the men who review a book a day month after month and year after year." Johnson, it seems, thought that he was finished with daily reviewing. He was wrong.[11]

He returned at the beginning of November and served in the same capacity for three more months. On January 31, 1945, saying farewell for the second time, he typically made a joke at his own expense and saluted his faithful audience: "To those resolute and durable readers . . . who have survived the

10. GWJ to H. L. Mencken, August 6, 1944, HLM Papers; Kathryn Johnson Sliger, telephone interview by author, from Valparaiso, Ind., June 18, 1997.

11. GWJ, "Books and Things," *NYHT,* August 11, 18, 23, 31, 1944.

last three months—yes, there are some—it is my pleasant task this morning to offer felicitations. Lewis Gannett, after a tour of duty in the war zone, has returned and will resume his rightful place tomorrow." Johnson told a correspondent that he was grateful for the experience but certainly did not want to repeat it.[12]

This year that began with Johnson happily completing his duty as a daily book reviewer proceeded to be a happy one for America, for him, and for his family. On May 8, 1945, the month after Roosevelt's death, the Allies celebrated victory in Europe. Japan surrendered on August 14, eight days after an atomic bomb was dropped on Hiroshima and five days after another was dropped on Nagasaki. Johnson fully supported President Truman's decision to employ this controversial weapon. The atomic bomb, he then explained, "killed civilians only where civilians had to be killed in order to stop the slaughter of our own forces." Nineteen years later, he spoke even more forcefully: "I have never been one of those hag-ridden by guilt over Hiroshima. . . . I believe that Hiroshima actually saved more Japanese lives than it destroyed—to say nothing of our own prospective losses."[13]

The American Civil Liberties Union honored Johnson in 1945 by appointing him to its National Executive Board. Moreover, he was asked to join the Century Club in New York City, that prestigious organization founded in 1847 to promote the arts. It proved a pleasant remembrance of things past that Earle Balch, the husband of Emily Clark, whose *Reviewer* had been graced decades before by Johnson's prose, was one of those who nominated him. Very proud of his membership in the Century Club, Johnson retained it until his death.[14]

Honored in New York City, Johnson found the home fires burning brightly in Baltimore. The daughters' education completed, the family was reunited. After two years at Oberlin, Kathryn returned to Baltimore to study at the Peabody Institute. After graduating, she took another degree at the Johns Hopkins University and began a teaching career in the Baltimore pub-

12. GWJ, "Books and Things," *NYHT*, January 31, 1945; GWJ to Charlotte Kohler, January 27, 1945, *Virginia Quarterly Review* Papers, Special Collections, Alderman Library, University of Virginia, Charlottesville, Va.

13. GWJ, "Lewis Mumford, a Philosopher in a Panic," *NYHTB*, April 7, 1946; GWJ, *Hod-Carrier: Notes of a Laborer on an Unfinished Cathedral* (New York: William Morrow, 1964), 175.

14. Jonathan Harding (archivist, Century Club), telephone interview by author, from New York City, June 8, 1995.

lic schools. Having graduated from Vassar, Dorothy returned to Baltimore, and in June 1945, she and her mother established the Ardlussa Kennels. (The name came from the home of one of Johnson's North Carolina relatives.) They began with miniature poodles; Dorothy did the obedience and the clipping, while Mrs. Johnson handled the showing. Later, the kennel switched to toy poodles, and one of the dogs won Best in Show in Madison Square Garden. The business lasted about twenty years, after which poodles were always kept as pets. The household, as R. P. Harriss has described it engagingly, could be lively: Johnson "continued to write, oblivious to the yapping of Kathryn's show-type poodles. They were not, of course, inaudible to his visitors, and as one of them thought herself to be Clare Boothe Luce, walked habitually on her hind legs and expressed strong opinions, visitors found conversation with Gerald difficult. He served good Scotch, which ameliorated the situation."[15] Baltimore's two most celebrated authors proved imaginative regarding their pets. While the Johnson poodle engendered a literary prototype, Mencken, who loved to scoff at Christian Science, named his pet turtle "Mrs. Mary Baker Eddy."

Johnson did not celebrate the book that he began in 1945 and saw published the following year. He wrote a biography of Adolph Simon Ochs, the publisher of the *New York Times,* who had died in 1935. Its publication marked the fiftieth anniversary of Ochs's purchase of the newspaper in August 1896. Johnson received an advance of $15,000—more than twice his highest annual salary as a journalist and a substantial sum in 1946 dollars. The newspaper put up $12,500 and Harper and Brothers the rest.[16]

Johnson surely understood that he was not being paid all this money to debunk this eminent figure in American journalistic history. While *An Honorable Titan* never degenerates into hagiography, it predictably proves quite laudatory. Johnson applauds Ochs's loyalty, courage, resiliency, grace under pressure, and his "intense vitality combined with an insatiable curiosity about men and events." Assessing his subject's politics, Johnson remarks appreciatively that Ochs grew more liberal as he aged, that "the man who couldn't stomach Bryan in 1896 was able to accept the Second Roosevelt in 1932." Johnson salutes Ochs's success in raising the *New York Times,* which was los-

15. Dorothy Johnson van den Honert to author, June 8, 1995; Kathryn Hayward Johnson, interview by author, Valparaiso, Ind., June 8, 1989; R. P. Harriss, "The Sage of Bolton Hill," *BS,* February 28, 1988.

16. Lester Markel (*New York Times*) to Frank S. MacGregor, January 22, 1945, Harper and Brothers Papers, Firestone Library, Princeton University, Princeton, N.J.

ing $2,500 a week when he bought it, to its place of prominence among American newspapers. Ochs's life provides a tale very much in the American tradition where a boy who began work at eleven and quit school at fourteen "[lifted] himself by his bootstraps" and conquered his profession.[17]

Unfortunately, it is a tale that Johnson could have told better. Too much editorializing slows the narrative; the biographer's penchant for stopping his story to argue with his subject's detractors proves bothersome. Some of the chapter titles seem elephantine, and Johnson, usually so masterful as a stylist, offers here a story full of chichés: "skating delicately and joyously over thin ice" and "once the cat was out of the bag," for example, and "getting too many irons in the fire" and "riding the high tide of success." The book's success was financial rather than literary. He had written far better books, but books for which he had been compensated far less handsomely.[18]

Johnson sensed that he could have done a better job, but his explanation to his editor, that "the real weakness of the book is [its] failure to emphasize [Ochs's] moral timidity," seems odd. Johnson overlooked the more obvious weaknesses of the bumpy narrative and the sloppiness of some of the prose. Moreover, it was a peculiar judgment to make about the career of a man who seemed both bold and highly principled. Timidity appalled Johnson; he had scorned it before, and it was very much on his mind at this time as he surveyed the American scene.[19]

Reviewing a book by Lewis Mumford, "a terrified man," Johnson proclaimed that "to live at all is dangerous, and the higher the form of life the more perilous its condition. Perhaps the safest of all living things are lichens; perhaps the least safe is the free man." In "The Liberal of 1946," the Johnsonian credo published in *The American Scholar,* he explains that the true liberal is "aware of the perils ahead and therefore alert but . . . is convinced that the opportunity is greater than the danger." While humankind can never be perfected, it can indeed be improved, and the true liberal believes "in the possibility of raising the general level of civilization of the masses." The true liberal, the hortatory Johnson concludes, is a "man unterrified." This idea would resound throughout his canon during the coming years, as other Americans grew jittery during an atomic age.[20]

17. GWJ, *An Honorable Titan: A Biographical Study of Adolph S. Ochs* (New York: Harper & Brothers, 1946), 21, 101, 69, 154, 83.

18. *Ibid.*, 142–69, 20, 60, 76, 101.

19. GWJ to Frank S. MacGregor, November 18, 1946, Harper and Brothers Papers.

20. GWJ, "Lewis Mumford"; GWJ, "The Liberal of 1946," in *America-Watching: Perspectives in the Course of an Incredible Century* (Owings Mills, Md.: Stemmer House, 1976), 155–59.

In his single book of 1947, Johnson told the story, on the bicentennial of John Paul Jones's birth, of precisely such a man unterrified. Born poor in Scotland, this "indomitable" man liked to say, "I propose to go in the way of danger." In 1778, he sailed into the Whitehaven Harbor and became "the first man since William the Conqueror to invade England and come away unharmed." The following year, with his ship, the *Bon Homme Richard,* badly damaged in battle with the British ship *Serapis,* he was asked to surrender and replied famously, "No, I have not yet begun to fight." He proceeded to win "the most brilliant [victory] in American naval annals up to that time." Dead at forty-five in 1792, he was buried in obscurity in a French cemetery, and it was only in 1913 that his remains were brought to America, the country for which he had risked everything. This story is full of those paradoxes that always fascinated Johnson. Moreover, it is the tale of an individual with whom he clearly sympathizes—a man full of new and good ideas that forced his contemporaries to question their old ones, "and there is nothing that men resent more bitterly than being forced to think along new lines."[21]

Johnson uses the work of one bold Scotsman as a model to tell the story of another. He wrote to his sister Kate that the book opens "with a cadenza for 48 trombones and a steam calliope. . . . My model is Carlyle's 'French Revolution,' the loudest book in the history of the English language. I am not so foolish as to try to imitate Carlyle's style, but maybe I can capture a bit of his noise." He could indeed. Jones "was a gaudy fellow," the volume opens. "He swung through the world raising so much dust and clatter that the people of his own time could rarely see what he was really like, and for a century after he was dead the most fantastic lies were still told about him and still believed." Never *pianissimo,* this volume, like *Jackson,* captures its readers right away. *Jones* finds Johnson emphasizing the novelty and the danger of the founding of America. The country's founders faced "the necessity of doing something unheard of, something without precedent, and the outcome . . . [could] not be predicted with any sort of assurance." At sixty-nine, Ben Franklin "cheerfully risked the hangman; he was an old man [who] was brave enough to face up to new conditions and new ideas." In the end, with *Jones* celebrating both its subject and the American experiment, Johnson offers a bracing story for which he felt there was pressing need.[22]

21. GWJ, *The First Captain: The Story of John Paul Jones* (New York: Coward-McCann, 1947), 125, 170, 177, 245, 251, 4.

22. GWJ to Katherine Johnson Parham, March 21, 1946, GWJ Papers; GWJ, *The First Captain,* 1, 65, 69.

He used "The Devil Is Dead, and What a Loss!" to speak more sharply to terrified Americans. "Strategically, economically, politically," he proclaims, "the United States enjoys in 1947 a security the like of which it has ever attained before. Yet terror is the order of the day." He deplores the fact that, in the midst of prosperity, Americans exhibit so little gumption. The civil libertarian proceeds to elaborate upon the decline of free speech and then, using a lively metaphor that he had employed before, fuses materialism and a religion that has been profaned: Americans are not supposed "to giggle in the Cathedral of the Holy Dividends." Johnson himself guffawed.[23]

That May, Johnson returned to North Carolina to speak in a very different voice than the one which excoriated terror and censorship. Elegiac rather than polemical, he addressed the Gerald Johnson Book Club in Red Springs. He talked not about his writing or his life in the big city as a figure of national import but rather about the people and the place that had shaped him. Nearing his fifty-seventh birthday, Johnson recalled his own lost youth of the century past and spoke of that magical time still glimmering for the children of the present: "For youth and life go on after we, who have had our share, must stand aside. There is still a path into the fairy haunted wood, even if our feet have stumbled and cannot find it again. The light that goodness and beauty once shed in the world does not fade, even if our eyes grow too dim to perceive its glow. The people whom I found so gentle and true have passed, but there are others whom today's children regard with shining eyes."[24] Like an American Lewis Carroll, Johnson was spinning out his own version of Wonderland. Also like Carroll, Johnson was very conscious of time's flight, of the sad fact that summer inevitably dies. The following summer, Johnson's younger daughter, that little girl to whom he had read *Tom Sawyer* and the *Arabian Nights,* that young musician who had gotten the keys of the piano dirty and helped to generate that wondrous chapter in *A Little Night Music,* would get married.

On June 12, 1948, Dorothy Johnson wed Leonard van den Honert, an electrical engineer. Born in Holland, he was raised in New Jersey; his family returned to Holland during the Depression. His "Ir" degree from the University of Delft was the equivalent of an American Ph.D. without the dissertation. The couple had met while Leonard was working at the Johns Hopkins

---

23. GWJ, "The Devil Is Dead, and What a Loss!" in *America-Watching: Perspectives in the Course of an Incredible Century* (Owings Mills, Md.: Stemmer House, 1976), 159–65.

24. GWJ, "The Lumbee River," *Pembroke Magazine* 15 (1983): 94–97

University. Johnson's four sisters traveled from North Carolina to Baltimore for the ceremony, after which the couple settled in Pittsfield, Massachusetts, where Leonard took a position with General Electric. So joyous for the couple, this occasion was, understandably, bittersweet for Gerald and Kathryn.[25]

Mencken sent the couple a generous gift of silver flatware, but fate proved far less generous to him. Time's passing became evident in a far more gruesome way than in the departure of a daughter and a new son-in-law. On November 23, 1948, Mencken suffered a stroke that robbed him of his ability to read and write. It came at a time when his reputation was ascendant once more. It was Mencken the raconteur, the mellow elegist rather than the caustic critic of the contemporary scene, who found pronounced success during the 1940s. His autobiographical trilogy (*Happy Days, Newspaper Days,* and *Heathen Days*) stands as one of Mencken's most memorable achievements, a moving paean to an age that, in his eyes, merited nostalgia. The prose here is, arguably, the finest writing of one of America's most distinguished stylists. In this elegy for a once-remarkable country now irrevocably lost, Mencken played a part that would have been unthinkable twenty-five years before: Prospero waving his wand. Such a role would, of course, always be unthinkable for Johnson.[26]

But this was hardly the time for disputation, and Johnson acknowledged the enormity of Mencken's achievement in the *Days* books. Through his letters, Johnson tried to cheer up his old friend. Moreover, he once more repaid his debt through the currency of his art. He explains, in his introduction to William Manchester's *Disturber of the Peace: The Life of H. L. Mencken,* that "one aspect of the man that is extremely difficult to define is yet one that can be overlooked by none that had dealings with him. It is his attitude toward other writers, particularly the young and obscure. To say that he was generous, even lavish, with his sympathy and assistance is true enough, but not the whole truth; he also gave the rarer gift of genuine admiration."[27] Such was

25. GWJ to Jonathan Daniels, October 5, 1948, Jonathan Daniels Papers, Southern Historical Collection, Wilson Library, University of North Carolina at Chapel Hill; Dorothy Johnson van den Honert, telephone interview by author, from Pittsfield, Mass., June 23, 1997.

26. Dorothy Johnson van den Honert to Mencken, [1948], HLM Papers; Vincent Fitzpatrick, *H. L. Mencken* (New York: Continuum, 1989), 99; H. L. Mencken, *Thirty-Five Years of Newspaper Work: A Memoir by H. L. Mencken,* ed. Fred Hobson, Vincent Fitzpatrick, and Bradford Jacobs (Baltimore: Johns Hopkins University Press, 1994), 373.

27. GWJ to H. L. Mencken, January 14, April 11, 1949, HLM Papers; GWJ, introduction to *Disturber of the Peace: The Life of H. L. Mencken,* by William Manchester (New York: Harper and Brothers, 1950), xiii.

the story of his own dealings with Mencken twenty-five years before, when the Baltimorean had been so magnanimous to a relatively obscure North Carolina writer seeking a larger reputation. Characteristically, Johnson proved a good man during bad times—a staunch friend to this craftsman, cruelly deprived of his tools, who would endure more than seven years of what he thought of as a living death.

Johnson's book projects during 1948, both of them workmanlike rather than inspired, engaged him far less emotionally than Mencken's plight did. Having succeeded with that pictorial biography of Woodrow Wilson four years before, Johnson and the editors of *Look* collaborated on *The Central Northeast,* part of the Look at America series. It was a testament to Johnson's growing stature as a freelancer that he received another hefty advance of $15,000—this time from the Eugene A. Filene Good Will Fund, which commissioned a book about its founder, the famous New England merchant who "built up an obscure woman's specialty shop into the greatest store of its kind in the world." Given Johnson's irreverence about wealth, it is hardly surprising that the book pays less attention to Filene the financier than to Filene the "social statesman." The volume proves less a conventional biography—the structure is topical rather than chronological—than a study of Filene's thought. Johnson applauds his subject's "acceptance of the inevitability of change" and explains that Filene's political and economic liberalism were based not upon sentimentality but rather upon "logical, unemotional reasoning." Significantly, Johnson applauds Filene as yet another man "unterrified," another example of courage for his readers in a timid age.[28]

That same year, Johnson dared to get involved with television, then a new and highly controversial medium. In late April 1948, Johnson served on a discussion panel aired on WBAL television in Baltimore. This initial involvement in television would culminate four years later in his own program that would air both locally and nationally. As he was wont to do in print, he would speak plainly about matters that many others either avoided or upon which they trod very softly.[29]

He also dared to sign on with a bold venture, the *New York Star.* This daily, whose first issue appeared on June 23, 1948, followed the controversial

28. GWJ to Frank S. MacGregor, February 6, 1947, Harper and Brothers Papers; GWJ, *A Liberal's Progress: Edward A. Filene, Shopkeeper to Social Statesman* (New York: Coward-McCann, 1947), 8, 134, 142.

29. "Diary of R. P. Harriss," April 26, 1948.

newspaper *PM.* The *Star* was, by its own account, "a liberal newspaper . . . [edited] for men and women who believe in the future of America." Johnson wrote fifty-three columns, averaging about 800 words, that ran two to three times each week on different days. For the most part, he discussed politics. He spoke as the *vox populi,* referring to himself colloquially as one of "us plain working stiffs."[30]

Writing for this Yankee newspaper, he identified himself as a Southerner and both defended and criticized his native land. Henry Wallace, the presidential candidate of the Progressive Party, was pelted with eggs while he spoke in Greensboro. Johnson condemned the two miscreants as "a couple of young limbs of Satan" but forcefully defended the integrity of the the city where he had lived eleven years. He had to be amused when this defense caused him to be assailed in the newspaper's editorial mail as "a typical southern reactionary who doesn't know that the Civil War is over." While he acknowledged that the South had its racial problems, he again grew tired of those sanctimonious Northerners who preached to the South about the error of its ways. "I doubt that the deepest recesses of racial prejudice in this country are in the South," he declared, "or that Negroes are hated as some other minority groups seem to be in other sections."[31]

He also spoke wrathfully about his native region. He complained that Mississippi was benighted and criticized those Southern Democrats who chose to be obstructionists about civil rights. The Dixiecrats enraged him most of all. He called them "reactionaries" and explained that "if you take [Strom] Thurmond you have to choose his Ku Klux friends." Using that adjective of which he was then so fond, Johnson scorned the Dixiecrats as "the party of terrified men." The comparative historian likened those supporting Thurmond in 1948 to those who had championed John C. Breckinridge back in 1860, and "their ruin was so complete that the South has never really recovered." Johnson could hardly have been more pleased when Truman beat Dewey in spite of those misguided individuals who split from their party and embarrassed civilized Southerners.[32]

30. David Margolick, "*PM's* Impossible Dream," *Vanity Fair,* no. 461 (January 1999): 132; Bartley C. Crum and Joseph Barnes, "The *Star* Suspends Publication," *NYS,* January 28, 1949, 1; GWJ, "We Could Use a Tom Jefferson Now," *NYS,* October 3, 1948, p. 11.

31. GWJ, "What Was Wallace Doing in Greensboro, N.C., Anyway?" *NYS,* September 5, 1948; GWJ, "It's All Henry Wallace's Fault," *NYS,* September 15, 1948; Harry I. Moore, "letter to the editor," *NYS,* September 12, 1948; GWJ, "Mr. Deutsch—What Kind of Facts?" *NYS,* September 30, 1948.

32. GWJ, "A Gresham's Law for Red Hunters," *NYS,* August 10, 1948; GWJ, "Civil

Actually, Johnson's support of Truman generated a column that proved as oracular as the one the previous decade that had predicted the Nazi-Soviet Pact. During July, when the overconfident Republicans were prematurely dividing the spoils, Johnson suggested that "Battling Harry," a man "with more guts than a fiddle-string factory," would actually win the election. When Truman prevailed on November 8, Johnson found himself "a great man." The *Star* was the only New York morning newspaper that had supported Truman, and Johnson was the only columnist who had actually "called the turn."[33]

Johnson's piece about the Truman inauguration, "All for the Little Guy with No Gold Braid," offered the most accomplished writing among these *Star* columns that were consistently of high quality. Once more celebrating the noble American experiment in democracy, Johnson explained that "Mr. Truman stands right there, not in his own right, but representing you and me and Joe Doakes down the street and Martha, his wife, and the kids playing baseball in a vacant lot. He represents a Negro and a Jew and an American-born Japanese. In reality, it is a Minnesota farmer taking the salute, a Georgia Cracker, a New York filing clerk in whose honor the bombers darken the sky and fill the air with thunder." The inauguration marked not Truman's victory alone but rather the triumph of that average American who "took matters into his own hands, regardless of the great lords in business and journalism, regardless of the experts and wiseacres." Like Walt Whitman, Johnson embraced multitudes, and he wrote about them so artfully that his writing hardly seemed art at all.[34]

Johnson came to harbor considerable hopes for his association with the *Star*. The paper planned to begin syndicating his column in early 1949, and he thought that this money would suffice to pay his monthly bills. However, these hopes were dashed. After seven months, despite increases in both advertising and circulation, the newspaper was still not self-supporting. On January 28, 1949, after 186 issues, the *Star* ceased publication. Johnson would

Rights: Ethical vs. Political Approach," *NYS*, July 14, 1948; GWJ, "Truman a Bargain by Comparison," *NYS*, September 12, 1948; GWJ, "Thurmond Nice? So Was Breckenridge [*sic*], and He Cost Plenty," *NYS*, August 18, 1948.

33. GWJ, "A Haberdasher Shows That a Tie Need Not Be a Noose," *NYS*, July 11, 1948; GWJ to Katherine Johnson Parham, November 8, 1948, GWJ Papers.

34. GWJ, "All for the Little Guy with No Gold Braid," *NYS*, January 20, 1949.

never again have a comparable journalistic forum to publish his political commentary on such a regular basis.[35]

While Mencken suffered on Hollins Street, his words remained very much on Johnson's mind. Writing to Howard Odum, Johnson passed along one of those piquant observations that Mencken had made in conversation: "The sad part of standing for freedom of speech is that you are always fighting for sons of bitches, because it is the son of a bitch who always gets into trouble first; but if you don't fight for him, the bars are down." Johnson thought the Communists odious but found them far less dangerous than those who tried to silence them. He worked against the passage of the Ober Act, Maryland's anti-subversive legislation. "It can be interpreted by unscrupulous persons," he explained, "to serve purposes which the Legislature never intended." Typically, Johnson thought more frequently about Big Brother than his fellow citizens did. The degree to which this matter of personal freedom preoccupied Johnson is evident in *Our English Heritage,* his single book of 1949. Writing about John Rolfe's activities during the seventeenth century, Johnson remarked, with absolutely no subtlety, that "he contracted a political marriage, an act which [now] might well incur the disapproval of the House Committee on Un-American Activities."[36]

Our English Heritage, written for J. B. Lippincott's The People of America series edited by Louis Adamic, does not purport to offer an exhaustive treatment of this broad subject. This would constitute the work of several lifetimes, Johnson explains, "and would result, not in a book, but in a library." Soundly structured, the book falls into two sections. The first, "The People," chronicles the three waves of British settlers ("The Expendables, "The Indispensables," and "The Gentlemen of Quality") who sailed to the New World. In the second section, "The Institutions," Johnson's wide range of knowledge permits him to explain the English influence upon America's language, legal system, religion, arts, sciences, and philosophy. Typically self-effacing, he calls himself "a mere chronicler." Actually, Johnson succeeds in making this large mass of material intelligible to the common reader without vulgarizing it.[37]

35. GWJ to Frank S. MacGregor, January 15, 1949, Harper and Brothers Papers; Crum and Barnes, "*Star* Suspends Publication."

36. GWJ to Howard W. Odum, June 6, 1949, HWO Papers; "Vote on the Ober Act, Johnson Urges," *BS,* May 4, 1949; GWJ, *Our English Heritage* (Philadelphia: J. B. Lippincott, 1949), 85.

37. GWJ, *Our English Heritage,* 83, 181.

Once more intrigued by the origins of America, Johnson the moralist again uses the past as a pulpit to preach to the present. The early settlers faced huge dangers—America was "a deadly country, even for the able-bodied"— but persevered to take control of their destiny. "Freedom is costly," Johnson opines. "If one generation doesn't pay its price another must." During its inception and its formative years, American proved no country for the cautious and complacent, and Johnson laments that "we are at this moment politically the most conservative of the great nations." As always, he thought "conservative American" an oxymoron.[38]

Johnson concludes by using a tapestry metaphor to discuss the future of the average American. The pessimists, he scoffs, argue that America's development "has come to its logical conclusion," and the tapestry's next panel will show the common man "beginning to quail before the glare of a dictator." Weaving a different scenario, Johnson says that "the pattern set by the English, far from having run out, is only now ready for its development with richer fabrics, more gorgeous hues and more daring designs than its originators ever possessed." The panel will show a common man raising "his eyes from the face of the ruler and [turning] them toward the stars." "My new book," he told Howard Odum, "is being praised by all the critics and bought by none of the public." *Incredible Tale,* his next venture, would both be praised in print and feed him far better.[39]

Johnson signed a contract with Harper and Brothers on May 3, 1949, received an advance of $4,000, and began work immediately. He found the book "a bitch to write" but pushed on resolutely. He told a correspondent that "if I ever expect to say anything, now is the time, so I am grimly determined." This remark suggests that he was not entirely satisfied with his writing up to this point. It also suggests that, approaching his fifty-ninth birthday, he was more aware than ever of his own mortality. (Mencken's plight was, of course, a painful and constant reminder of the dirty tricks that time can play upon the disciplined and the productive.) During that summer, Johnson devoted nearly every working hour to *Incredible Tale,* and the project proved "ruinous financially." He complete the manuscript in late September, thereby managing to finish a volume of nearly three hundred pages in under five months.[40]

38. *Ibid.,* 29, 12, 239.

39. *Ibid.,* 224–46; Donald H. Kirkley, "Man of 10 Million Words," *BS,* April 11, 1954; GWJ to Howard W. Odum, August 31, 1949, HWO Papers.

40. GWJ to Cass Canfield, May 10, 1949; GWJ to Frank S. MacGregor, August 12, 1949, Harper and Brothers Papers.

Unlike some other authors, he was not superstitious about discussing a work in progress or a completed manuscript not yet published. His correspondence shows the importance that he accorded this project and explains his methodology. He wrote his sister Kate that the book was "by longest odds the biggest thing I have ever undertaken" and called it "the confession of an unabashed liberal." He was writing a "Biography of Nobody," Johnson explained to his editor, "that is to say, the story of man of no importance, who knows only what he reads in the newspapers." He was less interested in conventional history than in "folklore." In a letter to the North Carolina playwright Paul Green, Johnson, who knew all too well about his penchant for moralizing, wryly referred to the book as "my new sermon." This homily, hardly a conventional one, saw print on March 15, 1959, and the congregation heartily approved. Johnson was honored as he had never been before.[41]

The book's title comes from an oration by Aeschines ("we are born to serve as a theme of incredible tales to posterity"), and his subtitle, *The Odyssey of the Average American in the Last Half Century,* shows yet again his interest in the common citizen. Johnson remarks that "the passing generation is a battered generation" experiencing "the freezing fear of total war." The average American of fifty has had "his hopes . . . shattered [and] his idealism chilled." Standing at the mid-point of a bloody and tumultuous history, Johnson offers reassurance, for he asserts confidently that "the worst has already happened."[42]

Returning to that structural trope with which he always felt comfortable, Johnson again draws history as a drama populated by heroes such as Wilson and Roosevelt and villains like Lenin ("a man of the library" imprisoned by Marxism), Stalin (the cold dictator tolerating "no crack in the monolithic state that he rules"), and Hitler ("one of the grisliest jokes the sardonic gods ever perpetrated upon mankind"). Johnson stresses that these immense men, who for better and for worse have shaped the course of the twentieth century and have embodied the upper limits of good and evil, have passed from the earth. Conversely, he explains that "the only immortal among us is the Average Man"—that average American who was bold enough to cast his lot with the dangerous American experiment, who has repulsed the attacks of those

41. GWJ to Katherine Johnson Parham, September 26, 1949, GWJ Papers; GWJ to Frank S. MacGregor, March 30, 1949, Harper and Brothers Papers; GWJ to Paul Green, December 30, 1949, Paul Green Papers, Southern Historical Collection, Wilson Library, University of North Carolina at Chapel Hill.

42. GWJ, *Incredible Tale: The Odyssey of the Average American in the Last Half Century* (New York: Harper and Brothers, 1950), 5, 244, 293.

determined to rob him of his civil liberties, and who has refused to profane the American dream by selling his soul in the pursuit of ephemeral wealth. The *New York Herald Tribune* called the book "inspirational," and another reviewer likened Johnson to a sanguine physician dispensing "a healthy and necessary anti-histamine for the sniffling which has too long and too seriously engaged our attention."[43]

That June, Johnson's uplifting tale was offered as a dual selection of the Book of the Month Club—"one of the fastest selections ever made by the jury," he exulted. His publisher hosted a celebratory lunch at Pierre's Restaurant in New York City. All of this gave Johnson "a great kick," and he remarked that "Harper's stubborn faith in me as a writer is beginning to pay off." The homage and royalties generated by *Incredible Tale* validated Johnson's decision to pursue such a lonely and challenging career, a career in which he had always labored well but not always lucratively. From now on, he would be "taken seriously by the business end of the literary establishment."[44]

When Johnson traveled south that spring and summer, he returned to his native state more famous than he had been three years before, when he had delighted the Gerald Johnson Book Club. On May 12, he spoke to the Friends of the Library in Chapel Hill on the occasion of a dinner honoring Dr. Louis Round Wilson, the esteemed librarian. Johnson returned in August to visit Riverton, happy as always with family and familiar places. That same month, he attended the first annual North Carolina Writers' Conference on Roanoke Island. Wearing a plumed hat and tights, he also made a guest appearance in Paul Green's *The Lost Colony* when the play was produced in Manteo.[45]

Family matters that year generated delight and melancholy. Gerald and Kathryn's first grandchild, Peter van den Honert, was born on April 11, 1950. They would spend that Thanksgiving in Pittsfield visiting the new family member and his parents. (Although neither grandfather nor grandson could then anticipate it, Peter would figure prominently in one of Johnson's most successful book projects.) On June 17, Kathryn Johnson wed Frederick Allen Sliger in Baltimore. A native Texan and chemical engineer, he worked for

43. *Ibid.*, 126, 123, 252, 149, 281; Joseph Barnes, "That Optimistic, Durable Fellow, the Average American," *NYHTB,* May 28, 1950; E. W. Kenworthy, "Fifty Years of America," *BES,* May 27, 1950.

44. GWJ to Katherine Johnson Parham, May 25, 1950, GWJ Papers; GWJ to Cass Canfield, March 3, 1950, Harper and Brothers Papers; GWJ to Katherine Johnson Parham, March 3, 1950, GWJ Papers.

45. "Johnson to be Guest at North Carolina Fete," *BS,* August 6, 1950; Jesse Glasgow, "Gerald Johnson: Man of the World," *Wake Forest* 27 (spring 1980): 13–16.

the American Oil Company, and the couple moved that year to Valparaiso, Indiana. Happy for his daughter and his new son-in-law, Johnson was melancholy for himself and his wife. Prior to the wedding, he told his sister Kate that he was "in a mood of depression, wondering just what, after [my daughter] leaves, Kathryn and I will find excuse for cumbering the earth any longer." As usual he found work, those damnably long days at the typewriter that proved the best salvation of all.[46]

Having taken a bold stand as a freelancer, Johnson had found freedom and fame during this first phase of his new career. During the next ten years, in Johnson's seventh decade, his reputation would ascend even higher. Much to his benefit, America would provide him with a writer's most valuable sort of opponents: public figures, revered by many, whose values he deplored and whose presence challenged him to speak forcefully for the adversary culture. On February 9, 1950, Senator Joseph McCarthy of Wisconsin spoke in Wheeling, West Virginia, and claimed that more than two hundred members of the State Department were also members of the Communist Party. Appalled, Johnson remarked contemptuously to Odum that "no doubt we shall meet shortly in the concentration camp, where Senator McCarthy is going to put everybody who objects to chattel slavery." While he would attack McCarthy as profoundly un-American, Johnson would also challenge the values of the war hero who won two presidential elections. Although Johnson the veteran admired Eisenhower the soldier, Johnson the writer thought Eisenhower the politician overmatched and misguided. Johnson would engage in a running battle with America's "thought police" and do his best to dispel "the fog of terror" shrouding the land. Manifesting an energy and radicalism that belied his years, Johnson would assault what he saw as the American Jericho—with its complacency and conformity, with its insufficient concern for life's unfortunates and its exaggerated respect for the corporate mentality, with its contempt for the reflective life and its assent to mindless materialism. He would not topple the walls, but to the delight of some and the outrage of others, he would make them shake a bit.[47]

46. GWJ to Lenoir Chambers, November 24, 1950, Lenoir Chambers Papers, Southern Historical Collection, Wilson Library, University of North Carolina at Chapel Hill; Kathryn Johnson Sliger, telephone interview by author, from Valparaiso, Ind., June 18, 1997; GWJ to Katherine Johnson Parham, May 25, 1950, GWJ Papers.

47. Thomas C. Reeves, *The Life and Times of Joe McCarthy: A Biography* (New York: Stein and Day, 1982), 224; GWJ to Howard W. Odum, May 8, 1950, HWO Papers; "Gerald Johnson Says People Will Keep Democracy Alive," *BS,* October 15, 1950; GWJ, "Prime Document for a Postponed Campaign," *NYHTB,* August 15, 1948, p. 5.

12   "The Critic and Conscience of Our Time"
1951–1960

> Every American of the past who is worth remembering by the present was once considered a subversive character. And they were rightly so regarded, for they did subvert many an entrenched wrong, many an ancient folly, many a hallowed evil. Washington, Jefferson, Jackson, Lincoln, Wilson and Roosevelt—all were controversial figures, all were enemies of the existing order, all were denounced as unsound men engaged in un-American activities. But all were free spirits and all extended, in one way or another, the boundaries of liberty, so now all stand as monumental while their detractors are forgotten or remembered only as painful examples of the folly into which otherwise sane men sometimes fall.
>
> —*Gerald Johnson, "Books and Citizenship"*

During his seventh decade, this writer who drew so frequently upon the Bible experienced firsthand the somber truths set forth in Ecclesiastes. A new generation was arriving. He and Kathryn celebrated the births of four more grandchildren: Christopher, Ann Kathryn, and Gerald van den Honert in Massachusetts; and Susan Kathryn Sliger in Indiana. On the other hand, an older one was passing from the earth. Richard Hayward, Kathryn's father, died at eighty-eight in 1958; now, both husband and wife faced the world as orphans. Two years later, Johnson suffered the loss of his older sister, Mary. Howard Odum died in late 1954, Mencken in early 1956. The invaluable services of literary agent George Bye ceased with his death the following year. In the midst of so much mortality, Johnson kept writing.

Moreover, he lectured in Canada and across the United States. For a short time, he returned to academic life, and he established a significant new forum with the *New Republic*. His venture into televison succeeded far beyond his expectations. As he approached his seventieth year, Johnson, again showing remarkable adaptability, completed his first book for a juvenile audience, a highly successful volume that would influence his authorship of books for years to come.

He continued to play the gadfly. Lamenting that Americans "have become prisoners of our doubts and fears," he explained that "we are reluctant to admit that we owe our liberties to men of a type that today we hate and fear—unruly men [and] disturbers of the peace." Disgusted with American materialism and mindlessness, he reduced them to the absurd: "To judge by the elaborate advertising in our magazines, the heart's desire of the American man . . . is to shut himself in a goldfish bowl mounted on a raft and proceed down the road at a hundred miles an hour; and that of the American woman is to escape any sort of useful work that might take her away from the bridge table or television set." He pointedly called American politics "the never-ceasing struggle to dethrone the privileged and enthrone the best." Predictably, he outraged the privileged and delighted the best. So decorous in society, Johnson was, in the realm of ideas, very much a disturber of the peace himself.[1]

The beginning of 1951 found a combative Johnson back in Greensboro, that city which he had defended so forcefully three years before. Addressing the Book and Author Luncheon, Johnson gave no safe and soporific speech. Instead, he snorted at those authors who chose to retreat to the proverbial ivory tower and argued that true men of words were politically engaged. Noting that "the safest man in the world is the slave," he declared that America's writers "should proclaim liberty, not security." Using a trope that would recur throughout the decade, he called for his fellow authors "to do their part in the war of ideas."[2]

Throughout the year, he warred with those guilty of racial prejudice, the invasion of privacy, and demagoguery. Johnson used the *Baltimore Evening Sun* to battle for better health care for the city's people of color and to call for greater opportunities for them to join the medical profession. Outraged by Senator McCarthy, Johnson decried the presence of "keyhole peepers" in a free republic and scorned the politician for "[making] government service almost impossible for an honorable man." Such criticism was leveled more than two years before Edward R. Murrow used *See It Now*, his popular television show on CBS, to launch the famous attack that so badly hurt the sena-

1. GWJ, "The Press and the Spirit of the People," *Southwest Review* 30 (August 1953): 318–23; GWJ, "Wading into Trouble," *NR* 135 (December 10, 1956): 10; GWJ to Wingate Johnson, July 5, 1952, GWJ Papers.

2. "Responsibility of Authors Outlined by Gerald W. Johnson Talk Here," *GDN*, February 4, 1951.

tor. Johnson's censure in 1951 proved the work of a bold man who told the truth as he saw it at considerable personal risk.[3]

This American People, Johnson's single book of the year, was the product of a collaboration between the American Library Association and Harper and Brothers. The volume exemplified the theme of the association's seventy-fifth anniversary celebration: "The Heritage of the United States of America in Times of Crisis." Published on October 3, the volume could just as well have been entitled *In Defense of Liberty* or, with a nod of thanks to John Stuart Mill, *On American Liberty.* Clearly, freedom was very much on Johnson's mind, for his eight chapters discuss such matters as free speech, freedom of conscience, free enterprise, freedom of inquiry, freedom of association, and freedom of opportunity. The book sets forth characteristically Johnsonian ideas tailored to a country experiencing, in his eyes, the jitters of the Atomic Age and hysteria about the threat of Communism.[4]

His preface, stridently entitled "Let's Get This Straight," explains that *This American People* is "an inquiry into the risks that a man must now run if he is to be thoroughly American." The true American must risk the danger inherent in challenging any government "that becomes destructive of liberty." He must conquer fear: "From Franklin's 'Hang together or hang separately' to Roosevelt's 'All we have to fear is fear itself,' the best counselors of this country have advised us to go ahead even if we are afraid." And he must cast his lot not with the powers of darkness but rather with those individuals who "flood the world with light."[5]

Reviewing the book in the *New York Herald Tribune,* Robert E. Sherwood both perceived Johnson's purpose and celebrated his success. "There are plenty of good people striding through the world today," Sherwood observed, "but it would be hard to find one with a clearer understanding of our national deficiencies as well advantages, or a better ability to state them simply and sensibly than Gerald W. Johnson." The reviewer proceeded to remark that "the mouthings of Joe McCarthy . . . may express some aspects of 'This American People.' But Gerald Johnson expresses the final, considered

3. GWJ, "The Needs of Provident Hospital," *BES,* September 4, 1951; GWJ, "The Revolting Era of Good Feeling," *This Week,* December 30, 1951, pp. 6–8; GWJ, "How Jefferson and Three Successors Administered the Government," *NYHTB,* September 16, 1951, p. 5; Thomas C. Reeves, *The Life and Times of Joe McCarthy: A Biography* (New York: Stein and Day, 1982), 564–65.

4. "Gerald Johnson Chooses to Write A.L.A. Book," *GDN,* March 4, 1951.

5. GWJ, *This American People* (New York: Harper and Brothers, 1951), x, 42, 85, 201.

truth. I hope that many Americans will read this book." Many did; *This American People* sold over eleven thousand copies its first year.[6]

Like its beginning, the end of 1951 found Johnson back in North Carolina. In early December, he traveled to Raleigh to receive an award presented by the North Carolina Society for the Preservation of Antiquities; he was honored for his accumulated writing on state history. Later that month, he visited his sister Kate (Mrs. Benjamin Parham) in Oxford, and the visit proved sufficiently newsworthy for the *Raleigh News and Observer* to cover it. Friends and neighbors came to mingle with the famous author. Questioned about the forthcoming election, Johnson said that he hoped that Dwight Eisenhower would not tarnish "the great and noble name" that he had made in the military by deciding to run for president.[7]

The following year, North Carolina's past figured prominently in *The Making of a Southern Industrialist: A Biographical Study of Simpson Bobo Tanner.* Tanner (1853–1924) founded the Henrietta Mills in 1887 and twenty years later became president of the American Cotton Manufacturers Association. In this monograph of eighty-four pages, Tanner joined Jackson, Randolph, Wilson, and Ochs as Southerners whose lives Johnson chronicled. Tanner differed from his predecessors in that he proved a figure of regional rather than national significance.

Kenneth Tanner, the subject's son, was responsible for this volume, which Johnson called "an act of filial piety." He admitted that he wrote this book because he "couldn't well get out of it." It is uncertain whether someone called in a favor, or whether someone made Johnson a financial offer that he could not refuse. In any event, this book that he began reluctantly came to interest him more as it progressed. He came to regard Tanner less as an individual than as a type, and the lives and work of the textile barons "were so important a point of the history of the South that the region cannot be understood unless they are taken into account."[8]

6. Robert E. Sherwood, "Our Government: The Brave Devised It for the Brave," *NYHTB,* October 28, 1951, pp. 1, 22; Frank S. MacGregor to Dr. Ralph E. E. Ellsworth, March 18, 1954, Harper and Brothers Papers, Firestone Library, Princeton University, Princeton, N.J.

7. "Gerald Johnson Gets Cannon Cup," *BES,* December 8, 1951; "Cannon Cup Awards Are Made," *Raleigh News and Observer,* December 7, 1951; "Gerald W. Johnson Visits Oxford Kin," *Raleigh News and Observer,* December 20, 1951.

8. GWJ to Wingate Johnson, November 27, 1952, GWJ Papers; GWJ, *The Making of a Southern Industrialist: A Biographical Study of Simpson Bobo Tanner* (Chapel Hill: University of North Carolina Press, 1952), 73.

Looking backward here, Johnson discusses aspects of Southern history that he had analyzed before in some of his more provocative essays. Echoing what he had explained in "Service in the Cotton Mills" (1925), Johnson depicts Tanner as one of that first wave of mill owners more interested in duty to their region than in financial profit for themselves. As he had done in "The Cadets of New Market," Johnson evocatively captures the hard times in the South after the war. Finally, as he had done after the publication of *I'll Take My Stand*, Johnson attacks those who romanticize the life of the land, "those townsmen whose contact with the soil is limited to golf courses and small flower-gardens." In this volume about the past, Johnson once more cannot help offering a lesson for the present. Tanner "faced a far worse situation than ours, but he pulled out of it; if we can't do as much under easier conditions, we shall not fail because the Russians are very terrible (or the labor unions, or the New Dealers, or the atheists—write your own ticket) but because we don't raise any more S. B. Tanners."[9]

Once again concerned with freedom during an age preoccupied with safety, Johnson fittingly called his second book of 1952 *Pattern for Liberty: The Story of Old Philadelphia*. Chronicling life in the city from 1776 until 1790, from the Declaration of Independence until the move of America's political capital to Washington, the volume offers "a plausible reconstruction of the environment in which the young republic grew from swaddling clothes to schoolboy garments." A study of the American character at its best, *Pattern for Liberty* celebrates "bold, brisk fellows in a bold, brisk city" and offers a tale of tolerance and humility for an age grown intolerant and highly unreasonable. Employing that luminary image once again, Johnson concludes by remarking that the contemporary citizen, wandering through Independence Hall, should "see there the symbol of a rising, not a setting sun."[10]

As a public speaker, Johnson used various forums to chastise those who walked in darkness. Addressing the Academy of Political Science in New York City, he criticized those who obstinately defended states' rights. Speaking to the Maryland Library Association, he lamented that "the concept of honor has largely disappeared from American life." A speech to the Alabama Library Association found Johnson even more pugnacious. Recounting the event to Odum, Johnson said with pride that "I tore into McCarthyism and

9. GWJ, *Making of a Southern Industrialist,* 20, 9.

10. GWJ to Wingate Johnson, November 9, 1952, GWJ Papers; GWJ, *Pattern for Liberty: The Story of Old Philadelphia* (New York: McGraw-Hill, 1952), 25, 130, 146.

such recklessly, wondering if I would escape with a whole skin. But they loved it. Swarms of them came up to me afterward, laughing and slapping me on the back and loudly thanking God that at last somebody had spoken up and called a skunk a skunk." Moreover, Johnson boldly used other fo-rums—the reviews in the *New York Herald Tribune* and his new television show—to continue his assault upon the senator, his followers, and those Americans he cowed.[11]

An element of the absurd marked Johnson's entry into television com-mentary. When he was first approached in the spring of 1952 by WAAM, Baltimore's ABC affiliate, Johnson did not even own a television himself. The station wanted him to analyze the presidential conventions, and Johnson protested that he "knew nothing about conventions and nothing about tele-vision commentary." All he knew, he proceeded to explain, "was what the folks on Bolton Street were saying." The station replied that this was pre-cisely what it wanted—"somebody to discuss the convention from the point of view of the plain, impartial citizen." Skeptical, but never averse to trying something new, he agreed to do four shows. By the time that he was finished, *How Things Look from Bolton Street* had aired more than 140 times, both lo-cally and nationally, and Johnson had received several prestigious awards. He talked about whatever interested him: local, national, and international poli-tics; the good life in Baltimore City and the sterility of suburbia; economics and education; journalism and literary criticism; race and religion; civil liberty and the perils of Big Brother. WAAM had the good sense to leave Johnson alone, and he was grateful that the station "never dictated one word uttered here."[12]

Johnson, on his part, had the good sense never to try to appear something other than what he was: a writer. The studio was outfitted to look like the study at 1310 Bolton Street. He labored for several days over each two-thou-sand-word script that filled fifteen minutes of air time; he called these scripts "the hardest work I've every done outside the Army." Without theatrics and

11. GWJ, "The Extension of Federal Powers at the Expense of State Powers," lecture delivered on May 24, 1952, at the Academy of Political Science, New York City, GWJ Papers; "Lack of Honor in Political Life Decried," *BS,* May 11, 1952; GWJ to Howard W. Odum, April 28, 1952, HWO Papers; GWJ, "The Case for Honor against Fear," *NYHTB,* January 6, 1952, p. 4; GWJ, "Mr. Shirer Looks Back at Europe in a Tumultuous Age," *NYHTB,* Septem-ber 14, 1952, p. 3, GWJ, *HTLFBS,* September 12, November 11, 1952, *HTLFBS* Papers.

12. Donald Kirkley, "Man of 10 Million Words," *BS,* April 11, 1954; GWJ to Wingate Johnson, June 28, 1952, GWJ Papers; GWJ, *HTLFBS,* July 4, 1954, *HTLFBS* Papers.

any sort of visual aids, he sat there and read his copy. Sensibly, he pictured himself addressing one representative viewer:

> He is not much interested and he is a little deaf . . . enough to make it necessary to speak very clearly. He is more than a little skeptical, having a strong suspicion that I am liable to make a fool of myself, a suspicion only too well founded. So I try to reason with him. It's no use to shout, and it's worse than useless to wave my arms and pound the table. I try not to do anything before the camera that I wouldn't do if I were talking in a living room. Above all, I try to assume that my man is too intelligent to swallow any obvious hooey.

Johnson had always admired President Roosevelt's huge skills as a communicator, and *How Things Look from Bolton Street* was the closest that Johnson ever came to FDR's "Fireside Chats."[13]

As he had done with the *New York Star,* Johnson talked as the *vox populi,* a sort of American Everyman. He spoke for the "plain people," and he explained that "the great bulk of us just manage to get along. . . . The very rich and very poor do not constitute America. The strength of the country is the great mass of in-betweens, and that's us." Mr. Johnson's neighborhood came alive in the viewer's imagination as a place of common sense and common decency, a place that cared about the underdog. And the station that had solicited Johnson's commentary had to be pleased when, instead of waxing grandiloquent, he used a homespun analogy to explain that "all the uproar over the [Democratic] nomination . . . will be more or less hollering down a rain-barrel."[14]

Typically, Johnson's loyalties were solidly Democratic during the 1952 presidential campaign. He thought Eisenhower unqualified to run the county, and he scoffed at Richard M. Nixon as "one of the chief architects of the witchcraft that has nearly abolished free speech in this country." On the other hand, Johnson proved highly enthusiastic about Adlai Stevenson. He saw this former governor of Illinois as highly intelligent and, in the tradi-

13. Kathryn Hayward Johnson, interview with author, Valparaiso, Ind., June 8, 1989; Kirkley, "Man of 10 Million Words"; GWJ, untitled address given on Wednesday, April 22, 1953, at the Associated Press Broadcasters' Meeting, National Press Club, Washington, D.C., GWJ Papers; Gilbert Sandler, "Gerald Johnson's 'Fireside Chats,' " *BES,* October 15, 1991.

14. GWJ, *HTLFBS,* March 28, 1954, December 2, 1952, July 18, 1952, *HTLFBS* Papers.

tion of Wilson and Franklin Roosevelt, a great communicator with "a genius for presenting a complex problem to the people in apparently simple terms."[15]

During the summer of 1952, Johnson traveled to Illinois to work on Stevenson's behalf. Although Johnson was hampered by his deafness, Stevenson was delighted to have him there, and Johnson contributed ideas, helped to plot strategy, and wrote speeches. On November 5, after Eisenhower's victory, Johnson sent Stevenson a telegram: "A battle is lost, but not the war. Liberalism under your leadership will yet save this country. Proud to have followed you." Nine days later, he wrote to account for the loss: "There were just five reasons for your defeat, to wit, Ike's five stars. Hero worship is the whole story." A grateful Stevenson said that it should be Johnson who drafted the manifesto for liberals at the mid-point of the twentieth century.[16] The men would do battle once again, and the friendship begun here would endure until Stevenson's death. In all, Johnson grew closer to Stevenson than to any president or any other presidential aspirant.

While Johnson was disappointed in the result of the election, he was pleased when the departing chief executive summoned him to Washington. Two years earlier, Truman had written a six-page letter in his own hand that was addressed to "Dear Gerald." In early December 1952, he called Johnson to the White House "to express his appreciation of my support and to chat about things."[17] During the next eight years, there would be no such friendly chats with President Eisenhower.

The following year, Johnson declined to undertake a biography of Eleanor Roosevelt, but he agreed to write about the residence of America's first president by focusing upon the efforts of those women who fought to preserve it. *Mount Vernon: The Story of a Shrine* celebrated the hundredth anniversary of the Mount Vernon Ladies' Association, "the first official restoration group in the United States and the first women's patriotic society." In 1853, Johnson explains, Mount Vernon was "a picture of neglect, decay, and desolation." A century later, with its million annual visitors, it was "by far the

15. GWJ, *HTLFBS,* July 18, 1952, *HTLFBS* Papers; GWJ to Adlai Stevenson, November 14, 1952, AES Papers.

16. Adlai Stevenson to Jonathan Daniels, August 5, 1952, Adlai Stevenson to Eric Sevareid, August 3, 1952, GWJ to Adlai Stevenson, November 5, 14, 1952, Adlai Stevenson to GWJ, November 10, December 28, 1952, AES Papers.

17. GWJ to Katherine Johnson Parham, January 30, 1950, December 2, 1952, GWJ Papers.

most important place of secular pilgrimage in the country." Johnson uses this monograph of about 25,000 words to attack gender stereotyping. The life of Ann Pamela Cunningham, the South Carolinian who organized the association, "stands as a shattering disproof of the old idea of a Southern lady as charming but brainless and not to be taken seriously." Moreover, he asserts that the history of this association "becomes a sort of epitome of the history of the intelligent American woman for the past half century." In the Johnsonian tradition, this volume extols those resolute individuals who push forward in the face of indifference and disapproval.[18]

Johnson resolutely told the harsh truth as he saw it when he spoke in Dallas during the spring of 1953. He gave one of the four addresses at Southern Methodist University in a program called the "Institute of American Freedom." After calling Alexander Hamilton a "born maverick," Johnson remarked pointedly that "he would have died rather than tell a Congressional investigating committee that he was not a Communist." Derived from his speech, Johnson's essay, "American Freedom and the Press," was published later that year in *The Present Danger: Four Essays on American Freedom,* a volume whose preface bemoans America's descent into "hysteria" and criticizes those misguided individuals "willing to cast overboard many of our traditional freedoms."[19]

The civil libertarian refers to Jefferson's famous declaration that a free press without a government is superior to a government without a free press. Freedom of the press, he asserts unequivocally, "is the measure of [American] liberty." While he acknowledges that a country "hag-ridden" by fear of communism cannot value a free press as much as it should, this particular fear, in Johnson's view, does not prove the sole destructive influence. He points as well to economics: "A modern metropolitan newspaper is Big Business. Only a great millionaire, or a millionaire corporation, can own a large-city newspaper now; and in all the world there is nothing more timorous than a million dollars, except ten millions. In revolutionary times the rich are always the people who are most afraid, and the press is rich." Once again, Johnson's values lay outside the mainstream of mercantile America. Money does not set

18. GWJ to Frank S. MacGregor, April 10, 1953, Harper and Brothers Papers; GWJ, *Mount Vernon: The Story of a Shrine* (New York: Random House, 1953), foreword (unnumbered page), 4, 46, 6.

19. GWJ, "American Freedom and the Press," in *The Present Danger: Four Essays on American Freedom,* ed. Allen Maxwell (Dallas: Southern Methodist University Press, 1953), 25, v.

one free; rather it imprisons—the greater the accumulation, the longer and more restrictive the incarceration.[20]

On November 23, 1953, when his first biweekly column ran in the *New Republic,* Johnson found a much larger audience for such iconoclasm. While he had been contributing to magazines for more than three decades, this was his first column to appear on a regular basis. Moreover, the *New Republic* offered Johnson his first regular print forum since the cessation of the *New York Star* back in early 1949. Typically self-effacing, Johnson called his column "The Superficial Aspect." Actually, it proved far from superficial. Frequently political in nature, this column of about a thousand words discussed national and international issues. As he had done on the *Star,* and as he was continuing to do with *How Things Look from Bolton Street,* Johnson played the part of *vox populi.* "I happen to live," he informed the magazine's readers in his first piece, "in a neighborhood inhabited by very commonplace people; in fact, I happen to be one of them. Bolton Street in Baltimore is, I am certain, exactly like a thousand streets in American cities." About six weeks later, he explained further that he and his neighbors were "small people, honest, patriotic and perfectly sane, but not intellectual giants."[21]

In fact, he was highly intellectual, a writer whose interests could hardly have been more diverse. He drew upon Shakespeare and T. S. Eliot, Thucydides and Rudyard Kipling, Greek and Roman myths and the Bible, popular comic strips and nursery rhymes, and he took full advantage of the freedom to frolic as he pleased. The decision of the New York City Board of Education to remove *The Adventures of Huckleberry Finn* from its required list of readings led Johnson to comment with wit and scorn: "Every work of art is offensive to someone, for a work of art is a protest against things as they are and a proclamation of things as they should be. Venus de Milo is an offense to every flat-chested woman in the world, and the Belvedere Apollo to every pot-bellied man. *Huckleberry Finn* is just as offensive to racism as Mark Twain could make it, regardless of whether the fascism is that of a white Troglodyte or a black Mrs. Grundy." Deftly, he made his opponents' positions untenable. Discussing political corruption, he used a colorful animal metaphor to lampoon venal politicians and the wealthy special-interest groups that tried to

20. *Ibid.,* 22, 26–27, 29, 33, 39.

21. "The Superficial Aspect," *NR* (November 23, 1953): 15; and 130 (January 4, 1954): 15. On June 30, 1955, Johnson began to give his articles individual titles, with "The Superficial Aspect" remaining the column's title.

purchase them: "The rumor circulated by the cynical that the oil and communications interests have invaded the stockyards, buying Congressmen in
carload lots, is certainly a canard. In the first place, a dozen head of prime
stock would probably meet every requirement; they don't need a carload. In
the second place, only the irrational would buy a steer that already bears the
company brand." Whether he was tweaking the Republican elephant that he
found ponderous and dim-witted, defending free speech against its sanctimonious detractors, or speaking eloquently for those incapable of articulating
their beliefs, Johnson distinguished himself in "The Superficial Aspect."
Many magazine articles date quickly—they seem archaic after five years to
say nothing of more than three decades—but a journey through Johnson's
writing for the *New Republic* is never boring. He offered his readers both instruction and delight.[22]

Beginning in the summer of 1953, Johnson delighted both Theodore
Roosevelt McKeldin and the crowds who listened to his speeches. Formerly
the mayor of Baltimore, McKeldin, a Republican, was then governor of
Maryland. (He would subsequently serve another term as mayor.) Johnson
wrote his first speech for McKeldin to honor the ninetieth anniversary of the
Battle of Gettysburg and thereafter crafted all his nonpolitical speeches. In
time, McKeldin won five Freedom Foundation awards, and he remarked
gratefully that all of these speeches had been written by Johnson.[23]

For those television scripts on which he worked so arduously, Johnson
received an award in his own name. On March 27, 1953, he was given the
Alfred I. du Pont Award for "meritorious service to the American people,"
the first non-network commentator to be so honored. He found himself
praised as "one of the most pungent, thoughtful, and knowledgeable com-
mentators in America today." On May 31, the show received its first network
exposure, and Johnson could hardly have been more pleased with the results.
"My television program," he told a correspondent that July, "has been explo-
sively successful. . . . [It has been] rated . . . as the top commentator's program
on TV, but . . . I understand that McCarthy's investigators are at work."
Johnson had recently used the show to accuse McCarthy of religious bigotry

22. GWJ, "Oh, for Mencken Now," *NR* 130 (September 30, 1957): 11; GWJ, "The
Formaldehyde Crew," *NR* (March 3, 1958): 16.
23. Lloyd Dennis, "Gerald Johnson: Man of Many Parts," *GDN,* March 22, 1964; R. P.
Harriss, "Will the Real Sage of Baltimore Stand Up and Take a Bow?" *Baltimore News American,*
August 4, 1985; Gerald Parshall, "Gerald Johnson Gets Tribute at City Hall," *BS,* August 6,
1970.

and to liken his followers to the infamous Know-Nothing Party of the nine-teenth century. It seems that Johnson was correct in his suspicion that his criticism was generating a counterattack.[24]

Critical acclaim continued—Johnson received both the George Foster Peabody Award and the Sidney Hellman Foundation Award for his commen-tary—but the show lost its national audience. ABC informed Johnson that the final network program would air on January 10, 1954. ABC expressed no dissatisfaction with his work but said that the change was merely a matter of rescheduling. Johnson thought differently. "I have been critical of McCar-thy," he wrote to Adlai Stevenson, "and McCarthy has two men on the FCC, which has the power of life and death over the networks." He pro-ceeded to express surprise that the show had lasted as long as it did.[25]

Stevenson wrote letters on Johnson's behalf, and the show's cancellation was criticized in print. While it did not appear again on national television, the program did air locally on WAAM, with one hiatus, until nearly three years after its inception. Johnson did not leave quietly. He used his final Inde-pendence Day program to observe that this was "[an] appropriate occasion on which to review the state of our liberties." He commended "those men in Philadelphia" for having "the nerve to do what was right in the teeth of a power relatively ten times as strong as Soviet Russia." "It took bold men," he declared, "to assert [the Right of Revolution], bolder men than we are; but being bold, they were free men, and I sometimes fear freer men than we are." Growing more caustic, he announced that "it is a curious and disap-pointing fact that on July 4, 1954, the United States appears to be more afraid of a handful of idiots who fell for the Communist flapdoodle than the design-ers of the Declaration were when one-third of the country was disloyal." The people of Bolton Street, he scoffed, "are getting pretty tired of crawling under the bed every time some witch-hunting plug-ugly says, 'Boo!'" Es-chewing all subtlety, he dared his fellow citizens to reclaim their liberty.[26] Once again, no one had any trouble understanding where Johnson stood.

24. "Gerald Johnson Gets Radio [*sic*] Award," *BS,* March 28, 1953; John Crosby, "Radio and Television," *BS,* May 31, 1953; GWJ to Frank S. MacGregor, July 14, 1953, Harper and Brothers Papers; GWJ, *HTLFBS,* July 5, 12, 1953, *HTLFBS* Papers. The show aired nationally under the title *Gerald W. Johnson* (*Variety* 190 [June 3, 1953]: 31). I am indebted to Lee Gordon of Baltimore for his kind assistance in determining how widely the television show aired.

25. GWJ to Wingate Johnson, December 26, 1953, GWJ Papers; GWJ to Adlai Steven-son, December 24, 1953, AES Papers.

26. Adlai Stevenson to Senator Mike Monroney, January 5, 14, 1954, AES Papers; John

In all, Johnson experienced a provocative and productive sojourn in television commentary. From his sixty-second through his sixty-fifth years, he showed that remarkable ability to adapt. In this new medium, he disturbed the peace many times. He challenged powerful opponents whom he had no real chance of defeating, but this, as he saw things, mattered not at all. It did matter very much, however, that while many other Americans capitulated and crept away, Johnson elected to stand and fight.

How Things Look from Bolton Street proved only one of several forums that Johnson used to respond to the Supreme Court's landmark decision on March 17, 1954, *Brown v. Board of Education of Topeka,* which superseded *Plessy v. Ferguson* and outlawed segregation in public schools. Johnson foresaw that this new ruling would have huge implications, negative as well as positive, for both whites and blacks. As we have seen, Johnson believed that the races could learn to live together peacefully, and, at this time, he remained a meliorist in racial matters. However, he did not believe that *Brown v. Board of Education,* which was "pretty much what everybody expected," would prove a panacea. He argued that "while all 48 states will get the credit, the poor old South will have to foot the bill. That's always the way." Not merely the white South would suffer, he opined, but the black South as well. "I hope and believe," he said, "that what [Southern Negroes] get will be worth all it costs and more, but let nobody think that for a minute that they are getting anything free." He predicted, for example, that black educators in historically black institutions would find their jobs imperiled. He explained that "from the standpoint of the country, the distress of all the South, white and black, is a small price, but it isn't small to the South." *Brown v. Board of Education* called for its ruling to be implemented "with all deliberate speed," but Johnson remarked ominously that the rest of the country should expect nothing miraculous: "Between 1865 and 1870 the North did expect miracles, and its exasperation when they did not occur was largely responsible for the troubles of the next 30 years. Let us not repeat that."[27]

It was not surprising that Johnson, who had left North Carolina twenty-eight years before, chose to respond to *Brown v. Board of Education* as a Southerner. Even though he had reservations about this decision, he knew that it had to be obeyed. "The only Southerners worth listening to," he asserted,

Crosby, "Farewell to Gerald Johnson," *NYHT,* January 3, 1954; GWJ, *HTLFBS,* July 4, 1954, *HTLFBS* Papers. The final program aired on June 19, 1955.

27. GWJ, *HTLFBS,* May 23, 1954, *HTLFBS* Papers.

"are those who face the fact that the decision has gone against them and who accordingly set themselves to adjust the life of the region to 20th Century conditions." And when some Southerners came to resist the integration of their public schools, he criticized them. In the end, Johnson offered a temperate response to a controversial decision, a response that made him vulnerable to attacks from both Northern liberals and Southern conservatives.[28]

The following year, marked by several speeches of note, proved serene in comparison to the tumult of 1954. On April 26, 1955, Johnson celebrated his Southern heritage as he addressed the Phi Beta Kappa Society of Davidson College. On August 31, 1837, Ralph Waldo Emerson had delivered his famous oration "The American Scholar" to the Phi Beta Kappa Society at Harvard. Narrowing the focus, Johnson called his talk "The Provincial Scholar." While Emerson discussed "Man Thinking," Johnson spoke of "the Southerner thinking." Such an individual, he explained, "must maintain the flavor, without the limitations, of his original provincialism." Declaring that "there are no citizens of the world, for the man whose allegiance is to the world is not a citizen of anything," Johnson said that "the question is one of making a North Carolina heritage an intellectual asset," and he proceeded to celebrate Dr. William Louis Poteat and Dr. Howard W. Odum.[29]

Johnson praised Odum for his "ability to spend a long life fighting for righteousness without any touch of the moral arrogance that is the besetting sin of most crusades." This life had concluded, with Odum's death at seventy, the previous November. The men had known each other closely for over three decades. Odum had praised Johnson's courage, smoothed his transition to Chapel Hill, published his essays, and, with *The Wasted Land,* had entrusted his writing to Johnson's skills as a synthesizer. It was no easy task for Johnson to speak of this most loyal of friends and this staunch comrade in the battle for intellectual freedom in the past tense.

The following month, the regionalist made way for the metaphysician as

28. GWJ, "Romanticism Run Mad," *NR* 134 (May 21, 1958): 8. See Morton Sosna, *In Search of the Silent South: Southern Liberals and the Issue of Race* (New York: Columbia University Press, 1977), 129: Virginius Dabney "was a middle-of-the road Southern liberal. He believed in justice for blacks but insisted that proponents of change still had to recognize the recognize the racial sensitivities of the vast majority of white Southerners." This captures Johnson's position as well.

29. Ralph Waldo Emerson, "The American Scholar," in *Selections from Ralph Waldo Emerson,* ed. Stephen E. Whicher (Boston: Houghton Mifflin, 1969), 65; GWJ, "The Provincial Scholar," GWJ Papers.

Johnson traveled to New York City to deliver the Felix Adler Memorial Lecture to the Society for Ethical Culture. In a talk entitled "The Ethical Emphasis of Modern Historians," Johnson the humanist questioned the supremacy of science—"the supreme triumph of the scientific method has been to endow us with the means of eliminating life from the planet, and with life the power of thought"—but praised ethics for producing "righteousness, courage, hope and love." He acknowledged that America was in a period of "crisis" but argued optimistically that it was "no plunge to Avernus." He took this opportunity to set forth, more clearly than anywhere else in the canon, his religious beliefs. Proclaiming that America will be saved "by the faith of [its] ordinary men and women," he explained that "I am not disposed to bind that faith in the chains of any narrow definition. Faith in our own and the country's destiny is a form of words; faith in God is another form; faith in the ideals of truth and justice is still another. All alike imply belief in the existence of some power other than and superior to the strength of man's own right arm, and I am indifferent to the form of words in which it is described." Johnson had traveled a long way from the faith of his father, and an even longer way from that of Daniel Whyte.[30]

The next month, he stayed home to deliver the commencement address at the Peabody Conservatory of Music. In "The Musician in a Time of Troubles," he discussed the role of the artist and the value of art in a world "where the only important art [seemed] the art of war." Rejecting art for art's sake, he explained that "the Ivory Tower is not of this world, and its inmates do not greatly interest the people of this world." Rejecting complacency and conformity, the gadfly asserted that "it is the social function of all artists . . . to foment discontent with the expedient." Echoing what he had said so winningly eighteen years before in *A Little Night Music,* Johnson remarked that "light and healing, what men call the good life, is the great, all-inclusive art," and searching for this must be the true artist's "central aspiration." Without such a goal, the artist will fall prey to narcissism or despair, withdraw from the world of men, and profane his craft.[31]

All three of these addresses proved typically homiletic. Johnson preached engagement rather than withdrawal, courage rather than fear, enlightenment rather than ignorance. America's worship of false gods appalled him, as did

30. GWJ, "The Ethical Emphasis of Modern Historians," delivered on May 4, 1955, GWJ Papers.

31. GWJ, "The Musician in a Time of Troubles," delivered on June 3, 1955, GWJ Papers.

the sword of annihilation dangling overhead, but the talks proved far more celebratory than funereal as he extolled "the Southerner thinking," the merits of the ethical life, and the redemptive qualities of art.

Unfortunately, soon after the new year dawned, Johnson faced the melancholy task of writing a funeral ode for one of America's most remarkable artists: a brave man who had never withdrawn and who had disturbed the peace for half a century, an author who had labored to make it possible for his fellow writers to discuss the subjects of their choice in the language that best suited their ends. About twenty weeks past his seventy-fifth birthday, H. L. Mencken died of a heart attack on January 29, 1956, and Johnson crafted an eloquent obituary for the *Saturday Review.* Johnson draws Mencken as "conspicuously kindly and polite," a man "too expansive, too free of envy, too obviously void of any disposition to grasp at personal advantage." Johnson remarks, as so many others had previously, upon his friend's huge energy; he had "the vitality of twenty men." Johnson does not speak here of his early dealings with Mencken, during the time before he left North Carolina, but describes instead what it was like to work on the Sunpapers with one of America's most eminent journalists. Typically, Johnson underplays his own significance and passes along a joke at his own expense: "To us smaller fry in the organization, [Mencken] was consistently genial and consistently helpful, although he could be sardonic. To me one day he observed blandly, '[Edmund Duffy] is a great cartoonist, but in politics, of course, Duffy is an idiot.' Since Duffy's politics and mine were identical, I got it, all right." Using a poignant trope that his friend would have appreciated, Johnson concludes that Mencken "caused a zest for life to be renewed in other men; [he] touched the dull fabric of our days and gave it a silken sheen." Mencken's passing generated considerable commentary—in Baltimore, throughout America, and abroad—but no one else wrote more gracefully about it than Johnson did. Mencken had done appreciably more for the North Carolinian's career than had any other individual, and Johnson, as his daughter Dorothy has remarked, "never forgot a favor."[32]

The month after Mencken's eulogy was published, Johnson traveled to the University of Washington for his second, and final, sojourn in academia. It had been almost thirty years since he had left Chapel Hill to sign on with

---

32. GWJ, "Henry L. Mencken (1880–1956)," in *America-Watching: Perspectives in the Course of an Incredible Century* (Owings Mills, Md.: Stemmer House, 1976), 199–202, and in *Critical Essays on H. L. Mencken,* ed. Douglas C. Stenerson (Boston: Hall, 1987), 33–37; Dorothy Johnson van den Honert to author, June 8, 1995.

the *Evening Sun*. From late March through the middle of May, 1956, Johnson served as the Walker-Ames Visiting Professor in the university's School of Communications. In his sixty-sixth year, he chose to live in a dormitory room. "They call me a visiting professor," he said modestly, "but I'm really a visiting student. I want to find out what these young people have in mind when they enter journalism."[33]

While he lived with his typical lack of ostentation, he communicated with his usual candor and flair as a lecturer, television commentator, and writer. Discussing how the journalist should treat the politician, Johnson remarked waggishly that "he should piously and prayerfully endeavor to let each candidate make a jackass of himself according to the dictates of his own folly, not according to that of the reporter." The commentator who had proven so successful with *How Things Look from Bolton Street* did four shows that aired, under the title *The Outside View*, on KCTS television in Seattle. Talking once more as the *vox populi*, Johnson spoke to his viewers of "you and me and all other plain citizens of the United States." He seized this opportunity to criticize President Eisenhower for "his hopeless inability to get anything worthwhile done." Writing for the *University of Washington Daily*, Johnson attacked loyalty oaths for teachers and called for "sharp and incessant criticism of all existing institutions, including the oldest and the most firmly established."[34]

This sojourn in Seattle benefited everyone involved. The University of Washington attracted a writer of national renown and a celebrated television commentator. Johnson's listeners and viewers experienced firsthand his piquant commentary. He received "a nice, fat fee" that he hoped would pay the grocery bills all summer, and he was able to draw upon this experience for a book that would be published two years later.[35]

During his trip to the West Coast in March, Johnson had stopped in Chicago to visit with Adlai Stevenson. Since their close interaction during the presidential campaign of 1952, the men had maintained a lively correspondence. Johnson offered advice on a variety of matters, and both commented upon what they saw as the foibles of the Republicans. If Stevenson decided

33. "Visiting Professor Says He Really Is 'Visiting Student,' " *Seattle Times,* March 16, 1956.

34. GWJ, "The Press and the Political Candidates," delivered to the Seattle Kiwanis Club, April 17, 1956, GWJ Papers; *The Outside View,* March 11, April 5, 12, 19, 1956, GWJ Papers; GWJ, "A Journalist Looks at Academic Freedom," *University of Washington Daily,* May 2, 1956.

35. GWJ to Frank S. MacGregor, March 21, 1956, Harper and Brothers Papers.

to run again, Johnson assured him that "anything I can do will be done." Johnson's advice, Stevenson replied, proved far more valuable than all the weighty memoranda that he received from others.[36]

Johnson viewed the campaign of 1956 as yet another struggle between the forces of light and the agents of darkness. The intelligent, urbane, and articulate Stevenson was opposed by the president whose administration "had [quaked] like an aspen with fear of McCarthy," the president who had managed to lose "in 18 months what it took 20 years to acquire." Recalling Theodore Roosevelt's "Square Deal" and FDR's "New Deal," Johnson lampooned Eisenhower's policies as the "Raw Deal." He was even more contemptuous of the vice-president, "Li'l Abner Nixon, that Red-blooded American Boy," who had managed to drive "even the ungodly to prayer. I estimate that not less than 67 percent was added both the frequency and to the fervor of their petitions for the continued good health of the President of the United States."[37]

Stevenson asked for both Johnson's ideas and his words to use in his acceptance speech at the Democratic National Convention and drew heavily upon this material. A master of the art by this time, Johnson also advised his friend how to speak most effectively on television. Despite their efforts, Stevenson lost by a larger margin than he had four years before. His "sane liberalism" proved, in Johnson's view, no match for the Republicans during a time of peace and plenty. Once again proving a good friend during difficult times, Johnson told Stevenson how glad he was to have helped. Looking ahead to four more years of the "Raw Deal" and "Li'l Abner," Johnson said that "I shall be still more glad with the passage of time." Responding with great warmth, Stevenson offered thanks and urged Johnson to keep sending along his ideas. Once again, Johnson had involved himself in what he saw as a righteous battle, but it was another fight that he had little real chance of winning.[38]

36. Adlai Stevenson to GWJ, June 22, 1954, GWJ to Adlai Stevenson, July 15, 1954, and August 11, 1955, Adlai Stevenson to GWJ, September 6, 1955, AES Papers.

37. GWJ, "Hail the Ornery Cuss," *NR* 132 (June 30, 1955): 16; GWJ, "The Superficial Aspect," *NR* 131 (July 5, 1954): 15; GWJ, *HTLFBS,* April 14, 1953, *HTLFBS* Papers; GWJ, "The Superficial Aspect," in *America-Watching: Perspectives in the Course of an Incredible Century* (Owings Mills, Md.: Stemmer House, 1976), 192–93.

38. GWJ, "Splitting the Party," *NR* 134 (April 23, 1956): 8; Adlai Stevenson to GWJ, June 25, July 31, 1956, GWJ to Adlai Stevenson, August 18, November 7, 1956, Adlai Stevenson to GWJ, December 15, 1956, AES Papers.

Johnson sent Stevenson proofs of his next book, *The Lunatic Fringe,* published in the late spring of 1957, and the politician praised it highly. Johnson's title alludes to Theodore Roosevelt's autobiography, and the first of the volume's three epigraphs is a pointed observation by John Stuart Mill: "The mere example of non-conformity is itself a service. Precisely because the tyranny of opinion is such as to make eccentricity a reproach, it is desirable, in order to break through that tyranny, that people should be eccentric." A celebration of nonconformity, *The Lunatic Fringe* is dedicated to "The Unterrified American If Any." Johnson's preface, "As You Like It," deplores the growth of timidity in America and scathingly assesses the most recent presidential election: "Suspicion of everything new and untried and distrust of most things that have been tried, is the prevalent mood, betraying us into such erratic action as the election of last November, when we stampeded into the sheltering arms of the Great White Father." Usually entertaining, sometimes uproariously funny, *The Lunatic Fringe,* with its menagerie of eccentrics, is far from subtle.[39]

Showing once more his facility with the character sketch, Johnson chronicles the stories of five women and nine men, all but two (John Peter Altgeld, governor of Illinois, and the Populist "Sockless Jerry" Simpson) native born, who lived during the eighteenth through the twentieth centuries. Presidents and lesser politicians and propagandists parade through Johnson's pages, as do newspaper editors and authors of books, economists and Abolitionists. What unites this curious cast of characters, Johnson explains, is the fact that all affected American political history. The book is enhanced by Johnson's range of knowledge and his usual interest in comparative history. (He likens the frightening fervor of the Temperance fanatic Carry Nation, "a six-foot woman with a hatchet and absolute certainty that she is the chosen instrument of the Lord," to the destructive certitude of Senator McCarthy.) Giving respect where it is due, he praises Sarah and Angelina Grimke, South Carolina sisters who "did much to break open the way to liberty for American women," and Horace Greeley, whose prominence as a journalist was equaled only by that of Ben Franklin. Relishing the absurd, he snorts at Victoria Claflin Woodhull, the spiritualist and mesmerist who sold elixirs and, like Mark Twain's King and Duke, preyed upon the credulity of the American

39. Adlai Stevenson to Edward W. White Jr. (publicity manager, J. B. Lippincott), April 19, 1957, AES Papers; GWJ, *The Lunatic Fringe* (Philadelphia: J. B. Lippincott, 1957), 4.

public. Her story, Johnson says, "is the most uproarious farce that the Lunatic Fringe has produced."[40]

Amidst the laughter and the respect, the chronicling of triumph and disaster, the didactic Johnson observes once more that change is the fundamental law of life, that what is seen as eccentricity, even madness, by one's contemporaries can seem something quite different to posterity. "The passage of time," he explains, "has demonstrated that, more often than not, the apparitions that frightened us should have been welcomed with relief, for they were not in fact hobgoblins, but guides pointing the way out of our difficulties." He uses the volume's conclusion to scoff at the "tyranny of fear" strangling America during the 1950s and to explain that, while the typical American is "grimly confident and briskly efficient" when confronting physical danger, "it is when he fears that he may have his head turned by the siren songs of characters that he classifies vaguely as 'subversives' that he falls into blind panic." Those readers who grasped the lessons of *The Lunatic Fringe,* the most significant and successful book that Johnson wrote for adults during this decade, did not join the stampede.[41]

Johnson was startled by the reviews. He told Stevenson that, while most reviewers treated *The Lunatic Fringe* kindly, they are "puzzled by my tacit assumption that independence of thought needs no defense. They seem to think that if a wise leader is available it is . . . dangerous folly to think for yourself." He proceeded to observe that "if this idea is abroad in the land I have been writing in Sanskrit under the impression that it is in English."[42]

Nobody had trouble understanding Johnson's response to the controversial events that occurred in Little Rock, Arkansas, later that year. In early September, in order to prevent Central High School from being integrated, Governor Orval Faubus had members of the state's National Guard block off the building. Later, facing a federal injunction, the governor withdrew the National Guard. After the nine black students who integrated the school were threatened, President Eisenhower sent in federal troops. Johnson used several articles in the *New Republic* to discuss these events. His first, "The Arkansas Toreador," ridicules the governor and scoffs at those Southerners who supported his "lame-brain leadership." Predictably, Johnson also attacks

40. GWJ, *The Lunatic Fringe,* 207, 215, 221, 56, 64, 105.

41. *Ibid.,* 222, 247, 239.

42. GWJ to Adlai Stevenson, August 8, 1957, AES Papers.

those sanctimonious Yankee reformers so fond of patronizing the South. Such reformers, he remarks acidly, "may learn that in race prejudice they are grappling a devil much more agile and sinewy than they believed, not one to be exorcized by spells and incantations alone. They may thus acquire a new respect for those Southerners who have been wrestling with the evil spirit these many years, not altogether in vain."[43] In the end, his published commentary about this "Moment of Truth" proved very much in keeping with what he had said before: the law must be obeyed; Southerners have blindly followed some dangerous leaders; and the racial situation in the South is more complicated than outsiders can perceive. As had been the case with his response to *Brown v. Board of Education*, his moderate position made him vulnerable to attack from both extremes.

Not surprisingly, Johnson continued to reflect upon these matters and, in a letter to Paul Green, spoke in a far more melancholy tone. Dismayed by "the impotence of the civilized minority of the white South," Johnson remarked that "the conspicuous figures are the troglodytes, represented by Faubus, on the one hand, and the Negro school children on the other. But there is a party of the third part, the civilized white man, who can't give to either of the others any of his valuable possessions, to wit, discretion, foresight, historical perspective, poise. He would gladly; but he cannot. And he, too, is pathetic."[44] The entire situation appalled Johnson: streets filled with hate; an elected official no better than a brutish beast; and a civilized minority, a *tertium quid,* incapable of preventing barbarism.

Race proved only one of several controversial issues that Johnson the orator discussed the following year as his travels took him north to Canada, his first trip outside the United States since 1938, and then back to the South on several occasions. On March 18, 1958, he delivered the "War Memorial Address" at McGill University in Montreal. He came, he explained, "to pay tribute to men who once were Canadian but whose story is now woven into the stuff of my life; for these men died for liberty and . . . became additions to the honor . . . of the human race." He proceeded to attack those who profaned such valor and sacrifice: "shallow thinkers . . . [who] in the name of democracy . . . have endeavored to suppress freedom of thought" and

43. GWJ, "The Arkansas Toreador," *NR* 137 (October 14, 1957): 10. See also Johnson's *NR* articles of July 21, 1958, and August 18, 1958.

44. GWJ to Paul Green, July 24, 1959, quoted in Paul Green, *A Southern Life: Letters of Paul Green, 1916–1981,* ed. Laurence G. Avery (Chapel Hill: University of North Carolina Press, 1994), 585n.4.

"leather-lunged fools . . . bellowing from every street corner that thinking is a crime." He saw fit to name names. Senator McCarthy had died the previous May, and Johnson scorned his former adversary as "a protagonist of terror."[45]

Later that year, he spoke on four occasions in North Carolina. On April 10, the delivered the Phi Beta Kappa Address, "The American Scholar in 1958," at Wake Forest. He gave thanks for his own intellectual liberation under Dr. William Louis Poteat and praised the school's willingness to engage in the "battle of ideas." Calling Johnson "one of the great expatriate North Carolinians of our day," the *Greensboro Daily News* printed most of the talk, which was also read into the *Congressional Record*. Speaking on the radio in Chapel Hill that July, Johnson urged his listeners to acknowledge the benefits of intellectual combat, for "it is precisely out of the clash of contending opinions that the truth at last emerges, and that, more than any other factor, accounts for the survival of the United States."[46]

He proved just as bellicose in delivering the Danforth Foundation lectures in November at East Carolina College (now East Carolina University) in Greenville. He used the first to talk at length about race and argued that "repression is not the way to raise the level of any people of any color." He remarked, as he had done before, that both races bore the responsibility to effect improvement, and he challenged his listeners to accept the inevitability of change, to do what had to be done "without tradition or precedent or the maxims of long-dead sages." In the second lecture the following day, the gadfly scoffed at philistine America. It was not the country's standard of living that mattered, he argued, but rather the country's standard of life. Creativity, he declared, is superior to productivity, and he warned his listeners not to become "slaves of gadgets."[47] In these public performances, this man who so relished paradox presented one himself: a benevolent-looking gentleman with silver hair, impeccably dressed, soft-spoken, contemptuous of all theatrics, deftly going about the business of unsettling people's minds.

45. GWJ, "War Memorial Address," GWJ Papers.

46. GWJ, "The American Scholar in 1958," GWJ Papers; "A College's Army: Arsenal of Ideas," *GDN,* May 11, 1958; GWJ untitled radio address delivered on July 5, 1958, GWJ Papers.

47. GWJ, "As of 1958—Tensions and Stereotypes," delivered on November 11, 1958; GWJ "As of 1958—Creativity and Productivity," delivered on November 12, 1958, GWJ Papers. On October 30, 1958, Johnson delivered "Personality in Journalism" at the University of Minnesota (see *America-Watching: Perspectives in the Course of an Incredible Century* (Owings Mills, Md.: Stemmer House 1976), 217–24).

Peril and Promise, Johnson's first book of 1958, evolved from his time at the University of Washington and aggressively defended freedom of the press. This volume of 110 pages proved the only book devoted entirely to journalism since *What Is News?* thirty-two years before. The lover of paradox remarks early on that "the peace that endures longest is to be sought precisely at the point where the battle of ideas rages with the most unrestrained fury." American journalism, which Johnson calls the best in the world, finds itself imperiled not during times of intellectual combat but rather during times of intellectual retreat and insipid silence. This proponent of the adversary culture argues that every large newspaper should have "at least one radical" on its staff. Despite the book's brevity, Johnson still finds the space to chastise those credulous Americans so easily duped by advertisers and propagandists and those unreflective citizens who run with the herd. Sounding much like Thoreau, Johnson explains that "there is no virtue in conformity."[48]

Johnson was dissatisfied with his second book of 1958, *The Lines Are Drawn: American Life since the First World War as Reflected in the Pulitzer Prize Cartoons.* The volume reproduces thirty-five cartoons, and Johnson contributes about fifty thousand words of copy: a substantial introduction, a briefer conclusion, highly impressionistic commentary on each cartoon, and a brief biographical sketch of each cartoonist. Johnson remarks that America "had it origins in the conviction of its founders that controversy is the very life of the mind," but he laments that "the persons charged with the duty of selecting a cartoon that meets the high approval of the American people have, practically without exception, chosen a noncontroversial one." Making this point more forcefully and colloquially in his correspondence, he criticized the cartoons' "namby-pamby quality." Always honest about his writing, he admitted that "I have written a namby-pamby book, never pouring the sulphuric acid on as I should. If I had, the book wouldn't have been published."[49] The dilemma of the free-lance writer could hardly have been more clear.

His work in progress, a book for juveniles that would appear the following year as *America Is Born,* proved considerably more significant, and more successful financially, than either *Peril and Promise* or *The Lines Are Drawn.* Johnson had first thought about writing an American history for children

---

48. GWJ, *Peril and Promise: An Inquiry into Freedom of the Press* (New York: Harper and Brothers, 1958), vii, 13, 38, 47, 64.

49. GWJ, *The Lines Are Drawn: American Life since the First World War as Reflected in the Pulitzer Prize Cartoons* (Philadelphia: J. B. Lippincott, 1958), 22; GWJ to Wingate Johnson, November 19, 1957, and May 6, 1958, GWJ Papers.

after the birth of his first grandchild, Peter van den Honert. This man who always embraced change came to believe, in his sixtieth year, that the author "who writes for children is perhaps the most important writer in the country." He searched a secondhand bookstore for a copy of Dickens's *A Child's History of England,* reread it for the first time since he was fourteen, and discovered that "all that [he] knew about the history of England [was] in that book." His purpose in *America Is Born,* he explained, was not to bombard Peter with facts but rather to provide him with a book that would allow him "to trace the element of greatness" in the history of his native land.[50]

Wisely, Johnson perceived that the book's appeal was hardly limited to children. "The simplicity" of *America Is Born,* he told a correspondent, "will be confined merely to the language. That, I hope to make intelligible to a boy of twelve; but not the ideas. He will begin to grasp them at 25, and will really get to them at 50." Although it fails to reach their stature, *America Is Born* can be placed in the tradition of such volumes as *Robinson Crusoe, Gulliver's Travels,* and *The Adventures of Huckleberry Finn,* books that are first encountered on the literal level by youngsters but whose figurative import is later grasped by adults.[51]

America Is Born contains, as Harold A. Williams has remarked, much of "Johnson's fundamental philosophy." The advocate of freedom rather than safety, Johnson explains that "sailing out of sight was pretty risky business" and that the men who reached Jamestown "were not careful men." Valuing work and competence rather than bloodlines and privilege, Johnson asserts that the experience of Jamestown has taught Americans that all people, even gentlemen, must work for their keep. Jamestown has also taught us, remarks the Southerner grown weary of advice from outsiders, that "the man on the spot knows better what to do than the man at a distance." Discussing an old theme, the ever-changing nature of the American experiment, he asserts that "it will never be finished. As long as a man lives he changes a little every day, and the same is true of a nation." In brief, *America Is Born* proves polemical throughout as Johnson relishes every opportunity to tweak the complacent, the meddlesome, and the reactionary.[52]

50. GWJ to Jonathan Daniels, August 27, 1959, Jonathan Daniels Papers, Southern Historical Collection, Wilson Library, University of North Carolina at Chapel Hill; GWJ to Paul Green, January 7, 1959, Paul Green Papers, Southern Historical Collection, Wilson Library, University of North Carolina at Chapel Hill.

51. GWJ to Frank S. MacGregor, June 1, 1953, Harper and Brothers Papers.

52. Harold A. Williams, interview by author, tape recording, Baltimore, June 4, 1990; GWJ, *America Is Born* (New York: William Morrow, 1959), 19, 116, 127, 130, 239–40.

The volume sold over 10,000 copies its first year. The United States In-formation Service placed the book in the "easy reading" section of its librar-ies abroad. Throughout 1959, Johnson labored to complete the companion volumes: *America Grows Up,* covering the period from the Declaration of In-dependence until World War I; and *America Moves Forward,* carrying up to what was then time present. Both volumes were published in 1960. Within two years, the *History for Peter* trilogy sold about 25,000 sets. Its first and third volumes were designated "Honor Books" in the annual competition for the Newbery Award for the best contribution to children's literature.[53]

Johnson's decision to write for this new audience largely freed him from the criticism leveled at his more "serious" writing: insufficient research, a tendency to oversimplify, the sacrifice of content for style, and a grating parti-sanship. Chronicling what intrigued him and ignoring what did not, he spun out a riveting tale for children.[54] (One ten-year-old boy in Baltimore, who decades later would find himself chronicling Johnson's life, found *America Is Born* so entrancing that he read it far into the night, long after his parents were convinced that he was asleep. The book was far more exciting, he de-cided, than anything that his teachers made him read for school.) Writing about voyages and frontiers, the devils within humankind and the enemies without, singing the immense possibilities of this New World for brave indi-viduals, Johnson engaged in American myth-making. His decision to write this history for his grandson proved one of the most felicitous decisions of his career.

The final year of this very busy decade found Johnson back on the road. During the spring of 1960, he lectured on journalism at the University of Illinois. With his contempt for the sanctimonious, he argued that "misunder-standing has brought more woe upon the world than vice ever did" and de-clared that the journalist, as an agent of communication, would find his importance increasing with time. While in Illinois, Johnson took the oppor-tunity to spend the night in the home of his old friend in Libertyville and discovered that he liked Adlai Stevenson "better than ever. His personal charm is even greater than Roosevelt's and he is far wittier."[55]

---

53. GWJ to Wingate Johnson, November 27, 1959, GWJ to Katherine Johnson Parham, August 6, 1959, GWJ to Mrs. G. T. Bullock, December 13, 1961, GWJ Papers; "Newbery Award Winners," http://www.jademountain.com/AWR/newbery.html, January 19, 1999.

54. Edward N. Todd, "New Books," *BES,* September 30, 1959.

55. GWJ, untitled lecture delivered at the University of Illinois, GWJ Papers; GWJ to Lois Johnson, May 3, 1960, GWJ Papers.

Johnson also returned to North Carolina to lecture in Laurinburg, a short drive from Riverton. Speaking during National Library Week, he declared that "we have not been sufficiently concerned with the non-material" and urged his listeners to pay more attention to books and less to banks. Turning to race, he lashed out at "hate, resentment, and terror" and scoffed at "nostalgia for the past." He urged his audience instead "to devote every energy to making the best of the conditions that exist." He also declared, as he had declared before, that "the situation has . . . been too much complicated by well-meant but ill-informed outside advice."[56] That summer, after he wrote his most important essay about the South in decades, he found himself criticized along much the same lines.

In choosing his title, Johnson, it would seem, was thinking about his battle with the Agrarians three decades before. He chose "To Live and Die in Dixie," the phrase that follows "I'll take my stand" in Daniel D. Emmett's famous song. It had been thirty-four years since Johnson moved north of the Potomac. Approaching his seventieth birthday, he thought it time to reassess his native land and his relationship with it. Writing here with unconcealed emotion, Johnson, as Fred Hobson has remarked, "perhaps best defines himself as [a] Southerner."[57]

Falling again between the polarities of the apologist and the doomsayer, Johnson details both the foibles and the glories of his region. Criticizing the South's complacency, he asserts that many Southerners, lured by the siren song of her beauty, fail to perceive her horrors. A decline in candor has brought with it a diminution in honor. Too many Southerners retreat into the literature of escape, and the region is hurt by its xenophobia. Speaking yet again on race, he asserts that blacks have been burdened with unjust expectations: "Shall we . . . brand the negro as inferior because he has not yet accomplished in ninety-five years what the white has not yet accomplished in more than seven centuries?"

As the essay progresses, however, Johnson turns from censure to approbation. The Southerner, he explains, shows special pride in his place of birth

56. GWJ, "O Fortunatos Nimium, Scotland County," *Raleigh News and Observer,* April 10, 1960.

57. GWJ, "To Live and Die in Dixie," in *South-Watching: Selected Essays by Gerald W. Johnson,* ed. Fred Hobson (Chapel Hill: University of North Carolina Press, 1983) 146–57; Fred Hobson, introduction to "To Live and Die in Dixie," by GWJ, in *South-Watching: Selected Essays by Gerald W. Johnson,* ed. Fred Hobson (Chapel Hill: University of North Carolina, 1983), 146.

because of the "difficulties" attached to it. Using a financial metaphor, he asserts proudly that "we are the sons of a land that has paid its way." Only the South has experienced "ten years of military occupation, thirty years of poverty and grinding toil, ninety years of harassment, anxiety, frustration, and moral deterioration. The South has been granted no favors. The South has paid in full." He concludes by declaring emphatically that "I am a Southerner, and I wish the fact to be known." Through the memories that he carried north with him and through the huge power of the imagination that was his art, he was as much a resident of Dixie as had been the boy in Riverton, the adolescent in Thomasville, the student at Wake Forest, the cub reporter in Lexington, the editorial writer in Greensboro, and the professor in Chapel Hill. For Johnson, the landscape of the imagination, not literal geography, best defined one's place of residence.

His performance drew mixed reviews. The *Raleigh News and Observer* proclaimed that "To Live and Die in Dixie" should be read by every Southerner. On the other hand, the *Richmond News Leader,* concentrating on Johnson's criticism of the South, lambasted him. This man who so often criticized the artist who withdraws to the ivory tower read that he was "cloud-touched," that "he writes with that beautiful detachment from reality that characterizes the genuinely irresponsible man," that he "is weaving tapestries," and that "the serenity of a Baltimore study" was a poor place from which to view the realities of the Southern scene. This censure proved as vituperative as the criticism generated by Johnson's censure of *I'll Take My Stand.* Moreover, he was attacked for much the same reason that he had attacked the writers of the Agrarian manifesto. He was, according to this newspaper, more dreamer than realist.[58]

Discussing the presidential campaign of 1960, his commentary made the Republicans just as unhappy as "To Live and Die in Dixie" made some of its Southern readers. Continuing to attack the record of the Eisenhower administration, he called the president "the pastmaster of Utter Confusion" and remarked that he was "capable of building Nothingness into an immense success." Johnson expressed no more confidence in the president's would-be successor, "Li'l Abner Nixon," than he had years before.[59]

Predictably, Johnson again supported Adlai Stevenson. "I suspect," he re-

58. "Southern Accent," *Raleigh News and Observer,* March 19, 1961; "Gerald Johnson on the South," *Richmond News Leader,* July 2, 1960, p. 8.

59. GWJ, "In Search of Identity," *NR* 143 (October 10, 1960): 20.

marked laughingly, "that when what Dr. Samuel Johnson called 'lapidary in-scriptions' are in order an appropriate epitaph on my tombstone would be, 'He voted for Stevenson until the cows came home.' " Initially, Johnson was not impressed by John Fitzgerald Kennedy; moreover, recalling Al Smith's problems back in 1928, Johnson predicted that Kennedy would be defeated by his Catholicism. After Kennedy was elected, Johnson changed his mind and predicted that the president "will be great." Prior to the inauguration of this politician whose administration of about a thousand days would be fre-quently likened to Arthurian legend, Johnson wrote, "Kennedy's foes are strong and ferocious, but his weapons are excellent. The trust of the people is the best blade that comes to the hand of any President, and when its metal has been tempered in the heats and pressure of religious strife, it is a very Excalibur."[60] Johnson at seventy proved oracular once more.

In *The Lunatic Fringe,* Johnson quoted with approbation Tom Paine's fa-mous remark "I thank God I fear not." Johnson could well have been speak-ing of himself, for such fearlessness had marked his own activities during this tumultuous decade. He had challenged both Senator McCarthy and President Eisenhower. He had talked candidly about *Brown v. Board of Education* and the events in Little Rock. He had decried the country's descent into mindlessness and materialism. Refusing to court public approval, he had stubbornly told the truth as he saw it in words accessible to all. When Adlai Stevenson spoke at Johnson's seventieth birthday party and called him "the critic and con-science of our time," the politician engaged in no special pleading for a friend but instead offered a fair assessment of Johnson's activities.[61]

In December 1960, Johnson closed out the decade by addressing his good friends at the Hamilton Street Club in Baltimore. He talked about how an old man best responds to time's flight. The onset of senility, he explained, "is signaled not by any physical sign, but by a man's loss of belief that there is something worth seeing around the next corner." He pointed out that Aga-memnon valued the venerable Nestor more highly than the warrior Ajax and said that the man with "an inquiring mind" could never grow old. He praised the salubrious qualities of laughter and gave thanks for the "imperturbability" brought by the passing of the years. "We will get to the next corner," he

60. GWJ, "I'm for Adlai Stevenson," in *America-Watching: Perspectives in the Course of an Incredible Century* (Owings Mills, Md.: Stemmer House, 1976), 239–40; GWJ, "In Search of Identity"; GWJ to Lois Johnson, June 20, 1960, GWJ Papers; GWJ, "He Will Be Great," *NR* 143 (November 21, 1960): 10.

61. GWJ, *The Lunatic Fringe,* 21.

concluded, "if we have to make it on a peg-leg or in a wheel-chair, yet we'll get there somehow." During his final two decades, he would manage, despite increasing physical problems, to reach that corner again and again. He would continue to to disturb the peace, but the iconoclast would often find himself regarded as something of an icon. Johnson as Nestor would be celebrated, in his adopted city and elsewhere, as a sort of public treasure.[62]

62. GWJ, *De Senectute* (Baltimore: Hamilton Street Club, 1961), 7–22.

13   America's Toboggan Slide
1961–1970

We have spent twenty-four billions to plant American footprints on the surface of the moon, but why, God only knows. In recent years our bombers have blown up a certain number of armed men in Vietnam, which may not be sensible, but is at least understandable. But it appears that the bombers at the same time have blown up a vastly greater number of old women and cows, which is incomprehensible. We have spent an incalculable number of billions building vast and magnificent cities and then allowed them to rot.

—*Gerald Johnson, "At Least It's Movement"*

During his eighth decade, the future continued to interest Johnson more than the past did. Blessed again as grandparents, he and Kathryn celebrated the births of Frederick W. Sliger and Louisa van den Honert, the last of their seven grandchildren. He surely astonished some of his contemporaries when he and Kathryn built a new house and moved in during his seventy-sixth year. Newspapers, magazines, and manuscripts covered his desk. Worlds remained to write. Fittingly, the study's large front window faced the east.

Complacency continued to appall him. "I am contrary enough to think it better to live as part of an experiment in progress," Johnson proclaimed, "than to enjoy the finished product. . . . Aldous Huxley was right in assuming that the only logical procedure for a man in Utopia is to hang himself. The Lord was gracious to Moses in not letting him discover what a damned dull place is Canaan." America during the 1960s—a land of immense aspirations and broken dreams, a country torn asunder by rioting and assassinations, a republic sharply divided by the most unpopular war in its history—was a long way from Canaan and anything but dull. Johnson criticized this country where "courage is next door to treason" and "indifference to money is close akin to forgetting God" and remarked that "an efficient gadfly is a useful creation." When North Carolina awarded Johnson a Gold Medal for his con-

tributions to literature, an alarmed businessman complained that "they're giving all these medals now to Socialists."[1] Even in the midst of homage,
Johnson managed to unsettle people's minds.

While he continued to analyze national and international issues, he wrote
with particular fervor about his native region. The South during the 1960s
was, as Fred Hobson has remarked, a land "both sinned against and sinning
in an outrageous manner." This man who, decades earlier, had criticized en-
forced silence in Dayton and excoriated violence in Gastonia now offered
arresting commentary upon events in Oxford and Albany, Birmingham and
Philadelphia.[2]

The beginning of 1961 found life imitating art. The speaker who had
talked the previous month at the Hamilton Street Club about reaching that
next corner on a crutch or in a wheelchair himself slipped on the ice on Liberty Street in downtown Baltimore and broke his hip. He was operated on
the next day, January 24, and remained in a wheelchair until late March. He
responded philosophically: "If you escape the pox in youth, you break a hip
at 70." The day after the operation, the Sunpapers wrote a preliminary obituary to remain in-house until its appearance was warranted—a standard procedure for figures of Johnson's magnitude. He would outlive it by more than
nineteen years.[3]

The month after Johnson's accident was marked by the publication of his
single book of the year, the first volume for adults since 1958. *The Man Who
Feels Left Behind* offers eight essays, four of which, including "To Live and
Die in Dixie," had appeared previously. The book's unifying motif is the idea
of how to deal with change, how to respond to a world where the established
footholds seem to be disappearing with frightening rapidity. "Like an old-
time cavalryman whose horse was shot from under him," explains the old

1. GWJ to Wingate Johnson, May 23, 1963, GWJ Papers; GWJ, "Gadflying with I. F.
Stone," *NR* 149 (December 11, 1963): 21; James Walt, "Tale of Another Liberal's Progress,"
Maryland English Journal 4 (fall 1965): 62.

2. Fred Hobson, introduction to *South-Watching: Selected Essays by Gerald W. Johnson,* ed.
Fred Hobson (Chapel Hill: University of North Carolina Press, 1983), xxv; see also Fred Hobson, *The Southern Writer in the Postmodern World* (Athens: University of Georgia Press, 1991), 7,
and *Tell About the South: The Southern Rage to Explain* (Baton Rouge: Louisiana State University
Press, 1983), 297.

3. "Author Breaks His Hip," *BES,* January 24, 1961; "Johnson Is Doing 'Very Well,'"
BES, January 25, 1961; GWJ to Jonathan Daniels, March 26, 1961, Jonathan Daniels Papers,
Southern Historical Collection, Wilson Library, University of North Carolina at Chapel Hill;
GWJ to Wingate Johnson, January 13, 1962, GWJ Papers.

veteran, "the intelligent but untutored man sees the battle of ideas whirling away toward the horizon, while he is left behind amid the wreckage of exploded theories and a litter of axioms dead or maimed." Acknowledging that America is in a "jam," Johnson admits that the third quarter of the twentieth century has been marked by "military insecurity, economic uncertainty, [and] social unrest."[4]

However, *The Man Who Feels Left Behind* concludes not as a dirge but as an exhortation. Johnson takes the title of his final chapter, "Thou Shouldst Be Living at This Hour," from Wordsworth's famous remark to a long-dead Milton. Johnson argues that his contemporaries, rather than capitulate to danger and uncertainty, should give thanks for the opportunity to live during such a challenging time. Always the realist, he graphically depicts the plight of the average American: "Since 1945, he has been suspended over Hell Gate, with the rope visibly unraveling." However, Johnson also declares that, despite such peril, "his hope of achievement is still greater than his fear of disaster."[5]

Johnson acknowledged that this volume was flawed. The essays vary appreciably in quality, and not surprisingly for a book of this nature, the reader gets bumped along from chapter to chapter. The *New York Times* scoffed at Johnson's "pull-up-your socks peroration." To his credit, however, Johnson accepted the responsibility of playing a role that, in his view, America needed at this time of rapid upheaval: someone to show the way. "All we need is a Voice," he remarks, "like that of the Baptist crying in the wilderness—or perhaps not a voice crying, but a translator reading in books of ancient wisdom and turning them into modern idiom." He himself is that translator, offering old wisdom in a lucid prose to a confused people. Johnson's readers found themselves in the presence of an author in the vanguard, a man who, despite his years, refused to be left behind himself.[6]

Characteristically, he refused to keep quiet and stirred up controversy throughout the the year. He urged universities not to become involved, except in cases of dire emergency, with the military-industrial establishment. Writing again on race, he distressed both white doomsayers and black militants by arguing that "the position of the black minority in this country has

4. GWJ, *The Man Who Feels Left Behind* (New York: William Morrow, 1961), 11, 19, 17.
5. *Ibid.*, 169, 168.
6. GWJ to Lois Johnson, March 7, 1961, GWJ Papers; Charles Poore, "Books of the Times," *New York Times,* March 7, 1962; GWJ, *The Man Who Feels Left Behind,* 101.

been immensely improved within the past seven years." He also spoke of the "wrath and amusement" generated among Southerners by hypocritical outside reformers who extolled blacks in the abstract but refused to shake their hands. He lamented that McCarthyism was being "revived in a more pestilential form" by the followers of John Birch, "a brainless character." After quoting Victor Hugo's observation that Napoleon fell because "God was bored by him," he remarked pointedly that "a nation afraid of itself is a greater bore than Napoleon."[7]

Fear and boredom were very much on Johnson's mind when he traveled to Chapel Hill in early October 1961 to deliver the thirty-second Mellett Lecture at the University of North Carolina's School of Journalism. Donald Round Mellett, editor of the *Canton (Ohio) Daily News,* had been shot to death in 1926 after he refused to stop attacking the city's gangsters and corrupt politicians. Johnson's argument in his speech, he told a correspondent, was that "the threat to this country in not Communism, but boredom." He told his audience that "we are passing through great tribulation because we, as a nation, have failed to muster enough of the kind of courage that kept Don Mellett's memory green." Johnson complained that America's "obsession with its own security has come to be an international scandal" and concluded by challenging others to follow the example set by this bold editor "who considered his duty ahead of his danger." This oratory received a "flattering reception," and the *Greensboro Daily News* reprinted lengthy excerpts.[8]

Because of the considerable success of *A History for Peter,* William Morrow contracted with Johnson to write another trilogy for children, "more or less supplemental to the history," on the three branches of the federal government. He completed both *The Presidency* and *The Supreme Court* by the end of 1961. In early 1962, he took a much-deserved vacation. While Kathryn visited the Sligers in Valparaiso, Gerald, upon the recommendation of his sister Ella, traveled to Radium Springs, Georgia. He liked the place so much that he returned early the following year.[9]

7. GWJ, "Appropriate Academic Dress," *NR* 144 (June 12, 1961): 16; GWJ "Pride and Prejudice," *NR* 145 (December 25, 1961): 10; GWJ, "God Was Bored," in *America-Watching: Perspectives in the Course of an Incredible Century* (Owings Mills: Stemmer House, 1976), 248–49.

8. GWJ, "The Republic's Second Chance," 32nd Don R. Mellett Lecture, delivered on October 4, 1961, GWJ Papers; GWJ to Jay Jenkins, October 12, 1961, GWJ Papers; GWJ, "Will U.S. Forfeit the Chance Athens Twice Forfeited?" *GDN,* October 15, 1961.

9. GWJ to Mrs. G. T. Bullock, December 13, 1961; GWJ to Wingate Johnson, February 21, 1962, GWJ Papers.

The two new books generated different responses. After *The Presidency* was published in the spring of 1962, President Kennedy wrote to Johnson and praised the book warmly. Thoroughly taken with the volume, a North Carolina reviewer remarked, "The idea is that eventually you give the book to the youngster of your choice. At least, that can be your excuse for buying it. But the real reason, of course, for getting your hands on it is so that you can read it yourself." On the other hand, Johnson found *The Supreme Court* difficult to write and expressed dissatisfaction with it. After remarking that "writing for children is no child's play," he told a correspondent that "I never [sweated] as much over any other book. . . . Imagine trying to explain the case of *Marbury vs. Madison* to a kid of 12!" His difficulties did not lead him, though, to offer bromides about racial matters. Commenting upon *Plessy v. Ferguson* and *Brown v. Board of Education*, he explains that "just as the 1896 decision was applied to a great many things other than trains, so the 1954 decision has been applied to a great many things other than schools." After stating that "racial integration is far more than something for lawyers to quarrel over in a courtroom," he observes, as he had previously, that it has proven "much harder for the Supreme Court to change custom than to change the law."[10]

Writing for the *New Republic,* he set forth his consternation over the events in Albany, Georgia. Protesting segregation in the city's bus system, seven hundred blacks, including the Reverend Dr. Martin Luther King, Jr., were arrested for parading without a license. After speaking of "the deadly danger of the situation," Johnson observes that "in the background is a third force that neither side [reasonable blacks and whites] cares to discuss. It is the irresponsible element in both races, held in check thus far, but for how much longer?" Subsequent violence, when cities burned and the streets ran red with blood, proved him oracular once more.[11]

Johnson's final "Superficial Aspect" article appeared in the *New Republic* on December 8, 1962. He had no quarrel with the magazine, which he felt had treated him quite well. Instead, President Kennedy, with whom Johnson was becoming increasingly disenchanted for not being more forthcoming about American involvement in Vietnam, proved the catalyst for the break.

10. GWJ to Kathryn Johnson Parham, July 14, 1962, GWJ Papers; Frances Griffin, "History for Us Children," *Winston-Salem Sentinel,* April 5, 1962; GWJ, *The Presidency* (New York: William Morrow, 1962), 56; GWJ to Mrs. G. T. Bullock, December 13, 1961, GWJ Papers; GWJ, *The Supreme Court* (New York: William Morrow, 1962), 34–35.

11. GWJ, "Trial of a Small Town," *NR* 146 (March 19, 1962): 6–7.

"I am very much afraid," Johnson told a correspondent, "that Kennedy is simply a light-weight who does not and cannot measure up. Yet there is no point in attacking him, because he is all we have; and that is why I am getting out of journalism." Despite the protests of the editor, Johnson refused to change his mind. He would continue, however, to contribute occasional essays and reviews to the magazine. He had made yet another decision based upon his principles, but he could not then anticipate that he would never find another comparable print forum to publish his writing on a regular basis.[12]

While some of his fellow citizens may well have been recovering from their excesses of the previous night, a caustic Johnson began the new year at his typewriter composing "Meditation on 1963." "Brilliant and bitter," opens the essay, "the New Year, the one hundred and first since Lincoln freed the slaves, opened with a cloudless sky overhead, hard-packed snow furnishing a treacherous surface underfoot, and a saw-toothed wind cutting between." After scoffing at the sound and fury of various politicians, Johnson turns to race and education, particularly James Meredith and the University of Mississippi, and his commentary is as savage as the wind outside. After remarking that "Meredith's purpose . . . was not the acquisition of knowledge," Johnson says that "a Negro who chooses to exercise a legal right to enter the University of Mississippi is not seriously in pursuit of an education, since he will not get it there. He seeks martyrdom, not instruction." This is invective, not reasoned analysis, and the commentary proves unfair both to Meredith and the university. Johnson proceeds to acknowledge the horrors of the arms race by decrying the "messengers of death" that the United States has pointed at its enemies.

Typically, however, "Meditation on 1963" speaks of promise as well as peril. Borrowing from the French poet and historian Jean Froissart, Johnson explains that this is an occasion "to encourage all valorous hearts, and to show them honorable examples." As he had done before, he encourages his readers to embrace the reflective life. He urges them to understand the past so that they can deal more intelligently with the present and to take up, in addition to their morning newspapers, the writing of authors long dead (Froissart, for example, and Shakespeare) whose commentaries remain so appropriate for the world of 1963. How little things have changed, observes the comparative historian; "the lady whose colors were worn by the winning knight was the Miss America of 1963." Concluding once more with a luminary image,

12. GWJ to Wingate Johnson, October 5, 1962, GWJ Papers.

Johnson acknowledges that the storied knights of the past were but "[tapers] in a great darkness," but he gives the final word to Portia, Shakespeare's emissary of mercy: "How far that little candle throws his beams." As we have seen, Johnson the newspaperman had earlier seized the occasion of the Nativity to write those poignant Christmas columns. He could, similarly, have seized the occasion of New Year's Day to write other annual essays about the state of the nation. Unfortunately, "Meditation on 1963" had no sequel.[13]

That spring, publication of *The Congress* completed the trilogy on the federal government. One of Johnson's editors told him that "there is hardly a school librarian or junior-high student in the country who does not know the name of Gerald Johnson." Again refusing to skirt controversy, he bludgeons Senator McCarthy without mentioning him by name: "It is indeed a dreadful thing to see a United States Senator wasting his time denouncing people on account of their race, or religion, or calling everybody who shows any intelligence a Communist. It makes the country look silly."[14] Johnson's readers, young and old alike, again received highly partisan commentary.

He proved equally partisan in his lengthy assessment of Ralph McGill's *The South and the Southerner,* a review which ran in the *Baltimore Sun* that spring. Because the "book is astringent," Johnson remarked, "fools below the Potomac will overlook the fact that it is also tonic and will denounce it as treasonable—that is, it will be denounced by the relative few who can read." He criticized the South's "flight from intelligence"—the clergymen, lawyers, and journalists who refused to step forward and lead after *Brown v. Board of Education*, and the demagogues who "burst into clamor." On the other hand, McGill, who faced public opprobrium and violence, was a Southern hero who "preferred truth to popularity."[15]

After the horrific event of November 22, 1963, Johnson discovered yet another hero. With the assassination causing him to put aside his earlier reservations about John F. Kennedy, Johnson calls him the "Young Chevalier" and explains that "there are times in the history of a nation when a symbol is worth more than a sage." It is evident, he concludes, "that the national pantheon has a new figure and a shining one. It is, above all, the ideal of youth."

13. GWJ, "Meditation on 1963," in *America-Watching: Perspectives in the Course of an Incredible Century* (Owings Mills, Md.: Stemmer House, 1976), 256–62.

14. Lloyd Dennis, "Gerald Johnson: Man of Many Parts," *GDN,* March 22, 1964; GWJ, *The Congress* (New York: William Morrow, 1963), 103–104.

15. GWJ, "Turbulence in the South," *BS,* March 24, 1963.

Kennedy proved the final president whom Johnson would elevate to the American Valhalla.[16]

While he had little to say about heroism the following year, he found much to scorn in racial prejudice, cowardice, murder, and a Republican presidential candidate whose ideas and followers disgusted him. In terms of his writing for books, Johnson proved especially productive throughout 1964. One of eight contributors to *Pittsburgh: The Story of An American City,* Johnson wrote a lengthy chapter entitled "The Muckraking Era." For this volume clearly intended as a municipal celebration, Johnson does not shrink from discussing the perils of life in an America without a safety net. Like the Muckrakers, he criticizes political corruption, the "lack of responsibility" on the part of owners, tainted food and shameful housing, and the plight of the immigrant.[17] He proved equally opinionated in both *Communism: An American's View* and *Hod-Carrier: Notes of a Laborer on an Unfinished Cathedral.*

Johnson explains that *Communism,* an illustrated monograph of about 25,000 words, is addressed primarily to "young Americans, who have little to say in public affairs today, but who will have great voting power a few years hence." He sets forth the huge differences between this ideology's theory and practice and argues that, the better people understand communism, the better will they be able to resist its wiles. A typically Johnsonian challenge resounds throughout the volume: Dare to know! "The will *not* to know is calamity," he proclaims, "for it is cowardice." The man appalled by the silencing of John Scopes nearly forty years before is appalled here because public-school teachers who discuss communism are accused "of trying to make Communists of their pupils." In his correspondence, he complained again about the difficulty of writing for juveniles and wondered how successful the book would be. Marked by common sense and clarity, *Communism* received the Junior Book Award from the Boys' Clubs of America.[18]

When *Hod-Carrier* appeared in April, it so captivated one Southern reviewer that he called Johnson "about the nearest combination of Dr. Samuel Johnson, H. L. Mencken and Walter Hines Page that North Carolina has produced. He is raconteur, philosophical gadfly and prose stylist par excel-

16. GWJ, " 'Once Touched by Romance,' " in *America-Watching: Perspectives in the Course of an Incredible Century* (Owings Mills, Md.: Stemmer House, 1976), 262–64.

17. GWJ, "The Muckraking Era," in *Pittsburgh: The Story of an American City,* ed. Stefan Lorant (Garden City, N.Y.: Doubleday, 1964), 261–319.

18. GWJ, *Communism: An American's View* (New York: William Morrow, 1964), 148, 152, 150; GWJ to Wingate Johnson, April 4, 1963, GWJ Papers.

lence." The book's genesis proved unusual. For the first time in his life, Johnson explained to Paul Green, he had "three months free and used them to write a book for myself alone, not even demanding an advance." It was a project, he said, that "I ask nobody to like." Actually, there is much to admire. Its sixteen chapters, three of which had appeared previously in the *Atlantic Monthly,* cover diverse aspects of the American experience during 1963: urban renewal and birth control, for example, education and race. The cathedral motif in the subtitle comes from Johnson's reading of Henry Adams's *Mont-Saint-Michel and Chartres* and his own viewing of that renowned house of God in the French city. The construction metaphor, applied to the unfinished American experiment, provides the book's structural trope. Self-effacing as usual, Johnson draws himself as a mere hod-carrier, a laborer hauling mortar. Actually, the volume shows him to be a master craftsman with words.[19]

Two characteristically Johnsonian ideas, the inevitability of change and the sanctity of freedom, serve as leitmotifs throughout the volume. The lover of paradox declares that "nothing is more changeable than the past" and argues that the great American "experiment" of 1776 is in a constant state of evolution. Calling for more personal liberty in America, he derides those who "are afraid to be free."[20]

Turning to race, he deplores the lack of freedom in both the past and present. The "one grave error" of those drafted the Constitution, he explains, was "the failure . . . to incorporate in the document provision for the eventual extinction of slavery by lawful means." And the subsequent passage of the Fourteenth Amendment (written in "the language of a drunk—confused, contradictory, and divorced from reality") has proven no panacea. Surveying the embattled land of his fathers, he complains that "in the spring of 1963 the South was still in the gutter, sitting on the Negro, albeit more and more shamefaced about being there." Appalled by the barbaric events in Birmingham—the bombing of the Sixteenth Street Baptist Church that killed four black girls and the "turning [of] fire hoses and police dogs on school children"—he declares that "the great need of Alabama and Missis-

19. GWJ to Lois Johnson, March 4, 1964, GWJ Papers; William D. Snider, "Gerald Johnson: Hod-Carrier and Philosophical Gadfly," *GDN,* July 19, 1964; GWJ to Paul Green, February 20, 1964, Paul Green Papers, Southern Historical Collection, Wilson Library, University of North Carolina at Chapel Hill.

20. GWJ, *Hod-Carrier: Notes of a Laborer on an Unfinished Cathedral* (New York: William Morrow, 1964), 115, 45, 20.

sippi is not freedom for Negroes, but for white men; for were they really free they would know that the progress of freedom among Negroes is the only effective guarantee of their own security." Besides arguing once more that the fates of the races are intertwined, Johnson the Southerner shows his usual contempt for sanctimonious outsiders. He snorts that "for Americans living north of the Potomac to curl the lip at Alabama and Tennessee is to repeat the sin of the Pharisee. He thanked God that he was not as other men; he was quite right. He was worse." With its vibrant prose, *Hod-Carrier* showcases the considerable skills of this writer who, despite advancing age, refused to go quietly into that good night.[21]

In his seventy-fourth year, Johnson here ruefully acknowledges time's passage. Recalling his Marvell he observes "So, now that the sound of Time's winged chariot hurrying near resolves into the admonition, 'If you have anything to say, man, say it now, for permanent silence it at hand.' I have taken heed." Permanent silence was not imminent, but *Hod-Carrier* would be the penultimate book that Johnson completed for an adult audience, and the final such volume that proved successful.[22]

The atrocities in Philadelphia, Mississippi, during the heated summer of 1964 angered Johnson as much as the atrocities in Birmingham had. Three young men working on a voter-registration drive (James E. Chaney, a black from Mississippi, and Andrew Goodman and Michael H. Schwerner, two civil rights activists from New York) were murdered and buried in a mud bank. Twenty-one people were arrested and subsequently released without being charged. After scorning Philadelphia as a "sardonically named town," Johnson calls the murders "homicide tainted with genocide" and "an assault upon civilization." Decrying the pernicious influence of demagogues upon "rednecks" and "lint-heads," he explains that "the legend of the Old South" has become "bedraggled and degraded." He calls it "the tragedy of the South that in the hands of second-raters it remained powerful, but as an engine of petty politics. It was potent to transform the yahoo, in his own eyes, into a *preux chevalier* inhabiting a realm of moonlight and magnolias instead of the moonshine and skunk cabbage of his actual ecology." Given the climate of the state, he asserts that such violence may well recur. One of Johnson's most strident indictments of the Deep South, "Judgment in Mississippi" concludes

21. *Ibid.*, 34, 118, 87, 120.
22. *Ibid.*, 10.

that the specter of murder and twenty-one "grinning" Neanderthals walking free "chills the blood of bystanders."[23]

The 1964 presidential campaign chilled him as well. He was astonished that a major political party could nominate Barry Goldwater. Johnson dismissed the Republican candidate as "an intellectual lightweight" and a figure "completely out of touch with modern times." After Lyndon Baines Johnson won easily—he received more electoral votes than any previous candidate with the exception of FDR in 1936—Johnson was appalled by "the downright maudlin hatred of the defeated Goldwaterites," one of whom had brayed that "a vote for Barry [is] a vote for Christ." "When fanaticism turns religious," Johnson observed, "it turns murderous." Though Gerald Johnson typically voted Democratic, he was no enthusiast for LBJ, and the writer's reservations would increase as the losses in Vietnam mounted. Johnson would come to conclude that the Texan was "the worst politician since Hoover."[24]

The following year, Johnson faced the sad task of eulogizing a politician whom he respected far more than either Goldwater or Johnson. Adlai Stevenson, whom President Kennedy had appointed American ambassador to the United Nations, died of a heart attack in London on July 14, 1965. Johnson's loyal service was indeed remembered, for he and Kathryn were asked to sit with the Stevenson family at the funeral held in the National Cathedral in Washington. On the day of Stevenson's death, Johnson struggled for ten hours to write an obituary for the *New Republic*. He called the piece "a wretched thing" and, far too hard on himself, remarked that "my failure in life is that when I am most strongly moved I am least able to write." Later, writing less hurriedly and at greater length, he did justice to his old compatriot. Johnson extols this "great non-doubter" for "raising the intellectual level of political dialogue in this country. . . . [I]n that work he was the most successful man of our generation, doing more than any other to accelerate the political maturity of the American people." The failure to elect Stevenson, Johnson concludes, was "a lost opportunity, a miserable stony and barren stretch in the path of our political development." Johnson himself suffered a

23. GWJ, "Judgment in Mississippi," *NR* 151 (December 16, 1964): 13.

24. GWJ, "Reviving the Two-Party System," *NR* 152 (January 2, 1965): 20; GWJ, "On Voting Democratic: Confession of a Party-Liner," *NR* 170 (June 22, 1974): 16–18; GWJ to Jonathan Daniels, November 20, 1964, Jonathan Daniels Papers; GWJ to Adlai Stevenson, June 8, 1965, AES Papers.

lost opportunity when he failed to complete the intellectual biography that he had planned to write about Stevenson, a project conceived prior to the politician's death and entirely supported by him. Johnson told his sister Kate that "for the rest of my life I shall be haunted by the feeling that it would have been a great book, *the* book of my career."[25]

While Stevenson's death generated a remembrance of things past, those gallant but doomed campaigns in 1952 and 1956, so did the fortieth anniversary of the publication of Johnson's first contribution, "A Tilt with Southern Windmills," to the *Virginia Quarterly Review.* In a sequel entitled "After Forty Years—Dixi" (the final term, the third principal part of the Latin verb *dico,* translates as "I have spoken" and also serves, of course, as a homonym for "Dixie"), Johnson assesses his earlier effort and finds it sound. Turning again to race relations, he criticizes the violence in Birmingham and Philadelphia and denounces "the reign of terror that has flailed the South ever since the Southern Negro began to make a serious claim to the rights guaranteed him by the Constitution." The essay, however, does not continue as a philippic. Instead, Johnson the meliorist praises the policy of "non-violent protest," remarks that "the Southern Negro has given, especially in the years 1963 and 1964, a demonstration of political maturity that is among the most impressive in all history," and declares that "the Southern Negro in 1965 is . . . better educated, less intimidated, and more spirited by far than the Southern Negro forty years ago." There is, he concludes, "a gleam of hope not apparent to an earlier generation."[26] Such optimism would not survive this turbulent decade.

When Johnson celebrated his seventy-fifth birthday in August, Baltimore feted its most famous living author. James H. Bready of the *Sun* wrote a column that made the birthday "a public event" and helped Johnson, the recipient of considerable homage, to experience "a wonderful day." Two months later, another party was held at the Enoch Pratt Free Library. He received

25. John Bartlow Martin, *Adlai Stevenson and the World: The Life of Adlai Stevenson* (Garden City, N.Y.: Doubleday, 1977), 862–63; GWJ to Katherine Johnson Parham, July 18, 15, 1965, GWJ Papers; GWJ, "Adlai Stevenson," *NR* 153 (July 24, 1965): 5–6; GWJ, "Lament of the Lame," *Michigan Quarterly Review* 6 (January 1967): 15–16; Adlai Stevenson to GWJ, October 27, 1964, GWJ to Adlai Stevenson, October 31, 1964, AES Papers.

26. GWJ, "After Forty Years—Dixi," in *South-Watching: Selected Essays by Gerald W. Johnson,* ed. Fred Hobson (Chapel Hill: University of North Carolina Press, 1983), 158–65. See John T. Kneebone, *Southern Liberal Journalists and the Issue of Race, 1920–1944* (Chapel Hill: University of North Carolina Press, 1983), 228.

bottles of Scotch whose ages totaled his own and heard it said that "he tells the truth as it is—naked." The man who could always laugh at himself wryly wrote his sister Kate that "I fully agree with a fellow I met on the street . . . who said, 'I am sure that you must find celebrating your 75th birthday an unexpected pleasure.' "[27]

The Christmas of 1965 was marked by an unusual gift that Gerald and Kathryn both cherished: a new home. They had rented 1310 Bolton Street since 1937, and, when the landlord reclaimed the house, they did not wish to leave the Bolton Hill neighborhood of which they had grown so fond. With the help of friend and prominent civic leader Walter Sondheim, Bolton Place was built a few blocks to the south, within easy walking distance. The development contained seventeen houses facing a common courtyard. Situated at the closed end, the Johnson house occupied the most prominent position.[28]

Gerald and Kathryn, who carefully planned their new home and oversaw the construction process, gained a distinctive, award-winning house that matched their needs. Its small grounds were distinguished by Kathryn's bonsai. The front of the house was graced by two terra-cotta medallions, taken from a former branch of the Enoch Pratt Free Library, that announced the intellectual life within. With much of the house concentrated on one floor, the writer who had broken his hip no longer had to climb stairs to his study. Although the house ended up costing 65 percent more than they had planned and left them "broke to the wide," he and Kathryn had no regrets.[29]

This move to 217 Bolton Place generated a pensive moment hidden from Johnson's reading public, a moment that found him far different from the confident figure who appeared in print. His reexamination of the thousands of volumes that had accumulated over the decades led him to assess the career that now stretched back more than half a century. The elderly man, surrounded by piles of books and preparing to leave the room where he had done his best work, wrote to his sister Kate that

27. James H. Bready, "Books and Authors," *BS,* August 1, 1965; GWJ to Katherine Johnson Parham, August 5, 6, 1965, GWJ Papers; "Gerald Johnson Paid Tribute by Friends on 75th Year," *BS,* October 18, 1965.

28. "Prime Mover," *BS,* March 29, 1980; "At Home with . . . Walter Sondheim," *Baltimore News American,* December 2, 1972; Virginia Tracy, interview by author, tape recording, Baltimore, November 15, 1990.

29. GWJ to Katherine Johnson Parham, July 24, 1965, GWJ Papers; author's visit to 217 Bolton Place and interview with then-current resident James Weitzel, July 16, 1991; GWJ to John C. Masten, January 25, 1966, GWJ Papers.

to tell the truth I find it somewhat depressing—so many projects that didn't work out, so many schemes that failed, so many hopes that blew up! Yesterday I put in a couple of hours stacking up some 300 volumes that I am going to sell to a second-hand book dealer; and that at least gave me the cold comfort of knowing that I am not the only writer of my generation that never got very far. I found first editions of such novels as 'The Green Hat,' 'The Hard-Boiled Virgin,' 'Moon-Calf,' and a couple of Dubose [*sic*] Heyward's. But Michael Arlen faded, I can't even remember the Atlanta gal's name [Frances Newman], Floyd Dell turned into a sourpuss and Heyward died.[30]

Such a tortured moment proved one of the nasty costs of the writing trade that he revered. Like some other authors—the elderly Edmund Wilson, for example, sometimes rose in the middle of the night to read reviews of his old books—Johnson could be plagued by self-doubt. But in saying that he "never got very far," he made far too harsh a judgment. With more than thirty books, his renown as an essayist, and his considerable stature as a journalist, he had succeeded far beyond what the cub on the *Lexington Dispatch* could possibly have imagined. Unlike Frances Newman, a suicide, he had managed to stay the course. His worst failing, he well understood, would have been silence, and he was never guilty of this. He made it to the desk every day and wrote as long as possible about what seemed important to him. His prose was pellucid, his output prodigious. None of this, however, could drive away the demons. As he gazed at these dusty volumes, he was staring into the abyss. But he persevered. Resilient once more, he turned away and made his way back to the typewriter.

The Cabinet, his single book of 1966, was offered by William Morrow as a sort of companion volume to the successful trilogy on the federal government. The United States Information Service regarded these volumes so highly that it had them translated into a variety of languages (among them Hindu and Arabic, Persian and Bengali) and placed them throughout the service's libraries abroad. About 500,000 copies were printed. It proved a considerable honor for him to be chosen as the official explicator of the fundamentals of American government.[31]

30. GWJ to Katherine Johnson Parham, August 16, 1965.

31. Jinny Voris, "According to Mr. Johnson: Some Insights on H. L. Mencken," HLM Papers; Jonathan Hereford, "Cultural Leaders to Be Honored," *BES,* May 1, 1968.

While Johnson was explaining the government to foreigners, he continued to criticize its foreign policy. He likened America's presence in Southeast Asia to Britain's fiasco in South Africa during the Boer War, and he remarked that the United States was in danger of "[losing] confidence in [its] own destiny." As he had done during Kennedy's presidency, Gerald Johnson relentlessly demanded more information about Vietnam: "What, exactly, is our commitment? To whom made? When, where, and by whom made? By what authority? Under what sanctions? Within what limits?" President Johnson's answers never satisfied him.[32]

Journeying back to North Carolina in late 1966, this iconoclast addressed the Greensboro Rotary Club. He mocked "the vast number of Americans who today walk briskly about the streets but who are dead from the neck up." He argued that "lack of money is not the worst form of poverty in America. Far more damaging . . . is poverty of ideas, poverty of vision, poverty of moral courage to abandon superstition and face the truth." The *Greensboro Daily News* reprinted the talk in its entirety. Clearly, Johnson retained a significant following in this city which he had graced as a journalist and later defended so forcefully. Proud of his achievements, the Women's College of the University of North Carolina (later the University of North Carolina, Greensboro) awarded him an honorary doctorate the following year.[33]

Johnson's lone book of 1967 deified a controversial American who, whatever his faults, certainly exhibited no poverty of ideas or vision or moral courage. As its subtitle suggests, *Franklin D. Roosevelt: Portrait of a Great Man* is outright hagiography, something which Johnson had tried to avoid in the first biography back in 1941. This "boy's life of Roosevelt," Johnson explained to his sister Lois, "looks at the whole thing the way one looks [at] the masterpieces of folklore. . . . [I]t is a yarn of Fortune's darling, suddenly and savagely mauled by Fate, but by that beating converted into a grim challenger of destiny." The book opens as a fairy tale: "Once there was a boy, born in 1882, named Franklin Delano Roosevelt, who had a great deal." After Johnson spins out a story full of moral lessons, he concludes in the same vein by remarking that "as long as men thrill to the story of one of their own

32. GWJ, "Another Boer Affair?" letter to the editor, *BS,* April 7, 1966; GWJ, "Commitment to Vietnam," letter to the editor, *BS,* March 2, 1966; See also GWJ, "No More Good Samaritans?" letter to the editor, *BS,* September 4, 1966.

33. GWJ, "The Revelations of 50 Years," *GDN,* November 20, 1966.

kind whom misfortune could not break and danger could not appall, they will listen to the story of Roosevelt, and each will wish that he were such a man." Not everyone agreed. Johnson attributed the "indignation" expressed by some reviewers to their "hatred of extraordinary duration" for the subject rather than to their reservations about the biographer's treatment.[34]

While Johnson wrote reverentially about this dead American hero, he spoke with censure and alarm as he assessed the contemporary scene. He concerned himself most with Vietnam and race relations. Lecturing in April at the E. E. Folk Journalism Workshop at Wake Forest, he praised Harrison Salisbury's reporting on Vietnam but challenged American journalists in general to do a better job of getting at the truth. He debunked the "domino theory" (if Vietnam were to fall to communism, then so would its neighbors), and he called for "every doubter to push to the front . . . [and] not allow dissent to be stifled." He was convinced, he told a correspondent, that "for the first time . . . the country is fighting for a cause not worth a war." As he surveyed violence in Cleveland and Detroit, Boston and New Haven, he decried the "race war sweeping like a forest fire through the cities" and wondered "how much longer [we can] rely on the police, as the hospitals and morgues fill up with policemen, fallen in the line of duty." In the final month of this tumultuous year, Johnson offered a literary parallel for America's predicament. He recalled Mrs. Jellyby, the deranged philanthropist in Dickens's *Bleak House,* who gazes afar while poverty and oppression fester beneath her feet. While 1967 sometimes found Johnson speaking *de profundis,* he grew even more alarmed the following year, part of which was spent in a burning city with barricades and snipers.[35]

Things fell apart; the center no longer held. As Willie Morris has remarked in *New York Days,* 1968 was, "with the exception of the Civil War years, surely the most tragic and cataclysmic in American history." American troops in Vietnam were pounded during the Tet Offensive, and a hundred Vietnamese were massacred at My Lai. Senator Robert Kennedy was assassi-

34. GWJ to Lois Johnson, August 6, 1966, GWJ Papers; GWJ, *Franklin D. Roosevelt: Portrait of a Great Man* (New York: William Morrow, 1967), 11, 184; GWJ to John Webb, July 2, 1967, GWJ Papers.

35. GWJ, untitled lecture, delivered on April 12, 1967, GWJ Papers; GWJ, "Laugh, Casca, Laugh!" in *America-Watching: Perspectives in the Course of an Incredible Century* (Owings Mills, Md.: Stemmer House, 1976), 274–77; GWJ, "Too Much Faith in Everything but Reason," letter to the editor, *BES,* August 9, 1967; GWJ to Ross Sanderson, July 19, 1967, GWJ Papers.

nated in Los Angeles, the Reverend Dr. Martin Luther King, Jr., in Memphis. Riots broke out in more than one hundred cities. Above all else a man of reason, Johnson confronted a world he had never made. He remarked sadly that "we are on the toboggan and the downslide has begun." Through his commentary on foreign policy, race relations, and the presidential campaign, he tried to slow the plunge.[36]

Perceiving a huge difference between America's professed aims and its activities in Vietnam, Johnson remarked bludgeoningly that "we have defended Christianity by acquiescing in the butchery of the Catholic, Diem, and supported the Buddhist, Ky. We have defended Capitalism by destroying the capital assets of Vietnam at a tremendous waste of our own." Infuriated by the increase in troops, he scorned President Johnson for deliberately misleading the American public. Disgusted with American military strategy, the old soldier called General William Westmoreland "the most incompetent general since Burnside lost an army at Fredericksburg." America he concluded, should "cut [its] losses and withdraw."[37]

While Vietnam continued to make him rage, the conflagration in Baltimore profoundly shook him. On Saturday, April 6, two days after Dr. King's death, rioting erupted. The National Guard and 2,000 federal troops worked to gain control of the city. By the time that the violence was quelled four days later, 6 people had been killed, 700 injured, and 6,000 arrested. The damage to businesses was estimated at $14 million. Three dogs in Bolton Place were poisoned, as were animals in the Baltimore Zoo. This man who had spent his life struggling that helpless creatures should come to no harm was appalled. As he stood at the back window of 217 Bolton Place, he could see seven of the more than a thousand fires that burned throughout the city. It was domestic violence of a magnitude far beyond what he had witnessed previously.[38]

Three months later, the *Evening Sun* sent a reporter to gather Johnson's

36. Willie Morris, *New York Days* (Boston: Little, Brown, 1993), 181–86; Stanley Karnow, *Vietnam: A History* (New York: Viking, 1983), 530; GWJ to John C. Masten, April 29, 1968, GWJ Papers.

37. GWJ, "The Superfluity of L.B.J.," *American Scholar* 37 (spring 1968): 221–26; GWJ, "Not the Draft," letter to the editor, *BS,* January 11, 1968; Lawrence Freeny, "Gerald Johnson: The Needle Gets Sharper," *Baltimore Magazine* 61 (October 1968): 25.

38. Sono Motoyama, "The Year Baltimore Burned," *Baltimore City Paper,* April 5, 1994, 14; GWJ, "The End of Incredulity," in *America-Watching: Perspectives in the Course of an Incredible Century* (Owings Mills, Md.: Stemmer House, 1976), 278–85; GWJ to John C. Masten, April 29, 1968, GWJ Papers; Frank Shivers, interview by author, Baltimore, June 3, 1991.

opinions. Until the rioting, Johnson explained, "I had looked with pride on Baltimore's race relations. But I suddenly recognized that the problem is above the level of ordinary human cognition." After speaking of "the clash between two entirely different and divergent cultures," he chose to end the interview optimistically. Perhaps he felt that the last thing a battered and shaky city needed was the voice of doom: "This country has always done what hasn't been tried or done before; that's how we got started. We have to find the solution to this problem, and we will. After all, the time has come when the miraculous is routine."[39] He did not sound entirely convinced, or convincing.

The following month his readers in the *Virginia Quarterly Review* received a jeremiad. After chastising both blacks and whites for their part in the violence, he speculates about the racial "future of this country" and then proceeds to answer his own question: "Nothing promising, we may be sure." The comparative historian raises the possibility of "another Jacquerie" and discusses America's racial problems in the context of Great Britain's dealings with the Irish Republican Army: "A handful, relatively speaking, of bold and agile Negro terrorists whom the rest of black America does not approve but will not betray could make Britain's trouble with IRA sink into insignificance historically."[40]

In the end, the violence in 1968 marked a watershed for Johnson's racial attitudes. He called the rioting "probably the second most senseless activity in which this country has been engaged, being topped, for sheer idiocy, only by the Civil War." He lost much of his former optimism about the races' ability to co-exist peacefully, and he toughened his earlier stance on social segregation. Even stricter separation of the races, he believed, would help to prevent another such catastrophe. This was a curious position for a writer so enamored of paradox, for Johnson failed to see the contradictions that seemed clear to a number of others: barriers don't protect; rather, they imperil by promoting fear and intolerance. Walling in and walling out will not make for good neighbors but will inevitably increase rather than diminish the threat of violence in the streets. So often the moralist, Johnson chose not to view segregation as a moral issue.[41]

39. Albert Scardino, "Historian Leans toward Pessimism on Education, Civil-Rights Problems," *BES,* July 12, 1968.

40. GWJ, "The End of Incredulity."

41. GWJ, "Black Power and the Turks' Millet," *BS,* August 25, 1968. See Morton Sosna, *In Search of the Silent South: Southern Liberals and the Issue of Race* (New York: Columbia University Press, 1977), 201: Howard Odum and Virginius Dabney "represent those Southern liberals

As he looked ahead to the presidential election, Johnson was not sanguine. "With foreign war in Vietnam," he told a correspondent, "civil war at home, and a terrific depression, what difference will it make who is president? Sir Galahad couldn't do us much good. Beelzebub couldn't do us much more harm." Writing for publication, however, he cast aside his gloom and cast his lot with Senator Eugene McCarthy, who made him think once more of chivalry. In "Hurrah for the Children's Crusade," Johnson used the luminary image once more to proclaim that McCarthy's campaign "has lighted the landscape with a blaze that has brought stark reality into view." Johnson spoke, he informed his readers, "for a large number of Americans of middle age and up who find McCarthy's call an invitation to a brighter and merrier, if not a better day." On the other hand, Johnson saw Hubert Humphrey as "Johnson's stooge" and called Humphrey's nomination in Chicago "the damnedest steal since 1912. It was the most cynical thing, the foulest thing I could imagine." Although he voted for Humphrey—in his view the lesser of two evils—he predicted that Nixon would win the election. After the Republican victory, Johnson faced, quite unhappily, four years of government under "Tricky Dick" ("Li'l Abner Nixon" was now a caricature of the past), Spiro T. Agnew, whose record in Maryland politics made Johnson shudder, and their platform of what he sardonically dubbed "lawnorder."[42]

Thankfully, 1969 proved less catastrophic. This writer who had been elected, the month after the rioting, to the Greater Baltimore Arts Council Hall of Fame found himself honored the following year by Loyola College (now Loyola College in Maryland) for his "contribution to the general welfare" and by Goucher College, which awarded him another honorary doctorate. Marked by homage, 1969 was also distinguished by the publication of *The British Empire: An American View of Its History from 1776 to 1945.* "The direct interest of Americans in this history," he explains in this volume of about sixty thousand words, "arises from the fact that we are left to pick up the pieces—not of the Empire, but of the world order that the Empire sustained for ninety-nine years. Americans need to know where the British Em-

who failed to see segregation as a moral problem." Likewise, Johnson chose not to view segregation in moral terms.

42. GWJ to Masten, April 29, 1968; Freeny, "Gerald Johnson: The Needle Gets Sharper," 24; GWJ, "Hurrah for the Children's Crusade," *NR* 157 (April 20, 1968): 12; GWJ, "Kennedy's Significance," letter to the editor, *BS,* June 13, 1968, GWJ, "Agnew Not Quite Unveiled," *BES,* October 11, 1968; GWJ, "The Agnew We Knew," *NR* 161 (November 29, 1969): 13–14.

pire failed in order not to stumble into the same error." In his conclusion to this cautionary tale, he argues that American "empery," if it is to prove stable and praiseworthy, must be sustained by something other than physical force. The last of the publications written for a juvenile audience, *The British Empire,* like its predecessors, offers a moral lesson.[43] In all, Johnson's decision to write that history for his grandson had provided him with a new forum in which he felt eminently comfortable, a forum where he wrote with considerable skill (the *Roosevelt* fiasco being the most notable exception), and a forum that generated the publication of ten books in eleven years. With this writing for juveniles, Johnson could hardly have asked for a more successful ancillary phase of his career.

The following year, a personal landmark, found him receiving additional acclaim. In June 1970, the Maryland Institute, College of Art, made Johnson an honorary doctor of letters, and the award's citation praised the octogenarian's youthful outlook and vitality. August 6, his eightieth birthday, was proclaimed "Gerald White Johnson Day" throughout Maryland. Johnson "has not feared," Baltimore mayor Thomas D'Alesandro remarked appreciatively, "to nettle the established and self-satisfied, or to give voices to the causes of the oppressed and overlooked."[44]

Johnson seized this occasion to write "Reflections at 80" for the *Baltimore Sun.* He talked about his century ("the century of iconoclasts," he called it) and the writing profession. Glancing backward, he gave thanks for the liveliness of his times: "After all, we have not been bored—dismayed, at times, and at other times infuriated, horrified, exalted, or dejected, but never bored." Borrowing from the speech that he had given at the Hamilton Street Club a decade earlier, he extolled curiosity and stressed the need to make it to that proverbial next corner. He wanted, of course, to stay around long enough to see what awaited him there, but at the beginning of his ninth decade, he acknowledged mortality and spoke of the most appropriate sort of death for the man who finds the world forever fresh: "Very Important Persons, with no more questions to ask, may die properly in bed, with a Doctor of Medicine on one side, and a Doctor of Divinity on the other, but the Inquiring

43. Hereford, "Cultural Leaders to Be Honored"; GWJ, *The British Empire: An American View of Its History from 1776 to 1945.* (New York: William Morrow, 1969), 150–52.

44. James H. Bready, "Books and Authors," *BS,* July 26, 1970; Gerald Parshall, "Gerald Johnson Gets Tribute at City Hall," *BS,* August 6, 1970.

Reporter should go out with a pencil in one hand and a wad of copy paper in the other."[45]

While Johnson's death lay nearly a decade away, his health was deteriorating. He described himself as "deaf in both ears, lame in one leg, and blind in one eye." The month after his eightieth birthday, he suffered a "heart flutter" that "immobilized him." The end of 1970 found him "utterly played out."[46] Like his inquiring reporter, however, Johnson would persevere to the end. One would have expected nothing less from this descendant of Catharine Campbell and those brave soldiers who fought on for the Confederacy long after any real chance of victory had died.

Johnson's valiant efforts during the decade to come, his difficult final decade, bring to mind Marcel Proust's memorable image for the elderly clergyman at the end of *The Past Recaptured,* the final volume of *Remembrance of Things Past.* This clergyman, Proust remarks, "advanced with difficulty, trembling like a leaf, upon the almost unmanageable summit of his eighty-three years, as though men spend their lives perched upon living stilts which never cease to grow until sometimes they become taller than church steeples, making it in the end both difficult and perilous for them to walk and raising them to an eminence from which they suddenly fall."[47] Certainly, Johnson would tremble, but he would never stop advancing until he fell. From the huge height of his ninth decade, he would continue to evaluate the past, assess the present, and speculate, with an optimism that became increasingly difficult, upon the future of his native land.

45. GWJ, "Reflections at 80," in *America-Watching: Perspectives in the Course of an Incredible Century* (Owings Mills, Md.: Stemmer House, 1976), 293–96.

46. GWJ to Betty Adler, December 21, 1967, BA Papers; GWJ to Katherine Johnson Parham, September 9, 1974, December 9, 1970, GWJ Papers.

47. Marcel Proust, *The Past Recaptured,* trans. Andreas Mayor (New York: Random House, 1991), 272.

14   Journey's End
1971–1980

I have not yet joined the ranks of the doomsday prophets. The twentieth century has undoubtedly gone sour—not here only, but in the rest of Western civilization as well. But it has happened before and the world eventually pulled out of it. I am persuaded that it will do so again—although I am not sure that I will live long enough to see the end of this nightmare.

—*Gerald Johnson to Katherine Johnson Parham, June 5, 1978*

Alluding to the seven-ages-of-man speech in Shakespeare's *As You Like It,* Johnson the octogenarian placed himself in the sixth age as the "lean and slippered pantaloon." He remarked this his memory reached "far back into ancient history." As he knew only too well, he was now confronting an enemy more pernicious than the Germans who had strafed and shelled him in France and the Klan which had tried to scare him in Greensboro. It was an opponent that Johnson, like all productive people, hated the most. The enemy was time.[1]

His health continued to decline. As a younger man, he had traveled throughout the United States and, an inveterate walker, had crisscrossed downtown Baltimore. Now, Baltimore's most distinguished living author became, in the words of his friend James H. Bready, "more or less a shut-in." While his mobility lessened, his deafness increased. Conversations could prove an adventure. Jesse Glasgow, fellow journalist and Wake Forest alumnus, has recalled that, while Johnson was "a great conversationalist," his hearing problems "brought some strange replies. A guest might say something about flowers and Johnson, rising and picking up the glasses, would say,

---

1. GWJ, "Mencken and the Art of Boob Bumping," *NR* 168 (May 19, 1973): 7.

'Good idea. Let's have another one!' " His friends understood, and he bore this infirmity with grace.[2]

Decades earlier, he had written his morning editorials for the *Evening Sun* and then returned to his study to write tirelessly until bedtime. He now complained that he could write for only two hours a day. "My head is buzzing with ideas about the contemporary scene," remarked this writer who had once moved so easily among books, essays, and journalism, "but to get them on paper in any coherent form is beyond me." He began five books; one was published. While he wrote more successfully in his shorter pieces, his market shrank, and this final decade found him communicating his ideas more frequently through letters to the editor—letters, as Mr. Bready has remarked, "where he gave away better stuff for free than what other writers of the same pages were paid for." A number of these letters proved eulogies for absent friends.[3]

Age hardly made him mellow about current events. Throughout 1971, he used this editorial mail to comment acidly on American foreign policy. He called the Vietnam War a cancer and bludgeoned Nixon and Agnew for their arrogance in refusing to listen to the American people. He spoke so forcefully that one correspondent claimed that Johnson had "joined the radical left."[4]

His manuscript in progress proved equally controversial. He called it *The Imperial Republic* and gave it a sobering subtitle: *Speculations on the Future, If Any, of the Third U.S.A.* Displeased, his editors at Liveright "ripped it to shreds," and Johnson rewrote the book. Published in 1972, this short volume of 122 pages divides American history into three periods. The first republic, which he labels "provisional," lasted from 1776 to 1789; the second, which he calls "national," ran from 1789 until the end of World War II. The final phase, the "imperial" one, extended from the end of the war until time present, "a quarter of a century deafened by such a clangor of brazen-lunged liars that rational, coherent thought is almost impossible." The issue that most concerns him here, Johnson explains, is "how to redesign a discredited form

2. James H. Bready, "Gerald Johnson: Looking Back over Thirty Years," *BS,* March 30, 1980; Jesse Glasgow, "Gerald Johnson: Man of the World," *Wake Forest* 27 (spring 1980): 15.

3. GWJ to Katherine Johnson Parham, December 5, 1971, February 28, 1972, GWJ Papers; Bready, "Looking Back over Thirty Years."

4. GWJ, " 'Cancerous' War," letter to the editor, *BES,* September 13, 1971; GWJ, "Reflection on the 'Provocation in Washington,' " letter to the editor, *BES,* May 15, 1971; W. S. Wertz, "Second Thoughts," letter to the editor, *BS,* May 23, 1971.

of government, imperialism, so that it will work. Every tub stands on its own bottom, and the tub represented by this book is bottomed on the assumption that today's question is the same as that of 1787—the renovation of an exploded political theory." This "tub" metaphor, the book's foundation, is hardly one of Johnson's more laudable analogies, and *The Imperial Republic* is marked too often by a talky, informal style that hinders the presentation of Johnson's ideas. While he complained that many reviewers failed to understand him, he also acknowledged that "when so many people miss the point it must be that I haven't made the point." The book earned only a little over $400, and Johnson called it a "flop." It was unfortunate that this volume, his final original book, did not prove a more pleasant and lucrative experience.[5]

Johnson was pleased, on the other hand, when he was contacted by Fred Hobson. Then a graduate student at the University of North Carolina, Chapel Hill, Hobson was writing a dissertation entitled "H. L. Mencken and the Southern Literary Renascence," a study in which Johnson figures prominently. The men corresponded at some length, and Johnson read excerpts from the dissertation. This led him to cast his mind on former days and evaluate, nearly half a century after the fact, his efforts in a significant phase of his career, that of Southern regional writer.

Johnson had erred in "The Congo, Mr. Mencken," he concluded, by predicting that the "Southern intellectual revival" would be led by North Carolina. He remained convinced that the "dynamite" planted by Mencken had done more good than harm: "You can't break a log-jam with an ice-pick. High explosives destroy some good timber, but to release the mass is more important than to destroy a log or two." Assessing his own commentary, Johnson said that "I have no apologies . . . although I know it was too violent to be really good writing. But I knew it at the time and in similar circumstances would do it again." Thus, he expressed no regret about his role as a liberator back in his salad days.[6]

When the dissertation was published as *Serpent in Eden: H. L. Mencken and the South,* Johnson wrote an eloquent, highly laudatory foreword. Employing the same demolition trope used in the correspondence, he says that

5. GWJ to Katherine Johnson Parham, May 16, 1971, GWJ Papers; GWJ, *The Imperial Republic: Speculations on the Future, If Any, of the Third U.S.A.* (New York: Liveright, 1972), 2, 4, 5, 45; GWJ to Charles Lambeth, June 1, 1972, January 21, 1974, July 19, 1972, in the possession of Mr. Lambeth, Thomasville, N.C.

6. GWJ to Fred Hobson, January 21, 1972 and May 18, 1972, in the possession of Dr. Hobson, Chapel Hill, N.C.

Mencken's "dynamite" made "the intellectual life of the South for a decade the most vigorous in the republic." While *Serpent* discusses both the Southern Agrarians and the response to *I'll Take My Stand,* Johnson does not use this foreword to refight old battles. This was hardly the place for such polemics. In all, this remembrance of things past gave Johnson "a lift," something which, he told his sister Kate, he "surely needed."[7]

The 1972 presidential campaign gave him no lift at all. He called it "the dullest since 1920 when Harding won sitting on his front porch." Continuing to despise Nixon, Johnson mocked the president's arrogance as "the turkey-gobbler strut" and dismissed his talk of peace in Vietnam as "an electioneering gimmick." Initially, Johnson supported Democratic senator Edmund S. Muskie of Maine "in a pretty languid way." After George S. McGovern received the Democratic nomination, Johnson, far from oracular, predicted that this senator from South Dakota would give Nixon "a scare." Actually, on November 7 Nixon received 521 electoral votes to McGovern's 17. While the election disappointed Johnson, the campaign would have ramifications that he could not then fully anticipate. On June 17, five people had been arrested for breaking into the executive headquarters of the Democratic National Committee at the Watergate complex in the nation's capital. In time, the Watergate scandal would rock the nation, topple the president, and provide the occasion for some of the most caustic prose of Johnson's final decade.[8]

Throughout 1973, this scandal infuriated Johnson and preoccupied him in both his writing for publication and in his correspondence. In "Watergate: One End, But Which?," a lengthy essay which appeared in the *American Scholar,* Johnson criticizes Nixon's "contempt . . . for the intelligence of the American people" and that people's catastrophic error in "[allowing] their sovereign power to be usurped." Johnson remarks colorfully that the White House has been "[defiled] into a thieves' kitchen were malefactors [gather] to plot burglary, bribery, forgery and slanderous defamation of honest men."

7. GWJ, foreword in *Serpent in Eden: H. L. Mencken and the South,* by Fred Hobson (Chapel Hill: University of North Carolina Press, 1974), ix–xi; GWJ to Katherine Johnson Parham, May 16, 1972, GWJ Papers.

8. GWJ to Katherine Johnson Parham, February 28, 1972; GWJ, "The Turkey-Gobbler Strut," in *America-Watching: Perspectives in the Course of an Incredible Century* (Owings Mills, Md.: Stemmer House, 1976), 296–301; GWJ to Katherine Johnson Parham, December 20, 1972, GWJ to John C. Masten, January 24, 1972, GWJ Papers; GWJ to Charles Lambeth, July 19, 1972.

Writing for the *Baltimore Sun,* he went so far as to call the scandal America's "third crisis" (the first two being the Constitutional Crisis of 1787 and the Civil War) and wondered whether Americans would view July 4, 1973, as a "festival or funeral." Appalled by Nixon's lack of honor, he upbraided the president for hiding "behind a woman's skirts when he laid the blame for the wrecked tapes on his secretary. That makes Bluebeard look like a gentleman." Johnson closed the year by declaring that responsible Republican leaders should urge Nixon's "voluntary withdrawal." A catastrophe for the country, the Watergate scandal proved a windfall for Johnson the essayist and journalist.[9]

The scandal, on the other hand, proved catastrophic for Johnson's book in progress, a volume celebrating America's forthcoming bicentennial in 1976. "The book will have to be rewritten," he lamented. "Watergate broke in while it was half done and that ruined the whole project." He pushed ahead with the manuscript, but William Morrow called for extensive revisions. Johnson postponed this task in the hope that there would come a time when "one can write about political affairs with some assurance that what you say will not be shot to pieces by the next edition of the newspapers." This bicentennial book was never completed. (Twelve years after Johnson's death, an excerpt would appear in the *Virginia Quarterly Review.*)[10]

While the following year was marked by another abortive book project, a volume "for teen-agers on the Bill of Rights," Johnson proved much more successful with his shorter pieces, and two graceful essays appeared in the *American Scholar* and the *New Republic.* In "Position Paper for the American Realist, 1974," a topic that could have proven ponderous in the hands of a lesser writer, Johnson uses rollicking animal metaphors and a felicitous allusion to capture his readers and lampoon his opponents. The American realist, he remarks laughingly, "is a jackass from the standpoint of our continent-sized Animal Farm, for he has only a languid interest in getting both forefeet, as well as his snout, into the swill trough." Extending the trope, he says that "this relative lack of interest is no proof of moral superiority, but is owing,

---

9. GWJ, "Watergate: One End, but Which?" in *America-Watching: Perspectives in the Course of an Incredible Century* (Owings Mills, Md.: Stemmer House, 1976), 302–308; GWJ, "America in Its Third Crisis," *BS,* July 8, 1973; GWJ to Katherine Johnson Parham, December 1, 1973, GWJ Papers; GWJ, "Nixon Adorers," letter to the editor, *BS,* December 30, 1973.

10. GWJ to Katherine Johnson Parham, June 23, 1972, and May 22, 1974, GWJ Papers; GWJ, "To Be Living at This Time: An Assessment of Values," edited, with a preface and postscript, by Vincent Fitzpatrick, *VQR* 68 (autumn 1992): 626–50.

chiefly, to to his observation that an animal as sinewy, swift, and surefooted as the jackass seems to enjoy life more and live longer than the fattest and greasiest of the swine." In "On Voting Democratic," he draws upon the traditional animal symbols to explain his preferences:

> When the donkey is high he usually takes off in the direction of the New Jerusalem, the elephant, in like condition, turns toward Tyre. Obviously, neither can arrive, because the New Jerusalem never was and the glories of Phoenicia never will be again. The practical problem is to determine which crash landing will have the better chance of survivors. There is no definite answer, but the historical facts are that the donkey's trip ended in Johnson's Great Society and McGovern, the elephant's in Watergate and Nixon. Which was the more terrific smash only time can tell, but my prediction is that the donkey will recover consciousness sooner than his rival will.[11]

This was the Johnson of old: an erudite man wearing his learning lightly, and a graceful stylist drawing upon a wide range of references to enliven his copy.

Nixon failed to recover from Watergate, and, after the president's resignation on August 9, 1974, Johnson wrote an essay scathingly entitled "The Nothing King" and argued that Americans had no choice but to engage in a "salvage operation." After President Ford pardoned his predecessor on September 8, Johnson complained that this act was "grossly immoral." Ford, in Johnson's view, had "his foot in his mouth more than any [other] president since Harding." However, Ford, unlike Nixon, generated an element of sympathy on Johnson's part: "He is so obviously a well-meaning bumbler that it is impossible to work up a rage against him."[12]

Johnson recovered, albeit more slowly than he wanted, from his first surgery since early 1961 when he had broken his hip. On June 21, 1974, he was operated on successfully for cancer of the throat, and he remained hospitalized for ten days. Nearly a year later, he complained that "I have not yet

11. GWJ to Katherine Johnson Parham, March 7, 1974, GWJ Papers; GWJ, "Position Paper on the American Realist," in *America-Watching: Perspectives in the Course of an Incredible Century* (Owings Mills, Md.: Stemmer House, 1976), 308–13; GWJ, "On Voting Democratic: Confession of a Party-Liner," in *America-Watching: Perspectives in the Course of an Incredible Century* (Owings Mills, Md.: Stemmer House, 1976), 314–18.

12. GWJ, "The Nothing King," in *America-Watching: Perspectives in the Course of an Incredible Century* (Owings Mills, Md.: Stemmer House, 1976), 318–19; GWJ to Katherine Johnson Parham, January 3, 1975, September 9, 1974, November 30, 1974, GWJ Papers.

managed to get back in trim. They all say that I am unreasonable, that eleven months is not bad for a comeback, but it is devil of a long time to me." Making no concessions to age and infirmity, he wanted to write as productively as he had when he was young.[13]

Like its predecessor, 1975 was marked by a project that Johnson failed to complete: "a small book on the Declaration of Independence." As he had done in 1974, however, he wrote quite skillfully in his essays. "The End of the Beginning" appeared in the fiftieth-anniversary issue of the *Virginia Quarterly Review*. Johnson the realist acknowledges America's parlous state: "The outlook at the beginning of 1975 is gloomy, and it is not merely silly to deny it, it is dangerous, for until we face our difficulties realistically we shall do nothing intelligent toward overcoming them." Again refusing to play the doomsayer, Johnson argues that these difficulties can be overcome. "To assume in advance that the trouble will be more than we can handle," he remarks while flaying an old enemy, "would be the equivalent of pleading *nolo contendere* before the case comes to trial, which may be the philosophy of Spiro Agnew [he had resigned under fire on August 10, 1973] but not that of Abraham Lincoln." Johnson sets forth several reasons for his optimism— among them the fact that Americans "have been here before" and the opinion that many of his fellow citizens have "a metaphysical faith" in the American. Johnson concludes, as his title suggests, that America is facing the end of its apprenticeship, not the beginning of its demise. "The End of the Beginning" proved his final contribution to the *Virginia Quarterly Review,* the journal for which he had written so effectively for half a century.[14]

He used the *New Republic* to send a final, heartfelt Christmas gift to an agnostic, dead nineteen years, who liked to celebrate the Nativity by pulling down the shades and having a few quiet drinks. "Reconsideration: H. L. Mencken" opens in 1926, the year in which, nearly half a century before, Johnson had signed on with the *Baltimore Evening Sun*. He details Mencken's generosity to younger writers and, using the demolition trope once more, discusses the reverberations of "The Sahara of the Bozart." After acknowledging Mencken's considerable influence as a social critic right after World

---

13. GWJ to Katherine Johnson Parham, June 11, 1974, GWJ Papers; GWJ to Fred Hobson, September 14, 1974, in the possession of Dr. Hobson; GWJ to Charles Lambeth, July 31, 1974 and June 7, 1975, in the possession of Mr. Lambeth.

14. GWJ to Katherine Johnson Parham, August 12, 1975, GWJ Papers; GWJ, "The End of the Beginning," in *America-Watching: Perspectives in the Course of an Incredible Century* (Owings Mills, Md.: Stemmer House, 1976), 325–32.

War I and throughout the 1920s, Johnson concludes by detailing the considerable difference between time past and present:

> The frauds of Mencken's day were adept at stealing credit to which they had no lawful claim and fairly good at stealing cash . . . under some pious pretense. But our modern felons are sterner stuff. They abscond with cash in fabulous qualities, but the great prize they aspire to is nothing short of the government itself—the sovereignty of the people. Against felons of that size a slapstick is useless and a policeman's club none too effective. What we need is a battering ram such as FDR constructed to stave in the gates of the castle of privilege. Mencken was a man of his time and a valuable one, but this is not his time. *Requiescat in pace.*

Fifty years before, when he had stirred up the animals all across America, Mencken had been regarded as America's most influential private citizen; now, Johnson finds his rollicking satire as archaic as a blunderbuss. Like Hamlet wandering in the graveyard and encountering poor Yorick's skull, Johnson is struck by that awful sense of time's flight. He manages here to offer a poignant farewell to that controversial figure who had exerted the greatest influence on his own career. For the North Carolinian, there would remain a few more gates to stave in before he rested peacefully.[15]

While no bicentennial book by Johnson was published in 1976, America's two hundredth anniversary was marked by the appearance of the only anthology of his writing to be published during his lifetime. Appropriately entitled *America-Watching,* this collection of more than three hundred pages offers seventy-one selections ranging from 1923 until 1975. The material was assembled and edited by Kathryn Johnson, who collected and preserved her husband's writing, and Barbara Holdridge, Johnson's publisher at Stemmer House, a firm in Owings Mills, outside Baltimore.[16]

Old readers as well as new ones were given easy access to essays from such periodicals as the long-defunct *Reviewer,* the *Virginia Quarterly Review, Harper's Magazine* ("The Cadets of New Market" was, of course, included), the

---

15. GWJ, "Reconsideration: H. L. Mencken," *NR* 173 (December 27, 1975): 32–33; William Manchester, *Disturber of the Peace: The Life of H. L. Mencken* (New York: Harper and Brothers, 1950), 158.

16. Barbara Holdridge, interview by author, tape recording, Owings Mills, Md., April 17, 1991; GWJ, acknowledgment to *America-Watching: Perspectives in the Course of an Incredible Century* (Owings Mills, Md.: Stemmer House, 1976), unnumbered page.

American Scholar, the *New Republic,* and the *Saturday Review of Literature.* From his journalism, *America-Watching* includes such diverse pieces as the polemical "One for Roosevelt," written during that tumultuous year, forty years before, when Johnson was at war with the Sunpapers, and the more whimsical "Reflections at 80." From his more than forty books, the anthology includes excerpts from the Jackson biography, *A Little Night Music, American Heroes and Hero-Worship,* and *Incredible Tale.* Kathryn Johnson and Barbara Holdridge had chosen well, for *America-Watching* captures Johnson's staggering productivity, his immense skill as a stylist, and his extraordinary range of interests.

His achievements were acknowledged. In his introduction, the distinguished historian Henry Steele Commager calls Johnson "not only a public figure but an institution" and explains that the "one theme" recurring throughout the canon is "the necessity of freedom and justice in our society." Commager concludes by remarking that Johnson "has been around now for two generations, and we tend to take him for granted; indeed, we can scarcely imagine the journalistic landscape without him. We should not take him for granted; we should thank our lucky stars that we have had him for so long and that we still have him." The Maryland Senate passed a resolution congratulating Johnson on the appearance of the anthology, and *America-Watching* was designated an "Ambassador Book" particularly suited to explaining America to residents of other countries.[17]

Throughout the year, Johnson watched America for *Long Island (N.Y.) Newsday.* He agreed to write a brief regular column (about five hundred words per installment) "dealing with the Bi-centennial but keyed on some current happening in light of the Declaration." Eight installments appeared from January to June. Later in 1976, he sold *Newsday* two more pieces, both recollective in nature. The first discussed his activities in France when the Armistice ended World War I; the second captured a child's Christmas in Riverton back in 1894. He welcomed the income from *Newsday,* of course, but remarked that "what is really important [is] getting back into big-time newspaper work once again."[18]

---

17. Henry Steele Commager, introduction to *America-Watching: Perspectives in the Course of an Incredible Century* (Owings Mills, Md.: Stemmer House, 1976), ix–xi; GWJ to Katherine Johnson Parham, February 1, 1977, GWJ Papers; Mary Ellen Moll (Books Across the Sea) to GWJ, October 29, 1979, in the possession of Barbara Holdridge, Owings Mills, MD.

18. GWJ to Katherine Johnson Parham, January 1, 1976, GWJ Papers. Three pieces appeared under the title "The Unanimous Declaration" in three issues of *New York Newsday,* January 1976. Five columns appeared under the generic title "Bicentennial Watch": "A New Stamp Act, an Old Insult," January 22, 1976; "Sounds of '76 in the Cacophony," February 17,

His ability to continue this newspaper work, indeed all of his writing, was seriously challenged on June 7, 1976, when he suffered a "mild stroke." His speech was affected, and he experienced weakness in his right arm. He was admitted to Baltimore's Union Memorial Hospital and remained there until early July. Both Gerald and Kathryn were understandably alarmed. With their financial situation hardly secure, they needed the income from his writing, and he acknowledged "the spectre that has haunted me . . . the suspicion that my earning power has been destroyed permanently by the stroke." However, as he had done after the operations for the broken hip and the cancer, he resolutely returned to the typewriter and produced some lively copy.[19]

The month after he left the hospital, Johnson used the *Sun* to comment on the forthcoming presidential election. After being asked how Mencken would have responded to the Democratic candidate, James Earl "Jimmy" Carter, Jr., the former governor of Georgia, Johnson at eighty-six deftly imitated the prose that he had aped as a far younger man: "Of course Carter is a star-spangled jackass, but so are all the others, and out of the herd, this one seems less likely to walk off with the White House spoons." Johnson was dismayed by what he saw as Carter's religious fundamentalism (he dubbed him a "snake handler") and told a correspondent that "it is hard for me to believe that an honest politician can possibly come out of Georgia." After Carter defeated Ford by forty-seven electoral votes, Johnson wrote that the Georgian had won "not because of beauty or brains, but because the Nixon administration stunk and Gerald Ford was mired in it right up to his neck." This marked Johnson's seventeenth and final presidential election as a voter and a commentator. There was a remarkable symmetry here for this critic who remained so interested in the affairs of his native region: Both the first election in 1912 and the final one in 1976 resulted in the victories of presidents born in the South. While Johnson's respect for Carter would increase, he would never raise him to that plateau on which he had elevated Woodrow Wilson.[20]

1976; "Quite a Bit Bigger, but Not Any Better," March 14, 1976; "A Revolution Long before '76," April 18, 1976; and "Flattery Will Get Us Nowhere," June 6, 1976. The recollective columns were "The War Is Over: Armistice Day 1918," November 11, 1976; and "The Indomitable Christmas Spirit," December 19, 1976.

19. Kathryn Hayward Johnson to Katherine Johnson Parham, June 8, 1976 and August 29, 1976; GWJ to Katherine Johnson Parham, August 29, 1976, GWJ Papers.

20. GWJ, "Mencken Would Have Been Speechless," *BS,* August 29, 1976; GWJ to Katherine Johnson Parham, October 19, 1976, GWJ Papers; GWJ to Charles Lambeth, April 28, 1976 and April 26, 1976, in the possession of Mr. Lambeth.

The following year found Johnson lionized once more. After Johnson wrote a moving tribute to Hubert Humphrey, who had been diagnosed with terminal cancer, Senator Charles Mathias of Maryland inserted the tribute into the *Congressional Record,* along with a "very flattering preface" about its author. Johns Hopkins University awarded Johnson an honorary doctorate, and the Maryland Senate proclaimed him "a great American journalist."[21]

In one of the more melancholy episodes of this final decade, this great American journalist on one occasion went unrecognized by the newspaper for which he had done his best writing. In May 1977, a frail-looking Johnson, wearing a hat and coat and leaning on a cane, napped on a bench in a small park near his home in Bolton Place. He was photographed, and the picture appeared in the *Evening Sun.* The caption beneath the photograph identified Baltimore's most famous living author as "an old man [dozing] on a bench." Such was one of the costs of a life where he appeared far less often in public.[22]

This episode was marked, however, by a happy coincidence. The picture was entitled "The Old Man and the Sun," an obvious play upon Hemingway's *The Old Man and the Sea.* The comparison, albeit unintentional, could hardly have been more appropriate. Johnson and Santiago, Hemingway's fisherman, were kindred spirits—brave old men who fought on with courage and skill and refused to surrender to the inevitable. For his part, Johnson would have a few more years in the sunshine before the shadows finally enveloped him.

In 1978, the humble Johnson accepted further accolades, and the bellicose one assaulted the establishment. He received yet another honorary doctorate, this one from Towson State University (now Towson University), and he was honored by the Friends of the Enoch Pratt Free Library. Respectful of the aristocracy of intellect but contemptuous of the aristocracy of money, he used the *Evening Sun* to proclaim that Baltimore was "in serious danger of being pillaged and ruined, not by an army of insane Russians, but by the fat-headed complacence of of so many possessors of old money—heirs of the third and fourth generation . . . who expect to spend the rest of their years living on tax-free municipals." He clearly relished this opportunity to stave in the gates of privilege.[23]

21. GWJ, "Humphrey Praised" letter to the editor, *BS,* September 14, 1977; GWJ to Charles Lambeth, September 26, 1977, in the possession of Mr. Lambeth.

22. "The Old Man and the Sun," *BES,* May 19, 1977.

23. GWJ, "Enough of Fat-Headed Complacence, Baltimore," *BES,* January 3, 1978.

For his next book project, he seized the opportunity to return to what had succeeded previously. At age eighty-eight, he began a fourth volume in the History for Peter series, a volume tentatively entitled "America, since Roosevelt." Just as Watergate had interrupted his progress on the bicentennial book five years before, the "unspeakable horror" in Guyana interrupted him here. More than nine hundred lost souls followed James Jones, the sort of spurious messiah whom Johnson had denounced for decades, to a foreign land and there committed mass suicide. Johnson remarked that such a catastrophe could "destroy the country." In fact, it hardly dented America, but it did blow the book in progress "out of existence," and Johnson was forced "to start all over again." After throwing away 50 pages, he wrote about 100 more and estimated that he was about two-thirds finished. "I don't kid myself that I have written a great hit," he told his sister Kate, "but even a small one . . . would make things pretty easy for Kathryn and me for the rest of our lives." "America, since Roosevelt" was never published, and Johnson attempted no more long-term projects. The American reading public, the beneficiary of more than forty volumes since 1925, would never again enjoy a new book by Gerald Johnson.[24]

The shadows were lengthening, and 1979 marked his final year at 217 Bolton Place. Breaking its long-established policy of not accepting likenesses of living persons, the Enoch Pratt Free Library honored Johnson by accepting a bust sculpted by the prominent Baltimore artist Reuben Kramer. It was displayed in the library's Central Hall, opposite a bust of George Bernard Shaw, another prolific author who lived long and refused to avoid controversy. Johnson wrote his final essay, and "A Sage Remembers" (surely not his title, for he was too modest to label himself such) would appear posthumously. He wrote no warm and rosy memory piece but instead talked candidly about the 1968 riots and argued that America's "great fault" was "the intellectual inertia that has allowed its science and technology to outstrip its philosophy."[25]

His final letter to the editor of the *Sun* appeared on November 19. Praising the president's handling of the Iranian crisis, Johnson wrote that "for the first 72 hours . . . President Carter, in spite of what must have been terrific

24. GWJ to Charles Lambeth, 10 May [1978], in the possession of Mr. Lambeth; GWJ to Katherine Johnson Parham, December 10, 1978, and January 1, 1979, GWJ Papers.

25. "Library Given Bust of Gerald Johnson," *BES,* July 3, 1979; "G. W. Johnson Dies at 89, Was Writer," *BS,* March 23, 1980, pp. A1, A4; GWJ, "A Sage Reminisces," in *Baltimore: A Living Renaissance,* ed. Lenora Heilig Nass, Laurence N. Kraus, and R. C. Monk (Baltimore: Historic Baltimore Society, 1982), 150–53.

pressure to play the star-spangled jackass, kept his head." It was fitting that this final piece of editorial mail extolled grace under pressure, a trait that marked Johnson's own career. It was also fitting that, with "star-spangled jackass," Johnson employed a Menckenian resonance, an acknowledgment of the man who, back in the days that surely seemed another lifetime ago— when Coolidge was president and before the stock market crashed—had brought the Southerner north to Baltimore to write his finest journalism.[26]

Johnson granted his final interview in December, and he and Kathryn were visited at 217 Bolton Place by Peter Kumpa of the *Evening Sun*. It was, he found, the home of a very bright man who refused to take himself too seriously, and Kumpa wrote of the many roles that Johnson had played, discussed his reading habits, and praised the remarkable prose "that has made us wiser, made us think, and entertained us at the same time." It was also the home of a man "in his fragile years." Gerald "has good days and bad days," Kathryn explained. "The doctor says that at 89, it's only natural." Four days after this feature appeared, Gerald and Kathryn spent their fifty-eighth, and final, Christmas together.[27]

The bad days increased. In January 1980, Johnson moved to the Edge-wood Nursing Home in North Baltimore. Understandably, his months in an assisted-living environment proved difficult for this man of fierce independence. The nurses did everything possible for their honored guest, but Johnson still plaintively asked a visitor: "Is there any way out of here?" In his ninetieth year, in failing health and with periods of confusion, he continued to think of himself as a writer and wanted to return to his books and papers.[28]

The relatives to whom he had been so faithful could not have been more generous or supportive, and his old friends came calling. In happier times, Johnson had been the groomsman in the wedding of Mr. and Mrs. Robert Preston Harriss; now, R. P. and Margery were his final visitors. Johnson "was very weak," Mr. Harriss has recalled, "and, toward the last, his mind sometimes wandered. But on our last visit . . . we found him lucid and cheerful. He called each of us by name. He even told one of his wonderful North Carolina stories." Seeing that Johnson was tired, the Harrisses prepared to leave. Johnson "raised his hand . . . and blew [Margery] a kiss. It was his

26. GWJ, "U.S. and Iran: Searching for Answers," letter to the editor, *BS,* November 19, 1979.

27. Peter Kumpa, "Gerald Johnson, in 90th Year, Still Keeps Avidly in Touch," *BES,* December 21, 1979.

28. Bready, "Gerald Johnson: Looking Back over Thirty Years."

good-bye to her and to us, and to the world he loved and made a better place by loving it." He died of pneumonia at noon on Saturday, March 22, 1980. That remarkable voice which for the greater part of the twentieth century had discussed seemingly everything under the sun, which had made his readers laugh and cry, and which had afflicted the comfortable and championed the unfortunate, was finally stilled.[29]

As he had wished, Johnson was cremated. Twenty-nine years before, the ashes of Mrs. Hayward, his mother-in-law, had been entombed in Baltimore's Green Mount Cemetery, and he and Kathryn had agreed that theirs would be placed here as well. Johnson had also expressed the wish that a marker would be placed for him in the Spring Hill Cemetery in North Carolina. On March 29, 1980, his ashes were entombed in the Undercroft of the Chapel in the cemetery whose centennial history he had written back in 1938. Green Mount Cemetery, he had then remarked, "represents journey's end for the great, for the famous, and for the merely notorious, it is true; but it is the resting-place of a vast number of others, who did nothing spectacular, who were merely honest men and virtuous women, whose work created no flaring headlines in the newspapers, created nothing except a great and powerful city rich, not merely in money, but also in honorable tradition." He had ably elegized these figures, both prominent and obscure, gathered there in silence, and now he had reached "journey's end" himself. This cemetery which, in life, he helped to distinguish with his prose he now, in death, further distinguished with his presence.[30]

His death generated considerable commentary. There were the inevitable comparisons with Mencken and the acknowledgment of those twelve wondrous years on the *Evening Sun* when the bourgeois Baltimorean and the liberal Southerner had cavorted in print on Mondays and Thursdays. *Time* magazine noted Johnson's passing, and both the *Washington Post* and the *New York Times* composed their own obituaries rather than rely on wire-service copy. North Carolina mourned his passing, and William D. Snider, editor of the *Greensboro Daily News,* saluted Johnson's courage and called him "one of the outstanding journalists of his time." Editorials in both the *Daily News* and the *Raleigh News and Observer* acknowledged his extraordinary skill as a stylist;

29. R. P. Harriss, eulogy delivered at the memorial service for Johnson, March 31, 1980, photocopy in possession of the author.

30. GWJ to Katherine Johnson Parham, March 7, 1974, GWJ Papers; GWJ, *Green Mount Cemetery: One-Hundredth Anniversary, 1838–1938* (Baltimore: Proprietors of the Green Mount Cemetery, 1938), 111.

he was a writer who offered "common sense set to music." On Sunday, March 23, the *Sun* ran a gargantuan obituary (forty-nine paragraphs, about 1,800 words) that began prominently on the front page. The newspaper's lead editorial the following day called Johnson "Baltimore's clarion voice of uncompromising conscience." The *Evening Sun* admitted that "the action of summing up comes hard" and speculated about how Johnson's writing would be viewed by posterity: "How much of his writing will endure is for any reader to guess, any lover of clear and flavorsome prose, any fancier of debate in the strongest terms—and on highest planes, with nary a personal foul." Johnson would have appreciated this, especially the final comment. He fought fairly—never descending into the mud, never bringing hidden agendas to his writing, never attacking those who could not defend themselves. He was a man of common decency, a writer who brought civility to a trade that, when practiced by lesser individuals, can prove very uncivil indeed.[31]

Family and friends gathered to say good-bye. A memorial service was held on Monday, March 31, 1980, at the Brown Memorial Presbyterian Church in Bolton Hill, the church where, during kinder days, Gerald and Kathryn had watched their daughters marry. "I don't believe my father ever harbored a truly malicious thought," Dorothy Johnson van den Honert remarked. "He not only admired the sonority of Lincoln's famous phrases, 'With malice toward none, with charity toward all,' but he made them the basis of the ethical framework within which he routinely lived." Johnson had touched many people during his fifty-four years in Baltimore, and it was an eminent and diverse group of Baltimoreans who rose to remember their friend: Walter Sondheim, businessman and prominent civic leader; Dr. Thomas B. Turner, dean emeritus of the Johns Hopkins School of Medicine; Dr. Curt B. Richter, professor emeritus of psychobiology at the Johns Hopkins School of Medicine; and fellow writers Louis Azrael, James H. Bready, and R. P. Harriss. They talked about the old days and more recent times and

---

31. "Milestones," *Time* 115 (April 7, 1980): 83; Richard Pearson, "Gerald W. Johnson Dies, Former Editorial Writer for Baltimore Newspapers," *Washington Post,* March 24, 1980; John L. Hess, "Like Mencken, a Sage," *New York Times,* March 24, 1980, p. B9; Bready, "Gerald W. Johnson: Looking Back over 30 Years"; "Noted Author and Historian Dies," *GDN,* March 24, 1980; "Gerald W. Johnson," *GDN,* March 24, 1980; "Common Sense Set to Music," *Raleigh News and Observer,* March 26, 1980; "G. W. Johnson Dies at 89, Was Writer"; "Gerald W. Johnson," *BS,* March 24, 1980, p. A16; "Gerald W. Johnson," *BES,* March 24, 1980, p. A10.

recalled Johnson as both man and writer. Mr. Bready marveled at his friend's work ethic, praised his concern for the underdog, and, employing that luminary image which Johnson had used so often and so well, called him "a force toward the light." Clergymen preach once a week, Bready remarked, but Johnson's purpose every day "was theocratic: to let you know which is right and which is wrong."[32]

For all of his homilies, Johnson, as we have seen, had never been conventionally religious. This world had always seemed more important to him than the next, and he had never viewed any church as his sanctuary. Rather, he found the most sacred place to be his study, a room where mourners could not have gathered because there was not sufficient space. Here he presided: with his desk and typewriter as his pulpit, his copy as his sermon, and his readers all across the land as his congregation. And it is this place which gives the most memorable and representative picture of Johnson at the end: a resolute old man—time destroyed but never defeated him—standing among his books and papers, facing the east, looking always toward the light.

32. Photocopies of the eulogies in possession of the author.

Epilogue
Home Again

There once was a man named Christopher Wren, whose body has been dust these two hundred years. Yet . . . two years ago, I stood on Fleet [S]treet looking toward Ludgate Hill, where above the tangled roofs of the city, the dome of St. Paul's floated against the sky, and saw before my eyes what was really important of Christopher Wren. As long as his work stands, he still moves the minds and hearts of men.

—*Gerald Johnson, "Argument for Ladies,"* Baltimore Evening Sun, *April 12, 1940*

"A man's true stature," Johnson once remarked, "is usually revealed, not by his corporeal presence, but by his ghost." It is hardly surprising that this reflective man pondered the matter of how his ghost might be perceived by posterity. After Johnson's death, the sands of life kept running—for those he loved and those he fought—and time, as always, won out in the end. Two of the most significant forums for which he had written, a magazine and a newspaper that had once captivated their readers, passed from the earth. Fittingly, Johnson returned, in spirit if not in body, to the land where he had been begotten, born, and shaped.[1]

During the remainder of the year of Johnson's death, he was celebrated several times in North Carolina. On April 13, 1980, the Thomasville Public Library dedicated the Gerald White Johnson shelf displaying all of his books. On April 26, the Board of Trustees at Wake Forest University passed a resolution honoring Johnson; that spring, the *Wake Forest* magazine ran a memorial issue containing several retrospectives. On October 31, Wake Forest dedicated its Gerald White Johnson Reading Room in the Z. Smith Reynolds Library. The room displayed, among other material which Mrs. Johnson had sent down from Baltimore, the colorful academic attire accompanying his

---

1. GWJ, *The Lunatic Fringe* (Philadelphia: J. B. Lippincott, 1957), 120.

many honorary degrees and the striking portrait painted back in 1939 by the Baltimore artist Stanislav Rembski. For Rembski, his subject's eyes "saw infinity in the present."[2]

On June 8, 1980, a farewell party was held for Kathryn Johnson in Bolton Place; she then moved to Valparaiso, Indiana, to live with the Sligers. There was, on the other hand, no farewell party for the *American Mercury*. With no notice of cessation, the magazine's final issue appeared that spring. At its best, during its early years under Mencken's editorship, when the young Johnson was contributing lively essays, this magazine, with its enlightened skepticism, was one of America's foremost periodicals. At its worst, it later drifted into the foul backwaters of fear and intolerance—denouncing efforts by homosexuals to gain equality under the law, extolling Adolf Hitler, and questioning the existence of the Holocaust. The lugubrious demise of the *Mercury* marked one of the more gruesome ironies in American literary history, a testament to that power of darkness which Johnson had witnessed during his career.[3]

In 1983, two years after the death of his sister Ella Johnson Webb at age eighty-four, the University of North Carolina Press published *South-Watching*. Edited by Fred Hobson, this collection of twenty-two essays provides easy access to such memorable pieces as "The Congo, Mr. Mencken," when Johnson was playing a part in the Southern literary renaissance; "No More Excuses," when he was battling the Southern Agrarians; and "To Live and Die in Dixie," when at seventy he was singing the virtues of his native land. The first anthology since *America-Watching* seven years before (and the final collection yet to appear), *South-Watching* captures Johnson's skill and attitudes as a regional writer. The volume received the Lillian Smith Award for Non-Fiction and generated considerable commentary throughout the South.

On June 15, 1984, Johnson was inducted into the North Carolina Journalism Hall of Fame in Chapel Hill. Dorothy Johnson van den Honert remarked during the ceremony that her father "would be immensely embarrassed and immensely pleased to be placed in such distinguished company." She glanced back to the hot summer of 1925, to that trial which had

2. Myra Thompson, "300 Gather at Library," *Thomasville (N.C.) Times,* April 14, 1980; Jesse Glasgow, "Gerald Johnson: Man of the World," *Wake Forest* 27 (spring 1980): 13–16; Russell Brantley, "Gerald Johnson: Man of Wake Forest," *Wake Forest* 27 (spring 1980): 10–12; Kathryn Hayward Johnson to author, February 14, 1989; Stanislav Rembski, interview with author, tape recording, Baltimore, October 13, 1990.

3. Vincent Fitzpatrick, "The *American Mercury*," in *American Literary Magazines: The Twentieth Century,* ed. Edward E. Chielens (Westport, Conn.: Greenwood Press, 1992), 11–12.

proven a watershed, and then speculated upon how the civil libertarian might respond to the present: "Gerald's early manhood was spent in the shadow of the Scopes trial, and the whole notion of mind-control became almost an obsession with him, which affected and directed his thinking to the day of his death. If he saw, today, the apathy with which this nation seems to be accepting the corrosion of its Bill of Rights . . . it might shake even the unshakable optimist that was Gerald Johnson."[4]

The following year, Johnson was placed in distinguished company once more. The University of North Carolina Press published John T. Kneebone's *Southern Liberal Journalists and the Issue of Race, 1920–1944.* In addition to Johnson, the volume concentrates upon George Fort Milton, Virginius Dabney, Ralph McGill, and Hodding Carter. Johnson, as we have seen, always thought it his duty to speak forthrightly about race, and this book offers a judicious, thoroughly documented assessment of his racial views, attitudes that could outrage both liberals and conservatives.

In February 1988, Johnson was inducted into the Maryland-Delaware Press Association Hall of Fame. The following year, however, was marked by censure rather than applause. In late 1989, *The Diary of H. L. Mencken* was published. This controversial volume, which caused a brouhaha on the American literary scene, treats Johnson acidly. Mencken had begun this book back in 1930 and continued it until his stroke in late 1948. In 1941 and 1942, he had written "Thirty-Five Years of Newspaper Work," a volume published under that title in 1994. Mencken's memoirs call Johnson a "second-rate Southerner" and argue, among other things, that as an editorial writer he wrote skillfully but had little of consequence to say. As an editor, he proved "quite incompetent for command." He had poor skills as a reporter and wrote feeble defenses of the New Deal. Recalling his editorship of the *Evening Sun* in 1938, Mencken says that he found Johnson "completely hopeless." Why, one wonders, did Mencken write such things? Perhaps the reason was in part political, a lingering resentment over Johnson's successful defense of President Roosevelt, a man whom Mencken never ceased to loathe. In any event, it should be pointed out that Johnson was hardly the sole recipient of such bilious commentary. Having suffered his wife's death and his own health problems, and having experienced that huge decline in his reputation

4. Dorothy Johnson van den Honert, remarks delivered at Chapel Hill, June 15, 1984, photocopy in possession of the author.

during the New Deal years, Mencken sometimes tended to be churlish in the writing that he consigned to time-lock. While Johnson never saw these remarks by the writer he lionized and the man he always considered a friend, *The Diary of H. L. Mencken* was published while Kathryn Johnson was alive. The Baltimorean who had, in life, proven so generous to Johnson turned petty in his memoirs. On the other hand, Johnson, the lesser of the two writers, remained gracious and thankful to the end.[5]

In August 1990, the Johnson centennial was celebrated in North Carolina and in Maryland. The occasion generated numerous retrospectives in the print media. Moreover, the Davidson County Historical Museum in Lexington, where the "unlicked cub" had learned his trade on the *Dispatch* more than sixty-five years before, devoted an exhibit to his career.[6]

Katherine Johnson Parham, Gerald's sister and frequent correspondent, died in 1991. On January 15 of that year, Kathryn Hayward Johnson died in Valparaiso at age ninety-two. It would be difficult to exaggerate the influence of this "woman of gusto and courage," as Barbara Holdridge has called her, upon her husband's career. She supported, despite its huge perils, his bold decision to leave the Sunpapers. She ran the household that helped to effect his immense productivity. As the keeper of his flame, she preserved her husband's work, thereby facilitating *America-Watching* and subsequent research about his career. She was cremated, and her ashes were entombed next to Gerald's in the Green Mount Cemetery. Lois Johnson, the former dean of women at Wake Forest, died on October 22, 1993, one month shy of her ninety-ninth birthday, and was buried with her parents in the Spring Hill

5. *The Diary of H. L. Mencken,* ed. Charles A. Fecher (New York: Knopf, 1989), 150; *Thirty-Five Years of Newspaper Work: A Memoir by H. L. Mencken,* ed. Fred Hobson, Vincent Fitzpatrick, and Bradford Jacobs (Baltimore: Johns Hopkins University Press, 1994), 296, 302, 304, 306. I never mentioned *The Diary of H. L. Mencken* to Kathryn Hayward Johnson, and she never indicated to me that she had read it.

6. Vincent Fitzpatrick, "Baltimore's Other Sage: A 'Hod-Carrier' in the Cathedral of American Life," *BS,* August 6, 1990; Roy Hoopes, "Gerald Johnson: The Second-Ranking Sage of Baltimore," *Maryland Magazine* 22–23 (summer 1990): 14–17; David DuBoison, "Gerald W. Johnson: Enemy of Boredom," *Greensboro News and Record,* August 5, 1990; Kathy Blomstrom, "Thomasville Native Featured in Exhibit," *Thomasville (N.C.) Times,* August 18, 1990; Paul F. Conley, " 'Local Boy Made Good,' " *Winston-Salem Journal,* August 19, 1990; Wint Capel, "Local Library Has Best Johnson Collection," *Thomasville (N.C.) Times,* August 30, 1990; Paul Dillon, "Museum Opens with 1918 Exhibit," *High Point (N.C.) Enterprise,* September 15, 1990.

Cemetery. Her death carried with it a sense of an ending, for she had been the last survivor among Flora and Archibald's five children.[7]

On September 15, 1995, the *Baltimore Evening Sun,* the victim of changing times, ceased publication during its eighty-sixth year. Johnson's finest journalism had appeared in a newspaper that no longer exists. In December of that year, Andrew Lytle died and was buried in Sewanee, Tennessee. He had been the last surviving member of the Southern Agrarians, that group which had generated, with the publication of *I'll Take My Stand* sixty-five years before, the most significant literary combat of Johnson's career. Any further commentary would have to come from someone other than the principals.[8]

On May 18, 1996, Johnson was among the first group, fifteen in all, inducted into the North Carolina Literary Hall of Fame. He joined, among others, Charles W. Chesnutt, Jonathan Daniels, Paul Green, O. Henry, Randall Jarrell, and Thomas Wolfe. The induction ceremony was held in Southern Pines, and Johnson's "presenter" was a man who knew his career well: Bynum Shaw, novelist, professor of journalism at Wake Forest, and a former member of the staff of the Sunpapers. Shaw remarked that, despite Johnson's long residence in Baltimore, "in his heart he was a Tar Heel every day of his ninety years."[9]

As Johnson had wished, a marker was place for him in the family plot in the Spring Hill Cemetery. He had also wanted his ashes interred there but had deferred to Kathryn's wish that they be entombed in Baltimore, so that she could join both her husband and mother in death. Johnson wanted "no monument" here in North Carolina, "just a simple stone with my name and date. I would like to think of it, not as a memorial to me, but as my last act of obedience to the Fifth Commandment, 'Honor thy father and thy mother.' " Such a marker now lies among the gravestones of his father (eulogized for posterity as the "Friend of the Fatherless"), his mother, and his sister Lois. Describing Gerald as the "Son of Flora McNeill and Archibald Johnson," the marker serves as a tribute to the parents rather than to their famous

7. "Kathryn H. Johnson, Raised Poodles," *BS,* January 19, 1991, p. A10; Barbara Holdridge, "A Woman of Gusto and Courage," letter to the editor, *BS,* January 25, 1991.

8. Jon Meacham, "Andrew Lytle: Powerful Voice Is Stilled," *Chattanooga Times,* December 16, 1995.

9. Bynum Shaw, remarks delivered at Southern Pines, N.C., May 18, 1996, photocopy in possession of the author.

son. Johnson could not have been more self-effacing, for there is no evidence here that he ever wrote a word.[10]

In spirit, Johnson had come home again, back to rural North Carolina—among the shades of Daniel Whyte and Catharine Campbell and John Charles McNeill, that poet who, long ago, had taught Gerald about the glory of Ovid. Johnson had traveled far—to the red fields of France, to England, and to positions elsewhere in the United States—but his journey back to this little patch of earth confirms, as T. S. Eliot has written so famously in "Little Gidding," that "the end of all our exploring / Will be to arrive at the place where we started / And know the place for the first time." For a final time, Johnson's career showed remarkable symmetry.[11]

The house where Johnson was born is gone. The House That Jack Built still stands and beckons to a new generation of children. Photographs of Flora and Archibald stand prominently on the front porch, lest anyone forget that the past is always present. For the most part, Johnson's land of lost content has withstood the onslaught of the twentieth century. No superhighways, no monolithic hotel chains, intrude here. Churches abound. It is hardly surprising that such a place, which has insisted upon going its own way and maintaining its own values, would produce a figure as determined and individualistic as Gerald White Johnson—a man who refused to run with the crowd and who refused to be seduced by the baubles that have entranced so many.[12]

He knew all about impermanence. Yesterday's subversives are today's heroes. Empires rise and fall. Presidents come and go. Attitudes that seem enlightened now may well seem laughable later. But this Southerner also knew that "some things are always in fashion." He knew that "if a man has the habit of speaking the truth, even if it costs him money, or prestige, or safety, he has something that can never become antiquated."[13] He had precisely such a habit. He refused to lie, and he refused to cower. He told the truth as he saw it in a plain language that no one could misconstrue. On occasions where a number of other Americans chose to creep away, he elected to stand and fight.

10. Dorothy Johnson van den Honert to author, October 14, 1994, June 8, 1995; GWJ to Katherine Johnson Parham, March 7, 1974, GWJ Papers.

11. T. S. Eliot, "Little Gidding," in *Four Quartets* (New York: Harcourt, Brace, and World), 1943), 59 (ll. 240–42).

12. Catharine Lambeth Carlton, interview by author, tape recording, Riverton, N.C., August 17, 1989.

13. GWJ, "Schooling for Ancestors: 2051 A.D.," *Vogue* 117 (February 1, 1951): 188.

Although Johnson left behind nothing so famous as Christopher Wren's cathedral, he did bequeath a considerable legacy in black ink. A bringer of light, he urged his fellow Southerners to resist the wiles of the past and to look ahead, and he taught his fellow Americans to think of possibilities rather than limitations. Perhaps most important, he offered a voice of affirmation during an obscenely destructive century. He was a healer. From the beginning, he found words sacred. And it was a remarkable journey which found that young boy, lying on his stomach in North Carolina and reading a book, becoming an author of national renown—an author always articulate; a brave writer who attacked the privileged and the powerful and defended those who could not defend themselves; and a bold man, a voyager to the end of his days, who learned by going where he had to go.

Selected Bibliography

Manuscript Collections

Adler, Betty. Papers. H. L. Mencken Collection. Enoch Pratt Free Library, Baltimore, Md.

Barrett Minor Authors Collection. Papers. Special Collections, Alderman Library, University of Virginia, Charlottesville, Va.

Bjorkman, Edwin August. Papers. Southern Historical Collection, Wilson Library, University of North Carolina at Chapel Hill.

Branson, Eugene Cunningham. Papers. Southern Historical Collection, Wilson Library, University of North Carolina at Chapel Hill.

Carlyle, Irving Edward. Papers. North Carolina Baptist Historical Collection, University Archives, Personal Collections, Z. Smith Reynolds Library, Wake Forest University, Winston-Salem, N.C.

Chambers, Lenoir. Papers. Southern Historical Collection, Wilson Library, University of North Carolina at Chapel Hill.

Coffin, Oscar Jackson. Papers. Southern Historical Collection, Wilson Library, University of North Carolina at Chapel Hill.

Cullom, Willis Richard. Papers. North Carolina Baptist Historical Collection, University Archives, Personal Collections, Z. Smith Reynolds Library, Wake Forest University, Winston-Salem, N.C.

Dabney, Virginius. Papers. Special Collections, Alderman Library, University of Virginia, Charlottesville, Va.

Daniels, Jonathan. Papers. Southern Historical Collection, Wilson Library, University of North Carolina at Chapel Hill.

Graham, Frank Porter. Papers. Southern Historical Collection, Wilson Library, University of North Carolina at Chapel Hill.

Green, Paul. Papers. Southern Historical Collection, Wilson Library, University of North Carolina at Chapel Hill.

Harper and Brothers (Selected Records). Papers. Firestone Library, Princeton University, Princeton, N.J.

Herring, Harriet L. Papers. Southern Historical Collection, Wilson Library, University of North Carolina at Chapel Hill.

Jaffé, Louis I. Papers. Special Collections, Alderman Library, University of Virginia, Charlottesville, Va.

Johnson, Gerald W. Papers. North Carolina Baptist Historical Collection, University Archives, Personal Collections, Z. Smith Reynolds Library, Wake Forest University, Winston-Salem, N.C.

Johnson, Livingston. Papers. North Carolina Baptist Historical Collection, University Archives, Personal Collections, Z. Smith Reynolds Library, Wake Forest University, Winston-Salem, N.C.

Johnson, Mary Lynch. Papers. North Carolina Baptist Historical Collection, University Archives, Personal Collections, Z. Smith Reynolds Library, Wake Forest University, Winston-Salem, N.C.

Johnson, Wingate Memory. Papers. North Carolina Baptist Historical Collection, University Archives, Personal Collections, Z. Smith Reynolds Library, Wake Forest University, Winston-Salem, N.C.

Langford, Gerald. Papers. Special Collections, Alderman Library, University of Virginia, Charlottesville, Va.

McAlister, Alexander Worth. Papers. Southern Historical Collection, Wilson Library, University of North Carolina at Chapel Hill.

Mencken, H. L. Papers. H. L. Mencken Collection, Enoch Pratt Free Library, Baltimore, Md.

Mitchell, Samuel Chiles. Papers. Southern Historical Collection, Wilson Library, University of North Carolina at Chapel Hill.

Odum, Howard W. Papers. Southern Historical Collection, Wilson Library, University of North Carolina at Chapel Hill.

Roosevelt, Franklin D. Papers. Correspondence concerning *Roosevelt: Dictator or Democrat?* among Gerald W. Johnson, President Franklin Roosevelt, the President's Aides, Harper and Brothers, and George T. Bye. Franklin D. Roosevelt Library, Hyde Park, N.Y.

Scribner's. Papers. Archives of Charles Scribner's Sons. Firestone Library, Princeton University, Princeton, N.J.

Southern Writers' Convention, University of Virginia, 1931. Papers. Special Collections, University of Virginia, Charlottesville, Va.

Stevenson, Adlai E. Papers. Seeley G. Mudd Manuscript Library, Princeton University, Princeton, N.J.

Virginia Quarterly Review. Papers. Editorial Correspondence. Special Collections, Alderman Library, University of Virginia, Charlottesville, Va.

Walser, Richard Gaither. Papers. Southern Historical Collection, Wilson Library, University of North Carolina at Chapel Hill.

Wilson, James Southall. Papers. Special Collections, Alderman Library, University of Virginia, Charlottesville, Va.

Wilson, Louis Round. Papers. Southern Historical Collection, Wilson Library, University of North Carolina at Chapel Hill.

Winston, Robert W. Papers. Southern Historical Collection, Wilson Library, University of North Carolina at Chapel Hill.

Newspapers

Baltimore Evening Sun, 1923–1980.

Baltimore Sun, 1925–1980.

Greensboro (N.C.) Daily News, 1913–1917, 1919–1923.

Lexington (N.C.) Dispatch, 1911–1913.

New York Herald Tribune, 1937–1965.

New York Star, 1948–1949.

Books and Pamphlets by Gerald W. Johnson (Chronological Listing)

The Story of Man's Work (with William Richard Hayward). New York: Minton, Balch, 1925.

What Is News?: A Tentative Outline. Borzoi Handbooks of Journalism. New York: Knopf, 1926.

The Undefeated. New York: Minton, Balch, 1927.

Andrew Jackson: An Epic in Homespun. New York: Minton, Balch, 1927.

Randolph of Roanoke: A Political Fantastic. Biographies of Unusual Americans Series. New York: Minton, Balch, 1929.

By Reason of Strength. New York: Minton, Balch, 1930. British edition published under the title *The Strength of Catharine Campbell.* London: G. P. Putnam's Sons, 1931.

Number Thirty-Six: A Novel. New York: Minton, Balch, 1933.

The Secession of the Southern States. Great Occasions Series. New York: G. P. Putnam's Sons, 1933.

A Little Night Music: Discoveries in the Exploitation of an Art. New York: Harper and Brothers, 1937.

The Sunpapers of Baltimore, 1837–1937 (with Frank R. Kent, H. L. Mencken, and Hamilton Owens). New York: Knopf, 1937.

The Wasted Land (with Howard W. Odum). Chapel Hill: University of North Carolina Press, 1937.

Green Mount Cemetery: One Hundredth Anniversary, 1838–1938. Baltimore: Proprietors of the Green Mount Cemetery, 1938.

America's Silver Age: The Statecraft of Clay-Webster-Calhoun. New York: Harper and Brothers, 1939.

Beware of the Dog! (written under the pseudonym Charles North). New York: William Morrow, 1939.

Roosevelt: Dictator or Democrat? New York: Harper and Brothers, 1941. British edition published under the title *Roosevelt: An American Study,* with introduction and notes by D. W. Brogan. London: H. Hamilton, 1942.

American Heroes and Hero-Worship. New York: Harper and Brothers, 1943.

Woodrow Wilson: The Unforgettable Figure Who Has Returned to Haunt Us (with the editors of *Look* magazine). *Look* Picture Books Series. New York: Harper and Brothers, 1944.

An Honorable Titan: A Biographical Study of Adolph S. Ochs. New York: Harper and Brothers, 1946.

The First Captain: The Story of John Paul Jones. New York: Coward-McCann, 1947.

Look at America: The Central Northeast (with the editors of *Look* magazine). Look at America Series. Boston: Houghton-Mifflin, 1948.

A Liberal's Progress: Edward A. Filene, Shopkeeper to Social Statesman. New York: Coward-McCann, 1948.

Our English Heritage. Philadelphia: J. B. Lippincott, 1949.

Incredible Tale: The Odyssey of the Average American in the Last Half Century. New York: Harper and Brothers, 1950.

This American People. New York: Harper and Brothers, 1951.

Pattern for Liberty: The Story of Old Philadelphia. New York: McGraw-Hill, 1952.

The Making of a Southern Industrialist: A Biographical Study of Simpson Bobo Tanner. Chapel Hill. University of North Carolina Press, 1952.

Mount Vernon: The Story of a Shrine. New York: Random House, 1953.

The Lunatic Fringe. Philadelphia: J. B. Lippincott, 1957.

Peril and Promise: An Inquiry into Freedom of the Press. New York: Harper and Brothers, 1958.

The Lines Are Drawn: American Life since the First World War as Reflected in the Pulitzer Prize Cartoons. Philadelphia: J. B. Lippincott, 1958.

America Is Born. A History for Peter Series. New York: William Morrow, 1959.

America Grows Up. A History for Peter Series. New York: William Morrow, 1960.

America Moves Forward. A History for Peter Series. New York: William Morrow, 1960.

The Man Who Feels Left Behind. New York: William Morrow, 1961.

De Senectute. Baltimore: Hamilton Street Club, 1961.

The Presidency. The Government Series. New York: William Morrow, 1962.

The Supreme Court. The Government Series. New York: William Morrow, 1962.

The Congress. Series: *The Government.* New York: William Morrow, 1963.

Communism: An American's View. New York: William Morrow, 1964.

Hod-Carrier: Notes of a Laborer on an Unfinished Cathedral. New York: William Morrow, 1964.

The Cabinet. The Government Series. New York: William Morrow, 1966.

Franklin D. Roosevelt: Portrait of a Great Man. New York: William Morrow, 1967.

The British Empire: An American View of Its History from 1776 to 1945. New York: William Morrow, 1969.

The Imperial Republic: Speculations on the Future, If Any, of the Third U.S.A. New York: Liveright, 1972.

America-Watching: Perspectives in the Course of an Incredible Century. Owings Mills, Md.: Stemmer House, 1976.

South-Watching: Selected Essays by Gerald W. Johnson. Ed. Fred Hobson. Chapel Hill: University of North Carolina Press, 1983.

Contributions by Gerald W. Johnson to Books (Chronological Listing)

"Woodrow Wilson." In *Southern Pioneers in Social Interpretation,* ed. Howard W. Odum, 29–49. Chapel Hill: University of North Carolina Press, 1925.

"The American Way: Two Fundamentals." In *The American Way,* ed. David Cushman Coyle, 141–71. New York: Harper and Brothers, 1938.

Introduction to *Disturber of the Peace: The Life of H. L. Mencken,* by William Manchester. New York: Harper and Brothers, 1950.

"American Freedom and the Press." In *The Present Danger: Four Essays on American Freedom,* ed. Allen Maxwell, 19–41. Dallas: Southern Methodist University Press, 1953.

"The Muckraking Era." In *Pittsburgh: the Story of an American City,* ed. Stefan Lorant, 261–319. Garden City, N.Y.: Doubleday, 1964.

Foreword to *William Louis Poteat: Prophet of Progress,* by Suzanne Cameron Linder. Chapel Hill: University of North Carolina Press, 1966.

Foreword to *Serpent in Eden: H. L. Mencken and the South,* by Fred C. Hobson, Jr. Chapel Hill: University of North Carolina Press, 1974.

"Fifty Years, Almost, in Hamilton Street." In *Fifty Years of the 14 West Hamilton Street Club,* by Walker Lewis, 43–48. Baltimore: 14 West Hamilton Street Club, 1975.

"A Sage Reminisces." In *Baltimore: A Living Renaissance,* ed. Lenora Heilig Nass, Laurence N. Krause, and R. C. Monk, 150–53. Baltimore: Historic Baltimore Society, 1982.

Magazine Articles by Gerald W. Johnson (Alphabetical Listing)

"Adlai Stevenson." *New Republic* 153 (July 24, 1965): 5–6.

"The Advancing South." *Virginia Quarterly Review* 2 (October 1926): 594–96.

"After Forty Years—Dixi." *Virginia Quarterly Review* 41 (spring 1965): 192–201.

"The Agnew We Knew." *New Republic* 161 (November 29, 1969): 13–14.

"The American Demagogue." *Transatlantic* 18 (February 1945): 49–51.

"Appropriate Academic Dress." *New Republic* 144 (June 12, 1961): 16.

"The Arkansas Toreador." *New Republic* 137 (October 14, 1957): 10.

"At Least It's Movement." *Wake Forest* 16 (November 1969): 78.

"Baltimore: A Very Great Lady Indeed." *Century Magazine* 116 (May 1928): 76–82.

"The Battling South." *Scribner's Magazine* 77 (March 1925): 302–307.

"Behind the Monster's Mask." *Survey Graphic* 50 (April 1923): 20–22.

"Below the Potomac." *New Republic* 104 (May 12, 1941): 673.

"Billy with the Red Necktie." *Virginia Quarterly Review* 19 (autumn 1943): 551–61.

"Books and Citizenship." *Maryland Libraries: Journal of the Maryland Library Association* (summer 1954): 3–8.

"Bryan, Thou Shouldst Be Living at This Hour." *Harper's Magazine* 163 (September 1931): 385–91.

"The Cadets of New Market." *Harper's Magazine* 160 (December 1929): 111–16.

"Call for a Custom-Built Poet." *Southwest Review* 2 (April 1925): 26–30.

"Chase of North Carolina." *American Mercury* 17 (June 1929): 183–90.

"A Commission from Raleigh." *Meredith College Quarterly Bulletin* 34 (March 1941): 1–14.

"The Congo, Mr. Mencken." *Reviewer* 3 (July 1923): 887–93.

"The Cotton Strike." *Survey Graphic* 46 (November 1921): 646–47.

"Critical Attitudes North and South." *Journal of Social Forces* 2 (May 1924): 575–79.

"The Curve of Sin." *American Mercury* 5 (July 1925): 363–67.

"The Dead Vote of the South." *Scribner's Magazine* 78 (July 1925): 38–43.

"The Devil Is Dead, and What a Loss!" *American Scholar* 16 (autumn 1947): 395–403.

"Dixie, My Dixie." *New Republic* 139 (September 22, 1958): 20.

"The End of Incredulity." *Virginia Quarterly Review* 44 (autumn 1968): 531–42.

"The End of the Beginning," *Virginia Quarterly Review* 51 (spring 1975): 186–198.

"An Excuse for Universities." *Harper's Magazine* 170 (fall 1935): 369–76.

"For Ignoble Pacifism." *Harper's Magazine* 163 (November 1931): 727–32.

"The Formaldehyde Crew." *New Republic* 138 (March 3, 1958): 16.

"Fourteen Equestrian Statues of Colonel Simmons." *Reviewer* 4 (October 1923): 20–26.

"Gadflying with I. F. Stone." *New Republic* 149 (December 11, 1963): 21.

"God Was Bored." *New Republic* 145 (September 11, 1961): 10.

"Greensboro, or What You Will." *Reviewer* 4 (April 1924): 169–75.

"Guess Work." *Menckeniana* 1 (spring 1962): no pagination.

"Hail the Ornery Cuss." *New Republic* 132 (June 30, 1955): 16.

"He Will Be Great." *New Republic* 143 (November 21, 1960): 10.

"Henry L. Mencken (1880–1956)." *Saturday Review of Literature* 39 (February 11, 1956): 12–13.

"The Horrible South." *Virginia Quarterly Review* 11 (January 1935): 201–17.

"Hurrah for the Children's Crusade." *New Republic* 157 (April 20, 1968): 12.

"I'm for Adlai Stevenson." *New Republic* 143 (July 11, 1960): 12.

"If Wilson Had Taken Lodge to Paris . . ." *Vogue* 105 (February 1, 1945): 116, 173–74.

"In Search of Identity." *New Republic* 143 (October 10, 1960): 20.

"Issachar Is a Strong Ass." *Journal of Social Forces* 2 (November 1923): 5–9.

"Journalism below the Potomac." *American Mercury* 9 (September 1926):77–82.

"Judgment in Mississippi." *New Republic* 151 (December 16, 1964): 13.

"The Ku Kluxer." *American Mercury* 1 (February 1924): 207–11.

"Lament of the Lame." *Michigan Quarterly Review* 6 (January 1967): 15–16.

"Laugh, Casca, Laugh." *Saturday Review of Literature* 150 (December 2, 1967): 16, 19.

"The Liberal of 1946." *American Scholar* 15 (spring 1946): 154–59.

"Live Demagogue or Dead Gentleman?" *Virginia Quarterly Review* 12 (January 1936): 1–15.

"The Lumbee River." *Pembroke Magazine* 15 (1983): 94–97.

"Meditation on 1963." *Virginia Quarterly Review* 39 (spring 1963): 161–71.

"Mencken and the Art of Boob Bumping." *New Republic* 168 (May 19, 1973): 7–8.

"Mill Men Who Were Statesmen." *Cotton and Its Products* 3 (July 1925): 72–73.

"Mr. Babbitt Arrives at Erzerum." *Journal of Social Forces* 1 (March 1923): 206–209.

"Mobilized Farm." *Country Gentleman* 114 (August 1944): 44–47.

"No More Excuses: A Southerner to Southerners." *Harper's Magazine* 160 (February 1931): 331–37.

"North Carolina in a New Phase." *Current History* 27 (March 1928): 843–48.

"Note on Race Prejudice." *North American Review* 233 (March 1932): 226–33.

"The Nothing King." *New Republic* 171 (September 21, 1974): 13.

"Oh, for Mencken Now." *New Republic* 130 (September 30, 1957): 11.

"Old Slick." *Virginia Quarterly Review* 26 (April 1950): 204–13.

"On Voting Democratic: Confession of a Party-Liner." *New Republic* 170 (June 22, 1974): 16–18.

" 'Once Touched by Romance.' " *New Republic* 149 (December 7, 1963): 15.

"Onion Salt." *Reviewer* 5 (January 1925): 60–63.

"The Policeman's Bed of Roses." *Harper's Magazine* 162 (May 1931): 735–39.

"Position Paper for the American Realist." *American Scholar* 43 (spring 1974): 248, 260–66.

"The Press and the Spirit of the People." *Southwest Review* 30 (autumn 1953): 318–23.

"Pride and Prejudice." *New Republic* 145 (December 25, 1961): 10.

"A Proud Tower in the Town." *Peabody Bulletin* 33 (May 1937): 7–13.

"Reconsideration: H. L. Mencken." *New Republic* 173 (December 27, 1975): 32–33.

"The Religious Refugee." *Century Magazine* 111 (February 1926): 399–404.

"Reviving the Two-Party System." *New Republic* 152 (January 2, 1965): 20.

"Romanticism Run Mad." *New Republic* 134 (May 21, 1958): 8.

"Saving Souls." *American Mercury* 2 (July 1924): 364–68.

"Schooling for Ancestors: 2051 A.D." *Vogue* 117 (February 1, 1951): 188.

"Senator Byrd of Virginia." *Life* 17 (August 1944): 81–86, 89–91.

"Service in the Cotton Mills." *American Mercury* 5 (June 1925): 219–23.

"Should Our Colleges Educate?" *Harper's Magazine* 155 (November 1927): 723–27.

"Since Wilson." *Virginia Quarterly Review* 8 (July 1932): 321–36.

"Sophocles in Georgia." *Century Magazine* 112 (September 1926): 565–71.

"The South Faces Itself." *Virginia Quarterly Review* 6 (January 1930): 152–57.

"The South Takes the Offensive." *American Mercury* 2 (May 1924): 70–78.

"Southern Image Breakers." *Virginia Quarterly Review* 4 (October 1928): 508–19.

"Southern Pioneers in Social Interpretation (VI. Woodrow Wilson: A Challenge to the Fighting South)." *Journal of Social Forces* 3 (January 1925): 231–36.

"Splitting the Party." *New Republic* 134 (April 23, 1956): 8.

"The Superfluity of L.B.J." *American Scholar* 37 (spring 1968): 221–26.

"Symbols of the South." *Saturday Review of Literature* 26 (January 23, 1943): 5–6.

"Take Heart." *New Republic* 146 (February 19, 1962): 9–10

"A Tar Heel Looks at Virginia." *North American Review* 228 (August 1929): 238–43.

"The Third Republic—And After." *Harper's Magazine* 156 (February 1928): 339–44.

"This Terrifying Freedom." *Harper's Magazine* 171 (November 1935): 754–60.

"A Tilt with Southern Windmills." *Virginia Quarterly Review* 1 (July 1925): 184–92.

"To Be Living at This Time: *An Assessment of Values*." Edited, with a Preface and Postscript, by Vincent Fitzpatrick. *Virginia Quarterly Review* 68 (autumn 1992): 626–50.

"To Live and Die in Dixie." *Atlantic Monthly* 206 (July 1960): 29–34.

"Trial of a Small Town." *New Republic* 146 (March 19, 1962): 6–7.

"Truman." *Life* 17 (November 6, 1944): 103, 111–14, 117.

"The Turkey-Gobbler Strut." *American Scholar* 41 (autumn 1972): 533–41.

"An Unfortunate Necessity." *Century Magazine* 112 (May 1926): 41–47.

"Wading into Trouble." *New Republic* 135 (December 10, 1956): 10.

"Watergate: One End, but Which?" *American Scholar* 42 (autumn 1973): 594–603.

"What an Old Girl Should Know." *Harper's Magazine* 168 (April 1934): 607–14.

"What Does the University Think?" *Century Magazine* 114 (June 1927): 111.

"When to Build a Barricade." *Virginia Quarterly Review* 14 (April 1938): 161–76.

"White House Hopes in Maryland." *North American Review* 229 (June 1930): 642–46.

"Why Men Work for Newspapers." *American Mercury* 17 (May 1929): 83–88.

"Why Not a Poetry Society for North Carolina?" *Carolina Magazine* 53 (December 1922): 2

Secondary Sources

Arnett, Ethel Stephens. *Greensboro, North Carolina: The County Seat of Guilford*. Chapel Hill: University of North Carolina Press, 1955.

Ayers, Edward L. *The Promise of the New South: Life after Reconstruction*. New York: Oxford University Press, 1992.

———. "A Southern Chronicle: *The Virginia Quarterly Review* and the American South, 1925–2000." *Virginia Quarterly Review* 76 (spring 2000): 189–202.

Barr, Stringfellow. "Shall Slavery Come South?" *Virginia Quarterly Review* 6 (October 1930): 481–94.

Bishop, Don. "Johnson Becomes Book Critic by Accident." *Greensboro (N.C.) Daily News,* May 9, 1948.

Blotner, Joseph. *Faulkner: A Biography*. New York: Random House, 1974.

Boney, Victoria. "Gerald Johnson Still Tar Heel Editor." *Greensboro (N.C.) Daily News* March 29, 1941.

Brantley, Russell. "Gerald Johnson: Man of Wake Forest." *Wake Forest* 27, no. 2 (spring 1980): 10–12.

Bready, James H. "Books and Authors." *Baltimore Sun,* August 1, 1965, July 26, 1970.

———. "Gerald W. Johnson: Looking Back over Thirty Years." *Baltimore Sun,* March 30, 1980.

———. "A Happy Birthyear to Gerald W. Johnson." *Baltimore Sun,* January 12, 1975.

Canfield, Cass. *Up and Down and Around: A Publisher Recollects the Time of His Life*. New York: Harper's Magazine Press, 1971.

Cash, W. J. *The Mind of the South*. New York: Knopf, 1941.

Cason, Clarence. *Ninety° in the Shade*. Chapel Hill: University of North Carolina Press, 1935.

Clark, Emily. *Innocence Abroad*. New York: Knopf, 1931.

Clayton, Bruce. *W. J. Cash: A Life*. Baton Rouge: Louisiana State University Press, 1991.

Conkin, Paul K. *The Southern Agrarians*. Knoxville: University of Tennessee Press, 1988.

———. *When All the Gods Trembled: Darwinism, Scopes, and American Intellectuals*. Lanham, Md.: Rowman and Littlefield, 1998.

Crosby, John. "Farewell to Gerald Johnson." *New York Herald Tribune,* January 3, 1954.

Dabney, Virginius. *Liberalism in the South*. Chapel Hill: University of North Carolina Press, 1932.

Daniels, Jonathan. *A Southerner Discovers the South*. New York: Macmillan, 1938.

———. *Tar Heels: A Portrait of North Carolina*. New York: Dodd, Mead, 1941.

Davidson, Donald. "The Artist as Southerner." *Saturday Review of Literature* 2 (May 15, 1926): 1–3.

———. "The Dilemma of Southern Liberals." *American Mercury* 31 (February 1934): 227–35.

———. "First Fruits of Dayton: The Intellectual Evolution in Dixie." *Forum* 79 (June 1928): 896–907.

———. "Howard Odum and the Sociological Proteus." *American Review* 8 (February 1937): 385–417.

———. " 'I'll Take My Stand': A History." *American Review* 5 (summer 1935): 301–21.

———. "Mr. Cash and the Proto-Dorian South." *Southern Review* 7 (summer 1941): 1–20.

———. *Southern Writers in the Modern World*. Athens: University of Georgia Press, 1958.

Davidson, Donald, and Allen Tate. *The Literary Correspondence of Donald Davidson and Allen Tate*. Ed. John Tyree Fain and Thomas Daniel Young. Athens: University of Georgia Press, 1974.

DeCamp, Lyon Sprague. *The Great Monkey Trial*. Garden City, N.Y.: Doubleday, 1968.

DelFattore, Joan. *What Johnny Shouldn't Read: Textbook Censorship in America*. New Haven: Yale University Press, 1992.

Dennis, Lloyd. "Gerald Johnson: Man of Many Parts." *Greensboro (N.C.) Daily News,* March 22, 1964.

Donald, David Herbert. *Look Homeward: A Life of Thomas Wolfe.* Boston: Little, Brown, 1987.

DuBoison, David. "Gerald W. Johnson: Enemy of Boredom." *Greensboro (N.C.) News and Record,* August 5, 1990.

Egerton, John. *Speak Now against the Day: The Generation before the Civil Rights Movement in the South.* New York: Knopf, 1994.

Eliot, T. S. *Four Quartets.* New York: Harcourt, Brace, and World, 1943.

Faulkner, William. *The Reivers.* New York: New American Library, 1962.

Fitzpatrick, Vincent. "The *American Mercury.*" In *American Literary Magazines: The Twentieth Century,* ed. Edward E. Chielens, 7–16. Westport, Conn.: Greeenwood Press, 1992.

———. "Baltimore's Other Sage: A 'Hod-Carrier' in the Cathedral of American Life." *Baltimore Sun,* August 6, 1990. Reprinted under the title "Baltimore's Second Sage," *Lexington (N.C.) Dispatch,* August 21, 1990.

———. *H. L. Mencken.* New York: Continuum, 1989.

———. Introduction to *By Reason of Strength,* by Gerald W. Johnson. Laurinburg, N.C.: St. Andrews College Press, 1994.

Foster, Gaines M. *Ghosts of the Confederacy: Defeat, the Lost Cause, and the Emergence of the New South, 1865–1913.* New York: Oxford University Press, 1987.

Freeny, Lawrence. "Gerald Johnson: The Needle Gets Sharper." *Baltimore Magazine* 61 (October 1968): 24–25, 90, 92, 95.

Fussell, Paul. *The Great War and Modern Memory.* New York: Oxford University Press, 1975.

G.B. "Brilliant Baltimore Writer Never Forgets He's a Tar Heel." *Greensboro (N.C.) Daily News,* September 1, 1940.

"Gerald White Johnson." Website: http://www.ncwriters.org/gjohnson.htm. December 9, 1999.

Gibson, Joyce M. *Scotland County Emerging, 1750–1900: The History of a Small Section of North Carolina.* Marceline, Mo.: Walsworth, 1995.

Glasgow, Jesse. "Gerald Johnson: Man of the World." *Wake Forest* 27, no. 2 (spring 1980): 13–16.

Green, Paul. *A Southern Life: Letters of Paul Green, 1916–1981.* Ed. Laurence G. Avery. Chapel Hill: University of North Carolina Press, 1994.

Hall, Randal L. *William Louis Poteat: A Leader of the Progressive-Era South.* Lexington: University Press of Kentucky, 2000.

Harrison, S. L. "Anatomy of the Scopes Trial: Mencken's Media Event." *Menckeniana* 135 (fall 1995): 1–6.

———. *The Editorial Art of Edmund Duffy.* Madison, N.J.: Fairleigh Dickinson University Press, 1998.

Harriss, R. P. "Gerald W. Johnson: Journalist and Author." *Gardens, Houses, and People* 22 (September 1947): 10–12.

———. "Gerald W. Johnson of Baltimore." *Baltimore News American,* February 4, 1961.

———. "Remembering a Great Editorial Page." *Baltimore Evening Sun,* April 29, 1980.

———. "The Sage of Bolton Hill." *Baltimore Sun,* February 28, 1988.

———. "Scotus/Germanicus." *Menckeniana* 76 (winter 1980): 4–11.

———. "Will the Real Sage of Baltimore Stand Up and Take a Bow?" *Baltimore News American,* August 4, 1985.

Hobson, Fred. "Gerald W. Johnson: The Southerner as Realist." *Virginia Quarterly Review* 58 (winter 1982): 1–25.

———. "Johnson, Gerald." In *Encyclopedia of Southern Culture,* ed. Charles Reagan Wilson and William Ferris, 960. Chapel Hill: University of North Carolina Press, 1989.

———. *Mencken: A Life.* New York: Random House, 1994.

———. *Serpent in Eden: H. L. Mencken and the South.* Chapel Hill: University of North Carolina Press, 1974.

———. *The Southern Writer in the Postmodern World.* Athens: University of Georgia Press, 1991.

———. *Tell About the South: The Southern Rage to Explain.* Baton Rouge: Louisiana State University Press, 1983.

Hodges, Robert M. "Gerald Johnson Not a Deserter." *Greensboro (N.C.) Daily News,* November 27, 1938.

Hoopes, Roy. "Gerald Johnson: 'The Second-Ranking Sage of Baltimore.' " *Maryland Magazine* 22–23 (summer 1990): 14–17.

Hynes, Samuel. *A War Imagined: The First World War and English Culture.* New York: Atheneum, 1991.

Jenkins, Jay. "All the Way with GWJ." *Southern Pines (N.C.) Pilot,* March 2, 1983.

Jones, Dr. H. G. "Tar Heel Native Considered Great Journalist." *High Point (N.C.) Enterprise,* June 11, 1980.

Karnow, Stanley. *Vietnam: A History.* New York: Viking, 1983.

Kemp, Roy Z. "Gerald Johnson and Wolfe." *Raleigh News and Observer,* September 20, 1959.

Kirkhorn, Michael. "Gerald W. Johnson (6 August 1890–22 March 1980)." In *Dictionary of Literary Biography,* vol. 29, *American Newspaper Journalists, 1926–1980,* ed. Perry J. Ashley, 132–38. Detroit: Gale Research, 1984.

Kirkley, Donald. "Man of 10 Million Words." *Baltimore Sun,* April 11, 1954.

Kneebone, John T. *Southern Liberal Journalists and the Issue of Race, 1920–1944.* Chapel Hill: University of North Carolina Press, 1985.

Kumpa, Peter. "Gerald Johnson, in 90th Year, Still Keeps Avidly in Touch." *Baltimore Evening Sun,* December 21, 1979.

Larson, Edward J. *Summer for the Gods: The Scopes Trial and America's Continuing Debate over Science and Religion.* New York: Basic Books, 1997.

Levin, Jack L. "A Less Arrogant Baltimore 'Sage.' " *Baltimore Evening Sun,* March 22, 1990.

Lewis, Walker. *14 West Hamilton Street Club: History, 1925–1975.* Baltimore: 14 West Hamilton Street Club, 1975.

Linder, Suzanne Cameron. *William Louis Poteat: Prophet of Progress.* Chapel Hill: University of North Carolina Press, 1966.

Lippman, Theo, Jr. "Was This Lucid Gerald Johnson Really a Southerner?" *Baltimore Evening Sun,* June 13, 1983.

Lockhart, William B., Yale Kamisar, and Jesse H. Choper. *Constitutional Law: Cases—Comments—Questions.* (3rd ed.). St. Paul: West, 1970.

Mabry, William Alexander. *The Negro in North Carolina Politics since Reconstruction.* 1940; reprint, New York: AMS Press, 1970.

Manchester, William. *Disturber of the Peace: The Life of H. L. Mencken.* New York: Harper and Brothers, 1950.

Marbury, William L. *In the Catbird Seat.* Baltimore: Maryland Historical Society, 1988.

Margolick, David. "*PM*'s Impossible Dream." *Vanity Fair,* no. 461 (January 1999): 115, 117–32.

Martin, John Bartlow. *Adlai Stevenson and the World: The Life of Adlai Stevenson.* Garden City, N.Y.: Doubleday, 1977.

Matthews, Mary Green, and M. Jewell Sink. *Wheels of Faith and Courage: A History of Thomasville, North Carolina.* High Point, N.C.: Hall Printing Co., 1952.

McLeod, John Angus. *From These Stones: Mars Hill College, 1865–1967.* Mars Hill, N.C.: Mars Hill College, 1968.

McNeill, Duncan. *Life of Reverend Daniel Whyte: With Incidents in Scotland and America.* Raleigh, N.C.: Broughton, 1879.

Mee, Charles L., Jr. *The End of Order: Versailles, 1919.* New York: E. P. Dutton, 1980.

Mencken, H. L. "Confederate Notes." *Baltimore Evening Sun,* November 26, 1922.

―――. *The Diary of H. L. Mencken.* Ed. Charles A. Fecher. New York: Knopf, 1989.

―――. *Dreiser-Mencken Letters: The Correspondence of Theodore Dreiser and H. L. Mencken.* 2 vols. Ed. Thomas P. Riggio. Philadelphia: University of Pennsylvania Press, 1986.

―――. *The Impossible H. L. Mencken: A Selection of His Best Newspaper Stories.* Ed. Marion E. Rodgers. New York: Doubleday, 1991.

―――. *In Defense of Women.* New York: Knopf, 1922.

―――. "The Sahara of the Bozart." In *Prejudices: Second Series.* New York: Knopf, 1920.

―――. "The South Astir." *Virginia Quarterly Review* 11 (January 1935): 47–60.

―――. "The South Begins to Mutter." *Smart Set* 65 (August 1921): 138–44.

―――. "The South Looks Ahead." *American Mercury* 8 (August 1926): 506–509.

―――. "The South Rebels Again." *Chicago Tribune,* December 7, 1924.

―――. *Thirty-Five Years of Newspaper Work: A Memoir by H. L. Mencken.* Ed. Fred Hobson, Vincent Fitzpatrick, and Bradford Jacobs. Baltimore: Johns Hopkins University Press, 1994.

―――. "Uprising in the Confederacy." *American Mercury* 22 (March 1931): 379–81.

―――. "Utopia Eat Utopia." *Baltimore Evening Sun,* July 13, 1925.

―――. "Yearning Mountaineers' Souls Need Reconversion Nightly, Mencken Finds." *Baltimore Evening Sun,* July 13, 1925.

Mencken, H. L., and Sara Haardt. *Mencken and Sara, a Life in Letters: The Private Correspondence of H. L. Mencken and Sara Haardt.* Ed. Marion Elizabeth Rodgers. New York: McGraw-Hill, 1987.

Mencken, H. L., and George Jean Nathan. "Repetition Generale." *Smart Set* 36 (September 1923): 32.

Mims, Edwin. *The Advancing South.* Garden City, N.Y.: Doubleday, Page and Co., 1926.

Mitchell, Broadus. *The Rise of the Cotton Mill in the South.* Baltimore: Johns Hopkins University Press, 1921.

Moreau, John Adam. "Gerald W. Johnson to Forego Memoirs as 'Indecent Exposure.' " *Baltimore Sun,* April 15, 1973.

Morris, Willie. *New York Days*. Boston: Little, Brown, 1993.

Morrison, Joseph L. *W. J. Cash: Southern Prophet*. New York: Knopf, 1967.

O'Brien, Michael. *The Idea of the American South, 1920–1941*. Baltimore: Johns Hopkins University Press, 1979.

————. *Rethinking the South: Essays in Intellectual History*. Baltimore: Johns Hopkins University Press, 1988.

Owens, Gwinn. "Reflections on the Legendary Years." *Baltimore Evening Sun,* April 18, 1995.

————. "When Baltimore Was a Swell Town." *Baltimore Evening Sun,* April 29, 1991.

Owens, Hamilton. "The Sunpapers' History." *Menckeniana* 12 (winter 1964): 3–10.

Owsley, Frank. "A Key to Southern Liberalism." *Southern Review* 3 (summer 1937): 28–38.

————. "The Pillars of Agrarianism." *American Review* 4 (March 1935): 529–47.

Parker, Roy, Jr. *Cumberland County: A Brief History*. Raleigh: Division of Archives and History, North Carolina Department of Cultural Resources, 1990.

Parshall, Gerald. "Gerald Johnson Gets Tribute at City Hall." *Baltimore Sun,* August 6, 1970.

Paschal, G. W. *A History of Wake Forest College,* vol. 1, *1834–1865,* vol. 2, *1865–1905,* vol. 3, *1905–1943*. Wake Forest, N.C.: Wake Forest College, 1935, 1943, 1943.

Percy, Walker. *Signposts in a Strange Land*. New York: Farrar, Straus, and Giroux, 1992.

Powers, Mary Rebecca Watson et al. *Our Clan of Johnsons*. Kinston, N.C.: 1940.

Proust, Marcel. *The Past Recaptured*. Trans. Andreas Mayor. New York: Random House, 1991.

Race and Education: Integration and Community Control (an American Education Publications Unit Book adapted from the Harvard Social Studies Project under the direction of Donald W. Oliver and Fred M. Newman). Middletown, Conn.: American Education Publications, 1969.

Rascovar, Barry. "Tribute Paid Gerald Johnson." *Baltimore Sun,* August 6, 1970.

Reeves, Thomas C. *The Life and Times of Joe McCarthy: A Biography*. New York: Stein and Day, 1982.

Rubin, Louis D., Jr. Introduction to the Torchbook Edition of *I'll Take My Stand: The South and the Agrarian Tradition,* by Twelve Southerners. New York: Harper and Row, 1962.

————. "W. J. Cash after Fifty Years." *Virginia Quarterly Review* 67 (spring 1991): 214–28.

Sandler, Gilbert. "Gerald Johnson's 'Fireside Chats.'" *Baltimore Evening Sun,* October 15, 1991.

Shank, Joseph E., and Lenoir Chambers. *Salt Water and Printer's Ink.* Chapel Hill: University of North Carolina Press, 1967.

Shaw, Bynum. *The History of Wake Forest College,* vol. 4, *1943–1967.* Winston-Salem: Wake Forest University, 1988.

Shirer, William. *The Rise and Fall of the Third Reich.* New York: Fawcett, 1966.

Shivers, Frank. *Maryland Wits and Baltimore Bards: A Literary History with Notes on Washington Writers.* Baltimore: Maclay, 1985.

Singleton, M. K. *H. L. Mencken and the American Mercury Adventure.* Durham: Duke University Press, 1962.

Sink, M. Jewell, and Mary Green Matthews. *Pathfinders Past and Present: A History of Davidson County, North Carolina.* Thomasville, N.C.: 1972.

Snider, William D. *Light on the Hill: A History of the University of North Carolina at Chapel Hill.* Chapel Hill: University of North Carolina Press, 1992.

Sosna, Morton. *In Search of the Silent South: Southern Liberals and the Issue of Race.* New York: Columbia University Press, 1977.

Spilman, Bernard Washington. *The Mills Home: A History of the Baptist Orphanage Movement in North Carolina, 1885–1932.* Thomasville, N.C.: Mills Home, 1976.

Stenerson, Douglas C., ed. *Critical Essays on H. L. Mencken.* Boston: G. K. Hall, 1987.

Timberg, Scott. "The Forgotten Curmudgeon." *Baltimore Magazine* 86 (September 1993): 9.

Turner, Thomas Bourne. *Part of Medicine, Part of Me: Musings of a Johns Hopkins Dean.* Baltimore: Johns Hopkins Medical School, 1981.

Twelve Southerners. *I'll Take My Stand: The South and the Agrarian Tradition.* New York: Harper and Brothers, 1962.

Walt, James. "Tale of Another Liberal's Progress." *Maryland English Journal* 4, no. 1 (fall 1965): 56–62.

West, Woody. "Gerald Johnson: Philosopher for Our Time." *Washington Sunday Star Magazine,* January 19, 1969.

Williams, Harold A. *The Baltimore Sun, 1837–1987.* Baltimore: Johns Hopkins University Press, 1987.

Wilson, Charles Reagan, and William Ferris, eds. *Encyclopedia of Southern Culture.* Chapel Hill: University of North Carolina Press, 1989.

Woodward, C. Vann. *The Burden of Southern History.* (3rd ed). Baton Rouge: Louisiana State University Press, 1993.

————. *Origins of the New South, 1877–1913,* vol. 9, *A History of the South.* Baton Rouge: Louisiana State University Press, 1951.

————. *The Strange Career of Jim Crow.* 3rd rev. ed. New York: Oxford University Press, 1974.

Yarbrough, Mrs. J. A. "Interesting Carolina People." *Charlotte Observer,* [1946].

Theses, Dissertations, and Other Unpublished Materials

Beall, R. L. "Notes on the History of the Greensboro News and Record, including the Greensboro Daily News. . . ." Photocopy in possession of the author.

Gordon, Lee. "The National TV Odyssey of Gerald W. Johnson." Paper written for "The Idea of America" course in the master of liberal arts program, Johns Hopkins University, fall 1997. Photocopy in possession of the author.

Harriss, Robert Preston. "Diary of R. P. Harriss." In the possession of Mrs. R. P. Harriss, Baltimore; photocopies of selected entries in possession of the author.

Hobson, Fred Colby, Jr. "H. L. Mencken and the Southern Literary Renaissance." Ph.D. diss., University of North Carolina at Chapel Hill, 1972.

Lambeth, Mary Johnson. "Sketch of the Life of Gerald Johnson by His Sister, Mamie, Mrs. Charles Lambeth of Thomasville, N.C., 1939." GWJ Papers.

Melvin, Robert Alfred. "Livingston Johnson: A Study of a Baptist Editor's Role in Controversial Issues." Master's thesis, Southeast Baptist Theological Seminary, 1952.

Turner, Thomas B. "A Few Steps Backward." Baltimore, 1997. In the possession of Dr. Turner, photocopies of selected pages in the possession of the author.

Index

Italicized page numbers refer to photographs. GWJ refers to Gerald W. Johnson.